PSALMS FOR LIFE

Hearing and Praying the Book of Psalms

John Eaton

First published in 2006 in Great Britain

Society for Promoting Christian Knowledge
36 Causton Street
London SW1P 4ST

The author's translations of the psalms first appeared in *The Psalms:
A Historical and Spiritual Commentary* (2003, 2005) and are reprinted
here by kind permission of T. & T. Clark/Continuum.

1 3 5 7 9 10 8 6 4 2

British Library Cataloguing-in-Publication Data
A catalogue record for this book is available from the British Library.

ISBN-13: 978–0–281–05844–0
ISBN-10: 0–281–05844–X

Typeset by Graphicraft Ltd, Hong Kong
Printed in Great Britain by Ashford Colour Press

Contents

————◆◆————

Contents

Contents

Contents

Contents

vii

Contents

Preface

I suppose the story of this book begins with St Michael and All Angels. That's a small church some nine hundred years old, tucked away down a country lane that leads on further only to a beautiful lake beloved of wild birds. The churchyard, with many an old tombstone, is a mass of snow-drops, daffodils and bluebells in their turn, and in summer old roses are abundant on the sunlit wall of the church. Sheep and lambs enjoy the rolling fields that border it and rise towards a line of wooded hills, where many a Birmingham dog insists on taking its owner for a daily romp. A few years ago I was invited to give a series of addresses on psalms through the spring and early summer in St Michael's at the evening service. And so the idea came to me that I might build up similar presentations of every psalm, not omitting the difficult ones.

Here, then, each of the one hundred and fifty psalms is presented in a talk that ends by drawing on the psalm for a meditative prayer. I respect the character of each psalm in itself, but aim chiefly to relate the psalm to our life today. We listen for its message to us, and let it lead our prayer. Jesus is said never to have spoken of God without a parable, and it has seemed best for us also to begin each piece with a kind of parable or story to help us move easily over the great space of the centuries and feel the fresh force of old but ever-living words. And then our concluding prayer-thoughts, echoing words and impulses from the psalm, help us to come before God with our own cares and hopes lifted up by the same Spirit who was surely at work in the psalm.

In all this we join a great tradition, for the psalms have been the chief resource of Christian prayer and praise from the very first. In the New Testament no other scripture is quoted as often as the psalms, for they were found to be supremely prophetic of Christ and his kingdom. Already in Old Testament times the roots of this understanding were strong, for the ideals and visions expressed in worship in the time of the anointed kings (1000–587 BC) had come to be seen as foreshadowing the coming of the Messiah, the bringer of the kingdom of God.

But not just the length and weight of that tradition recommended the psalms to the Church of Christ. The psalms themselves have qualities which have made them pre-eminent in the resources of worship. Being words of deep feeling and vision, they were formed as poetry and, as customary in worship, were lifted to God in musical chant. Before the mighty and mysterious Creator they yet speak simply and directly, straight from the heart. So they lead us also into a true relationship, a sincere communion with the Holy One, when we might otherwise have remained tongue-tied, ignorant, baffled.

My presentations here will not be a commentary, where every point in a psalm would be dealt with, and some readers may wish to press on further into detailed study. For that purpose they might like to use my commentary *The Psalms* (2003, 2005) or its smaller version *Meditating on the Psalms* (2004), both published by T. & T. Clark/Continuum. With the kind agreement of T. & T. Clark, the translation which I made for that commentary is generally the one I use when I quote psalm verses in the present work. (I give psalm numbers according to the main tradition in English; likewise verse numbers, supplied only for long psalms.)

Although there were gifted women prophets, musicians and singers in biblical times, for the Book of Psalms the tradition of the male 'psalmist' (especially David and other royal or priestly figures) is probably correct, and when the psalmist has to be mentioned, I have thought it best to keep to this tradition. But I hope to have set out the prayers, teachings, emotions and visions in their universal force, transcending gender, race and era.

I cannot express my gratitude to all who taught me, prayed for me and helped me on my way. I mention only here, as precious encouragers, Bishop Keith Sutton, my sister Muriel, Rebecca Mulhearn at SPCK, and my wife Margaret. It is to Margaret and in memory of our parents that I dedicate this book.

John Eaton

Psalm 1

Taking God's word to heart

———◆◆◆———

It was one of the great piano concertos. Such a cascade of notes from the young pianist, and all from memory! What dedication, to have absorbed all that music at her age, adding it to an already large repertoire! It would be foolish to think the playing from memory was just to dazzle the audience. The fact is that the player can only be one with the music when memorization is perfected. The role of every finger, the weight of the hand and arm, the flow of the phrases, the meaning of the whole – all depends on that taking of the music into the heart by memorization. It is a most patient work of repetition, a dwelling on phrase by phrase, a deep living with the music in respect and love. And there is no question here of a current fashion or theory. For thousands of years musicians had little or no recourse to written music. Memory was paramount, and all was passed down from heart to heart.

Something like this can happen with scripture and the great sentences that resound in the prayer and praises of the Church. The printed page is very serviceable, but for the life in God it is only a beginning. This 'word of God' is a music we can render well only as it has entered our memory and heart, becoming part of us. And should we not think it a music as worthy of dedication and love as ever were the concertos played by our young pianist?

Now it so happens that something of this thought was deliberately placed at the very head of the Psalms, placed there in the shape of Psalm 1. The little song holds before us a portrait of the truly happy person. But first it insists, three times over, on what this person will *not* do. We see that dedication has a negative side to it; right at the outset there has to be a turning from what can only lead astray. There has to be a brave and sustained determination not to be swept along by the currents of bad influence. So the psalm begins:

> Happy the one who does not walk in the counsel of the wicked,
> or stand in the way of sinners, or sit in the circle of scoffers.

The tempters, as still today, employ as their best strategy the offer of pleasure. But real delight, says the psalm, lies elsewhere:

> [Happy the one] whose delight is in the teaching of the LORD,
>   meditating in his teaching day and night.

Such 'meditating' originally was a murmured reciting of teaching which might be written on a scroll, a murmuring line by line, to learn by heart and deeply take it in. It was a way of communion with the Lord, being attentive to his voice, open to his will. At the centre of it all was, not the teaching as a thing in itself, but the Teacher, the divine Guide. And so it was a truly absorbing occupation, the greatest pleasure and delight.

The psalm now makes a striking comparison with a tree. Fruit trees need special care in the hot, dry lands. An ideal position would be beside irrigation channels running perpetually from a fountain. A tree deeply planted there would be firm against winds and always well nourished, as its roots drew up the life-giving moisture. With such a tree our psalm compares the person who delights in the Lord's teaching. Here is someone deeply rooted in the living water of the word of God, strong against tempests, offering shelter, nourishment and healing to others. As the psalm says:

> Such a one shall be like a tree well planted by channels of water,
>   giving its fruit at its proper time, its leaves never withering –
>   yes, all this person does will be fruitful.

In contrast to this picture of fruitfulness the psalm sets pictures of waste and futility, to characterize the lives of those who ignore the Lord. In Palestine, as the hot earth cools quickly in the evening, a regular breeze blows in from the sea. The farmer tosses up the threshed crops into the breeze, and the good, heavy grain falls into a golden heap, while the light waste is whirled away towards the desert. Such in the end, says the psalm, is the fate of the wicked life – like the chaff which the wind drives away. Such a life cannot endure the divine judgement, which is never far away. And the song ends with another picture of contrasts: the good way in company with the Lord, and a false way without him, losing itself in a wasteland. With all its vivid pictures the psalm warmly commends to us a constant mindfulness of our Lord's teaching, a constant taking of his word into our heart.

From early times the Church saw the ideal of this psalm as fulfilled by Jesus. He was compassionate to those labelled 'sinners' by the authorities, but brave against the forces of corruption. He delighted in the will of his Father, and through the tree of his cross he bears the eternal fruit of God, the sheltering, healing and blessing of all creation. So the Church sometimes added a Christian refrain to their singing of this psalm, so putting the voice and the presence of Christ at the very beginning of the Psalms, thus:

> I Am that I Am, and my counsel is not with the wicked,
> but in the law of the LORD is my delight. Alleluia.

Though we ever fall short of his ideal, we would hold to him and let him show us how to absorb and delight in God's word, and take the way of ever-deepening knowledge of him, our Teacher, our Lord and our Saviour.

Lord, help me so to delight in your word that your teachings become part of my being.
Like a firm and fruitful tree, may I be constantly nourished by your living water.
Help me to discern and refuse the seductions of evil, and to be fulfilled in the happiness of being ever with you.

Psalm 2

An urgent message to the nations

There is no doubt that Millie's favourite composer was Handel. That was because he composed *Messiah*. Millie had been born near Manchester in 1895; her mother died at the birth and Millie went to be brought up by an aunt on Merseyside. It was common in those parts for many to find their greatest musical experience in local performances of Handel's great oratorio. Famous singers used to serve on these occasions. The modern preference for light resources of orchestra and choir had not yet come in, and the performers were a great host, seeming to want their sound to go out unto all lands.

Why were these performances found so thrilling and uplifting, beyond all other music? It must have been partly because the work draws on such mighty themes and weaves them together into a powerful whole. The dawn of the kingdom of God is made real to all present as they hear the prophecies of the Messiah, and the story of his birth, suffering, death and resurrection, and the final consummation. With dramatic force the messianic passages break from the lips of prophets and evangelists, and the glory of the Lord and his kingdom shines over all the assembly.

Among the scriptures which the singers set forth, Psalm 2 is especially dramatic. 'Why do the nations so furiously rage together?' thunders the bass. Defiantly, the rebellious multitude of the choir keeps plotting: 'Let us break their bonds asunder and cast away their cords from us.' But divine authority rings from the tenor: 'Thou shalt dash them in pieces like a potter's vessel.'

Such tremendous renderings of Handel's *Messiah* were not unworthy of the ancient vision in the climax of the year's worship in royal Jerusalem. Pilgrims gathered in great numbers and with eager expectations for the holy days leading in the autumnal new year. As with Handel's oratorio, the ancient theme was the new reign or kingdom of God. In that setting a king might be crowned or his office renewed. Psalm 2 is an example of what would then be said and sung. The ideal king is portrayed – prophesied, we might say – as one intimate with God, chosen to serve him as his servant and steward. Whatever multitudes rise against God's kingdom, says the psalm, they will be defeated by this his Anointed One. The Anointed himself speaks to the rebellious rulers in an imaginary drama. From his deeds of office he quotes God's promise to give him victory in his capacity as God's intimate, his 'son'. He urges the rulers to be wise and return to the fear of the Lord. And he ends: 'O the happiness of all who shelter in him!'

Still today the psalm calls out to the nations. Why do they consult and league together in harmful ways? Why do they disregard the only true kingdom, the kingdom of God? Are they not still adding to the misdeeds of greed, cruelty and destructiveness with which they ruin the earth and its creatures? The psalm may be heard to foreshadow the voice of Christ, calling to the nations to ponder the cross on Zion's hill. By this divine work, evil will be shattered. It is the supreme sign of love, given through the Son begotten in the 'day' of eternity. But it is a love terrible to evil, utterly certain in its final conquest. Wise are the peoples and rulers who acknowledge God the King and bow to him. Happy are all who come to trust and shelter in him. So cries the psalm to every generation.

Millie's love of Handel's *Messiah* was reflected in her way of life. After ten years of happy marriage she was widowed and left with four small children, and little enough to keep them. But duty and kindness, hope and happiness marked her days. The kingdom shone about her steps, as she followed the Messiah, the Christ, who on the holy hill of Zion had overcome the darkness and called nations and every one of us into his marvellous light.

Grant, O God, that the vision of your kingdom may shine into our hearts and homes.
May rulers and peoples turn back from folly, and humbly seek your guidance along ways of justice and compassion, for the good of all the earth.

Psalm 3

Trust and courage in face of many foes

Because they live on an island, the British have lots of coastline to enjoy. With all the varieties of rugged cliffs and coves, sandy stretches, marshlands teeming with birds, grassy fields that reach to coastal paths, there are the constants of fresh, clear air and the spaciousness of the great seas. But an even greater advantage of their sea borders has been protection against invasion. It is amazing to think they have not been invaded since the Normans came across the Channel in AD 1066.

How different the land of the Hebrews in biblical times! Invasions were frequent, whether from great empires or from small neighbouring countries, or even from wild hordes sweeping in from the deserts. And when there were internal troubles, foreign powers often had a hand in stirring them up. So it is not surprising that many of the psalms are prayers in face of warfare, and some verses reflect violent or gruesome scenes.

The very first prayer in the book, Psalm 3, is overshadowed by fear of battle. The heading actually places it in the time when King David and his bodyguard had to flee for their lives from Jerusalem, in face of a vast uprising led by his glamorous and ambitious son Absalom. Such headings are usually reckoned to be not so much accurate information as suggestions made by the scribes who preserved the psalms. But even so, our psalm has every appearance of being a king's prayer during warfare. It unfolds in a customary manner, though with fresh passion, and it is remarkable that we, some three thousand years later, can still learn a lot from this manner of prayer.

First, the name of God is called upon, the name 'Yahweh', usually translated 'Lord'. Story told how God had revealed this name to Moses, that he might indeed be called upon. It is the same for us: when we cry 'Lord' or 'Jesus', we are no longer calling into a void, but addressing One who has

5

made himself known to us, forged a bond, and encouraged us so to pray. Already when we first utter that name, the darkness parts.

Then the psalm continues with an account of the troubles. It is poured out to the Lord, as though to engage his concern, his pity. We see that biblical prayer has something childlike about it. You tell God frankly about your fears; you describe the trouble with undisguised alarm. So the king in the psalm tells the Lord how the enemies ever increase. They spread rumours that God will no longer support him, and all are looking to their own advantage. He says:

> Lord, how my foes increase!
> So many are rising against me!
> Many are those who say of my soul,
> He will have no salvation from God.

Against this scene of trouble the prayer now sets the promises of God. The king tells the Lord that he still relies on those promises given when he was first called. For the task of shepherding God's people, he was to be shielded by God in battle and he was assured that his prayers would be heard. He recalls these promises thus:

> But you, Lord, are a shield about me,
> my glory, and the one who lifts up my head.
> When I cry with my voice to the Lord,
> he hears me from his holy mountain.

And the king continues to affirm in his prayer that he trusts. Even in that most dangerous time for kings, when defenceless in sleep, he trusts in God's care:

> I lie down and sleep;
> I wake again, because the Lord sustains me.
> I will not be afraid of a host of ten thousands,
> which is arrayed against me.

Of course, it strengthens our trust when we speak so in prayer, echoing God's promises, though fears rise up. But childlike still, the king is also pressing the Lord to vindicate such trust. Surely God will not fail in these promises!

Only now comes actual prayer, in the sense of direct asking. The psalm began with invocation of the name, and continued with telling God the nature of the trouble, and then how the gracious promises were relied on. But now the petition, the request. The king is picturing the enemies as wild beasts, monsters even, as he cries:

Rise, LORD. Save me, my God.
O smite the jaws of all my enemies and break the fangs of the cruel.
Salvation is from the LORD.
Your blessing be upon your people!

So the little psalm ends. If we agree it is instructive, we may still wonder why Christians from very early times and all down the centuries recited such psalms night and day. It was because they linked them especially with Christ. At a deep level, such psalms could be seen to express prophetically Christ's sufferings, Christ's faith, Christ's strong prayer, Christ's salvation. To recite this psalm was to invoke his power against evil forces. So the psalm can become our praying in and through Christ when *our* foes increase, but also when we would fight with Christ against evil throughout the world. As we contemplate the cruelties, greed and ruinous ways across the earth, we may well pray that God will arise and smite the jaws of such evil, break the grip of such cruelty. As for the *people* who serve such evil, we should ask for the destruction, not of them, but of their bondage to evil, so that they may find a new birth as God's servants. And always through the psalm we join the ancient Christians in renewing our trust in the death and rising again of our Saviour as we recite:

I lie down and sleep;
I wake again, because the LORD sustains me.

One last thought: many of our Bibles put the mysterious word *Selah* here and there throughout the psalms, and in Psalm 3 three times. This Hebrew term was some instruction about the chanting of the psalms in ancient times, and no one now knows for certain what it means. It may well have signalled a 'pause' or 'interval' for an act of adoration. Perhaps the worshippers bowed low and murmured a response of assent or praise. At any rate, it can remind us that it is good, even in earnest prayer, to pause and wait in stillness before the glory and mercy of God.

So altogether the little psalm has suggested deep matters for us to explore. Not least how we may pray with Christ for his salvation to overcome the hosts of wickedness. Also how we may express trust in his great Sleep and Rising Again. And as we pray, often to pause and realize his power and his mercy, his wisdom and his love.

Father, many are the forces that make for evil. Many are those who seek only selfish gain, ignoring the gospel of your Son Jesus.

7

*We hold before you all who suffer their cruelty, and in the name of your risen
Son we cry to you to break the fangs of the cruel.
From you, the only Saviour, may blessing fall on all your world.*

Psalm 4
Trust when many despair

How often, as the shadows lengthen and the evening falls, has a day's last
gathering for prayer included Psalm 4! Thus, for many, the beautiful words
have stilled worries and brought peace: 'Stand in awe and sin not; commune with your own heart and in your chamber and be still . . . I will lay
me down in peace and take my rest, for it is thou, LORD, only, that makest
me dwell in safety.' But we need to ponder the psalm as a whole to appreciate how this was a peace given in the midst of trouble.

To begin such pondering, we may reflect on the plight of those modern
governments that have to choose an election date. They tend to go for a
pleasant time of year, often early summer. It is as though they get the
credit for the sunshine and birds, the flowers and springing growth.
And what a help also if the national soccer team wins through! A lucky
goal or a desperate save could get them millions of votes. But then, how
quickly support will fall away if the fortunes of weather or sport turn
against them! Unfair and irrational as all this may seem, it is a vestige of
profound and once widespread beliefs. Rulers were supposed to be in harmony with heaven and the cosmic order. When everything went awry, they
might be blamed for losing their role as mediators of blessing, and so face
an uprising.

The voice in our psalm is best taken as that of a king in such a dangerous situation. He first calls to God to answer his prayer of distress. From
all that presses in on him, 'Give me room,' he says; 'have pity on me and
hear my prayer.' And then he speaks to his people, exhorting them with
authority. Many may hear him now, others at second hand; and for others
again there may be only some mysterious influence, as when words of
prophecy are borne far by the divine Spirit. So his voice rings out:

How long, fine people, must my glory be scorned,
    while you love what is worthless and set your heart on a lie?

Yet know that the LORD wonderfully answers
    the one who is close to him;
the LORD will hear when I call to him.

Tremble then and sin no longer;
commune with your heart upon your couch, and be still.

Offer the sacrifices that make for peace,
and put your trust in the LORD.

His message is clear. In this time of hardship, many are scorning his glory as the Lord's Anointed and are turning to worthless and deceitful helps. They should remember the power of prayer that the Lord has given him and put away disloyal thoughts. In this time of sufferings they should meditate and wait quietly on the Lord; they should worship the Lord with offerings that make for peace with him, trusting him as the only Saviour.

Turning to God again, the psalmist describes to him the bad situation:

Many are saying, O that we might see good!
The light of your face has fled from us, O LORD.

It seems that harvests have failed for several years. Where has that light fled, people ask, the light of God's favour? Thus the psalmist has laid the agony before the Lord, and now he concludes with expressions of hope and trust:

You will put joy in my heart again,
    more than when their corn and wine abound.

In peace I will both lie down and sleep,
    for only you, LORD, make me dwell in safety.

In modern life there are famines of various kinds. In some countries physical starvation is known only too well. In others there is a famine of the word of God, the famine of the spirit. The fine people, those with power and privilege, will often be the first to resort to hollow and deceitful substitutes for the good faith. In such a time it is good to hear an eternal voice in the psalm, the voice of Christ. Though many despise his glory, his prayer for the world's salvation is mighty. He teaches us to fear God and hold to the good, to commune with our heart to find depth and quietness, and to offer our lives in loving service. When many are losing faith and courage, those who heed him will know an incomparable joy. And they will rest trustingly in God's hands, even when the last night falls. 'In peace I will both lie down and sleep, for only you, LORD, make me dwell in safety.'

*Lord, many seek what is worthless and set their heart on what will prove to
be a lie.*

*Teach our generation again to be in awe of your mighty reality, to turn from
sin and ponder the deep things before you.*

*Help us to offer ourselves for the making of your peace, and through trust to
know your joy in our hearts.*

Psalm 5
Finding the way

Not everyone relishes getting up in the morning. Some need coaxing with
melodious alarm clocks, or gentle music sounding at the set time, or an
obliging machine that makes the tea. Some are inclined to leave getting up
as late as possible, only to find they have given themselves a frantic task
to catch up with the clock. And there seems so much to do to make ready
for the day's obligations – to make ourselves ready, to make ready for the
family.

In Psalm 5 we meet a worshipper who says to God: 'Early in the morning I will make ready for you.' It would seem that the night has not quite
ended, and this person, quite likely the king, is much troubled by problems. He has been lamenting over them with prayer to the Lord, and his
hope is that God's help will come with the approaching day, sending light
into his darkness. This is how he begins his prayer:

> Listen to my words, O Lord;
> take heed of my lamentation.
>
> Attend to the voice of my crying, my King and my God,
> for to you alone I pray.
>
> Lord, in the morning you will hear my voice;
> early in the morning I will make ready for you, and will look up.

The worshipper considers how the Lord abhors the arrogant and cruel. He
himself approaches with trust in God's gracious promises, as he says:

> You put an end to those who speak falsehood;
> a murderous and deceitful man the Lord abhors.

As for me, in the abundance of your faithful love
  I will come into your house;
I will bow down towards your holy shrine in awe of you.

The day is dawning, but how difficult and dangerous seems the way ahead for this worshipper! How to face all the ill will and plots prepared against him? So he prays in those great but simple words that have been repeated so often down to our own times:

Lead me, LORD, in your goodness
  against those who lie in wait for me;
make your way plain before my face.

The prospect for the coming day might seem uncertain and beset by hidden enemies. Attackers might spring suddenly from hiding. But fears are stilled as the worshipper prays that the Lord in his goodness will lead the way, and indeed choose the way. May the Lord lead, and make the way 'plain' – that is, clear it of rocks and ambushers. The Lord is to lead in his 'goodness', and this may mean through his angel, the embodiment of his love sent out from heaven.

Coming back now to our world of alarm clocks, timed music and tea machines, our mornings of haste and perhaps of fears – is there a pattern of faith in the psalm that can help us? Certainly we too know not what a day will bring, or whether sudden attacks may come upon our peace. Sometimes great worries do beset us in a night of distress. Then we should learn from the psalm and put the coming day in God's care: 'LORD, in the morning you will hear my voice; early in the morning I will make ready for you, and will look up.' Perhaps he will send an angel to go before us – and angels take many forms. But whatever God's method, he will be there in his goodness. It is for us sincerely to want him to choose and make plain the way, and we must not close up our hearts in our own plans and desires.

Also, it is for us to be in harmony with his goodness, putting away all that is abhorrent to him. As the psalm says:

For you are not a god pleased with wickedness;
evil shall not dwell with you.

The arrogant shall not stand before your eyes;
you abhor all those who do harm . . .

For you, LORD, will bless your faithful one;
you will encircle this one with your favour as with a shield.

11

That last verse about the encircling of the faithful one with divine favour – that has seemed to the Church to speak of Jesus. The old royal prayers of David's house came to be seen as prophetic of Christ, the fulfilment. So Christians would enter the hope of this last verse through Jesus. After all, we in ourselves are not so just and faithful. But we grow in nearness to God as we grow in Christ. His mind, his humility, his harmony with the Father embrace and permeate his disciples. In this way, then, through our Lord Jesus, we take the end of the psalm to ourselves:

> Let all who shelter in you rejoice and ever sing for joy,
>> that you are a wall about them;
> and let those who love your name exult in you.

> For you, LORD, will bless your faithful one;
> you will encircle this one with your favour as with a shield.

How strongly the psalm prays for the downfall of the enemies! Here again the Church has thought of Christ and his defence of the little ones from their oppressors. It is good for us through such psalms to enter this work of prayer, for callous and ruthless servants of evil still abound. In the Christian tradition, however, we hold open the possibility that the wicked should turn and find a new existence in the service of God's kingdom – may they be frustrated and finished as evildoers, and be born again in Christ.

Samuel Sebastian Wesley, the grandson of English hymn writer Charles Wesley, was a great organist, serving in a number of cathedrals. One of his most popular anthems, still much in use, pinpoints one line of our psalm. The anthem goes: 'Lead me, Lord, lead me in thy righteousness; make thy way plain before my face.' Wesley did well to etch these vital words into our minds with his melody. But as we have seen, there is much more in this psalm to help us in God's way. And especially in times of sorrow or worry we may take to ourselves the preparation for a new day: 'LORD, in the morning, you will hear my voice; early in the morning I will make ready for you and will look up.'

Father, I do not see my way, and am troubled by barriers and adversaries.
Grant that I may be united with your faithful Son, and so be encircled with
the shield of your grace.
May I look up to you every morning and prepare for your coming as my
guide.
Lead me, Lord, in your goodness, and make your way plain before my face.

Psalm 6
Suffering and hope

From time to time it is felt that our hymn books should be updated, and it is interesting to see how their style and mood change over the years. The hymns today are certainly shorter. They have simpler words. But perhaps the biggest difference is that they are less mournful, dwelling less on the hardships and sorrows that life brings. Few now will recall singing about 'the long and weary way we tread' where sorrows 'crown each lingering year'. How quickly, so the old hymn reminded us, the living join the dead! How soon we too would be lying 'each within our narrow bed'!

No doubt to people today such hymns may seem to have dwelt unduly on the sorrows of the human lot. And yet few are as deeply tragic as some of the psalms. In the case of Psalm 6 it seems that the original musical accompaniment also had a tragic quality, for the heading calls for music from flutes, an instrument used when mourners wailed over the dead.

This little psalm appeals to the Lord to have pity on one who is sorely troubled in body and soul:

> LORD, do not in your anger rebuke me,
> or correct me in your wrath.

> Have pity on me, LORD, for I am weak;
> heal me, LORD, for my bones are troubled.

> My soul also is sorely troubled,
> but you, LORD – O how long?

In that last line words seem to fail; there is only the sense that in the long ordeal only God can help: 'But you, LORD – O how long?' Then the prayer flows again, strengthened by the thought of God's faithfulness:

> Return, LORD, rescue my soul;
> save me for the sake of your faithful love.

But death seems near, and it is urged that in death (according to the general Old Testament view) the sufferer would not be able to praise God:

> For there is no remembrance of your name in the land of death,
> and in the great darkness who will give thanks to you?

The sufferer then goes on to put before God all those nights of distress:

> I am weary from my groaning;
> every night I wash my bed and water my couch with my tears.
>
> My eye is wasted with grief,
> grown old because of all my foes.

Yes, there are 'foes'. In a time of such suffering, enemies seemed to abound and rejoice. Their ill will heightened the suffering. But now there comes strength against them through trust in the Lord. The prayer expresses a trust which the faithful God will not ignore. The forces of malice are bidden to scatter and flee away:

> Get away from me, all you that work evil,
> for the LORD will hear the voice of my weeping.
>
> The LORD will hear my pleading;
> the LORD will accept my prayer.
>
> All my enemies shall be put to shame and confusion;
> they shall suddenly turn back in shame.

We may learn from this psalm that we do not have to hide our grief from the Lord. Let our newer hymn books, if they will, leave out the tragic verses, descriptions of a life that is painful, crushing, and a long, long ordeal – the psalms still invite us to pour out our sorrows to him: 'The LORD will hear the voice of my weeping.'

Some years ago, in a great university, candidates for the degree in philosophy were sitting their examination in logic. The paper included a deceptively simple question: 'How do we know that a cat is pleased when it purrs?' No doubt, to the good student, the question would bring all the forces of logic into play. But for most people it is a matter of instinct; the purring is a language easily understood by all.

No less instantly eloquent is the language of tears. When words fail, the voice of weeping speaks from deep in the heart straight to the heart of compassion – 'The LORD will hear the voice of my weeping.' The nineteenth-century Baptist preacher Charles Spurgeon reflected on this 'voice'. The voice of weeping, he said, was in a universal language, understood all over the earth and in heaven also. How good to know that our tears are understood though our words fail!

We come to deeper levels in the psalm when we note that it is twice quoted by Jesus (John 12.27; Matt. 7.23; Luke 12.27). Such quotations of psalms sometimes come at key moments in the Gospels because the psalms were understood as foreshadowing the sufferings and victory of the Messiah. The quotation is a sign that God's ancient purpose is reaching its climax of fulfilment. In St John's account of Jesus in his final days in Jerusalem, we hear how certain Greeks, present in Jerusalem for the Passover, ask to see Jesus. Jesus finds here a sign that he is soon to be glorified through giving up his life, and he echoes our psalm, 'Now is my soul troubled.' Through this use of the psalm Jesus indicates that he is entering the time of his Passion when he will suffer the wounds that bring the world's healing, but at the last will overcome the forces of wickedness, and the Father will have glorified his name.

Naturally, then, the Church continued to see special importance in this psalm. It was often appointed for Ash Wednesday to help the worshippers enter the Lenten season of penitence and self-denial, but all in the power of our Saviour's example – he who suffered in faith that thereby evil forces would be scattered and God's glorious purpose achieved.

As so often, we see that a small psalm may contain a great deal more than we noticed at first. We have seen that in the first place it leads us to pour out our agonies to the Lord without disguise. And we saw that it leads us then to recall the promises of our Lord and to hold on with trust in his faithfulness. And deepest of all, it reminds us of the sufferings and faith of the Lord Jesus himself. We rest in him who has fulfilled the psalm and who, beyond the land of death and all its darkness, has established the kingdom of praise and thanksgiving.

Father, have pity on me in my weakness and my troubles, and save me in your faithful love.
O Christ, whose soul was sorely troubled and body wasted in the grief of your Passion, come quickly to the help of those who are weary from weeping and groaning.
Return, Lord, rescue my soul; renew my life, that I may evermore give thanks to you and bless your holy name.

Psalm 7

The Lion of the tribe of Judah

Between humans and animals there has often been much fear and hostility. Against this, mercifully, come experiences of wonderful friendship, such as we find in stories about hermits. St Macarius answered a knock at his door only to find his visitor was a hyena. She had a cub in her mouth; she had brought it to be cured of blindness. St Colman was friendly with a fly, which would help him keep his place in his holy book. Sometimes these stories of friendship tell of lions. A monk was once walking by the jungle of the River Jordan, when a lion came out and showed him a sore paw. The monk drew out a thorn, washed and bound the paw, and expected the lion to vanish into the jungle. But it would not leave him, and stayed with him years until the monk died. And then the lion would only lie on his good friend's grave and soon himself died of grief.

In the Bible lions appear in some passages as noble, brave, faithful servants of God. A title of Christ in the vision of the Book of Revelation is 'the Lion that is of the tribe of Judah' (Rev. 5.5). But often, too, the lion is an image of something terrifying. St Peter's letter warns us, 'Be sober, be watchful, for your adversary the devil, as a roaring lion, walks about, seeking whom he may devour' (1 Pet. 5.8).

In Psalm 7 a king is suffering from enemies as terrible as this and prays passionately:

> Lord, my God, I take shelter in you;
> save me from all who pursue me, and deliver me,
>
> or they will tear my soul like a lion,
> rending me, with none to deliver.

What a vivid impression this gives of someone running to seek safety from a lion that would tear him to pieces! Such are the enemies, and only the Lord can give refuge from their ferocity.

The prayer then brings out another aspect of the evil situation. The enmity is unjust, based on fraudulent accusations. And the sincerity of this worshipper is evident as he protests his innocence, for he hangs a terrible curse over his own head, to take effect if he lies:

LORD, my God, if I have done this,
if there is guilt upon my hands,

if I have done harm to one at peace with me,
or plundered my foe without cause,

then let my enemy pursue and overtake my soul,
tread my life to the ground and lay my glory in the dust!

Yes, this worshipper is surely being attacked unjustly, and so he can boldly appeal to the Judge of all nations, confident of the outcome:

Rise up, LORD, in your wrath,
    be exalted against the raging of my foes,
and rouse up for me the judgement you have commanded.

Let the assembly of the nations gather about you,
and over it take your seat on high.

LORD, Judge of the peoples, give judgement for the rightness of my
    cause,
and according to the innocence that is in me.

May the evil of the wicked come to an end,
    but establish the one who is just,
for you try the hearts and inner thoughts, O God of justice.

This passionate prayer leads us to call to God for shelter when enemies would devour us, or any adversity terrify us. And it leads us especially to call upon the just judgement of God when we are unfairly accused or condemned. The psalm assures us that in his own time and way he does save those who are true of heart. And in God's time, too, those who invent and perpetrate wrongs find the mischief returning and landing on their own head. Yes, in time of terror or unjust persecution the disciple of the Lord must call upon him who upholds the right. So we too will be able to say with the psalm:

For my shield I trust in God,
who saves those that are true of heart.

God is a judge who does right,
and a God who condemns evil every day . . .

I will give thanks to the LORD for his justice,
and will make music to the name of the LORD Most High.

17

Not the lion of terror will then take hold of us, but the strong and gracious Saviour, the Lion of Judah. 'Weep not,' says the Book of Revelation (5.5), 'Behold the Lion that is of the tribe of Judah, the Root of David, has overcome.' There is an ancient prayer that draws together our meditation on Psalm 7:

> O God, great, powerful and merciful, deliver us from the roaring
>   lion
> who goes about seeking whom he may devour,
> that through the victory of the Lion of the tribe of Judah,
> the hosts of all our enemies may be put to flight.

Lord, terrible are the murderous ones who in many lands prey upon your
  people.
O Christ, Lion of Judah, protect your little ones from the ruthless and violent.
Give us courage, Lord, to live justly, firm in the faith of your victory.

Psalm 8

A royal mission

O the glory and the tragedy of a king! These two opposing aspects are well expressed by Shakespeare in his *Richard II* (Act 3.2):

> Not all the water in the rough rude sea
> can wash the balm from an anointed king;
> the breath of worldly men cannot depose
> the deputy elected by the Lord.
>
> For God's sake let us sit upon the ground
> and tell sad stories of the death of kings;
> how some have been deposed, some slain in war,
> some haunted by the ghosts they have deposed,
> some poisoned by their wives, some sleeping killed;
> all murdered, for within the hollow crown
> that rounds the mortal temples of a king
> keeps Death his court.

It was hardly a promising plot for the stage – Richard deposed and murdered. But the poet's genius made it an enthralling drama. In many an eloquent passage the calling of a king is reflected on – its glory and fragility. Today it may be that there is less urgent concern with the powers and problems of monarchy, and yet in one respect every person on earth, in every country, should be deeply concerned.

This is evident as we ponder Psalm 8. According to this little song of praise, the human being, and so every human being, is a king crowned by God:

> What is man . . . ?
> You have given him little less than the angels
> and crowned him with glory and honour.
>
> You gave him rule over the works of your hands;
> you put everything under his feet.

Such is the royal wealth and glory given to the human being, says the psalm, that it is little short of what the heavenly beings have. All earthly creatures are subject to this rule:

> flocks and herds of every kind,
> even animals of the wild,
>
> birds of the heavens and fish of the sea,
> and all that moves along the paths of the seas.

Our singer reflects how wonderful it is that the God who created the vast world and wrought with his fingers the countless bodies of the night sky should have such thought and care for puny human beings as to give them this royal glory. This seems to be the singer's chief thought in this particular moment of worship. And a mighty thought it is, not less so today, as little human beings are able to measure and manipulate in the mysteries of space.

But it is important to note the whole pattern of the psalmist's beliefs. There are three things that must be mentioned.

First, the psalm teaches that we best serve God, not in pride and strength, but in humility and praise. The Creator's work to overcome chaos and evil is accomplished through the praises of his little ones. The worship offered by his humble servants – he has made it a bulwark against such chaos:

> Out of the mouths of babes at the breast you have founded a
>   stronghold,
> to counter your foes and still the enemy and the avenger.

Second, the psalm requires us to see that as the Lord our Ruler is ever thoughtful and caring towards us, so must we be also to those over whom we rule. In our turn, we have the royal mission to love and care for the works of God's hand, for living things of every kind.

Third, we must note that the pattern of the psalmist's thought is rounded out in the refrain which opens and closes the song: 'O LORD, our Lord, how glorious is your name in all the earth!' Here it is plain that the true king, the master and lord of all that is, is God. When our inner eye is opened, we see a world full of his glorious majesty. His 'name', shining out gloriously, is his revelation of himself. He is the only king of supreme majesty, and we have been appointed his stewards. Woe to human beings if they presume to rule earth and her creatures in their own will and power, for their own desire! Then the human crown would be hollow indeed.

But our psalm has a brighter vision. It sees the ideal which the apostles later recognized in Christ, the royal man who reigns as the Father wills (Heb. 2.6–8). Christ leads us in our royal destiny, fulfilling the whole pattern of the psalm. So his humility is indeed the stronghold against the enemy. And he teaches us ever to show to the little ones in our charge the kindness we ourselves have received from our Master. Most fundamentally, he teaches us that the kingdom is God's alone – the kingdom, the power and the glory – and our destiny is to do his will. Such is our crown, our royal function, and well may the song be ever on our lips: 'O LORD, our Lord, how glorious is *your* name in all the earth!'

Lord, you have crowned our race with glory, that we may in humility and
    simplicity sing your praise.
You put earth's creatures in our power, that we may care for them on your
    behalf in faithful love, as you have cared for us.
O Lord, our King, the royal Name belongs to you alone. Subdue the enemy
    and still all powers of cruelty, that we and all your subjects may walk
    humbly and kindly in the beauty of your wondrous creation.

Psalms 9–10

The melody that never ceases

There was once a cartoon film – it may have been from Hungary – used frequently on television to fill a few spare minutes. It showed an orchestra on board ship, playing under their conductor for all their worth. The sea grew rough, and still they played. Tempest raged, but they were undeterred. The ship sank, and they played on beneath the waves. When rescue came by some fantastic means, they were still playing with undiminished vigour. A similar idea is suggested by the rather enigmatic Jewish tradition of the fiddler on the roof – the melody continues through all the ups and downs of daily life and even when disaster strikes.

Such illustrations of 'holding on to the music' come to mind as we read Psalms 9 and 10 – one great prayer in two parts. It is at first sight quite surprising that the same composition should on the one hand raise music of thankfulness to the Lord, and on the other hand should also call on him to look with pity at the terrible situation and hasten to the rescue. It sounds contradictory as we hear such verses as these:

> I will give thanks, Lord, with all my heart;
> I will tell of all your marvellous works.
>
> I will be glad and rejoice in you;
> I will make music to your name, Most High.
>
> Make music to the Lord enthroned in Zion;
> tell among the peoples the things that he has done.
>
> Have pity on me, Lord; see what I suffer from those set against me,
> you that lift me up from the gates of death.
>
> Rise up, Lord, let not man prevail;
> let the nations be judged before your face.
>
> Why, Lord, do you stand far off,
> and hide yourself in times of need?
>
> Surely you must see the trouble and misery –
>   you regard it and will take it into your hands;
> the helpless throws himself upon you,
>   for you are the helper of the fatherless.

Yes, the piece seems to abound in contradictions, yet it is a way of prayer that we find in several psalms. The singer sees oppression and suffering all around, yet frames a sharp appeal to God with verses of praise and thanksgiving. It is a way of holding up the contradiction before the Lord himself. Can he really leave in such suffering those who have cherished the message of his faithful love, those who indeed recognize his power and justice?

Yes, such prayer is pointed. But deep down it carries with it the strength of faith that the good will of God must and will prevail. People who pray like this are part of a great alliance, the alliance of all who in one way or another stake their lives on the victory of goodness. Within this alliance are those who in calamity do not lose hope, but find a way to create something good.

An artist, Anton Drucker, was driven from Vienna by the Nazi occupation. He did not despair. He founded a Viennese patisserie opposite the church in Moseley Village, England, and also kept up his painting. As the years passed, many people found it a good place to sit awhile, a place with a kindly spirit. More and more branches have opened, and his son has inherited and maintained the tradition. Drucker's paintings have ever more walls to enliven. In one branch hangs his painting of the fiddler on the roof. His fiddler, perched on the roof tops, seems to be at once a figure of comedy and of pain, and beyond him, in the distance, is shown a Drucker's patisserie. The thought is near that Anton Drucker himself was one who kept the melody sounding – one of those refugees who lost all, yet did not despair, passing on the music of hope and beauty to generations to come.

Within the great alliance of hope, some know the light through art and the arts, and some through the melodies of duty and human kindness. And some, like our psalmist, find the fullness of hope as through every situation they sing thankful praise to God with all their heart. They thus enclose all experience in the faith that the Lord does see, and does not forget any of his creatures – he, the Creator of all faithfulness, will in his own time make all things well.

What a great theme has sounded from the psalm – thanksgiving in the midst of tragedy, thanksgiving that lightens tragedy with hope! It is a theme that points up the words repeated so often in Christian worship:

The Lord Jesus
in the night in which he was betrayed
took bread,
and when he had given thanks

he brake it and said,
This is my body . . .

And so our act of commemoration, the service of holy communion, is called 'the Eucharist', meaning the Thanksgiving. As long as this death is proclaimed, this life raised up, the music will never cease. Whatever tragedies befall, let us trust, and hope, and give thanks. Let us sing with the psalmist, both in the music of worship and in the deeds of daily life: 'I will give thanks, LORD, with all my heart; I will tell of all your marvellous works. I will be glad and rejoice in you; I will make music to your name, Most High. The LORD will be a high tower for the oppressed, a high tower in times of need. Make music to the LORD enthroned in Zion.'

*Lord, still in our time they move in dark places to murder the innocent. The
   helpless fall by their might. The ruthless take no account of you.*
Let not the hope of the poor be lost for ever.
*Blessed are those who nurse the light of hope. By your Spirit we will ever make
   music to your name, Most High.*
Father, who raised the Lord Jesus, raise me also from the gates of death.

Psalm 11

When you long to fly far away

'How can you say to my soul, Flee to the mountains like a bird?' So asks the singer of Psalm 11. For birds there was not as much cover around the towns of the Bible as we provide with our parks and gardens. Some birds found their best havens deep in the mountainous wilderness. Such was the dove – the rock-dove, ancestor of our pigeons. Flying swiftly on its long wings, it would cover great distances daily to gather food in the more fertile regions, and then return to its home on the ledge of some remote mountain crag.

The singer of our psalm has been advised to follow the bird's example and take refuge in the wilderness. It was a policy often followed in times of danger. The Bible tells of many who fled to those remote cliffs – warriors, kings, prophets. Still today the visitor is struck by the remains of fortresses and dwellings in almost inaccessible places hardly able to support life.

There is the grand fortress of Masada, high on a cliff that rises from low ground near the Dead Sea like the hulk of a gigantic battleship. Again, there are the dwellings of the idealist community of Qumran, the mysterious people of the Dead Sea Scrolls, at the base of crags beside the Dead Sea. And still in use are ancient monasteries perched on mountain ledges, such as that founded by St Sabas near Bethlehem – not for those who suffer from vertigo. Monks and hermits were seeking refuge from the distractions and corruptions of human societies, to dedicate themselves to God in lives of prayer. Kings like Herod were seeking a security they could not feel in their cities.

But most common were those who had fled from sudden enemies – invaders or political rivals. Such a situation may lie behind Psalm 11. David or a later king faces a great peril. His counsellors recommend flight from his capital, flight into the recesses of the craggy wilderness. 'For look,' they say,

> For look how the wicked bend their bow;
> they set their arrows on the string
> > to shoot from darkness at the true of heart;
>
> if the foundations are ruined,
> what can the faithful do?

But the psalmist is unwilling to follow the counsel. Is not the Lord his crag, his fortress? Will not the just God act against the evildoers? So he responds to the counsellors by recalling the chief reality in every situation – the Lord, sovereign, just and ever present:

> The LORD is in his holy temple, the LORD has his throne in heaven;
> his eyes see, his very eyelids try the children of earth.
>
> The LORD tries the good and the bad,
> and his soul abhors the lover of violence.
>
> On the wicked he will rain coals of fire and brimstone,
> and a scorching wind shall be the portion for their cup.

All this interchange between the king and his counsellors is reported in the little psalm. There is no prayer or praise in the song – no address to God. Instead it is like a little drama, condensed in the form of a brave and trustful answer to the counsellors who advise flight. But being a *psalm*, a song offered up in worship, this little snatch of drama is after all an indirect prayer. It seems to say to God, without using the actual words, 'See how I am trusting in you in this awful situation; please do not forsake me.'

Counsellors are much heard of nowadays. Individuals in misfortune are formally offered counselling. Governments add scores of special advisers to their regular hosts of administrators. But in the end we have the responsibility for our own decisions. And sometimes, like the psalmist, we may have to disagree with the advice given, and follow our better instinct. There are also times when counsellors within our own hearts would have us run away from a difficult, even dangerous, situation, and we need to stand firm and face the trouble, and say with the psalm, 'In the LORD I shelter, in the LORD is my trust.'

There is a key moment in the gospel story when Jesus resolves to go to Jerusalem, though it is a hotbed of his antagonists: 'And it came to pass, when the days were well nigh come that he should be received up, he steadfastly set his face to go to Jerusalem' (Luke 9.51). When *we* have to resolve not to hide away, not to 'flee to the mountains like a bird', it is this Jesus who will help us. Trusting in him, with our hand in his, we too will be able to set our face towards that place of destiny, ready with him to be received up.

The last words of our psalm give assurance:

> For the LORD is good and loves good deeds;
> the true of heart shall see his face.

Our prayer is then that the good Lord may put his faithfulness in us. May we be found among those true of heart who shall see his face, and so have perfect joy.

Lord, we see foundations ruined, and it seems there is nothing the faithful can do.

But you reign from your throne in heaven, and your eyes search and try all the children of earth. You love just deeds and abhor the lover of violence.

Grant us such faithful hearts that we do not despair and flee away. Waiting upon you, may we see the beauty of your face in the love of our Lord Jesus Christ, and want no more.

Psalm 12
Praying in a world of trickery and deception

Did you ever witness one of those old market traders in full flow? There was an outstanding maestro selling chinaware in the former Birmingham Rag Market. His plates, cups and dishes would be stacked in high-rising piles in front of the end wall of the market, and he would ascend among them on to a table. A large crowd would gather before him, and he would engage with them and hold their attention as skilfully as could any great actor or comedian. The subjects of his discourse were the special bargains he was offering. Such a bargain sounded attractive at its first revelation, but that was only a beginning. In humorous dialogue with women in the crowd, he would lead his proposal through stages of increasing wonder, till with a flourish he reached his final offer, evoking a gasp of astonishment. No doubt such old market traders were full of tricks and subterfuges, but no harm was intended; good will had to be maintained, and customers were generally well satisfied.

But it is another matter when deception is the weapon of the cruel. A characteristic of Hitler's Nazis was their ruthless use of falsehood to achieve their ends. They would make treaties of friendship only to prepare the destruction of those they had thus duped. Their ministry of propaganda was dedicated to spreading falsehood at home and abroad. Those caught in this vast web of treachery might well have echoed these words of Psalm 12:

> Help, LORD, for there is not a faithful person left;
> the trustworthy have vanished from among the children of earth.
>
> They speak falsely to their neighbour;
> with flattering lips they speak, and a double heart.
>
> May the LORD cut off all flattering lips
> and the tongue that speaks great boasts.
>
> For they say, 'With our tongue we will prevail;
> our lips fight for us – who will be our master?'

26

The modern victims of such a tyranny of deceit might, as they prayed, have felt the conviction that God must and would intervene. So at any rate felt the worshippers in the psalm, and they treasured this word of God that had come to them:

> For the plundering of the poor, for the groaning of the needy,
>   now I will rise up, says the LORD;
> I will place the hunted one in safety.

We know that retribution fell on the Nazis. But in this and so many oppressions the relief did not come soon enough for many of the sufferers. In the psalm, too, the promise of the Lord was followed by waiting. We see the worshippers waiting for his action. They keep before the Lord his promise, while expressing their trust and their continuing need:

> The words of the LORD are words so pure –
> silver refined in a furnace, seven times purified to the ground.

> You, LORD, will keep us,
> you will ever guard us from this generation.

> On every side the wicked strut,
>   as vileness is exalted among the children of earth.

This description of society seems very up to date. In many countries today, oppression and exploitation are practised with the use of deception and breaking of faith. Even in the more peaceful and liberal regions there is yet a great epidemic of untrustworthiness and fraud. A factor must be the development of commerce into vast empires which devour others. Their ruthless procedures are enhanced by the powers of information technology and multi-media advertising. The world seems filled with incessant propaganda with little care for honesty. Indeed the best brains are employed to devise the images and language of deception. The epidemic spreads into every walk of life, and the values of faithfulness and truth recede.

The psalmist was so appalled at the treachery of his day that he could only utter the briefest of prayers: 'Help, LORD' ('Save, LORD'). And often we too may well find words fail us, and we must just say 'Help, Lord'. The great nineteenth-century Baptist preacher Charles Spurgeon compared this prayer to the angel's sword, to be turned every way and used on all occasions. He also compared it to the little boat which can enter a harbour where big vessels cannot go – so the short cry 'Help, Lord' could trade with heaven when the stream of grace seemed too low to float a grander prayer.

The psalm also guides us well in its praise of the word of the Lord – gleaming as the purest of silver in this shadowed world of untruths. In the long waiting for the Lord's arising to make all well, we treasure the Word he has already given us, his Word made flesh in Jesus Christ. Here is already given us purifying and cleansing, truth and the faithfulness of God. In him we are renewed, through him hope shines brightly as we commend to him day by day the plundered poor, the groaning ones, and the little one that is hunted by the callous. 'Help, Lord,' we cry, and hold to Jesus, the pure and precious Word, with hope and faith.

Lord, we pray to you for the plundered and for the hunted one. Rise up for them and place them in safety.

As a means of power, a means to success, people on every hand speak falsely, with flattering lips and a double heart. Vileness is praised and exalted.

Save, Lord. Help, Lord. Hold us in the truth of your silver-pure words. Save us by your faithful Word that is Jesus Christ.

Psalm 13
A comforting word in a long ordeal

The young girl was known as 'a bad traveller'. What a misery for her was a journey by bus or train! Her world contracted into a prison of horrible feeling and fear of sickness. Effective tablets for the condition had not yet been devised, but her mother would encourage her with assurances that it was not much longer to the destination – just a station or two. Her kindly assurances were a help, although she may have been inclined to under-estimate the journey remaining. The fact is that in any suffering it is a relief to know that the end is coming into view. Blessings on the dentist who thinks to say, 'You are doing very well; we are nearly there.'

Already long before the time of the psalms there was in the Middle East a style of prayer in which the sufferer would raise to heaven the cry 'How long?' – how much longer must the ordeal be endured? Indeed, in one example from Babylon, the question 'How long?' comes four times. Now this fourfold 'How long?' is just what we find centuries later in the small Psalm 13:

How long, Lord, will you utterly forget me,
how long will you hide your face from me?

How long shall I have anguish in my soul
   and sorrow in my heart all day,
how long shall my enemy be exalted over me?

Yes, distress at an ordeal with no good end in sight is both an ancient and a universal experience. But it is striking also how the psalm concentrates on God. The sufferer relates everything to the intentions of God. In this sorrow it seemed that the Lord had utterly forgotten his worshipper and turned away his face. O that he would remember and turn again and look with pity on his servant:

Look down and answer me, Lord my God;
give light to my eyes or I shall sleep in death,

and my enemy shall say, I have prevailed against him,
and my foes rejoice that I am overthrown.

So far the prayer has expressed to God the depth of the anguish. But now a vital consideration is added; the sufferer speaks of God's faithfulness and declares trust in it:

But I trust in your faithful love;
may my heart rejoice in your salvation.

Then I will sing of the Lord,
that he has dealt so lovingly with me.

With the mention of God's faithful love, a light has broken into the darkness. It is as though hope is born in that moment. Despite all the weakness due to suffering, the certainty of a good end is grasped and held. The long ordeal will not be for ever, and the outcome will be a thankful joy in the Lord.

The features of this small but moving psalm often occur in the biblical prayers. There is a turning to God with the belief that all depends on him. Then appeal is made with passionate frankness, the heart allowed to speak freely to God of its pain. And finally, the mention of the Lord's faithful love – the commitment he has made as Creator and as Saviour, the utter reliability of his word – in this alone the sufferer trusts.

It is a way we may follow still in our sufferings. Only now, the faithful love has its focus, its burning heart, in Jesus. He himself knew the seeming hiddenness of the Father – the 'forsaking', the turning away. But he kept the way of trust and faithfulness, and the ordeal at last gave way to peace and new life. United to him, we too can hold on to trust, until God's faithful love turns the sorrow into peace and joy. So, by the strength of Christ, let us say: 'I trust in your faithful love; may my heart rejoice in your salvation. Then I will sing of the LORD, that he has dealt so lovingly with me.'

Lord, in many places they cry 'How long?' It seems to them that you have turned away your face and forgotten them.
Many a sufferer cries, 'Look down and answer me, Lord my God; give light to my eyes, or I shall sleep in death.'
Grant to us and to every sufferer trust in your faithful love, and hasten the time of salvation and the song of thankfulness.

Psalm 14
Damage and restoration

The most interesting windows in the row of shops were those of Mr Tyler, restorer of antique furniture. There one could see an ever-changing display of restored chairs, couches, tables, cabinets, desks and boxes. Visible behind the furniture, a staircase led to the upstairs rooms, where Mr Tyler and his two doughty sons transformed sorry old pieces – damaged and decrepit – into beautiful furniture, as good as new. Indeed it was better than new. Not only did it represent the finest styles of old masters, but also, though in perfect condition, it bore an air of maturity and experience, a depth of beauty which a brand new piece could not have.

'Damaged' and 'decrepit' are not the words used by Psalm 14 for the moral condition of the human race, but just as strongly the psalm says:

They are corrupt and vile in all they do,
there is no one that does good.

This sad verdict is not presented as a personal opinion, but rather as a prophetic insight, corroborated by God himself. The singer tells how the Lord in heaven has looked down upon our race with searching eye and has seen a general evil:

> The Lord has looked down from heaven upon the children of earth,
> to see if there is anyone acting wisely and seeking God.

> But all have turned aside, all alike corrupted;
> there is no one that does good, not even one.

The psalm gives the root of this corrupt behaviour in the memorable opening line:

> The fool says in his heart, There is no God.

That's a very strong sense of the word 'fool'. So blind to reality, so insensitive to all that is good, this 'fool' is absorbed in evil ways and is heading for disaster. When he 'says in his heart, There is no God', the point is that this, in practice, is how he acts, for he leaves God, the just Judge, out of consideration. Forget what this foolish one purports to be – a respectable citizen, even a leading religious figure. The psalm refers only to what he is in practice – a person who in daily actions leaves God out of the reckoning. Tragically, he is not an isolated case. The singer sees – and he believes the Lord sees too – that, right across the earth, 'all have turned aside, all alike corrupt; there is no one that does good, not even one'.

But the psalm is not in the end all about universal sin. It is about oppression. It is about cruelty to God's people, done with total disregard of the Lord's concern and of his presence within the circle of the ill-treated. This is the foolishness which is lamented, as pinpointed in a speech of God himself:

> Are all the evildoers without understanding,
> that they eat up my people as though they ate bread,
>> and do not call on the LORD?

> But there shall they fear with great fear,
> for God is in the circle of the just.
> Though you would confound the counsel of one who is poor,
> yet the LORD shall be his refuge.

As the psalm nears its end, the situation especially troubling the worshippers becomes clearer. God's servants, his 'Israel', are downtrodden, ill-treated, and they look with longing for the Saviour to come from 'Zion', as from the gate of heaven:

> O that the salvation of Israel were given from Zion!
> When the LORD restores the life of his people,
>> Jacob shall rejoice and Israel be merry.

31

They are praying for their life to be restored. Older translations have, 'When the LORD turns the captivity of his people.' Some modern Bibles have, 'When the LORD restores the fortunes of his people.' The thought is of a great turning, a transformation. The Lord is to take up his creatures from the pit of suffering and death, and make their life new and beautiful. It is a miracle of restoration, but, as with Mr Tyler's furniture, it is even more than that. The restored ones will be better than new, for they will have a depth of beauty from all they have been through. They will be perfected in communion with their Creator.

Can we enter into the deep simplicity of the psalm's vision today? Can we imagine that searching gaze of the Lord passing through our race, assessing the corruption, resolving on action? But who today would be the 'fool' who in practice leaves God out of account, daily exploiting and ill-treating those in his or her power? Who today are the callous exploiters, and who are the downtrodden 'people' of the Lord, the 'circle of the just'? The more obvious application has its truth, for still on earth are the tyrants and bullies, in practice ignoring the justice of God; and still there is a 'people', a Church of God, circles of the devout who suffer from the attacks of a hostile, greed-centred world.

But perhaps there is a more urgent application of the psalm that we should make. For are there not many who claim to serve God, but who in practice are callous about his 'people' in the sense of his vulnerable creatures – exploited populations, animals, plants, beings he has created and which are ever dear to his heart? The eye of God the Judge does not fail to see the widespread exploitation in all its foolishness, callousness and corruption. We may be sure that his 'people', his loved and cherished ones, has this wider sense when it comes to his sympathy for the circle of his abused creatures. His indignation burns for all his vulnerable ones as he cries: 'Are all the evildoers without understanding, that they eat up my people as though they ate bread, and do not call on the LORD? But there shall they fear with great fear, for God is in the circle of the just.'

Yes, a time of fear and repentance is fitting for this generation, especially the prosperous. New ways of thoughtfulness and care of all God has entrusted to humanity – these are urgent and imperative. But beyond this, the psalm teaches us to set our hope on the action of God, the great Restorer. From 'Zion', gate of heaven, salvation will come. The Lord will turn everything back to its first beauty – and yet more, for it will have a beauty enriched by suffering, a beauty ultimately wrought by the cross of Christ. Then Jacob shall indeed rejoice and Israel make merry, for all will live for him and through him for ever.

*You see, Lord, how they eat up your people as though they ate bread, and do
not call on you, or take you into account. But we believe you are in the
circle of the humble, and you are the refuge of the poor.*
*We believe that you will turn the life of your people, you will restore your crea-
tures. In the great salvation, your world shall be merry.*
Come, Lord. Turn our captivity. Come, Lord Jesus.

Psalm 15
Rules for guests in the holy place

Approaching someone's front door, you often find a message there for you
or any other caller. Sometimes it is written on the mat: 'Friends are always
welcome', or it might say, 'O no, not you again!' A lot of houses with front
gates used to have a notice, 'No hawkers, no circulars', which puzzled some
callers and made them feel uneasy, in case it applied to them in some way.
Even the common 'Beware of the dog' may leave the caller wondering how
to do that, short of beating a hasty retreat.

In the ancient world there would probably be a big notice written on the
gateway of a temple, warning visitors of the requirements of the god of this
place – purity, truth and so on. The same point might be made by sacred
singers as processions were about to enter the temple gates. Something
of this singing custom seems to underlie Psalm 15. But the psalm also reflects another practice, when a question might be brought to a temple
for an answer by God through a prophet. Both the customs are brought
together, as our psalm's question is about God's requirements of his
visitors.

The solemn question is directed straight to God:

> Lord, who will be welcome in your tent,
> who may stay on your holy mountain?

It was certainly felt to be an awesome thing to arrive at the temple
gates. The presence of the Lord was sensed very keenly; the mountain
was 'holy' – full of that presence. The temple was his 'tent' where he was
present in the form of his 'glory' and his 'name'. The worshippers would
be coming as pilgrims to a great festival lasting quite a number of days.

Who was worthy, who could come with impunity to stay in that holy presence?

The singer then gives God's answer. This describes the character of the person he would welcome to his house. It seems to be a list of ten require-ments, though the translators have not been quite sure where one ends and another begins. The first requirement underlies all the rest: this welcome person 'walks whole'. Some translators have 'walks blamelessly', others 'walks uprightly'; but the sense is literally 'walks whole', meaning to live day by day wholehearted towards the Lord.

The list of requirements then states that those welcome on the holy hill 'do right'; they don't just say 'Lord, Lord', but *do* what is just and kind in the eyes of God. Moreover, they speak truth not just with their lips, but in and from their heart; their thoughts and speech are all faithfulness, reliable, true.

Most of the remaining requirements are put negatively – what the wel-come person does *not* do. The value of these 'do nots' is that they focus sharply on kinds of conduct that God abhors. We sometimes see the same approach on buses; the many notices around the entrance do not say pos-itively, 'Please behave decently' or 'Show consideration for others'. They achieve more impact with negatives, such as 'No spitting', or 'Do not dis-tract the driver'. Indeed, the front of a bus can seem plastered with such prohibitions. So the psalm too strikes home with negatives: those welcome in God's house do not spread slander, they do no harm to others, they raise no abuse against a neighbour. Positively again, they are lowly in their own eyes, while quick to honour those who fear the Lord. Then back to the neg-ative – even though their promise works out to their disadvantage, they do not go back on their word. They do not take interest on money that they lend (the situation in mind for this remarkable ban on interest will be a loan to help someone in desperate need, perhaps a family facing starva-tion). Nor will they take a bribe to get an innocent person condemned. And so the whole is rounded off: whoever keeps to these requirements will not be overthrown – will not be cast out of God's presence in the temple, nor in the daily life that follows.

The psalm surely has something important to say to us. It reminds us that we should not think to crash into God's presence without pausing in awe, as it were at the gates. Am I welcome in his house, may I abide on his holy mountain? In that solemn pause we recall his requirements and test our lives with them. Have I been walking whole, loving the Lord with a whole heart? Have I been humble, preferring others who fear the Lord to have the honour? Sure enough, we shall have fallen short somewhere in the list, and so it is that we enter the temple of prayer only in confession and penitence, seeking grace to amend our lives.

But what an incentive! To be welcomed by our Lord, to stay with him, now and ever to have his support and his blessing!

At the gate of prayer, on the hill of worship, Father, I read again your wish for
*   me: daily to walk whole, true in my inner being, without words of malice*
*   or deeds of harm; lowly, respecting those who fear you; keeping my word,*
*   generous with money, taking no reward to hurt the innocent.*
Forgive and cleanse me.
By your Spirit may I grow in the life of your Son, to dwell close to you for ever.

Psalm 16

A prayer like an acorn

Many a great piece of music is just the development of a simple phrase. Beethoven was a master at this. One of his piano sonatas, for instance, begins with a descent of three notes, *doh, soh, me*; anyone could have written it. But then the little phrase is developed into a long movement, lively and arresting, enthralling in its transformations. In such works one feels that an acorn has grown into a mighty oak.

The beginning of Psalm 16 is an acorn of prayer. Here are the only words of request in the entire psalm: 'Keep me, God.' What a short prayer! From what suffering or danger did it arise? It is not told. Only the cry to God, to be guarded, to be watched over – 'Keep me, God.' But from this acorn grows an oak so rich and strong that centuries later the apostles were preaching from it of the resurrection of Christ.

This 'Keep me, God' sounds such a simple prayer, one that anyone might say. But it can contain a great deal when prayed with all one's soul. As our psalm continues, it begins to reveal from its little acorn a wealth of trust and of valuing the Lord above all other powers. Here are the opening lines:

Keep me, God,
    for I shelter in you.

I say: LORD, you are my Lord;
I have no good apart from you.

As for spirits below and lords that others delight in,
many shall be the troubles of those who turn back after them.

Their drink-offerings of blood I will not offer,
nor will I take their names upon my lips.

It seems that in the psalmist's time there were temptations to worship
other gods, as though to make up deficiencies in the Lord's power; people
would offer these spirits sacrifices and call out their names for help. For us
the temptation might be to give attention and energy to anything that
detracts from commitment to the Lord, diminishing our trust in him. Do
we 'turn back' to worship false gods of money, prestige, fashionable but
selfish pleasure? Is our commitment to God diluted by such fashions?
Rather we should say with the psalmist:

The LORD is my portion and my cup;
it is you that hold my lot.

My share has fallen in pleasant land;
my heritage shines fair upon me.

In other words: let others think some worldly power, some human
resource, is the provider of their life, the shaper of their lot and their destiny. We, with the psalmist, are to know the Lord as our 'portion', the
ground of our life, its meaning and resource. It is he that holds our lot, the
shaping of our destiny.

Already, then, we see what a wealth the psalm is unfolding from the
little prayer 'Keep me, God.' What faith, what commitment to the Lord
alone, burns in the heart that utters this cry sincerely!

Now when you have a problem, perhaps a difficult decision to make or
a tangle of affairs to unravel, do you sometimes say, 'I'll sleep on it'? The
fact is that difficulties often unravel as we sleep. We wake with a fresh per-
ception of the matter, and of any action that should be taken. Our psalmist
knew of such benefit in sleep, all the more since, when he lay down, he
placed himself trustfully in God's care. In the depth of the night he experienced the Lord's counselling and instruction. And with the guidance came
also a strengthening of faith and hope. As he says:

I will bless the LORD that he counsels me,
and in the depth of the night instructs my heart.

I will set the LORD always before me;
with him at my right hand, I shall not be overthrown.

Therefore my heart shall rejoice and my glory be glad,
and my flesh shall abide in safety.

And as the psalm draws to an end, its expression of faith goes yet further. In the depth of the night conviction comes to the worshipper that the Lord will not leave his soul in hell – will not abandon his life to the dominion of death.

In this great poetry of faith the apostles saw the link with Christ (Acts 2.25f.; 13.35); the words shine for them as a prophecy of the resurrection:

For you will not abandon my soul to the land of death;
you will not hand over your faithful one to see the abyss.

You will cause me to know the path of life,
fullness of joy before your face,
   and pleasures in your right hand for ever.

Through the darkest night, the faithfulness of Christ held firm and the light of the resurrection broke. The psalm can lead us to follow him, through our nights to his dawning. When in danger or distress we are moved to pray 'Keep me, God', let Christ lead us on through the psalm's unfolding of the little prayer, lead us on to the place of new life in him. 'Keep me, God,' we shall say, 'for you, LORD, are my Lord; I have no good apart from you. You are my portion, the ground of my being, the well-spring of my life, the guide of my destiny. In the depth of this night you will counsel me. You are beside me to uphold me, to drive away my confusions. You descended to the abyss and rose again, and now you will not forsake me, but bring me up also, to walk the path of life and know the fullness of joy with you for ever.'

Keep me, God, as I shelter in you. I have no good apart from you.
Many offer gains which prove false. But you shall be my portion, you alone.
I bless you, Lord, that you counsel me and instruct me through my nights.
You will not abandon me. O grant me to live before your face for ever.

37

Psalm 17
Safe in the eye of God

A baby spends much time gazing into its mother's eyes. When the child laughs and shows great interest as it gazes, it may be because it has seen its own reflection in the pupil of the mother's eye. Our own word 'pupil' comes from the Latin for a little child, *pupilla*, and hence the small figure reflected in the eye. And then in our language, 'pupil of the eye' became 'apple of the eye' (as in 'You are the apple of my eye'), someone specially dear. Yes, the glistening eye holding within it the tiny reflection of someone very close – that is an expressive symbol of care and love.

We find the very thing in Psalm 17, verse 8, where the traditional translation is 'Keep me as the apple of an eye.' More clearly we may render, 'Keep me as the little one mirrored in your eye.' What a tender and intimate thought, and this is addressed to the Almighty God, Creator and Lord of all! 'Keep me as the little one mirrored in your eye' – the prayer not of someone wholly withdrawn from the world, but, so it seems, of a king daily carrying the burden of the nation's affairs and now facing a bitter conflict. As enemies ravage all around, he has drawn near to God to make special prayer. He tells of the enemies:

> They have closed their heart to all feeling;
> they speak in arrogance with their mouth.

> Now they hem in our steps all around;
> they set their eyes to spread into our land.

> They are like a lion thirsting for the prey,
> a hunting lion crouched in a covert.

It is in the face of this fearsome peril that the people's leader and representative cries to his God:

> As I call to you, O God, surely you will answer me;
> turn your ear to me and hear my words.

> Show the marvels of your faithful love,
> O Saviour of those who take refuge from rebels against your hand.

Keep me as the little one mirrored in your eye;
hide me in the shadow of your wings,

from the wicked who ravage me,
from my enemies that greedily surround me.

Yes, it is the language of close and tender relationship – to be kept like a young bird hiding under its parent's wing, like the tiny one at home in the Beloved's eye. But the beginning of the psalm also points to the awesome nature of coming so close to God. The psalmist seems to be preparing to sleep in the sanctuary and expects that in the night God will come and test the sincerity of his heart. He says:

You shall try my heart when you visit me in the night;
test me, and you will find in me no evil purpose.

My mouth has not transgressed for human rewards;
I have kept to the word of your lips.

My steps have held to the way of your commandment;
my feet have not stumbled from your paths.

It is clear from this that the psalmist fully recognizes that the one who would so closely encounter the Holy One must be sure that his cause is just, his lips without deceit, his heart free of evil purpose, his steps holding to God's way. Then from sincerity and innocence the prayer for the overthrow of the enemy can be raised:

Rise up, Lord, confront and subdue him;
by your sword deliver my soul from the evil one.

At the end of the psalm, the next to last verse is of uncertain meaning and may have been damaged. But the last verse is a fitting end to a wonderful psalm. On the eve of conflict the king submits himself to God's judgement. In sincerity and trust he lies down to sleep in the dread holy place, where the Lord will visit him and try his heart. So in faith his prayer concludes:

I, found true, shall see your face;
Awaking, I shall be replenished by vision of your form.

His hope is that in a dream of the night he may see the face and form of God – a manifestation of God in love. Then indeed he will be 'satisfied' – sated with God's goodness, replenished by his grace, able to face the conflicts of the new day, assured of salvation.

There is much in this psalm to guide and uplift us in times of conflict and danger. We ourselves may face bitter opponents or harsh trouble. And at all times we must unite in the sympathy of prayer with the victims of evil across the world. For ourselves or for all these little ones we take up the psalm to draw near to God in awe and love – in *awe* that makes us put away unworthy thoughts and ways, opening our hearts to God's scrutiny, and in *love* that moves us to come very close for his sheltering and blessing. Through the Lord Jesus we may be bold to pray those tender words, 'Keep me as the little one mirrored in your eye, hide me in the shadow of your wings.'

But will God come through our night and show us his face and his form in token of his grace and salvation? Yes, in Jesus we have that all-satisfying sight of God's face and form, for Jesus is the showing forth of the Father, the outshining of his glory, the imprint of his very being. As we trust in him, we know him as the light in our darkness, the One who will guard us from all enemies. The humble, trusting disciple may indeed pray to be kept as the little one in the eye of God, and the prayer will be answered, as it was for Christ, in the mystery of God's eternal love.

Almighty Father, let me come to you in this night through the innocence of your Son Jesus.

Then keep me as the little one mirrored in your eye; hide me under the shelter of your wings.

Grant that I may see your loving face in Jesus and so be filled with your eternal peace.

Psalm 18

Victory over death

————◆————

A couple were choosing a wallpaper and wanted something 'a bit different'. And so it came about that halls and stairways were covered with scenes from the paintings of ancient Egyptian tombs and temples. The wallpaper came from Scandinavia, and it was the colouring and design that were so pleasing. If one paused to consider the detail, one could enjoy, for example, scenes of flute players sitting before their conductor, who signalled the notes with his hands. But one scene jarred – the earliest pharaoh, Narmer, raising high his club as he held a kneeling enemy by the hair.

This was an example of a common theme in Egyptian paintings: the conquering power of the pharaoh. These symbolic scenes were meant to convey a message and indeed a power: the rule given by heaven through the pharaoh would be strong enough to conquer the forces of evil. The pictures were drastic in their strength because there must be no doubt that the power given to the pharaoh would succeed against the most deadly enemies.

So here was a modern wallpaper carrying beliefs from the dawn of civilization. And perhaps also it will help us now to approach the thought of Psalm 18, which is a magnificent, but in a way terrible, psalm.

This extensive song is a thanksgiving and testimony to the Lord from his Anointed, his servant king. The king tells vividly of being rescued from death and given victory over foes, victory bestowed and effected by the Lord in faithfulness. The scenes of rescue and victory are highly imaginative and would themselves make tremendous wall paintings – only, the Israelites on principle painted with words rather than brushes. Death caught the Lord's Anointed in its deadly snare; the grim waters of the pit of destruction raged over him. But the Lord answered his cry and came riding to the rescue on a heavenly steed, riding through the skies, hurling lightnings and hurricanes at the foe:

> Then he reached from on high and took me;
> he drew me out of the mighty waters.
>
> He delivered me from my cruel enemy,
> and from my foes that were too strong for me.
> (vv. 16–17)

Later in the long psalm we find scenes of the king victorious amid 'the strife of peoples'. Some translators take these as past events, real battles already accomplished. But it is better to see here God's promise of victory to come. The king says:

> He makes my feet like the feet of a deer,
> and makes me firm upon the heights.
>
> He trains my hands for battles,
> and my arms shall bend even a bow of bronze.
>
> . . . your right hand upholds me,
> and your grace has made me great . . .

41

> I shall pursue my enemies and overtake them,
> and shall not turn back till they are at an end.
>
> (vv. 33–35, 37)

The prospect of conquest is then expressed with harsh strength – the enemy is to be utterly finished. As the Church has used the psalm down the centuries, these harsh passages are developed in their symbolic sense. Christ, the Messiah who fulfils the promises to the Lord's servant king, is sure of utter victory over all that opposes the good purposes of God. But the end of all is reconciliation, when all is made well in the new creation. In this way the psalm is sung as a vivid celebration of God's salvation wrought through Christ. Though death threw its cords around him, he was raised up to life eternal. So we sing to God:

> With the one who is faithful you show yourself faithful;
> with the one who is true you show yourself true;
> with the one who is pure you show yourself pure.
>
> (vv. 25–26)

We can indeed say that the dramatic events celebrated in the psalm are on a cosmic scale. The poetry has prophetic power and truly, as it says, 'The springs of the ocean are seen, and the foundations of the earth uncovered' (v. 15). It rings with divine certainty that the Messiah will succeed; the new kingdom, the perfect creation, will be established. All the same, there is much in the psalm to apply to our lives now. Already we may enter the salvation of Christ, enter already by way of trust and humility. Holding to Christ, we too have God's guiding light in times of darkness, and strength to face hardships and rise above barriers:

> For you will save a humble people,
> but haughty eyes you will bring low.
>
> You will light my candle;
> the LORD my God will make my darkness bright.
>
> For by you I shall run at a host of foes;
> with the help of my God I can leap over a wall.
>
> (vv. 27–29)

All in all, this is a psalm of great meaning for us. It leads us to meditate on the destiny of Christ as Servant King to suffer to the utter depths, and be raised up with great power, to lead a humble people on the way of purity, faithfulness and praise, and finally to achieve complete victory. And further, the psalm gives us a poetry to hearten us on our own pilgrimage. In dark places God will light our candle. Beyond stumbling he will give us sure feet like the feet of a mountain deer. Led by the psalm we shall give thanks to join the testimony that rings through all the ages:

> The LORD lives! And blessed be my Rock,
> and praised be the God of my salvation . . .

> Therefore I will give you thanks, LORD, among the nations,
> and make melody to your name,

> the One who has given salvation to his king
> and shown faithful love to his Anointed.

(vv. 46, 49, 50)

*Almighty God, you drew up your faithful Son from the waters of death. We
   thank you for his victory.*
Give us through him a surpassing love for you.
*Send out your arrows to scatter the wicked and violent, that their hearts may
   be turned, and together we may ever make music to your name.*

Psalm 19

The Creator – my Rock and my Redeemer!

How often have ponderous sermons been introduced by the verse, 'May the words of my mouth and the meditation of my heart be acceptable . . .'?! Yes, many a ponderous discourse – we are thinking of the old days, of course. These much used words are the last verse of Psalm 19, but there the reference is not to any sermon, but to the psalm itself – a poetic song and its music. The word translated 'meditation' here means rather 'resounding music, reverberation'. The singer may have been kneeling with his harp or lyre pressed to his body, and his instrument seemed to express the very music of his heart as he offered his chant to God and concluded:

> May the words of my mouth find favour,
>   and the music of my heart rise before you,
> LORD, my Rock and my Redeemer.

So no ponderous sermon here in Psalm 19, but a song-like meditation of great beauty and depth, sent up to heaven in the light air of morning, to please the God who is the sure Rock and merciful Redeemer of the singer's soul.

We may imagine the singer waiting already before dawn, waiting in the open court of the temple under Jerusalem's starry sky. Inspired, he hears beyond ordinary hearing, for he hears hymns of praise and testimony resounding in the heavens, he hears the great elements of the universe praising their Creator, pouring out, like ecstatic prophets, the tale of his creative work. They are teaching and encouraging each other to be centred on God and so fulfil their life and function. Day teaches its following day, night its following night. So his song begins:

> The heavens are telling the glory of God,
>   and the sky-vault recounts the work of his hands.
>
> One day pours out the story to the next,
>   one night to another unfolds the knowledge.
>
> They use no earthly speech or words,
>   their voice cannot be heard.
>
> Yet their music goes out through all the earth,
>   and their words to the edge of the world.

In due course the sun rises, and our singer reflects on its bold joy, its vast track from end to end of the heavens, and its reaching to every creature with its warmth:

> God has put a tent among them for the sun,
>   who comes out like a bridegroom from his bower,
>   and rejoices as a champion to run the track.
>
> At one end of the heavens is his rising,
>   and his circuit passes over their farthest bound,
>   and nothing is hidden from his heat.

Our singer has dwelt on the wonder of the sun because it is a sign to him of a yet greater breaking forth of light from God – the bright-shining word of God to his people, given in his teaching, his guidance, his law, his commandments. Our singer knows that this word of the Lord has many rays of healthful counsel, and establishes the life of communion with God; it is the true light of the world. Upon the Lord's people his word sheds light, life and wisdom, gladdening, reviving, steadfast and true, a gold beyond all gold, a honey sweeter than honey. So our singer praises the various forms in which God's word touches us:

> The LORD's teaching is perfect, reviving the soul;
> the LORD's testimony is trustworthy, making the simple wise.
>
> The LORD's precepts are right and gladden the heart;
> the LORD's command is radiant, giving light to the eyes.
>
> The fear of the LORD is pure and continues for ever;
> the LORD's commandments are true and altogether just,
>
> more desirable than gold, even much fine gold,
> and sweeter than honey flowing from the comb.

As God sends us his word, he sends us himself. All those bright rays of teaching and commandment awaken us to a bond with him. So now in the psalm, as God's presence is felt ever nearer, the singer at last addresses him directly:

> Your servant also has light from [your commandments];
> in keeping them there is great reward.

Then in the nearness of God he feels utterly unworthy, so he continues:

> Who can discern their unwitting errors?
> O cleanse me from my hidden faults.
>
> Hold back your servant also from deliberate sins;
>   may they not rule over me.
> Then I shall be whole, and innocent of great offence.

Such is the prayer that ever rises as we grow aware of God. O to be purified and made whole in love of him!

The meditation is over. Perhaps the priests serving in the open court are now making the morning offering. So our singer concludes with prayer that this offering of poetry and music, sincerely wrought from the depth of his heart, may rise to the heavens and please the Lord who is his fortress and his deliverer: 'May the words of my mouth find favour, and this music of my heart rise before you, LORD, my Rock and my Redeemer.'

Yes, a beautiful psalm – and what a lot it has to teach us! Most obviously it says to us: offer to God your art, knowing he will have pleasure in it. Your poems, your songs, your music, all that you do to make beauty and order, the poem that is your daily life – offer it to him, for his pleasure.

And again, the psalm says to us: grasp the unity of creation and religion. See together the joy of starry skies, mountains, seas *and* the Spirit's work in the Church. So we shall ponder deeply, to know that the Word of God that carried forth God's thought and power to effect creation is the same Word who came to us as Jesus Christ, to revive us, gladden our heart, and give light to all our being.

And for good measure the psalm further teaches us: as you praise and thank God in your worship, know that we humans are but a part of the congregation of all creatures. The heavens are telling, night and day, sun and all identities are telling the glory of God, and in that find life.

O the wonder that this God, the Lord of all, should be 'my Rock and my Redeemer'! God, lead us more and more into the depths of this experience.

O Jesus, Word of the Father, you are adored by the skies, their lights and their darks.

Help me to embrace your law. Cleanse me from my sins. Fill me with your light.

May I worship you in the congregation of all creation, and know you as my Rock and my Redeemer.

Psalm 20

The holy Name

What a valuable gift it is if you are good at remembering the names of those you meet! It is especially useful for pastors and teachers to be able to recognize and address by name those in their care. Only when the name is spoken does the person feel known and valued. With knowledge of the name there is the basis for a genuine relationship.

And when there is romance in the air, how the name of the beloved ever rings in the lover's heart! With every mention of that name the beloved seems near. Certainly there would not be much prospect of romance until the name was taken to heart. It would not be convincing to say, 'I love you, er, thingummybob.' No, the name is necessary for genuine knowledge, and to speak it is to reach out to the real person.

Names are very important in the Bible, and not least the name of God. In the stories of Moses it is said that God revealed to him his name, so that his people could call to him by this name. With this name (for which our English Bibles usually put 'LORD') they could cry for help, or call to him in praise and thanksgiving. In effect this name is the self-giving of God; in it he makes himself available and comes to us as Saviour.

One of the passages where we can see the importance of God's name is Psalm 20. The singer is leading the people in prayer for the king. They ask that his prayers be answered and his plans guided to success. And again and again they see the help as coming through the name of God. They say:

The LORD answer you on the day of distress;
the name of the God of Jacob set you up on high.

May he send you help from the holy place,
and from Zion may he uphold you.

May he remember all your offerings,
and receive your sacrifice with favour.

May he grant you the purpose of your heart,
fulfilling all your counsel.

May we rejoice in your salvation,
and in the name of our God set up our banners;
the LORD fulfil all your petitions . . .

Some look to their chariots and some to their horses,
but we will call upon the name of the LORD our God.

We gather that king and people expect conflict with powerful enemies. These enemies will be equipped with the superior weapons of rich nations – in those days that meant chariots and horses. But the worshippers affirm that for their defence they rely only on the name of the Lord. In the power of this name they will raise their banners. By calling upon this name they will overcome the foe.

For Christians, this powerful name that alone can save is the name of Jesus. In him we recognize all the meaning of the name of God. For Jesus is the outgoing of God, God making himself known. Jesus is the Lord ready to hear our cries. Through Jesus God shines into our lives in grace and salvation.

Let us look again at the psalm with this in mind. As we hear what the psalm says of the name of God, we relate it to all that he does in Jesus. Through the name of Jesus, God will answer us on the day of distress, lift us from the pit and set us up on high. As we believe in the name of Jesus,

God will send help from his holy throne. He will be mindful of our sufferings and sacrifices, and through Jesus receive them with favour. As we love Jesus and centre our life in him, God will grant fulfilment to our counsel and petitions and to the very purpose of our heart. Our longing will be only for the will of God, and our trusting prayer through Jesus will be a mighty force for good.

Yes, in the blessed name of Jesus God comes to his world with power and comfort. As our hymns have it, 'All hail the power of Jesu's name' and 'How sweet the name of Jesus sounds in a believer's ear; it soothes his sorrow, heals his wounds and drives away his fear.' But our psalm prompts us again and again to call upon this name given us by the mercy of God. In our days of distress we must call out this name, and trust this name. With the name of Jesus on our lips and in our heart we shall know God near, and all the grace of heaven upholding us.

In the name of Jesus, O God, answer us in the day of our troubles.
As we call on this name, send us help from your throne, and accept our
sufferings as a sacrifice to you.
Breathe into our hearts your counsel, and save us by the mighty name of your
Son, our Lord Jesus Christ.

Psalm 21
The source of strength

A young woman from Egypt was spending several years in Cambridge, England. She was working for a doctorate in English studies. Her strength of mind and her dedication already pointed to a successful outcome. She was strong also in kindness and friendship. One of her friends was an elderly Jewish refugee whose great scholarship included Arabic literature, and they had much delight in perusing Arabic tomes together. The Egyptian woman's name was Azzah – the Arabic word suggests 'strength' and 'comforting', and it was a name that suited the strength of her vitality and her kind heart. The related word in Hebrew stands, significantly enough, both in the opening and in the closing verses of Psalm 21, where it refers to the strength of God, ever mighty to save and comfort.

Strength is still much prized today, in spite of all our machines to do the muscle work. Especially in games and athletics, people strive, through exercise, diet and various substances, to add that extra strength that will give victory. The psalm has much to say about victory, but the only strength it mentions is that which comes from God.

It is a beautifully worded psalm, and was probably composed for the beginning or renewal of a king's reign. First it addresses God, thanking him for what he has just done in the sacred ceremony. In a kind of sacrament, God has filled this his chosen Servant with his strength and salvation, and he has answered his prayer for life and strength for the royal task:

> LORD, in your strength the king is glad,
> and in your salvation how greatly he rejoices!
>
> You have granted him the desire of his heart,
> and have not withheld the request of his lips.
>
> For you came to meet him with blessings of good;
> you placed a crown of pure gold upon his head.
>
> When he asked you for life, you gave it to him –
> length of days, everlasting and for ever.
>
> Great is his glory in your salvation;
> splendour and majesty you have laid upon him.
>
> Truly you have appointed him blessings for ever;
> you have gladdened him with joy before your face.

What a wealth of blessing! And now the singer makes it clear that all springs from an ideal relationship. On the king's side there is trust, and on the Lord's side there is the love pledged by the faithful God to the house of David. As the psalm has it:

> For the king trusts in the LORD,
> and through the faithful love of the Most High
>   he will not be overthrown.

The singer now turns to the king and, in the manner of a prophet, bestows on him God's promise of victory – so the king will have strength to defend his realm from evil forces:

> Your hand shall find all your enemies;
> your right hand shall find your foes . . .

49

For though they intend mischief against you and purpose evil,
yet they will not prevail.

The psalm recognizes that all will depend on God's readiness to show his power to secure his people in joy, and so it ends with a prayer that this may be so:

Be exalted, Lord, in your strength;
so shall we make music and sing of your power.

This kind of psalm tells us nothing about a particular king, but rather presents an ideal – almost a vision of the true Anointed of the Lord, one who prays and trusts, and so receives blessings that will overflow upon the people; in effect, he will be granted an abundant, unending *life*, life in close communion with God. No wonder the psalm came to be taken as prophetic of that ideal king who is our Lord Jesus Christ. In and through him flows that strength of God that overcomes evil and gives the 'blessings of good'. Through his trusting and loving relationship with the Father, new life comes to all who are joined to him.

In all the rich promise of the psalm, perhaps it is the message of 'strength' which especially addresses our need. In many ways we may feel our lack of strength – strength for the demands of every day, strength to overcome adversities, to overcome evil, strength to rejoice and be glad; strength to live a life of usefulness for others. In search of such strength, we turn to all sorts of human helps – holidays and recreations, tablets and potions, doctors and counsellors. Whole industries thrive on their promise of strength. They do give some help. But how hard it is to find that strength to live in gladness, how hard to find true life!

The psalm turns us again to the fundamental answer. The Lord alone is the source of strength, as he is of life itself. If we hold daily to Christ in trust and love, we share in the strength of God that is in him, the strength that (as St Paul found) is made perfect in our very weakness (2 Cor. 12.9). Finding Christ in the psalm, we say: 'Lord, in your strength through Christ we are glad; in your salvation how greatly we rejoice! Through him you have granted the desire of our heart and have not withheld the request of our lips. You came to meet us with blessings of good; you give us life in your salvation.' And then, as our Lord taught us to pray 'Thy kingdom come', we pray with the psalm for the help of all the world: 'Be exalted, Lord, in your strength; so shall we make music and sing of your power.'

May the strength of Christ sustain us.
May the life of Christ flow in us.

May the joy of Christ gladden us.
May Christ come to meet us with blessings of good, this day and always.

Psalm 22

When all the ends of the earth remember and return

It was said of St Francis that if he saw a worm on the path, exposed to danger, he would gently pick it up and place it in safety. And he would remind his brethren that our Saviour said, 'I am a worm and not a man.' These words are actually from Psalm 22, a psalm which from early times was applied to Christ.

It is not known what circumstances originally gave rise to the psalm, but several clues support the tradition that this is a royal figure, God's Chosen One, who cries out; the servant king cries to God from the lowest depths of suffering and contempt, and somehow holds on to trust. And then in the second part of the psalm, without explanation, there is an abrupt change of circumstance. He gives praise and testimony that God has answered his prayer. Around him are gathered all the people, celebrating the salvation in a festive meal of communion and thanksgiving before God. The royal figure sees the story of his salvation and new life echoing across the world and down the ages, prompting all nations to turn to the Lord. And he sees the salvation as even embracing the dead; and they too will worship the Lord.

An amazing psalm indeed! Sounding from depths of suffering and the victory of faith, it is somehow of a piece with the death and new life of Christ, somehow prophetic of his destiny. It is as though the voice of the Crucified could echo through centuries *before* as well as *after* those days under Pontius Pilate. And so we recognize in Christ's salvation a light that shines to the Beginning as well as to the End. We recognize the eternal dimension of the divine sacrifice, the Lamb slain from the foundation of the world.

It is especially touching that the disciples remembered how Jesus on the cross uttered the opening words of our psalm, not in the Hebrew, but in his mother tongue, Aramaic: 'Eloi, Eloi, lama sabachthani' – 'My God, my

God, why have you forsaken me?' These are sharp words indeed. 'My God', repeated in the opening verses three times, was an expression for God as bound to the worshipper in promise and trust, pledge and faithfulness. And now against this clashes the dreadful word 'forsaken':

> My God, my God, why have you forsaken me,
> and are so far from my salvation and from the words of my crying?

> My God, I call out by day and you do not answer,
> by night and I find no rest.

Yes, sharp words, but not the words of one who has turned from God and rants in barren bitterness. On the contrary, this sufferer is wholly turned to God, addressing urgent cries to him. God may seem silent and distant, but still the sufferer strives and prays for an answer. To the Lord, still, he goes on to describe his plight:

> And you sit enthroned as the Holy One,
> as the glorious splendour of Israel . . .

> But I am a worm and not a man,
> the scorn of all, despised by the people.

> All that see me mock me;
> they curl their lips and wag their heads.

> He relied on the LORD [they say] that he would deliver him;
> then let him save him, since he delights in him!

> But you were the one who drew me from the womb,
> and laid me on my mother's breast.

> On you I was cast at birth;
> from my mother's womb you have been my God.

> Do not stay far from me, for trouble is near,
> and there is none to help.

As the sufferer continues to describe his plight to God, it seems that the grasp of death has grown strong. The words match the hour when God's Beloved, the Light of the World, seemed overcome by the darkness. He tells of the demons of death that loom before him in the shape of monstrous bulls, lions and a pack of wild dogs which pierce his hands and feet. His bones come apart. Already his garments, as clothes of the dead, are being shared out as spoil. The psalm indeed cries to the Father for the Crucified:

Great bulls have come about me;
the mighty ones of Bashan have surrounded me.

They gape upon me with their mouths,
like a lion that rends and roars.

I am poured out like water, and all my bones are come apart;
my heart has become like wax, melting through my body.

My strength is dried up like a potsherd,
   and my tongue cleaves to my jaws;
and you have laid me in the dust of death.

Yes, the dogs are all about me, the deadly pack have surrounded
   me;
they pierce my hands and my feet.

I can count all my bones,
for they stare and gaze upon me.

My garments they divide among them,
and they cast lots for my clothing.

But you, LORD, do not stay far away;
O my Help, come quickly to my aid.

Deliver my soul from the sword,
my poor life from the grip of the dog.

Save me from the lion's mouth,
and from the horns of the wild oxen you will surely answer me.

'You will surely answer me' – yes, these last words of the prayer show that, in spite of all, trust is not extinguished. So we too, in union with our Lord Jesus, are strengthened to follow his way. In the bitterest sufferings, when we seem betrayed by an uncaring God, we will then still turn to the Lord, cry and pray to him, and in the depth of our heart hold on to the faith that he hears us and will, beyond all we can now see, make all things right.

And now, suddenly, this amazing psalm leads us out into a place of light and music. The whole community of God is assembled in worship and thanksgiving. Still addressing the Lord, the royal voice rings out – but now in praise and gladness:

I will tell of your name to those who worship with me;
in the festal assembly I will praise you.

You that fear the LORD, praise him;
    all you seed of Jacob, glorify him;
stand in awe of him, all you seed of Israel.

For he has not despised or abhorred the suffering of the sufferer,
and did not hide his face from him,
    but heard when he cried to him.

From you comes my praise in the great assembly;
    my vows I fulfil in the presence of those who fear him.

In this happy scene a meal is being shared in the presence of God. Such was the custom when the healed or rescued gave thanks for answered prayer. But in our psalm this act of communion and testimony has a vast outreach. Something has happened that is crucial for the whole world. The impulse of new life goes out to all that lives and also to the dead:

The poor eat and are satisfied;
those who seek the LORD praise him [and say to one another],
    May your heart live for evermore.

Let all the ends of the earth remember and return to the LORD,
and all the families of the nations worship before you.

For the kingdom is the LORD's,
and he is ruler over the nations.

All the living shall eat together and worship,
    and all gone down to death's dust shall bow before him,
for he has made my soul live again to him.

As the psalm comes to its end, it focuses on the witness – we might say the gospel – which will carry the effects of this salvation to all ages and regions. It will be an enduring testimony, borne through the generations by the seed of God's Beloved One. Christians may think here of the seed sown by Christ's work, the disciples who will ever arise to testify to his salvation. As the psalmist says:

My seed shall serve him;
witness shall be borne to the LORD for ever.

They shall come and declare his saving work,
telling a people yet to be born that he has done it.

Yes, he has done it. God has acted and accomplished the great salvation. It is finished. How these words resonate with the story of the Crucified! More and more our psalm appears as a poem that penetrates deep layers of truth, a prophecy most pregnant. It has joined with the truth of the Christ, the innocent One scorned and crucified, then delivered from death's hold and raised in glory. This gospel, as the psalm divines, is to be told so that all the ends of the earth shall remember and return to the Lord. And in this work of witness, we too, as seed of the Lord's sowing, have a part to play.

And thank God also for St Francis, who was granted the love to know that our Saviour's light was not for humankind alone, but for all creation. May we too have some of that love and insight. May we too lift the worm to safety, and remember, and return to the Lord.

For the suffering and the scorned ones, for the dying and the dead, we cry to you, Father: Eloi, Eloi, lama sabachthani.

By the agonies of your Son, we pray you to turn back the mocking forces of death.

By the strength of your Beloved One in his trust and his love, I call on you to come quickly. O my Help, come quickly to my aid.

Praise be to God that he has done it. Your salvation is accomplished. Our hearts live again, and the gospel rings out to the end of time.

All your creatures shall remember and return. All your families shall worship and rejoice before you. Blessed be God for ever!

Psalm 23

The light breaking through darkness

In the grand tearoom of Birmingham's art gallery there hangs a large and richly dark painting by Stanhope Forbes, an artist of the Cornish Newlyn School. It is called *The Village Philharmonic* and is dated 1881. The faces and instruments of the village musicians in the little room emerge in the glimmer of the oil lamps. It is as though the artist wanted us, not to see a spectacle, but to sense the mood of simple fellowship and devotion to the music. Painters in fact have often won striking effects of light by surrounding it with much darkness. For colours, too, contrast plays an essential part. Vincent van Gogh is only one of the many who were gifted in enhancing one colour by setting beside it a striking opposite.

In the best known of the psalms, Psalm 23, there are a number of beautiful images, such as the green pastures, the still waters, the shepherd and his staff, and the brimming cup. These images too are most effective when we recognize the contrasts in the background, contrasts which the ancient worshippers were aware of without prompting.

First of all here, we must note that the good shepherding by the Lord is done in the setting of a harsh terrain. At a Christian hostel in North Wales years ago, it was the custom before meals to sing a verse of the hymn 'Guide me, O thou great Jehovah', but the warden changed the next words from 'pilgrim through this barren land' to 'pilgrim through this bounteous land'. It was out of consideration for the good fare she was providing and for the beauty of the Welsh landscape. But the change from 'this barren' to 'this bounteous land' destroyed the contrast, for the hymn draws on the story of God's grace to his people in the wilderness, and it was in *that* setting that his provision was so wonderful. In fact, fierce and jagged wilderness presses into the east and south of the land of Judah, to the very outskirts of Jerusalem and Bethlehem. The shepherd ranging across that wilderness with his goats and sheep faced a struggle with want and danger. It is against this background that the psalm strikingly begins:

> With the LORD as my shepherd,
> I shall not be in want.

What a wonder that in such a terrain this shepherd can find places of greenery and a rare mountain brook, whose water he can dam with rocks into a safe pool:

> In green pastures he will let me lie;
> by still waters he will lead me.

On the burnt-up mountainsides exhaustion threatens life itself, but this shepherd can revive those in his care and lead them on a good way in new strength and contentment – all in accordance with his commitment:

> He will restore my soul;
> he will guide me in ways of salvation for his name's sake.

Contrast is still there in the famous verse about the valley of the shadow of death. This brings out the wonder of the good shepherd and his care by putting forward a contrasting figure – King Death, who would shepherd the flock into the deep shadow of his dominion, taking them for ever from the light of life. The psalm tells of the faithfulness and superior strength of the King of Life, the good shepherd; he will accompany his protected one through that dangerous place, the valley of Death's shadow, and in the end defeat the great predator:

> Even though I walk through the valley of the shadow of death,
>   I will fear no evil;
> for you will be with me,
>   your rod and your crook will comfort me.

In the rest of the psalm the portrayals of God's goodness are still enhanced by a contrasting backdrop – threats of danger and hostility. When the Lord lays a table and prepares good things for his beloved, it is still in the sight of enemies close by:

> You have prepared a table before me, a sign to my foes;
> you have anointed my head with oil, my cup runs over.

The enemies will lurk wherever God's disciple goes, and only his angels of grace and faithfulness will keep them at bay, until the final safety is reached, the homecoming to the Lord:

> Truly, goodness and love will follow me all the days of my life,
> and I shall come home to the house of the LORD for ever.

Yes, the psalm's message of God's care stands out against a backdrop of hardship and danger. Sooner or later we all know these troubles well. And when we know what it is to be lonely and longing for a strong protector, we treasure the assurance of those opening words, 'The LORD is my shepherd.' When we know what it is to be in a desolate region of life, starved in soul if not in body, we welcome the message of the green pastures and the still waters of rest and refreshment. When we know what it is to be exhausted, or how life seems full of enemies, the psalm speaks deeply to us of God's reviving power and protective love. And when the figure of Death threatens to destroy all the good we have known, how gladly we hear of the Lord who will be with us in that dark valley!

In all such times of suffering, the Church's witness rings out – into all this sorrow our Saviour entered; he walked in the great wilderness and against its terrors proved the love of his Father, and overcame the evil dominion. And we best experience the comfort of the psalm as we are joined to Christ. Through Jesus we come to know the pastures and pools of prayer, the revival of our soul, trust in defiance of death and all enemies. Through Jesus we are blessed with the communion of table and cup. Through every day we have the angels of his faithful love in close attendance, until our pilgrim's journey is completed, the hardships left behind, and we come home to the house of the Lord for ever.

Jesus, Lamb of God and Good Shepherd, grant that through you I may know
   the revival of my soul and the nourishment of your grace.
May your Spirit attend me all my days in goodness and mercy.
Grant me to trust that, even in the last valley of my earthly pilgrimage, you
   are with me, and will bring me home for ever.

Psalm 24

Everlasting doors

New people had moved into a neighbouring house. They at once began making alterations. At the front stood a skip, which was rapidly filling up with rejected furnishings – kitchen fittings, window frames and even a front door. The door in fact was only a couple of years old, but it had to go. If it had feelings, it might take comfort in the thought that its replacement probably would not survive long. Another new owner, and it too would be thrown out with the rubbish. A wasteful fashion indeed – but in any case such doors were not made to last. Gone were the days of properly seasoned timber.

By contrast, we hear in Psalm 24 of 'everlasting doors'. What a threat that would be to our industry! But these were the great doors that gave access to the courts of the temple in ancient Jerusalem. *Everlasting* doors? Well, the wood and the craftsmanship truly would be of the very best for the sacred place; but even so, could they really be everlasting doors?

The explanation is that they were symbolic. Like the other features of the temple, they represented things in heaven; the realities in the eternal realm were reflected here in miniature. And so they could be called 'everlasting' or 'eternal' doors. They were doors to heaven. When worshippers entered through them, they felt they were treading the very courts of God's heavenly dwelling; they were in touch with the heart of eternal reality – an awesome experience!

When we enter a church today, we can hardly share the awe of those ancient pilgrims entering Jerusalem's holy gates. We will hardly have so deep a sense of the merging of heaven and earth in the sacred place. But we can learn from them what is always right at the entering in for worship or any act of prayer. We can learn to subdue human clamour, human busyness, human initiatives, and so enter the holy presence with hearts aware of the Lord's majesty, ready to hear him. Yes, from the ancient words of Psalm 24 we can learn to enter before him by way of the everlasting doors, the doors that lead to true encounter with the Lord.

So what thoughts would the psalm commend to us at this entering in? First, it insists on the thought that the Lord God is the owner of the whole world and all that fills it; to him belongs every member of every species. And he is Lord of all because he alone created all, conquering every obstacle to beauty, order and life. As the psalm has it:

> To the LORD belongs the earth and all its fullness,
> the world and all that live in it.
>
> For it was he who founded it on the seas,
> and made it firm upon the floods.

The second thought which the psalm puts to everyone entering the sanctuary of prayer is the need for sincerity. To be welcome in God's holy place we must bring under his judgement our actions and our intentions:

> Who shall ascend the hill of the LORD,
> and who shall stand in his holy place?
>
> The clean of hands and the pure in heart,
> who have not lifted up their soul to false things,
> or sworn only to deceive.
>
> These shall carry home blessing from the LORD,
> and goodness from God their Saviour.
>
> May such be those now seeking him,
> seeking the face of the God of Jacob.

The third great thought which the psalm offers as we would go through the doors of prayer is that of the triumph of the kingdom of the Lord. For the ancient worshippers their procession through the gates symbolized the heavenly ascent of the Lord fresh from victory. He entered as King of Glory, conqueror of chaos, sovereign of life. For Christians this is now unfolded as the ascension of Christ, victorious through his faithful suffering and now reigning in the glory of Father. We are to ascend with him, blessed with the fruits of his conquest. So the psalm has a new relevance when it says:

Lift up your heads, O gates,
    and be lifted up, you everlasting doors,
and the King of Glory shall come in.

Who is the King of Glory?
The LORD, strong and mighty,
    the LORD who is mighty in battle . . .

The LORD of Hosts, he is the King of Glory.

Yes, there is much in this psalm to prepare our hearts when we too would ascend the hill of the Lord and enter before him in worship or prayer. We hear the psalm remind us that we come to the Creator who owns the world and every creature in it. We hear also the message that he is the source of truth and goodness, and requires us to love and live by what is good. And finally we hear, with the Church's tradition, that it is Christ who has ascended and entered before us, proved as King of Glory through his suffering and rising again. He will cleanse us and bring us safely into the holy place. He enables us to worship and bears up our prayers. As followers of Christ, the King of Glory, we too may pass through the everlasting doors, worship and carry home blessing from the Lord, goodness from God our Saviour.

Lord, how shall we pass through the everlasting doors and approach your holy
    presence, for we are not clean of hands or pure in heart. We have lifted up
    our soul to false things and failed in our promises. How could we abide on
    your holy hill and carry home blessings from you?
But the gates lift up their heads, and the King of Glory passes through. May
    we enter with him, made clean by his goodness, made new by his love?
Take me with you, Lord Jesus, that I may tread the eternal ground and wor-
    ship in the beauty of the Father, the Son and the Holy Spirit.

Psalm 25

A great secret

When all is said and done, we are but microscopic creatures, and it is not that obvious how we should address the Creator of the cosmos. The Psalms have always been our chief guide, and in our various times of need they offer strong and simple words to carry our prayers straight to the Saviour's heart.

There are many examples in Psalm 25. When we are down, the psalm leads us to pray, 'To you, LORD, I lift my soul.' To whom can we turn? The psalm leads us again: 'My God, I trust in you.' Are we unable to see which way to take? The psalm gives us this prayer: 'LORD, make me to know your ways and ever teach me your paths.'

Or again, if we are troubled by our sins, we can pray from the psalm, 'For the sake of your name, O LORD, forgive my sin which is so great.' And again, 'Remember not the errors of my youth and my sins; think of me according to your faithful love.' Or more briefly, 'Put away all my sins.' And when we come to one of those deserts in life where we feel alone and abandoned, we may pray, 'Turn to me and be gracious to me, for I am alone and very troubled.' Yes, in so many situations, a psalm such as this will help us wonderfully to find the right dispositions and the right words for prayer.

But in addition to its wealth of short prayers, Psalm 25 also contains wise counsel, summarizing what generations of the Lord's followers have found to be true. After all, we are not the first to explore the great territory of life and try the ways of God. Let us be encouraged by these short testimonies of good folk who have gone before us. Concerning the finding of the best way, they urge:

> The LORD is generous and true;
> therefore he teaches sinners in the way.
>
> He will guide the humble in judgement,
> and will teach the lowly his way.
>
> All the paths of the LORD are faithful love and truth
> to those who keep his covenant and his testimonies . . .
>
> Who is he that fears the LORD?
> Him will he teach in the way that he should choose.

But the most striking testimony of our psalm comes in verse 14. The old Prayer Book translation sounds intriguing here: 'The secret of the Lord is among them that fear him.' What can this 'secret of the Lord' be? More recent translations usually have, 'The friendship of the LORD is for those who fear him.' This seems rather different, but the link is the idea of trust and intimacy. The Hebrew word (*sod*) in fact indicates a trusted circle of friends.

It so happens that a circle of this kind has been meeting monthly for several years in a convenient living room. These half-dozen women begin by each telling of recent experiences – pleasant or problematic. They pass on to share thoughts on agreed spiritual reading. They end with silence and prayer – sometimes the late evening service of Compline. Not quite 'end', because, as they prepare to leave, they chat more freely, time goes by, and the house shakes with gales of laughter, while the old grey and white cat, familiar with these proceedings and settling in her armchair for the night, just opens her eyes wide.

The women always sit in the same places. If anyone is missing, the loss is tangible. There's a cross in the room, and they light a candle before it. So this circle of friends and intimates has a deep dimension. It is the Lord's circle, those who regularly meet together with him, each valued, all counted by him as his close friends.

This is near to what the psalm means. Those who 'fear' him, who constantly acknowledge his reality, to such he gives a place in his intimate circle, a fellowship of trust and kindness, where sorrows are eased and faith renewed, where hope shines out upon the path for coming days. In that circle, says the psalm, 'he will make known to them his covenant'; this is the bond of love and faithfulness, the bond which was given us anew in our Lord Jesus.

And the psalm has one last treasure for us. That lonely one who lifts heart and soul to the Lord, and that intimate circle gathering like the disciples with their Master – all the grace they know is to be reflected out upon God's community. Society's troubles and perplexities are not forgotten. Light shines out from the solitary and from the circle, and so the psalm ends by drawing the whole community into its prayer:

> Redeem Israel, O God,
> from the midst of all his troubles.

The psalm has indeed a great secret for us, the secret of the Lord, for it invites us into his friendship, his circle of trust and fellowship. There we are valued and filled with hope, and there we learn to lay our concerns before the Lord and to live in the strength of prayer.

To you, Lord, I lift my soul; my God I trust in you.
My eyes are continually towards you, for you will deliver my feet from the net.
Relieve the distresses of my heart, and bring me out of my sufferings.
In your friendship, Lord, is my comfort and all my hope. Ever more deeply
    make me to know your covenant of love.
Redeem your Church from all her troubles. Save your world from all the
    enemies of life.
Glory to the Father, generous and true,
and to the Son, the Way in whom sinners are taught,
and to the Spirit, the Secret and the Friendship of God.

Psalm 26

Washed by his innocence

What a lot of sayings we have about *washing* – usually suggesting something thorough, even drastic. 'It's a wash-out', we might say, or, 'I feel washed out.' 'Look what the tide's washed up', says someone in surprise. And how often things 'get lost in the wash'! Someone whose advice is ignored might say, 'I wash my hands of it.'

But here another word has chipped in – *hand*, a word used in dozens and dozens of sayings. All hands on deck, hand in hand, an old hand, a dab hand, a dead hand, hands on, hands off, handout, second-hand, cap in hand, hands down, hands up, offhand, a free hand, the upper hand, out of hand, hand in glove – the list seem endless. The fact is that our hands are at the forefront of our deeds. The hands represent the person in action.

These thoughts prepare us for a very forceful expression in Psalm 26, using the ideas both of washing and of hands. The singer declares:

> I have washed my hands in innocence,
>   that I might go around your altar, O LORD,
>
> to sing aloud with the voice of thanksgiving,
>   and to tell of all your wonders.

To get the picture here we have to remember that the main altar did not stand inside the temple but outside in the great court. It was in the court that the pilgrim worshippers assembled during the festivals. The ceremonies of worship included passing in procession around the altar, sometimes with a dancing step. In such a circling procession the people gave thanks for help they had received from the Lord.

But our singer has not yet reached that joyful moment. Rather, he is deep in trouble and prays to God to rescue him from a heavy distress. He has come to the temple to be close to the Lord's presence. There he will make his most earnest and solemn plea for help. He begins his prayer by inviting God's scrutiny of his heart and conduct:

Judge me, LORD, for I have walked in sincerity;
I have trusted in the LORD and have not wavered.

Prove me, LORD, and test me;
try my heart and inward thoughts.

We see how this worshipper recognizes the seriousness of the Lord's requirements. Not that he claims to have lived a good life in his own strength. He believes rather that he has responded to the Lord's goodness to him. He has kept before his eyes God's faithfulness and 'truth', trustworthiness. It is this grace of the Lord that has kept him in a bond of loyalty – as he puts it:

Your faithful love has been before my eyes,
and I have walked ever in your truth.

Thus he has taken no part in the circle of the wicked, he says, but has washed his hands in innocence – that is, he has kept to the way of purity before God. For only by this way could he expect to be among those giving thanks at the altar for the blessings of God's help. In the bond of faithfulness he has loved the Lord's sanctuary, praying for it, caring for it in practical ways. As he says:

LORD, I have loved the dwelling of your house,
the place where your glory abides.

So the singer comes to the heart of his prayer: 'Redeem me, LORD, and have pity on me.' And as the psalm closes, he looks forward in hope to standing again on firm and pleasant ground and to the time of thanksgiving in the assembly.

This psalm has been used times beyond all counting in Christian history. As priests have ceremonially rinsed their hands in preparation for their service at the Lord's table, they have taken to themselves that thought of washing the hands in innocence to go up to the altar of God. Other verses in the psalm, however, may have seemed more difficult to use. They bring home to us the awesome nature of that coming close to the Holy One to make our plea. Does he not look for a sincere heart, a heart that has had no part in the corruptions of the world, its selfish ways of living? Have we kept the Lord's faithful love and truth ever before our eyes and responded with an answering love? Have we, in the psalm's words, washed our hands in innocence?

We take courage as we remember that the very foundation of the Christian life is our baptism. This is a mighty sign for the washing through which we come to God in Christ. Christ washes us from our sins and nurtures us in his innocence. Through his washing of our hands and our souls, through his continuing grace, we *can* draw near to God in prayer, our feet resting on that firm and beautiful ground where we see his glory. And as the psalmist went around the altar singing with the voice of thanksgiving, we too in our own way will give thanks, blessing the name of the Lord who has washed away our sins and redeemed us from darkness and despair.

Father, as I come to ask your help in my troubles, cleanse me. Cleanse me by him who walked in sincerity, fully trusted in you and did not waver. Wash my hands and my heart in the innocence of Jesus.

Through him may I come to be a joyful witness to your wonders and your faithful love.

For his sake may I always love the dwelling of your house, the place where your glory shines out. May my feet walk firmly in the lovely land of your presence.

Psalm 27
One thing have I asked

When you are assailed by many troubles and dangers, it is natural to plunge straight into prayer for help. This is often the case in the Psalms, but Psalm 27 is an example of another approach. Start first with tribute to what you have already known of God's protection. Focus all your need and desire upon the supreme desire of knowing him. Pledge yourself to bring offerings and thankful music to him in the sure time beyond the present peril. And only after all this come to your cry for help.

Such a preparation for your cry will surely summon up from your soul all the resources of faith and past experience, strengthening your trust, simplifying your desire. But also it will add strength to your prayer, which will rest now on the divine promise and work, on the grace of our Lord and Saviour.

Well, how does this approach work out in Psalm 27? The cry for help is held back till verse 7, and all the first six verses are words of praise and trust. It seems that a king of David's line is here recalling all the grace of the God who has anointed him to defend his people. He sings:

> The LORD is my light and my salvation – whom shall I fear?
> The LORD is the stronghold of my life – of whom shall I be afraid?

The harsh world of battles and invasions is reflected in his words:

> When deadly ones draw near to me to eat up my flesh,
> my adversaries and my foes – see, they shall stumble and fall.

> Though a host encamp against me, my heart shall not fear;
> though the line of battle rise upon me, even then I shall trust.

And now this worshipper brings to focus what it is that he asks of the Lord – safety, of course, but as an opportunity to know the Lord in his beauty and wisdom. He concentrates all his need and desire into this 'one thing':

> One thing I ask of the LORD, and that alone I seek –
> that I may dwell in the house of the LORD all the days of my life,
>
> to look upon the beauty of the LORD,
> and seek guidance in his temple.

The king's residence adjoined the temple on the holy hill of Zion, for his calling was to serve and express the kingdom of God. His prayer then will be to live out his days peacefully in this closeness to the holy presence, seeing the glory of the Lord in visions and being guided to do God's will. There he will be sheltered 'in the day of trouble', hidden 'in the covering of his tent', safe upon the rock of God from all his enemies round about. And there too in thankfulness he will make offerings with music and songs of testimony and praise.

In these first six verses, then, the singer has expressed his faith and purified his desire. He now comes to his request and lets an urgent cry sound forth:

> Lord, hear my voice;
> as I call, have pity and answer me.

He is asking for a merciful and favourable reception – that God should not hide his face or forsake him. Has not God invited his prayers? Thus he sings:

> My heart recalls your word: Seek my face.
> So, Lord, your face now I do seek.
>
> Do not hide your face from me,
> or turn your servant away in displeasure.
>
> You have been my helper;
> do not leave me or forsake me, O God my Saviour.
>
> Though father and mother forsake me,
> the Lord will take me up.

We see how, even through such statements of trust, he is making earnest entreaty: may the Lord indeed take him up as his own child! And he asks to be led on a way through all the perils, and to be defended from the false-hoods and curses that the enemy's spin doctors and witch doctors pour out and puff out against him. His prayer ends with another great word of trust and hope:

> I believe that I shall see
> the goodness of the Lord in the land of the living.

The psalm's concluding verse seems to come from another voice or a choir; it is like the inspired word of comfort we sometimes get from a friend or from scripture:

> Wait for the Lord, be strong and let your heart take courage;
> yes, wait in hope for the Lord.

Such, then, is our psalm. Do you think it is one we can take to our hearts, even from those distant days of battle? Will we be glad to use it in urgent prayer for ourselves and for others? Its pattern is remarkable. While it speaks from a time of danger and consternation, yet it is prefaced and penetrated with recollections of God's promises and saving power. If in our distresses we seem to oscillate between trust and alarm, it is clear we are not the first to do so. So let us be encouraged by this beautiful psalm to express our fears to God, while beginning and ending with recollection of his mighty and loving protection. And through the words of the psalm let us, in all our bewilderment, rediscover the one thing needful – communion with him.

Lord, you are my light and my salvation. Banish my fear.
Beyond all my needs and duties, there is only one need. That one thing I ask,
  Lord, that one thing I seek – to be with you. Grant me that closeness where
  I see your beauty and know your guidance.
I believe that I shall see the goodness of the Lord in his land of life.
Wait for the Lord, O my soul. Be strong and let your heart take courage. In
  hope and trust, wait for the Lord.

Psalm 28

Uplifted hands

Sometimes a piece of music will end with an echo of its beginning. In a great symphony or concerto this will have deep significance, often enhanced by a new turn given to the phrase when it comes back. In the Psalms also we sometimes find that the ending has words that link with the opening. This is the case in Psalm 28. Its opening appeal includes this prayer:

> Hear the voice of my supplication as I cry to you,
>   as I *lift up* my hands to your holy dwelling.

The word for 'lift up' also occurs at the end of the psalm. Some will know it well as quoted in the Te Deum, thus:

> O LORD, save thy people and bless thine heritage;
>   govern them and *lift them up* for ever.

Only a little echo, you might think, and easily missed. But it catches that precious link of heaven and earth – the movement to and fro of prayer and blessing, intercession and answering grace. When God *lifts up* his creatures, it answers the *lifting up of hands* to him in supplication. On occasions when we have experienced his lifting up above some distress or destruction, we may wonder what hands were lifted up for us. But only in a fuller light shall we know of all those saving prayers.

The way our psalm is quoted in that traditional Te Deum has a further message for us in the word 'govern' – 'Govern them and lift them up for ever.' Much governing or ruling in human society is about subjecting, sub-jugating, putting down, putting under. But our verse asks for God's rule, a governing which lifts up and saves: 'O LORD, save thy people; govern them and lift them up for ever.' And wherever we have power and authority – in our own little dominions or on a larger scale – there should be a govern-ing that saves and blesses, a rule that ever lifts up the entrusted ones.

So this last verse of Psalm 28 is quite fruitful. But a closer translation shows even more, for it asks the Lord to be like the eastern shepherd, who guided the flock through harsh mountains to find green pastures, and carried the lambs in his bosom over the rough and weary ways. This trans-lation gives:

> O save your people and bless your heritage;
> shepherd them and carry them for ever.

Here still, even more strongly, God's rule over us is shown as his care, his constant loving care, tender and dedicated.

It does not always seem so, as we know only too well. At the outset of this very psalm we see how the worshipper is in great distress. The cry goes up to God with urgency. Death may not be far away:

> To you, LORD, I call; my Rock, do not be deaf to me.
> If you are silent to me, I shall be as those gone down into the Abyss.

Later, however, the singer strengthens his prayer by expressing confidence that the Lord will come to save:

> Blessed be the LORD,
> for he will surely hear the voice of my supplication.

> The LORD is my glory and my shield,
>   my heart trusts in him,
> and when I am saved my heart shall exult,
>   and with my song I will thank him.

These expressions of confidence in the Saviour give force to the plea, for how could such a trusting one be forsaken? And one more big considera-tion supports the prayer. This is that the one here raising imploring hands is the Lord's Anointed – the person sent by God to rule for him, sent with every promise of support. The people he rules are God's people. Surely then God must hear and act. These considerations give strength to the end of the intercession:

> The glory is the LORD's,
> and he is the stronghold of salvation for his Anointed.
>
> O save your people and bless your heritage;
> shepherd them and carry them for ever.

This figure who has here lifted up hands in prayer has been seen by the Church as foreshadowing Christ, the true Anointed. We picture him raising the hands of intercession for all kept in his heart, for all committed to him by the Father, for all creatures. He ever asks the Father to deliver us from evil and bless us, to shepherd his sheep and carry the little ones over the rocks and pits in the way. We picture him so, but are also encouraged by the psalm to stand with him and raise our hands also for the needs that are especially laid on our hearts. And so the psalm becomes a constant voice for us, leading prayer against evil and calling down blessings upon the humble. Ours are now the words: 'Hear the voice of my supplication as I cry out to you, as I lift up my hands to your holy dwelling . . . O save your people and bless your heritage; be their shepherd and carry them for ever.'

And only God knows how much is owed to the interceding hands, the hands that raise the world's sufferings up to heaven and draw down blessings and salvation. With this thought, a woman comes to mind – she has grown old and infirm, rather solitary and withdrawn. In the world's eyes she has nothing now to contribute. She might as well be gone. But, almost secretly, she has a ministry of prayer. She notes the needs of those with whom she still has some contact. She picks up scraps of international news. She has information about prisoners awaiting execution. Through the reality of her faith and her caring heart she fulfils a calling to pray. She is a strong intercessor. Daily she passes through the everlasting doors and lifts up her hands towards the Presence. Who can calculate the help that has gone out from that 'stronghold of salvation' because of her prayer?

Father, hear the voice of my supplication – for myself, for my dear ones, for my country, for your world. Hear as I cry out to you and lift my hands to your holy dwelling.
Hear the supplication of your Anointed, your Son Jesus. Turn the hearts of those who mean harm to your creatures.

O save and bless your heritage, shepherd your little ones, and carry them in
your arms beyond the chasm of death.
The Lord is my glory and my shield. My heart trusts in him.

Psalm 29

The Word that shatters

In many an old chapel, in a window or on a wall or woodwork, you would see a line taken from Psalm 29: 'Worship the LORD in the beauty of holiness.' One might feel that the minister, elders and sidesmen were trying to live up to this injunction with their immaculate, highly polished appearance and their reverential manners – the organ, too, with its subdued and mellifluous tones. It was indeed a common understanding of the line that it was calling for 'holiness' in our worship. As the old Prayer Book translation has it, 'Worship the Lord with holy worship.'

But the original meaning of the psalm was rather different. The singer is calling to the mighty beings of heaven, the angelic hosts, and bidding them fall down before the holiness of *God*. This 'holiness' is a beautiful but terrifying radiance, expressive of God's unique nature and power as Lord and Creator of all that exists. The singer's vision is that this radiance of God is now especially blazing out because he has conquered chaos, ordered the living world and entered on his reign. So the call goes out:

Give to the LORD, you powers above,
give to the LORD the glory and strength.

Give to the LORD the glory of his name;
bow low to the LORD [manifest] in the beauty of [his] holiness . . .

Now in his temple all cry, Glory!
The LORD has taken his seat above the ocean of heaven,
enthroned as king for ever.

The singer means that the angelic beings should acknowledge that they are no real gods in comparison with the Lord. They are to attribute to him all divine glory and strength. As they prostrate themselves before his radiance, they confess that they are only his minions.

71

In very ancient times the psalm rang out in the great festival at Jerusalem as the new agricultural round began. How readily those ancient pilgrims felt united with the worship in heaven! For them the earthly temple was like a window into heaven, and through it was streaming the 'holiness' of God, the splendour of his glory. The singer can call to the angels because heaven seems all around and over the temple courts. Earthly worshippers and angels alike, one vast congregation, bow low together, and together they cry out that the glory belongs to the Lord alone.

The special excitement and exaltation of the moment arose from a sense of drama in the worship. Great events are signified. God has conquered and is present to impart the gifts of life. The autumnal turn of the year, with expectation of storms to break the long summer drought – this turn of the year is echoing the creation's Beginning. For the earnest worshippers, the vision of a new world arises, a perfect reign of God.

In an ancient style of poetry, our singer pays tribute to the victorious Creator by recollecting how his mighty word, his thunder-voice, has quelled the raging waters and made them serve his purpose of life. In this tribute the singer does not draw directly on the stories of creation, but rather on recollection of winter storms. Thunder and tempest signified the ancient battle with chaos, and how the Lord ensured new life, peace and plenty. This is how the dramatic poem unfolds:

> The voice of the Lord against the waters –
>   the God of glory thundered,
> the LORD against the waters.
>
> The voice of the LORD with might,
>   the voice of the LORD with majesty,
>
> the voice of the LORD breaking cedar trees –
> so the LORD broke the cedars of Lebanon.
>
> And he made Mount Lebanon skip like a calf,
> and Sirion like a young wild-ox.
>
> The voice of the LORD cleaving flames of fire –
>   the voice of the Lord made the wilderness whirl,
> the LORD set whirling the wilderness of Kadesh.
>
> The voice of the LORD bowed the oak-trees,
> and stripped the forests bare . . .
>
> The LORD will give strength to his people;
> the LORD will bless his people with peace.

Does this all seem a long way from the serene chapels, with their polished wood, soft blue carpets and sweet organs? Perhaps. But the whole psalm, and not just one line of it, has much to give the Church today. For one thing, it invites us to deepen our experience in worship. The Christian year, too, has its sense of drama, with its climaxes at Christmas, Easter and Pentecost. There we too are called to experience anew the impact of divine events, and to be filled with the joy of their eternal significance. The psalm reminds us that in worship we also are joined to a universal throng of heaven and earth, all ascribing glory to the Lord alone, all drawing from him alone the strength of life, blessing and peace.

Then again, we are struck by the fact that, in the psalm, the terrifying, shattering thunderclap is 'the voice of the LORD' – so it is said seven times! This leads us also to discern his voice in the storms and upheavals of modern life. And what is his voice but his mighty Word, the Word that took our nature in Christ? So the psalm reminds us that our Saviour is the outgoing of God's creative being, a mighty force to break down and master chaos – in order to give life and blessing. In the times of shattering – storms in world affairs or in our own lives – the voice of the Lord, the Word that is Christ, is supreme and working to prepare good. With the psalm we pray and believe that, beyond the storms, the Lord will give us new life and bless us with his everlasting peace.

The voice of the Lord with might, the voice of the Lord with majesty! In the times of shattering, Lord, grant we may know your voice. Help us to trust that there is meaning – your meaning, your Word that prepares the blessings of peace.

In our worship may we know we are joined to the throng that worships you above the ocean of heaven, you that rule over the forces of life, you who alone are radiant with holiness. May we too in your temple cry 'Glory!' Thine is the kingdom, the power and the glory.

So bless us year by year and day by day, until your creation is perfected beyond the storms, and we see you for ever in the beauty of your holiness.

Psalm 30
The morning of healing

———◆◆◆———

It was a fine procession up the aisle. Two by two, the robed figures advanced, culminating in the splendidly clad bishop. From the organ pealed Henry Purcell's trumpet tune, so bright in tone, so infectious in rhythm. You could almost see the robed figures breaking into a dancing step. Almost. But not quite. No, the reality was that their pace did not quicken. There was no skip or dance to be seen. As in most European tradition, the unity of body and mind had long been lost, the unity which would have made the feet move with the joy of the heart.

It was different in the worship where Psalm 30 was composed. The singer means it fairly literally when he gives thanks to the Lord and says, 'You turned my sorrowing into dancing; you took off my sackcloth and girded me with joy.' He had worn sackcloth, fasted and wept before God, praying in great need. But now, in the time of salvation, he wears festive garments and moves with dancing step, as he sings thanks and testimony in the temple to his Saviour.

As a testimony, the singer outlines his story to the gathering of the faithful. Looking back, he sees that pleasant circumstances had led to complacency, a feeling that no trouble would ever happen to him. Suddenly it seemed that the Lord had hidden his face. Trouble came in plenty. Then the sufferer cried out to the Lord with all the penitence of the custom of sackcloth and ashes. He pleaded with a childlike earnestness. What advantage would it be to the Lord if he fell into the abyss of death? For that would be the end to his thanks and praise in the temple. He had said:

> What gain is there in my blood if I go down into the Abyss?
> Can dust thank you? Will it tell of your faithfulness?
>
> So hear, LORD, and have pity on me;
> come, LORD, as my strong helper.

Thus he pleaded, and at last his prayer was answered:

> You turned my sorrowing into dancing;
> you took off my sackcloth and girded me with joy,
>
> that in glory I should make music to you and not be silent.
> O LORD, my God, I will give thanks to you for ever.

74

Psalms usually have headings. We might think that this one would be headed, 'A song of one that is healed'. But no. Surprisingly the heading runs, 'A song at the dedication of the house'. This agrees with a Jewish tradition which tells that the psalm was chanted at the rededication of the temple in Maccabean times. An individual's story, it seems, came to be taken as a picture of the community. The community of the faithful had become complacent, driving away the favour of the Lord. They fell into troubles, reaching a death-like state. But penitence and prayer had been answered, and so the community's life was renewed. The great 'house' of worship was rededicated with joyous praise and dance.

And the Christian Church too has sometimes taken an individual's story to its heart. Whenever the Magnificat is sung, the Church enters into the pattern of faith shown by Mary. And how strongly the pattern of John Wesley's experience of Christ has characterized the whole Methodist community, as is still evident in the drastic self-offering spelt out in the annual Covenant Service.

But less dramatically, all humble believers are contributing to the total faith and hope of the Church. As living stones, each one is built into Christ's temple, helping to renew its life beyond every shadow of death that may fall upon it. An individual's thankful testimony makes a great contribution. Let each one of us be inspired by the psalm. Let us consider how our Lord has drawn us up from great darkness, how a night-time of tears has been followed by joy in the morning of Christ's light. Then we too will want to give thanks, and with that wholeheartedness which is symbolized in music and dance. As the psalm has it:

> In glory I shall make music to you and not be silent;
> O LORD, my God, I will give thanks to you for ever.

Lord, is this the Church's story, is this my story? A time of ease, my hill so strong, complacency. Then your face was hidden, and I was troubled.
But in your compassion you heard my cry. You drew me up. You healed me. You brought my soul out of darkness.
In Christ my sorrowing has become dancing. My soul shall make music to you. O Lord, my God, let me give thanks to you for ever.

75

Psalm 31
Not discarded

———◆◆◆———

There was once a little girl called Emma who liked to play 'shop'. Her emporium was a shed in the backyard. Her goods were carefully priced, and the friends who were her customers were all provided with token money. For this 'money' she had collected a great amount of broken crockery. The fragments were sorted according to quality, and the different grades represented coins of various values. The highest values were the pieces with gold rims or rings. Such treasuring of broken vessels is rare. Fragments of pottery are usually discarded as useless. Only archaeologists, hundreds or thousands of years later, find the pieces useful as clues to the date of a layer of remains.

The person praying in Psalm 31 felt like a broken vessel, useless, discarded, forgotten:

> Have pity on me, LORD, for I am distressed;
>   my eye is wasted with grief, my body and soul alike.
>
> For my days are consumed with sorrow and my eyes with sighing;
>   my strength fails through my suffering,
>   and my bones, they waste away . . .
>
> I am forgotten like a dead man passed from mind,
>   discarded like a broken pot.

In our own time it is not uncommon for people in various situations to feel 'discarded like a broken pot'. Some feel like this when their work is brought to an abrupt end, whether through illness, redundancy or retirement. Whatever strains and stresses that work might have entailed, one's life was poured into it – one's best energies, physical, mental, emotional. It provided that role, that identity, which people need. And for all the kind gestures at the leaving ceremony, there comes a sense of being soon forgotten, dispensed with. More severe is the forlornness that comes with incapacity, whether through some illness or accident, or through inexorable ageing. Now the hitherto useful and appreciated vessel is really shattered. As the psalmist says, one feels a burden to those who are near. The real person seems forgotten like the dead who have passed from mind, seems indeed discarded like a broken pot. As the psalm has it, days are consumed with sorrow and years with sighing.

But the psalm will not leave us there. The sufferer is wholly turned to the Lord, and verse after verse declares trust and hope:

> But I trust in you alone, O LORD;
> I have said, You are my God.
>
> My times are in your hand – O deliver me . . .
>
> Make your face to shine upon your servant;
> save me in your faithful love.

Such trust does not go unanswered. Mysteriously, the angels of the Lord's help steal about the sufferer. The conviction of God's goodness and continuing love grows strong:

> How great is your goodness, LORD,
>   which you have stored up for those who fear you,
> and openly accomplish for those who shelter in you . . .
>
> Blessed be the LORD,
> who in a besieged city wonderfully shows his love for me.

Yes, there is much in the psalm to kindle hope even when in a deep, deep valley of suffering. But one verse especially has been treasured as leading to a trust that brings profound relief:

> Into your hand I commit my spirit;
> you will redeem me, LORD and faithful God.

The 'spirit' committed here is in effect one's life, one's very being. The psalmist commits his life into the hand of God, giving God the charge of it. The psalmist releases his own anxious grip, entrusting the outcome to God. He commits his spirit, his life, into the Lord's hand, confident that the Lord is his faithful Redeemer, the One who will ever stay close – not treating him as a broken, useless pot, but reassuring him, and at last restoring him in beauty and joy.

Now it so happens that in St Luke's account of the death of Jesus, the very last words of our Lord are drawn from this verse, with the characteristic addition of 'Father'. Luke writes:

> And when Jesus had cried with a loud voice, he said, 'Father, into your hand I commit my spirit.' And having said this, he breathed his last.
>
> (Luke 23.46)

In the Gospels, whenever Jesus speaks from the Psalms it is a sign that he is taking the way revealed in ancient prophecy, the way destined for God's Messiah. The quotation of our verse shows the Messiah going trustingly into death, confident of the great redemption. And through this verse Christ, the Messiah, embraces us also. Our spirit he would commit also into the Father's hand, that we too should be redeemed by that love shown wonderfully 'in a besieged city'. When we are near to death, we do well to say this verse after him. But more – every day of our life we should say this verse, in youth and in age, and so gradually die to self and live for and through our Redeemer. We give him daily the charge of our spirit. Our times, our way, our destiny – all is rested in his hand.

The little girl who played 'shop' in the shed in the backyard was a sign, as children often are. The broken cups and dishes were not rubbish to Emma. She treasured them, and in the reality of her imagination gave them a vital role. May her story prompt us in the time of brokenness to turn to the One who will not discard us, but treasure and redeem us. So may we come gladly to embrace the daily dying – dying to all distance from him, making our life over into his possession.

My Jesus, may I stay near you – as they lay the net for you, when your strength
fails through your suffering, when you are become the scorn of all your foes
and your acquaintance flee from you, when you are discarded like a broken
pot?
My Jesus, may I pray the trusting words with you: O God, my times are in
your hand, in the covering of your presence you will hide me, you alone are
my crag and defence.
Day by day, and at my ending, Jesus, may I say with you: Father, into your
hand I commit my spirit; you will redeem me, Lord and faithful God.

Psalm 32

Confession and counsel

An elderly professor, who still had little sense of direction, used to recall how, one day in early childhood, he had got lost in the seaside town of Blackpool. Clad only in swimming shorts, he had been coming up the steps with his family from the beach to the esplanade. It was August in the

1930s, and the throngs around the beach were immense. His mother's eye lost him in the crush. When he reached the road, he set off in the wrong direction. Being already of a meditative turn of mind, he had covered a mile or more before suspecting all was not well. He consulted an elderly man, who led him to further consultations. At length a policeman committed him to the care of a tram conductor for a free ride back down the esplanade and a fortunate reunion with his family, who were out searching. The whole episode had arisen from his being hidden a moment from his mother's caring eye.

We may not warm to the idea that all our life we need such a caring, watchful eye always upon us, but there comes a time when we know that God's vigilant care and constant guidance are most precious and indeed essential. We may only reach this knowledge after some time of misery, as indeed happened to the singer of Psalm 32. Finding God after a period of estrangement, this worshipper hears God's own promise:

> I will instruct you and guide you in the way you should go;
> I will counsel you, with my eye watching over you.

Taking this promise to ourselves, we come to treasure it more and more – to be instructed and guided in a good and fruitful way, counselled at every turn by the kind wisdom of our Lord, and guarded by his wakeful eye. But a relationship is involved, so from our side there must be a continuing response. As the divine word in the psalm has it:

> Do not be like a horse or mule that will not give heed,
> whose course must be checked with bit and bridle,
> or they will not come with you.

While yet untrained, the animals will not give heed, but then they come to learn trust. Likewise there must be, from our side, trust in the divine Master, so that we are happy to go with him.

We get a glimpse of how this happy situation was reached in the case of the psalmist. There had been a time of great strain, probably illness, where it seemed that the joy of life had dried up. As the psalm puts it:

> Day and night your hand was heavy upon me;
> the springs of life within me turned to summer drought.

And so the conviction grew that the prime need was to get right with God:

> Then I acknowledged to you my transgression,
> and no longer hid my wrongdoing;

> I said, I will confess my sin to the LORD,
>> and you put away the guilt of my transgression.

In this new openness to God there was great relief. Health revived. The strain was lifted. The conclusion from the experience is not that all sufferers have an unacknowledged sin to confess. On the contrary, we know that there are the sufferings of self-sacrifice, and many more, that are a mystery hidden with God. But the psalmist does most warmly commend the value of confessing wrongdoing and receiving forgiveness:

> Happy the one whose sin is forgiven,
>> and whose transgression is covered.

> Happy the person to whom the LORD no longer imputes wrong,
>> and in whose spirit is no deceit . . .

> Therefore let every faithful soul pray to you while you may be
>> found;
> even when the great waters surge, they will not overwhelm him.

The psalm, we see, is emphatic in its counsel for real happiness, and it ends also on a glad note:

> Rejoice in the LORD, you faithful, and be glad;
>> sing out, all that are true of heart.

This reminds us of St Paul's 'Rejoice in the Lord always, and again I say, Rejoice' (Phil. 4.4). And indeed the joy of the Christian pilgrim also arises from the lifting of the burden of sin and the subsequent close walk with the Lord. The psalm thus speaks very much to the point. Confession is an opening towards our gracious Lord, and trust is an acceptance of his faithful love. By trusting in the cross of Jesus, and being willing to hear his counsel and walk with him all our life, we find a happiness beyond compare.

O my God, help me to be open towards you. May I be ready to acknowledge to you my wrongdoing. May I be willing to hear and to follow your instruction.

May your eye ever watch over me. May the waters of trouble not overwhelm me.

You are my shelter to guard me from trouble. You surround me with faithful love.

Happy the one whose sin is forgiven! O my soul, rejoice in the Lord always, and again I say, Rejoice.

Psalm 33

Our greatest discovery

————·•·————

The beginning of the world has been pictured vividly in science no less than in religions. Scientists in recent times have spoken of a beginning in a tremendous cosmic explosion. With that Big Bang, some 15 billion years ago, an expansion began and is still going on. Galaxies outside our own Milky Way move ever further from us. These scientists plot the development of matter in the first seconds after the explosion, then again in the first hundreds of thousands of years. And so they trace the formation of heavenly bodies through millions of years. In all this the mind has to grapple with protons and neutrons, electrons and positrons, quanta of light, helium and hydrogen, and many other mysteries.

It seems much simpler when Psalm 33 depicts the beginning, and yet what it says – or rather, sings – is of inexhaustible depth. The basic image used in the psalm's imaginative picture is indeed only the speaking of a word, with the passing of a breath from the mouth. But this word at the beginning is the word of God, the out-breathing of the One who transcends all existence and all our understanding. This is how the psalm puts it:

> By the word of the LORD the heavens were made,
>   and all their hosts by the breath of his mouth . . .

> For he but spoke, and it was so;
>   he commanded, and it was established.

This idea of a word of creation is indeed inexhaustible. But we can understand it in the first place as an expression of authority and power. In the ancient world they might say of a mighty ruler, 'He has only to speak and it is done.' Such was his authority. Applying this thought to God, we hear the psalm calling to mind his power and dominion beyond all our conceiving.

But we can also understand the Creator's word in terms of his self-giving. Any artist or writer will readily appreciate this. God's own thought went forth in that word – something of his mind, his very soul, laden with his beauty, his sense of rightness, his faithfulness, his love. As the psalmist sings:

81

> For the word of the LORD is true,
> and all his work is in faithfulness.
>
> He loves right and justice;
> the earth is full of the faithful love of the LORD.

Here our psalm has gone into depths beyond the capacity of natural science. The psalmist sees through the marvels of the physical world to the faithfulness of the Lord. According to this insight, we encounter in the world not only the Creator's power and wisdom, but, most wonderfully of all, his faithful love. For our psalm, the beginning of the world and the nature of the world – these are a matter of meeting the Creator, and responding to him in worship and trust. Along this way of response, the psalm teaches the vanity of human boasts, the falsehood of human arrogance:

> The LORD made null the counsel of the nations;
> he brought to nothing the plans of the peoples.
>
> The counsel of the LORD will stand for ever,
> the plans of his heart to all generations . . .
>
> The LORD looks down from heaven,
> he sees all the people of earth.
>
> From the place of his throne he peers down
> upon all that dwell in the world,
>
> he who has formed the hearts of each one,
> and understands all their deeds.
>
> A king is not saved by the greatness of an army;
> a warrior is not delivered by greatness of strength . . .
>
> But the eye of the LORD is on those who fear him,
> on those who wait for his faithful love,
>
> to deliver their soul from death,
> and to keep them alive in famine.

So the psalm would have us turn from reliance on earthly wealth and power, and rather meet the Creator with trust. We are to 'wait' for him – that is, always to remember that his action is decisive, not ours. We are to wait trustfully on him, and in all our troubles ask for the help of his faithful love. So the conclusion of the song rings out:

> Our soul has waited for the LORD,
> for he is our help and our shield.
>
> Our heart will rejoice in him,
> for we have trusted in his holy name.
>
> LORD, may your faithful love be upon us,
> as we ever wait for you.

With this thought of 'waiting for the Lord' the psalm ends. But we ought not to end without noting the way the psalm began. It's a call for music. Remarkably, music has quite a big role even in our technological world. Admittedly, some of it is aggressive and ugly, and the motivation behind it is to sell something or make huge profits. But our psalm, which has such deep thoughts about creation and life with the Creator, has a simple view of music. It thinks of music as played for God, in joy and thanksgiving:

> Rejoice in the LORD, you faithful;
> beautiful is praise from the true of heart.
>
> Give praise to the LORD with the lyre;
> with the ten-stringed harp make music for him.
>
> Sing to him a new song;
> raise the music of strings with shouts of joy.

And what is the cause of the joy? It is flowing from the greatest of all discoveries about the cosmic order, about the universe's beginning and continuing – the discovery that the world is full of the faithful love of the One who willed and spoke it into being, and ever upholds it by the breath of his mouth. To share in this discovery is indeed to see all things new, and to be made new, and so with thankful joy to sing to him 'a new song'.

O God, the Father, the Word, and the Breath, you that create and sustain all
things, grant us to know your faithful love that fills the world.
Grant us the depth of trust always to wait for your faithful love, always to
wait for you.
For you our soul has waited, for you are our help and shield.
In you our heart rejoices, for we trust in your holy name, Father, Word and
Breath.

Psalm 34
The test of experience

————◆◆◆————

One of the great figures of early Christianity was St Columba. With twelve companions he founded a community on the island of Iona in the inner Hebrides. From that base he did much to bring the gospel to Scotland. In his last hours, at the age of 76, he was copying out the Psalms. The last words he was able to write were from Psalm 34, verse 10. Completing a page, he wrote, 'Those who seek the LORD shall not lack anything good.' His brother monks thought the verse was fitting to Columba. He would surely lack nothing of God's eternal goodness.

The psalm has several statements of such warm testimony to God's goodness. Being an 'alphabetic' psalm, with a verse for every letter of the Hebrew alphabet, it tends to have verses almost complete in themselves, rather like proverbs easily remembered.

> Those who look to him are filled with light,
> their faces no longer downcast.

> The angel of the LORD encamps around those who fear him,
> that he may deliver them.

> O taste and see that the LORD is good;
> happy the person who shelters in him.

> The eyes of the LORD are towards the faithful,
> and his ears are open to their cry.

> The LORD is near to the broken-hearted,
> and he saves those that are crushed in spirit.

Such is the testimony of the psalm to the Lord as faithful Saviour. The singer has the warmth of experience and speaks personally:

> I sought the LORD and he heard me,
> and delivered me from all my fears . . .

> Here was a sufferer who called, and the LORD heard his cry,
> and saved him from all his troubles.

84

Such testimony has echoed the experience of many, and the New Testament writers obviously loved the psalm, quoting seven of its verses (John 19.36; 1 Pet. 2.3; 3.10–12; cf. Rom. 14.19; Heb. 12.14).

Yet many too are the situations when the protection or healing of the Lord are not to be seen. Then the faithful pray, it seems, to no avail. St Columba himself, in his long life of hardship, will have known many such situations. How is it, then, that the praise of the Lord's faithfulness still rings true in the depths of the soul?

For the Christian, the way through all the contradictions has to be in union with Christ. No angels seemed to camp about him and ward off his executioners. No miracle answered the prayer in Gethsemane to drive away the looming cross. And yet in a mysterious and mighty way the prayer *was* answered, and the power of heaven proved a sure defence until the victory was won.

In our own sufferings also, our prayer in the name of Jesus will be answered in God's way. The waiting may be long indeed. Perhaps only in the fullness of the ages the fruit of our sufferings will be seen and his faithfulness manifested. But already in our present troubled life our souls may be lit by the light of Christ's resurrection. In daily feeding on his grace we may prove the truth of the ancient words of our psalm: 'O taste and see that the LORD is good – happy the person who shelters in him!' Once alive to the love of the Lord, we shall gladly join in the psalmist's thanksgiving without waiting for all suffering and perplexity to be removed. Those warm opening verses will ring true for us:

> I will bless the LORD at all times;
> his praise shall ever be in my mouth.
>
> My soul shall glory in the LORD;
> the humble will hear it and be glad.
>
> Tell out the greatness of the LORD with me,
> and let us exalt his name together.

Lord, I am eager for life. I long for days to enjoy what is good. Help me then to follow the way of the psalm – learning to fear you, turning away from evil, doing good, pursuing peace. Help me to look to you and reflect your light. Lead me to taste and see that you are good.

You hear the cry of the faithful. You are near the broken-hearted. As I watch with Jesus, who was faithful to death, may I know that you will deliver me out of all my troubles.

Father, your angels are encamped about those who fear you. Those who fear you shall lack nothing. As I watch with Jesus, may I see into the mystery and believe the faithfulness and eternity of your goodness.

Psalm 35

Praying with your bones

People nowadays often speak of 'body language'. What gave rise to the fashionable phrase may not be clear to us, but we instantly can imagine its meaning. 'Body language' – without words, just with a movement of the head or the carriage of the body, you can speak volumes. Cats do it a lot. With head-rubbing and ground-pawing they give more than a hint to their food-provider. With expanding tail they convey to an unwelcome cat 'Get lost'.

Needless to say, the psalms long ago knew all about body language. A good example comes in Psalm 35. The singer promises to worship the Lord with praise and thanksgiving when delivered from his oppressor, and he says:

> All my bones shall say, LORD, Who is like you,
> delivering the afflicted from one who is too strong for him,
>> the poor and needy person from one that would despoil him?

'All my bones shall say' – the psalmist is probably thinking of the supreme body language, dancing. Through the dancing step around the altar of the Lord, he will express joy in the Saviour and bear witness to his faithfulness. Dance in those days, it has been said, was 'a praying with the bones' ('ein Beten mit den Beinen' – Heinrich Heine).

But that happy outcome of celebration still seems a long way off for our singer. At present he suffers the bitterness of receiving much evil in return for good. As he puts it:

> They repay me evil for good,
> to the desolation of my soul.
>
> Yet when they were sick I put on sackcloth;
> I afflicted my soul with fasting.

86

And when my prayer returned empty to my bosom,
it was as though I grieved for friend or brother.

I went about as if mourning my own mother,
and I was bowed down with grief.

But when I stumbled they rejoiced and gathered,
    they gathered against me;
smiting me unawares, they tore at me without ceasing.

In this bitter situation, the singer puts it all to the Lord:

LORD, how long will you look on?
Restore my soul from their ravages,
    my precious one from among the lions . . .

You see it, LORD – do not keep silence;
O Lord, do not stay far from me.

The prayer is raised with great urgency. The psalmist is very likely a king who is betrayed by former allies, and he calls on the Lord to come as the supreme warrior to fight off these attackers:

Lay hold of shield and buckler;
rise up and come to my help.

Draw spear and javelin against my pursuers;
say to my soul, I am your salvation . . .

May they be like chaff before the wind,
with the angel of the LORD driving them away.

May their path be dark and slippery,
with the angel of the LORD pursuing them.

For without any cause they have hidden a pit for me;
without cause they have dug their trap for my soul.

A forceful prayer indeed! And it may be that we too should sometimes similarly urge the Lord mightily to drive away evil forces that beset us or our loved ones. But a greater meaning opens out when we note that the psalm is taken up by Christ in St John's Gospel (15.18–25). Here it appears that the psalm was prophetic of Christ, the Messiah hated without a cause. So when we recite it, we may feel we are giving expression to Christ's continuing prayer against the oppressors and abusers, the deceitful and cruel – his unceasing intercession to protect 'the quiet in the land', the humble and faithful ones.

But further, we see that John's Gospel here links the psalm to Christ's whole destiny in suffering and victory. And so the routing of the evil ones is not the last word. The 'angel of the LORD' that pursues the wicked is at last seen to be Christ's Spirit of forgiveness, that desires them to turn and be made new. That miracle of repentance and new birth will indeed fulfil the peace which the psalmist desires; that will be the great peace of Christ's kingdom. What joyful dance then, what body language – 'all my bones shall say, LORD, who is like you?'

Fight, O God, against those that would ruin your creation. Do not stay far from the victims of those lies and cruelties.

Pursue the ruthless with your angels of judgement, until they turn and in penitence are made new.

Then my soul shall be joyful in you, and all my bones shall say, Lord, who is like you? For you deliver the afflicted from those too strong for them. Blessed be the Lord, who desired that his Servant have peace.

Psalm 36

The Saviour of humans and animals alike

You may know that charming French book for children of all ages, *The Little Prince*. In that rather deep story it is a fox who confides his special secret, 'You only see well with the heart.' How useful this word 'heart' is! It often stands for 'love' or other deep feelings. In the Bible it often stands for the springs of thought and will, the place where plans are made. This useful word 'heart' comes in a rather eerie verse that begins Psalm 36: 'Sin whispers to the wicked man in the depth of his heart.'

The singer is lamenting to God about an evil oppressor who at present is causing much suffering. This tyrant is a rebel against the good God. Perhaps he did once act well and wisely. But he has become hardened to God, no longer conscious of God's awesome reality. He worships only the god that is his own evil impulse. And deep within the man's heart this bogus god, in effect 'sin', whispers his oracles – ideas for wicked conduct which will be readily obeyed. As the psalm has it:

> Sin whispers to the wicked man in the depth of his heart;
> there is no dread of God before his eyes.
>
> For he flatters himself in his own eyes,
> that his hateful wrongdoing will not be found out.
>
> The words of his mouth are harm and deceit,
> he has ceased to act wisely and do good.
>
> He devises harm upon his bed;
> he sets himself on a path of wrong and refuses no evil.

Against this great doer of harm there is as yet no outright prayer. But the description of his heart and conduct carries in itself an appeal to the just and good God.

And now suddenly the singer opens up quite another prospect. This is truly something seen by the heart. It is a vision of beautiful life in the shelter of God's love. And as the singer tells of it, it is his way of expressing trust in that love, and of calling forth its power against the oppressor he has just described. He is now speaking directly to God as he unfolds the vision thus:

> LORD, your steadfast love is high as the heavens;
> your faithfulness reaches to the clouds.
>
> Your goodness is like the towering mountains,
>   your justice like the great deep;
> humankind and animals alike, LORD, you will save.

It is a wonderful picture – the world in perfection; one great household, God's house, in a landscape of pure river and mountains that reach to the clouds. To drink of the river is to delight in God's gift of life. To behold the mountains is to wonder at the surpassing greatness of his goodness, his love, his faithfulness. The whole human family is as one, gathered together under the shelter of the wings of God. But all the animals are there too, for he is their Saviour also. For all his creatures his household is a place of peace. The river of life is fed from a fountain that springs in the presence of the Lord. The light of life that blesses the eyes of his creatures is the outshining of the light from God.

It is indeed an inspired glimpse of an ideal world around its Creator. It is a vision of something yet to be, yet even now revealing the present love and faithfulness of God. How is such vision given? In ancient times it was nourished by the yearly round of worship, culminating in vivid thoughts of God's new reign, his kingdom of peace. Our singer depicts it as he speaks to God in order to press for its fulfilment. May the Lord make this faithful love and justice effective in the present crisis! As the singer passes on, he comes to his direct petitions:

> O continue your love to those who know you,
> and your goodness to the true of heart.
>
> May the foot of pride not come upon me,
> nor the hand of the wicked drive me away.
>
> Truly the evildoers shall fall;
> they shall be thrust down, unable to rise.

In our world today it is not difficult to find examples of the wicked person depicted in our psalm. Still there are oppressors of nations. More subtly, there are people at all levels of our society who fit the description – ignoring God, following selfish impulses, setting themselves on a path of wrong, and sometimes, it seems, refusing no evil. And alas, there is in our own hearts a person who may listen too willingly to the whispers of sin.

How the world needs – how we all need – the purifying vision of the Saviour, the One who gives light and life, and shelters his creatures from harm. In worship still today, as in olden times, this light of faith and hope is imparted. Especially at Christmas and Easter, and always in Holy Communion, that world of light and peace appears – a perfect world yet to come, but already shining upon us as we wait before God, share communion and pray.

Our psalm leads us to cherish this wonderful vision, to set against the oracles of sin that whisper in the depths of the heart. Here is a light of God's love to flood our hearts and to strengthen our prayers. It is a light to carry into every evil situation of daily life. What blessing God gives through that person who, in daily work and service, carries such a vision in the heart – that faith, that hope which is radiant with the light of God's own face! In that light we shall indeed see well – see with the heart, as the Little Prince's fox has it. Beyond all the sorrows of this world, we shall see and believe in that reality of goodness and love in the presence of the Lord. This is the true world, our home, now and for ever.

Lord, sin whispers still in the depths of the heart, and many obey without restraint. May the foot of pride not trample for ever in defiance of your will.

Guard me against the evil impulse. Strengthen me with the vision of your precious love.

In the hour of worship satisfy your people with the good things of your house. Refresh them at your well of life. Give them drink from the river of your delights.

In your light may we learn to see all your creatures with the heart of love, O faithful Saviour of people and animals alike.

Shelter me under your wings, O Love high as the heavens, O Goodness like the great deep.

Psalm 37

To possess the land of contentment

When the elderly dispute with the young, they have the advantage of being able to say, 'I have been young, as you are now. I understand how it all seems to you. Now I am old and have an extra perspective, which you haven't got.' A good argument. But the young person can hardly believe that the old one was ever young, and if it was indeed so, well, the world was a very different place then; and anyway, it was so long ago the old person has forgotten what it was like. The singer of Psalm 37 sounds like such an elderly person:

> I have been young and now am old,
>> yet I never saw a good person forsaken
>>> or his children searching for bread.
>
> (v. 25)

He is trying to persuade the younger ones not to envy people of bad ways who seem to prosper. But perhaps he doesn't remember too well. Has he *never* seen a good person fallen into such poverty that his or her family lack food? Yes, one may find fault with some of this psalmist's assertions.

And yet we would be wise to respect the core of what he is teaching, his message that the only way of happiness is to walk with the Lord – to delight in him, lay one's burdens on him, trust in him. There was once a woman of very little education who was widowed early and had several children to bring up. They received education far beyond what she had known, and in any arguments that arose could score points easily. But in later life, when they looked back, they could recognize her fundamental wisdom and their own fallibility. As we hear the elderly sage speaking in this psalm, we could be right to query the way he sometimes puts things – he seems to have oversimplified matters in his earnestness to keep the young from a disastrous path. But we would be wise to respect his fundamental wisdom and the warmth of his testimony to God's wonderful help. After all, Jesus himself seems to have known the psalm well, for he takes up words from it in his Sermon on the Mount (Matt. 5.5; cf. Ps. 37.11).

The psalm is made up of many memorable statements, almost complete in themselves. This is because of its special form as an alphabetic poem. The first letters of the verses take us through the Hebrew alphabet; there are usually two verses for each letter of the alphabet, and hence we have quite a long psalm of forty verses. It is all giving counsel in a time when people were often driven from their land – dispossessed or exiled. The psalm insists that it is those who patiently trust the Lord who will in the end 'possess the land' (or, as we can translate, 'inherit the earth').

There is an echo here of the idea of 'the promised land', the dream of the restless nomads. For ourselves, we can interpret it now to mean the place of life with our Lord, the only worthwhile life, the land of contentment with him. And we then hear the singer with profit as he teaches:

> Do not be indignant at the evildoers,
> nor envious of those that do wrong;
>
> for like grass they will quickly wither,
> and like the green herb fade away.
>
> But trust in the LORD and do good;
> dwell on the land and feed on his truth.
>
> It is those who wait on the LORD
>   who shall possess the land.
>
> The humble shall possess the land,
> and they shall delight in abundance of peace.
>   (vv. 1–3, 9b, 11)

And our singer challenges us to change our ways:

> Turn from evil and do good,
> and so abide for evermore.

> The just shall possess the land,
>   and shall dwell on it for ever.
>
> Wait for the LORD and keep his way,
>   and he will raise you up to possess the land;
>   when the wicked are uprooted you will see it.
>
> Keep innocence and heed the thing that is right,
>   for that will bring you peace at the last.
>   (vv. 27, 29, 34, 37)

In our day we are bombarded by advertising. It is not surprising that people are enticed into false ways to get happiness or riches, to 'possess the land' of comfort and fulfilment. And then they find they have been deceived. In Britain, we recently heard that research on the electorate had identified a new class of voters, numerous enough to cause an electoral upset. They are termed 'Meldrews' after Victor Meldrew, a rather sour character in the British sitcom *One Foot in the Grave*. They are affluent middle class, living comfortably in the suburbs. But they are constantly discontented, even angry, with the things of daily life. Perhaps they have been seeking happiness from the wrong source. Perhaps the wisdom of our psalmist is not outdated as he counsels:

> A little that a good person has
>   is better than great riches of the godless.
>
> Let your delight be in the LORD,
>   and he will give you the request of your heart.
>   (vv. 16, 4)

The singer takes account of our hardships; he knows that he is counselling sufferers, deeply troubled. He would comfort and encourage as he says:

> Put the burden of your way on the LORD;
>   trust in him and he will act.
>
> When someone's steps are guided by the LORD,
>   and they delight in his way,
>
> though they fall, they will not be flung from the path,
>   for the LORD has hold of their hand.
>   (vv. 8, 23–24)

Surely here in Psalm 37 is a counsellor worth heeding. No wonder some of his words were adopted by our Lord Jesus. Happy are those, Jesus said, happy are those right with God through humble trust, for they shall inherit the earth – they shall possess the land that means joy in the presence of God.

Lord, how shall I find your land of contentment? How can I dwell there in the abundance of your peace?

Bring into my heart your simple but hard counsels. Help me to trust in you and do good. To wait for you in stillness. To put away envious indignation.

To let you guide my steps. To be generous and show kindness. To have your teaching in my heart and speak what is right.

To put the burdens of my way on you. To be humble and happy with a little.

Lord, let me possess the land of blessing and contentment. Let my delight be ever in you.

Psalm 38
The prayer of the wounded world

How brave are those who nurse sufferers from contagious diseases! These carers were especially heroic in centuries gone by, when there were no protective treatments to be had. In the Middle Ages there were plagues which killed half or more of some communities. We must admire the devotion of those who nursed the sick and buried the dead, knowing always that their caring actions might well be fatal to themselves.

A different response to the suffering is sometimes depicted in the Psalms – those who hurry by or stand far off, anxious to avoid the contamination of evil fortune. An example comes in Psalm 38 (one of the Church's selection of 'Penitential Psalms' especially used in Lent). Here a sufferer tells God of such experience of being avoided, forsaken: 'My friends and companions stand away from my misfortune, and my neighbours stay far off.' Yet his need is great enough. The illness is severe indeed. As he tells God:

My bones are full of burning,
and there is no whole part in my body.

> I am utterly feeble and crushed;
> I roar at the disquiet of my heart . . .

> My heart throbs, and my strength has left me,
> and even the light of my eyes has gone from me.

> My friends and companions stand away from my misfortune,
> and my neighbours stay far off.

But not only is this sufferer troubled by the friends who keep well away. There are also rank ill-wishers – though to their evil words he makes no reply:

> Those who would harm me speak evil
> and mutter falsehood all the day long . . .

> Yet I am like one who does not hear,
> in whose mouth are no reproaches.

In the old city of Jerusalem a common sight used to be the porters. They carried goods through the narrow streets, where the many steps rendered vehicles and carts useless. They were characterful figures, these porters – like a race apart. On their heads they wore white skullcaps. Over their shoulders and back hung a thick draping. Their loins were girded up, leaving their legs bare. Strapped to their backs were high wooden frames into which could be stacked boxes of wares, one above another. It would all amount to a formidable load, rising well above the head, probably more than was good for the porter's gaunt and stooping body. The psalmist may have known such men thousands of years before, for he speaks of the heavy load of his offences in this fashion:

> My offences have risen over my head;
> like a great burden, they are too heavy for me.

Some people may be more inclined than others to feel guilty. But the psalmist is really thinking here about the *effects* of his sins. The *results* of his wrongdoing are like a burden too heavy to carry. Yet he is ready enough to admit his faults. He says to God:

> I confess my wrongdoing,
> and am sorry for my sin.

It is a sombre psalm, this prayer of a sufferer. But it is not without an undercurrent – or better, a foundation – of faith. All is said in hope, as appears in a few verses:

Truly, I wait for you, O LORD;
you will answer, Lord, my God . . .

Do not forsake me, LORD;
my God, do not stay far from me.

Hasten to my help,
my Lord and my salvation.

It may be that many worshippers today would say, 'This psalm does not really match my situation. I have troubles, but not as bad as this.' It is valuable, therefore, to note how the psalm was used in times long ago. Long before the coming of Christ it was applied to the community. It had some set use on the Sabbath at gatherings for worship, and possibly in the regular offerings at the temple. It was then a prayer from a sick and wounded society. Later, the early Christians related it to the Passion of Christ. We see the link in St Luke's Gospel, when it is said that as Jesus died 'all his acquaintance stood far off, seeing these things' (Luke 23.49). And some of the ancient translations use phrases for the suffering that suggest the crucifixion.

So all down the centuries to our own day, the psalm has fruitfully been used in Lent and Holy Week. Here it helps individuals to make vivid before God their troubles and their penitence, holding on to faith in the Saviour. But it can also help us to stand with Christ as he carries the burden of a wounded world and raises strong prayer for its healing. If we set out to pray for the world on the strength of our own compassion and faith we shall hardly be equal to the weight of it all. Rather we must use the psalm as an expression of *his* sympathy and *his* continuing prayer – how he entered into the world's wounding and bore the impossible burden of its sins, and through it all sustained his hope and faith in the Father. Through the psalm we voice his strong prayer, and we put our trust in his mission to save the world. Through the psalm we expose before God how terrible are the wounds and the offences in present-day society, but we also in Christ's name call down upon them the mercy that will at last make all things well.

This Lenten psalm then certainly reminds us how in this season a great work of prayer lies before us. This is especially a time when Jesus says to us, 'Watch with me; share the burden with me, until the Easter dawn.'

Lord, all my longing is before you and my groans are not hidden from you.
Look with pity on the wounds of your world.

See the burning bones, the throbbing hearts, the darkened eyes, the loneliness,
the snares of the destroyers, the burdens of sin, the want of health and
peace.
Do not you forsake us, sinful as we are. For the sake of the sufferings and faith
of your Son Jesus, come quickly to save what you have made.
Hasten to my help, my Lord and my salvation. In the name of Jesus. Amen.

Psalm 39
A prayer that blazed up

As you enter the Birmingham city art gallery, an assemblage of paintings rises on your left. Among them is an attractive, sunny scene – B.W. Leader's *An English Hayfield*. Ahead of you, towards the right, hangs a very large painting by the same artist – his *February Fill Dyke* of 1881. By contrast, this large work may seem at first to be rather lugubrious. Around the cluster of humble cottages, the church, the bare trees and sodden fields are dark areas. It is only a wintry evening light which picks out the great puddles over fields and pathways. Yet as you grow familiar with this wet and darkening prospect, you find it holds much beauty and, what is more, hope. You see that the wintry colours are rich and subtle, the tracery of branches delicate. The few people seem stoical and companionable. Above all, there is a sense of good life in preparation in the saturated earth and the gleams of evening light. It is the preparation for the harvest in due season.

Our first impression of Psalm 39 might well be that it is a lugubrious canvas, a thoroughly sorrowful prayer. Might we find hope here also, and the preparation of good? The psalm expresses an experience of long illness, now only worsening – a sense of coming near to death. The unusual beginning of the psalm may remind us of the story of Job, who at first tried not to complain when heavy troubles fell upon him, but in the end broke out in bitter lamentation. So the sufferer in the psalm at first held back all complaint, anxious not to seem to blame God and be overheard by the irreligious:

> I kept still and silent;
> I held my peace, to no avail.

For my pain increased,
  my heart grew hot within me;
through my sighs the fire blazed up,
  and I have spoken with my tongue.

Yes, we may say that in all suffering there is a time for quiet waiting and patience; but there also may come a time for releasing the inner fires and speaking out with all sincerity. Then it is good if someone can offer a ministry of sympathetic hearing. A friend or counsellor listens and so takes up some of this heat of distress. In the psalm, it is to the Lord himself that the story is told, and it is from him that help is sought.

Unlike Job, this sufferer can readily admit that wrongdoing has led to this plight. It is seen as a common fate:

You chasten man with rebukes for wrongdoing,
  and like a moth you consume his beauty.

So the psalm ends:

Look away from me, that I may again have cheer,
  before I depart and am no more.

This concluding prayer is in effect that the searching eye of God may turn away, judgement may be abated, and life may yet hold a little time of comfort and smiling. Here again, there is a great depth of sadness, for the underlying thought is of the brevity of human life. As the psalm has it:

I am but a visitor with you,
  passing on, like all my fathers . . .

See, you have appointed my days as hand-breaths,
  and my time is as nothing in your sight;
for even in the prime of life man is but a fleeting thing.

And beyond that brief span of life, according to the beliefs of that ancient time, there was no more real existence. The sufferer would 'depart and be no more'.

To enter into this sad prayer may bring a sense of purification. It's a little like when someone close to us dies. Somehow, that nearness to death purifies us of false values and wrong priorities that have crept in and come to govern our days. As we hold the hand of this psalmist near to death, we feel how we have been in some way missing reality – we hear the force of these lines:

Each one walks about like a shadow,
　and they are in turmoil for nothing;
they heap up, but do not know who will gather.

Such 'turmoil for nothing', such chasing after mere shadows, gives place to a quiet wisdom. But it is all in sadness until we can say with the psalmist:

And now, for what do I wait, O Lord?
My hope is only in you.

And these wonderful words were words of a very sick person, who knew how fleeting is life, and had no knowledge of a life hereafter! 'My hope is only in you' – these words are like a precious seed. How much is contained there which can yet mature and open as a most beautiful plant! However much the vision of heaven and resurrection-life develops in later times, however rich the Christian experience of life in the risen Christ, we never outgrow this ancient prayer from the darkness: 'And now, for what do I wait, O LORD? My hope is only in you.'

This ancient sufferer held on to the Lord alone, held on through patient silence, held on through blazing outspokenness and sorrowful pleading. Having hope in the Lord alone, this sufferer was one of the multitude who went before and prepared for the unfolding of faith in the risen Christ. In that faith we are no longer just passing strangers on earth, visitors before God who must soon leave the land of light. Through Christ it is seen that we pass on as strangers and *pilgrims*. We are passing through the hard way of this life en route to the heavenly city, a better country, our eternal home with God (Heb. 11.13–16).

Lord, let me know my end. Let me acknowledge how quickly all human life passes, how short my time must be.

Let me not spend my days in turmoil to heap up wealth, or to chase vain shadows.

O deliver me from all my sins. Turn the eye of condemnation from me, that I may know days of peace and cheer among the good gifts you have provided on earth.

Help me along my pilgrim way, looking to Jesus, who has prepared our abiding home.

For what do I wait, Lord? My hope is only in you.

Psalm 40
The red berry

———•+•———

One misty morning in November, someone was very busy in the garden. It was a squirrel, all her movements quick. She would nip off a sprig of holly from the hedge and carry it to the middle of the garden. Again and again she would take off a red berry, carry it to a flower bed, dig briskly with her front paws, bury it and cover it over. Alert and mindful, she would know exactly where to find each berry when food became scarce. Apart from the wonderful foresight, it was the vigour and intensity of her digging that caught the attention.

On the same misty morning, an old countryman trudged down the lane, somewhat stiff with rheumatism and heavy-footed in his Wellington boots. Soon he would be digging in a vegetable patch under the wooded hill, digging row after row with vigour and application to make a great area of loose, rich brown soil. His technique was different from the squirrel's, but for both animal and man digging was a matter of energetic and close involvement.

But it seems that the earliest translators of the Hebrew scriptures did not like to speak of God digging. They were learned Jews working in the Greek-style city of Alexandria at least two centuries before Christ. As they rendered the Hebrew books into Greek, they were always inclined to spiritualize earthy expressions about God. So when they came to Psalm 40, verse 6, they put something rather different from the Hebrew as we have it. The Hebrew says to God, 'Ears have you dug for me' – a quaint way of saying, 'You opened deep my ears to hear your word', a hearing beyond ordinary powers. Our English translations soften this 'Ears have you dug for me', for example as 'You have given me an open ear' (NRSV). But the ancient translation into Greek has moved further, giving 'A body you prepared for me'. And this is the translation of the verse accepted and quoted in the New Testament. The Letter to the Hebrews, chapter 10, pictures Christ, when he has come into the world, saying to the Father, 'A body you have prepared for me'. The letter says that, since Christ was willing to offer himself, 'we have been sanctified through the offering of the body of Jesus Christ once for all' (Heb. 10.10).

Those first translators into Greek came to be regarded as prompted and guided by God. And certainly in their rendering of that line in Psalm 40, we may think that the Holy Spirit buried a precious red berry, waiting for the time that it could serve the gospel of Christ.

Actually, Psalm 40 as a whole is spiritually a very rich psalm, whether we read it in its original sense or as it came to be fulfilled by Christ. Let us just take a little from each of these levels of meaning. First, then, the original situation. This figure in great distress is most likely the king, the anointed servant of the Lord. In the first part of his prayer he recalls the salvation God has shown him in the past. He focuses on ceremonies at the temple, where God's promises were set forth and the king himself taught and proclaimed the faithfulness of God. In accordance with God's word, revealed deep in his ear, he offered himself, ready to follow God's will.

What an awful contrast, then, the present situation! He declares that 'troubles without number have come about me'. He feels his offences must have been many, for now the consequences overtake him and his heart fails him. Before the Lord he is but poor and wretched, but he prays:

> May the Lord think of me.
> You are my help and my deliverer; O my God, do not delay.

It is an experience which many can match today. In worship we sing and speak of God's help and blessings, and the joy of life with him – and then we may have to go out into sufferings without an end in sight! Worse still, we may be leaders in that worship, expending our soul-energy on witness to God's faithful love and power, and afterwards going out to experience bitter blows. In such a case, the original sense of the psalm can speak for us and lead us to put it all to God, saying for ourselves, 'May the LORD think of me. You are my help and my deliverer, O my God, do not delay.'

But then, when the psalm is read as foreshadowing Christ, there is blessing for all times and situations. 'I waited, waited for the LORD, and he inclined to me and heard my cry' – yes, Christ, above all, waited for the Father in trust and was 'brought up from the raging pit'. He truly offered himself, his very body, and was the supreme witness to the Father's love and power. Not his offences, but ours, were the burden he bore. Through the offering of his body we were sanctified, that is, restored to communion with God and fellowship with all that is good. Through him the Father has indeed multiplied his wonders and shown thoughts for us that are beyond compare. And this Christ, who held to the Father's grace along the path of suffering, this same Christ embraces us in our troubles and is one with us in the great plea: 'Hasten to my help . . . my help and my deliverer, O my God, do not delay.' We may be sure that our witness to his faithful love will not be in vain. The salvation wrought through Christ will have the last word.

Dig deep, Lord, that our hearts' ears may be open to your word.
Deep in our souls plant your teaching and your will.
Keep us ever in Christ's body – prepared, offered, and taken up into your
*   eternal kingdom of joy.*
Put a new song in my mouth, having brought me up from the raging pit, up
*   from the miry clay, and set my feet on the rock, and made my steps secure.*

Psalm 41
Betrayal and blessing

———◆◆◆———

Even her mother said she was 'a little Hitler'. Such was her authoritative and decisive manner as she cared for the sick. She was a nurse in a famous London hospital. And very good she was too, tackling every difficulty briskly and with courage. Not of great stature, she would lift patients or turn beds while others might yet be considering the possibility. And the patients were very glad of her commitment. When she approached, they knew help was on the way.

Remarkably, the picture of a good nurse lifting the patient and remaking the bed is applied in Psalm 41 to God. The psalm has begun with an echo of proverbial wisdom: those who care for the needy will themselves be cared for by the Lord when they are suffering in their turn. The Lord will remember those past kindnesses and will now reward such a person with his restoring care. Indeed, says the psalm,

> The LORD will support him on his sickbed;
>   you will turn over all his bed in his illness.

Such teaching was hammering away especially at the powerful, the rulers, drumming in their duty to defend the defenceless and take care of the poor and needy. But of course, the Lord's rewards do not always come so pat when the need arises. And this is what the troubled king praying in this psalm has found – the nurse is slow to come. So having echoed the traditional promise of God, he goes on to beg it be applied now to him. For he has looked after the needy, and now in his own troubles, how greatly he needs the Lord to keep him from enemies and to nurse him in his sickness!

The worst of it is that some are glad of his illness. They cannot wait to be rid of him. He even suspects that some who make a show of concern and visit him are really sizing up their opportunities, and going out to spread damaging reports:

> My enemies speak evil against me:
> When will he die and his name for ever perish?

> And if they come to see me they speak falsely;
> their heart gathers mischief,
>   and they go out and speak it abroad.

Among these treacherous folk is one who was a trusted ally, but now has turned against him in the hour of need:

> Even one who was my ally,
>   one whom I trusted and who ate of my bread,
>   has lifted up his heel against me.

All this is put to the Lord, and the prayer ends in the hope that he will vindicate his king as still his Chosen One, set before the face of God for ever.

When the Book of Psalms was eventually completed and ordered, it happened that this psalm fell at the end of the first great section, Psalms 1–41. In the symphony of psalms, we might say, this section was the first movement. So what was its mood and its meaning?

The movement had opened with great promises of God. Psalm 1 presented the one immersed in God's will – he would be a green and fruitful tree. Psalm 2 showed the Lord's Anointed, God's Son, his king assured of victory. Then many psalms had the royal figure facing enemies and terrible troubles, but fighting back with trust in God's pledges. But now at the end of this first movement, in Psalm 41, the royal one is betrayed, and by a man who ate bread with him; judgement is foreshadowed for that traitor, and the prayer holds on to hope in God's purpose. God's love for his Chosen One will be shown when he raises him up to life before his face for ever. No wonder that in St John's Gospel (13.18; 17.12) the psalm is seen as prophetic of Christ's Passion and its outcome.

But well before the coming of Christ, the arrangers of the psalms had already signalled here the triumph of God's work. Here at the end of the first movement of their symphony of psalms they placed a kind of Gloria. It is a great amen of thanksgiving, lifting our hearts to the eternal God, lest the sorrow of so many psalms from suffering obscure the final glory. And as the Church gladly takes up the heritage of the Psalms, she finds in this great amen the light that shines over all suffering. It affirms that the good purpose, the good meaning, will never be lost. It declares that the Lord revealed and worshipped in his Church is the Eternal, and the bond formed in praise is from everlasting to everlasting. Whatever our sufferings, whatever the betrayals of this world, let us stand with his Messiah, his Christ, and with our amens be part of that eternal thanksgiving:

> BLESSED BE THE LORD, THE GOD OF ISRAEL,
>   FROM EVERLASTING TO EVERLASTING,
>   AMEN AND AMEN.

We thank you, Lord, for those who nurse the sick. They are your hands and
your heart of love. You will remember and bless them.
Have pity on me, Lord. Heal my soul, for I have sinned against you.
Lord Jesus, betrayed by a friend, amidst judgement you seek mercy and
forgiveness even for those who have committed great sin.
Uphold me amid all the deceits and treacheries of this passing world, to
follow in your steps, caring for the needy, forgiving my enemies, and with
all my life saying amen to the eternal Thanksgiving.

Psalms 42–43
Deep calls to deep

'Come on, Margaret. Get a grip on yourself, girl. Come on now, little Margaret, pull yourself together.' Margaret was not offended by these blunt exhortations. They were uttered by herself – to herself. Her husband also often addressed himself. Sometimes he would give himself advice, beginning, 'Now, if I were you'. Then he would recollect himself and say, 'But I *am* you'. After a moment's pause to recover from this setback he would continue, 'Anyway, I think you had better do such and such.'

There was nothing extraordinary in this habit of talking to oneself and seeing oneself, as it were, from a little distance. The ancient Hebrews often addressed themselves by picturing their soul as a distinct person. This happens obviously in Psalms 42 and 43, one prayer in two parts. There is a beautiful refrain verse which comes three times. Here the singer exhorts his own soul as though it were a mourner in front of him, weeping and bowing low to the ground. He wants to urge himself – his soul – not to give up on God, and three times he speaks thus:

> How you are bowed down, my soul,
>   and how you moan before me!
> Wait still for God, for I will yet give him thanks,
>   my Saviour and my God.

The situation must have been very bad, but the likelihood is that it was not a purely personal sorrow. The singer seems to speak as representative for his people – a king who carries them all in his heart. They are oppressed by an enemy, described as an unfaithful nation, headed by a deceitful and wicked man. So instead of coming to the temple with songs of joy and thanksgiving as in past days, they worship some way off in a penitential manner. That meant fasting, wearing sackcloth, weeping and crouching to the ground – all meant to show the Lord with body and spirit that they were indeed in a pitiable state, but were penitent and turned to him. Our singer contributes to this penitential worship by appealing to the Lord with a series of touching images.

The first is especially moving. The suffering people, represented by their leader, are compared to a fallow deer dying of thirst in a drought, desperately snuffing the air for a scent of water:

> As a hind pants for rills of water,
> so pants my soul for you, O God.
>
> My soul thirsts for God, for the living God;
> when shall I come and see the face of God?

Another picture of the suffering uses a contrasting image. Not a drought now, but a drowning in cascades of water. It is a picture of the waters of death, imagined as surging in the mouth of the underworld. The singer pictures his cry to God as coming from the base of the mighty Mount Hermon, where waters cascade and the River Jordan takes its rise. The scene is like an opening of the underworld, and the singer puts it to the Lord that he is nearly submerged:

> I call your name, Lord, from Jordan's source,
>   from Hermon's slopes and Mount Mizar.

Deep calls to deep with the roar of your waterspouts,
and all your breakers and billows sweep over me.

In such strong images, then, the distress is put before the Lord. The cry goes up like the gasping of animals in a fierce drought. The situation seems utterly without the living water of God's grace and help. Or again, the cry is like that of the drowning. Troubles roll over the sufferer like great waves from the land of death. No wonder that outsiders ask, 'Where now is your God?'

With these pictures of tragedy the singer presses upon the Lord. But he presses also by holding on to trust and hope. As he reaches his final prayer, he paints another moving scene, but now its strength is in its beauty of hope and dedication to God's praise. He is asking God to send forth his angels of light and truth to escort him through every difficulty to the holy hill. So he will ascend to God's dwelling and give thanks with the beauty of song and music. So he prays:

O send out your light and your truth that they may lead me,
and bring me to your holy hill and to your dwelling,

that I may come to the altar of God, to God my joy and gladness,
and with the lyre I will praise you, O God, my God.

And after this prayer, the eloquent psalm ends with the refrain, the singer once more urging his own soul to be patient, for God will prove true: 'How you are bowed down, my soul, and how you moan before me! Wait still for God, for I will yet give him thanks, my Saviour and my God.'

We may have often thought the psalm beautiful, especially the image of the hind that longs for water. But now we have recognized it as a cry from the extremes of suffering. There may be times when we ourselves know such depth of distress. There are certainly times when our prayer through the psalm can sound for those who pine away for lack of God's help – like the deer that gasps for water. Or with another image – the prayer can sound for those submerged in deadly troubles, sinking in the roar of the waterspouts, swept over by the breakers and billows of misfortune. Then the words of the psalmist live afresh: 'God my Rock, why have you forgotten me? God my Refuge, why have you rejected me?'

For Jesus, too, the psalm spoke. After the Last Supper, when he came to the place called Gethsemane, he said to his disciples, 'Sit here while I pray.' He took with him Peter, James and John. He was deeply troubled and said to them, using words from our psalm, 'My soul is bowed down with sorrow, even to death.' He went forward a little and fell to the ground, and he prayed that, if it were possible, the hour might pass from him.

The echoing of the psalm in our Lord's words tells us that he has entered the agony depicted long ago. In the Father's purpose it was necessary for his Son Jesus also to become like the deer crying for water, or like the one swept by the breakers and billows of death. So our Lord Jesus shares all that we can suffer. He falls to the ground with us, and prays that the hour may pass from us. We must hold to him through everything, until he leads us up the mountain way to the altar of God and the music of thanksgiving.

For many centuries those hopeful, yearning lines have been used before the Eucharist with its 'altar', its 'light' and its 'gladness'. Countless times, in preparation for the Holy Communion, the prayer has risen: 'O send out your light and your truth that they may lead me, and bring me to your holy hill and to your dwelling.' For, seen truly, it can be a daunting way for us, troubled as we are by cares of this world. How we need those angels of God's light and truth to encourage us and lead us! Have these been our parents, our teachers, our true friends? God's angels take many forms. But the psalm, at all events, has prompted us to ask for them, and in the mercy of Christ his angels have come, and will come.

As a hind pants for rills of water, so pants my soul for you, O God.
How you are bowed down, my soul! Wait still for God.
Lord, send me angels of your light and truth, that they may lead me and bring
*   me to your holy hill.*
So may I come to your altar, and know you as my joy and gladness, and offer
*   you the poetry and music of my thankfulness.*
My soul, wait still for God. For I will yet give him thanks as my Saviour and
*   my God.*

Psalm 44
Killed all day for God's sake

———◆———

A young father spoke to his children, giving them good advice. Afterwards he chuckled as he thought to himself, 'I'm beginning to sound like my own father!' It was true. Those grave counsels and cautions, which from his own father had seemed to him of doubtful worth, were now flowing from his own lips with earnest conviction.

It's a common experience. Hard-won wisdom is preserved and passed down the generations, as parents accept responsibility to pass on the precious insights handed down to them. So the rising generation, perhaps to its surprise, finds itself sounding like its own parents.

This chain of wisdom linking successive generations was important for the people of the Bible. We hear of it at the beginning of Psalm 44. First comes the theme of 'what our parents told us':

> O God, with our own ears we have heard,
> for our fathers have told us,
> all that you did in their days,
> in days long ago.
>
> By your hand you planted them,
> having driven out peoples;
> you spread them abroad,
> where you had broken nations.
>
> Not by their sword did they take the land,
> nor did their own arm save them;
>
> but it was your right hand and your arm
> and the light of your presence . . .

But then we hear the singer 'beginning to sound like his own father' as he continues:

> By you we drove back our foes;
> by your arm we thrust down those that rose against us.
>
> For I did not trust in my bow,
> nor could my sword deliver me.
>
> But you saved us from our adversaries,
> and put our foes to shame.

Yes, the psalmist (probably the king) has well learnt to attribute success not to himself, but to the decisive power of God. He pictures all his people as having acknowledged this in hymns of praise and thanksgiving:

> We gloried in God all the day long,
> and were ever praising your name.

108

So far we might think this is a contented psalm, from a well-contented people. But quite the contrary. All the song so far turns out to have been leading up to a very bitter prayer. In the past God saved, and his people duly acknowledged it. But now, O what a contrast, as the singer continues:

> But now you have rejected us and brought us to shame,
> and have not gone out with our armies.

> You have made us turn our backs to the foe,
> and our enemies have despoiled us.

> You have made us as sheep to be slaughtered,
> and have scattered us among the nations.

The heavy grief is all the worse because the people feel they have kept their side of the covenant. They have worshipped the Lord alone and kept his way. If it were not so, the Lord would have shown them their error, for example by a prophet. But no –

> All this has come upon us though we have not forgotten you,
> and have not been false to your covenant.

> Our hearts have not turned back,
> nor our steps gone out of your way.

> Yet you have crushed us in the place of desolation,
> and covered us with the shadow of death.

> If we had forgotten the name of our God,
> and to some strange god spread out our hands,

> would not God have searched it out?
> For he knows the secrets of the heart.

And now the prayer comes to its sharpest point. They suffer not just *in spite of* loyalty, but *because of* it. As the singer puts it:

> For your sake we are killed all the day long,
> and counted as sheep for slaughter.

It seems that, as they tried to keep the laws of the Lord, they were marked off from neighbouring religions and peoples. They easily attracted hostility. It could come to this situation, where they could say, 'For your sake we are killed all the day long.' It was a bitter burden to bear.

In the Christian ideal, the disciple bears the burden gladly. Christ's followers gladly give up all for his sake. They face hostility for his sake.

They take up their cross for his sake, and for his sake they will die. What gives this willingness to the heroes of faith? What leads them gladly to sacrifice all for Jesus' sake? The psalm gives the key in its final phrase. The last verse runs:

> Arise, LORD, come to our help,
> and redeem us for the sake of your faithful love.

Indeed it is the faithful love of our Redeemer which inspires our self-offering. Because of that love, the sacrifice will not be in vain. No suffering will separate us from that divine faithfulness. So, when St Paul quoted our psalm's words about being 'slain all the day long', he was inspired to one of his greatest utterances about God's love. In his courageous ministry, he certainly knew what it was to be 'slain all the day long', but he writes in his Letter to the Romans, chapter 8:

> Who shall separate us from the love of Christ? Shall tribulation, or anguish, or persecution, or famine, or nakedness, or peril, or sword? Even as it is written, 'For your sake we are killed all the day long; we were accounted as sheep for the slaughter.' No, in all these things we are more than conquerors through him who loved us. For I am persuaded that neither death, nor life, nor angels, nor principalities, nor things present, nor things to come, nor powers, nor height, nor depth, nor any other creature, shall be able to separate us from the love of God, which is in Christ Jesus our Lord.

That is a sublime assurance. But there will be times when the cry of the psalm must be raised with frank expression of perplexity, even the sense of forsakenness. And yet the last word is still given to God's faithful love: 'Why do you hide your face? Arise, LORD, come to our help, and redeem us for the sake of your faithful love.'

O God, we have been taught stories of your salvation, and have known your gifts of success and deliverance. And then in times of sorrow and failure we feel rejected and forgotten by you. Then the ancient words speak for us – 'You have crushed us in the place of desolation.'
Arise, Lord, come to our help. Redeem us for the sake of your faithful love.
Grant that as the words of Paul have been handed down and commended to us, we also may find their truth. So may we in our turn testify that no horror, no pain, no desolation, can separate us from your faithful love in Christ Jesus our Lord.

Psalm 45
The bride of Christ

Sometimes a child comes home from school bursting with news. In the happy excitement, eyes shine, cheeks glow, words tumble out in a mad chase. For adults too, when the heart is astir through some inspiring event, the words come tumbling out, impatient of rounded sentences.

It's similar for authors and composers. An unproductive time suddenly gives way to a time of inspiration. There is a seething within. Poems or music are driven up and expressed at an extraordinary speed. Robert Schumann can be considered as one of the two or three greatest composers of songs. A large part of his best work poured out in one year, 1840. It was the year he married his beloved Clara, herself an outstanding musician. He was inspired by love. His heart was stirred as never before, and the compositions, so original, so perfect, came chasing one after the other.

It was similar too for the great bards of olden times. Surrounded by rapt listeners, they would pass from a still concentration to a sudden freedom of inspiration. The poetry would flow from the heart and lips like silver from a glowing furnace. Thus one Scandinavian bard began his epic, 'Words melt in my mouth. One presses upon another. They rush over my tongue, on to my lips and over my mouth' (Epic of Kalewala, Finland).

Psalm 45 begins in just such a fashion. The poet's heart is fired to create what the psalm's heading calls 'a song of love'. He delivers it as the climax of the royal wedding approaches. But his inspiration is not just the romance of the occasion. It is a work of the divine Spirit. His poem is an oracle, a blessing – a good word of God both to the Lord's Anointed and also to the lovely bride. So the Hebrew bard steps forward and begins:

> My heart seethes with a gracious word;
>   as I speak my poem for the king,
>   my tongue darts like the pen of a rapid writer.

Then the words flow indeed, glowing with the good will of God. And first to the king:

> You are fair above the children of earth;
>   grace is poured on your lips,
>   for God has blessed you for ever . . .

111

> In your majesty ride on victorious,
> because of truth, humility and justice.

The Lord's Anointed is thus destined to conquer evil, but his way will be marked by humility and goodness. His anointing has been from the very hand of God, appointing him, bestowing the Spirit. So he will reign on earth for God, his throne belonging to God:

> Your throne is of God, for ever and ever;
> the sceptre of your kingdom is the sceptre of justice.
>
> As you have loved right and hated wrong,
> God, your God, has anointed you
>   with the oil of gladness above your fellows.

And now for the bride the poet has an earnest word. If she will give loving devotion, surpassing all former ties, she will have great honour and authority. The poetry then reflects her part in the progress of the wedding ceremony. In a robing room – 'within' – the bride is splendidly attired in a garment wrought with gold. In procession with her bridesmaids she passes into the king's palace, where stringed instruments are softly playing. The poet concludes with the prospect of the blessing that will give children to continue the life and reign of the Lord's Anointed.

The written record of the poem might have become just a historical curiosity, but later generations found in it a prophetic force. Already before the birth of Jesus the Jews had taken the psalm to foretell the coming Messiah. His 'bride' was understood to be his people, who were to be devoted to him in love and reverence.

The Church followed on, hearing the psalm speak of Christ – it is quoted in this sense in the New Testament (Hebrews 1). Christ was the king depicted in the psalm, the one who would have the anointing and the Spirit to reign from God's throne. His bride was to be the Church and each believing soul.

Along these lines we can still hear a word of God in this ancient poem, this inspired 'song of love'. The figure of Christ is here exalted, alone worthy of the throne of God. He appears as sure conqueror of evil, but by way of truth, humility and goodness. God's word in the psalm directs us to him – to love and honour him, and, 'forsaking all other', to cleave to him beyond all other claims. And through such devotion of the Church and her members Christ's name resounds through the generations and his royal work is continued evermore.

*Almighty God, grant to your Church to be renewed in devotion to your Son
  Jesus, forsaking all that is not of him.*
*In the likeness of his truth, humility and goodness may she be strong against
  evil. May she be clad in the gold of his grace. May she be one with him in
  the beauty of love.*
*O Jesus, may my heart be astir with love for you and with the inspiration to
  witness for you. May my tongue have warm words to tell of your glory.*

Psalm 46

Stillness and knowledge

The politicians were continually talking of 'weapons of mass destruction'.
One of the lesser nations was said to be accumulating them. The rhythmic
phrase was beginning to sound like an incantation, a kind of spell against
the foe – 'weapons of mass destruction!' Some speakers shortened it to
'WMDs', while others more expansively accused the renegade country of
acquiring 'chemical, biological and nuclear weapons'. The accused country
was told to destroy the offending weapons. In some spacious desert the
piles were to be collected, broken, burned or buried in the sight of international inspectors.

While all the speeches were resounding through the airwaves, the little
Quaker meeting house round the corner added a fresh poster to the thought-
provoking notices it habitually displayed to passers-by. The poster said:
'Destroy all weapons of mass destruction everywhere.' This simple senti-
ment would be rather disruptive if acted upon. The accusing speeches had
usually passed over the fact that quite a number of nations, including the
accusers and their client states, possessed massively destructive weapons
in some abundance. The inconvenient Quakers were also habitually pointing out the horrors of more normal weapons – the cluster bombs, mega-
bombs, missiles, multiple rockets, mines, shells and bullets. We die as
individuals, and an arrow or a spear, a club or a sword, may then seem as
terrible as any WMD.

So one comes to see that the most horrible thing of all is the spirit that
lies behind these weapons – the sin that hurts and destroys through all
society, the chaos of fear and jealousy, arrogance, revenge and greed.

This thought leads us to the message of a well-known scripture, Psalm 46. Here too we find the idea of the destruction of weapons. The psalm indeed pictures a worldwide breaking and burning of weapons, but it links it to a mighty act of God and his destruction of war itself.

We get inside the thought of the psalm as we appreciate that it will have come from the climax of the annual round of worship at the temple. A vast array of pilgrims has gathered at the time of the autumnal new year, when the agricultural cycle began. The ceremonies express the danger to the living order, the threat of death and chaos across the earth. But also they express the faith that the Creator has the good will and power to secure life and peace. The chanted poetry of the psalm takes up these great themes of danger and hope:

> God is our refuge and stronghold,
> our help in troubles, and very ready to be found.
>
> Therefore we shall not fear though earth sways,
> and mountains reel in the depths of the sea,
> though its waters roar and foam,
> and the mountains quake at its roaring pride.

Then the psalm pictures God's work among the nations. The chaos that would ruin the living order emerges in the aggression of the peoples. They rage and attack each other in constant wars. But against all this is a 'city of God', a centre of hope and peace and true life which he will ever guard. As the psalm puts it:

> There is a river
> that gladdens with its streams the city of God,
> the holy dwelling of God Most High.
>
> Since God is in her midst, she will not be shaken;
> God helps her as morning breaks.
>
> When the nations rage and the kingdoms reel,
> he utters his voice, and earth melts in consternation.
>
> The Lord of Hosts is with us,
> the God of Jacob is our stronghold.

But where is this 'city of God'? What is she? She is the stronghold of hope and faith that is formed around the Presence of God. She is known wherever there is worship and prayer, devotion and service to the Lord.

114

In the bright vision of our psalm, she is the centre of God's new creation, his new world. Come and see it, invites the psalm; come and see the new world of peace:

> Come, see the acts of the LORD,
> the destructions he makes on earth.

> He puts an end to wars to the bounds of the earth;
> he breaks the bow and snaps the spear,
>   and the shields he burns in the fire.

Then comes a message to 'be still'. It is a summons from God, not to devout individuals, but to the chaotic nations:

> Be still and know that I am God;
> I will be exalted over the nations,
>   I will be exalted over the earth.

'Be still', or more exactly, 'Desist' – desist from your schemes and ambitions, and in the stillness know where power and reality lie. Know with whom lies the decision. Know who alone is God.

The psalm ends with its refrain, a song of confidence. It is as though the new world were already achieved. The worshippers sing that the Lord has proved to be with them and for them, a sure defence against the evil forces: 'The LORD of Hosts is with us, the God of Jacob is our stronghold.'

The chant of 'God with us' was common in the great moments of celebration. It acknowledged that without him nothing could be achieved; without him there could be no joy, no true life. And there was a name that encapsulated this truth, the name 'Immanuel', meaning 'God with us'. It was the name of the hoped-for deliverer. It became a name we give to our Lord Jesus. For through him the morning of God's help has broken. Through him the river of life has flowed to gladden the city of faith, hope and love. Through him God has let himself be found, a 'very present help' – Jesus our Immanuel, God With Us. As we love and hold to him, the vision sustains us and becomes ever more assured. The weapons will be burnt, the evil chaos will be defeated and God will be exalted, to reign in peace over all.

O River of Grace, gladden us with new life.
O Morning Star, herald God's mercy for the city of faith.
O Immanuel, God With Us, be our stronghold when earth sways and nations rage.

Lord of Hosts, put an end to wars, break the weapons of hate. Be exalted over the nations.

May we be still and know that you are God. You alone are God, Creator, Ruler, Saviour.

We shall rejoice in the River, that gladdens with his streams the city of God.

Psalm 47
A time to clap and sing praise

A newspaper told of a blaze in a Methodist church. It was reported that the mayor congratulated the firemen on their reverence in removing their helmets before entering the smoke-filled building. Yes – it happened quite a while ago, when attitudes to church premises differed from those of our time. In those days, when sacred music was performed in church you would hear no applause. The interactive sermon with its lively contributions from the pews was unknown, indeed unthinkable. In such situations, the congregation maintained a stony silence.

But then things changed. It became customary to welcome the newly baptized into the fellowship with applauding hands. And when the new archbishop was installed in his cathedral chair, the congregation clapped and smiled. Altogether it was plain that applause, laughter and excitement were no longer thought irreverent in the place of worship. Support for the new attitude was found in the Psalms. The ancient congregations, it seems from the Psalms, were prone to utter loud shouts, dance with joy and vigorously clap their hands. Psalm 47 takes us straight there, for it begins:

> Clap your hands, all you peoples;
> acclaim God with joyful voice.

But in spite of the examples in the Bible, some may have misgivings about such applaudings in church. For it is a fact that also in our time television shows have cultivated an atmosphere of applause and enthusiasm. Studio audiences are rehearsed in the technique. Suitable noise can even be provided from machines. Presenters make their entrance to a jubilant applause, which they charmingly affect to moderate. Their every attempt at humour, however feeble, is met with tumults of laughter. People become insensitive to the falsehood of it all. Might such artificiality creep into the churches?

Psalm 47 is worlds away from this false excitement. Every verse centres on God, every line lit by the dread glory of his appearing, the dawn of his kingdom:

> Clap your hands, all you peoples . . .
> for the LORD Most High has appeared in dread majesty,
> Great King over all the earth.
>
> God has gone up with the shout of praise,
> the LORD, with the voice of the trumpet.
>
> Sing praises to God, sing praises;
> sing praises to our King, sing praises.
>
> For God is King of all the earth;
> sing praises with a psalm.
>
> God reigns over the nations;
> God has taken his holy throne . . .
>
> the shields of the earth belong to God,
> and he is very highly exalted.

But how are we to understand this dramatic moment when 'God has gone up' with shouts and trumpet blasts? It was the high moment in the year of worship. There has been a ceremony of procession and the lifting up of the ark, the symbol of his presence, back to its most holy shrine. A vision seizes the people. God is known as present in power and mercy, renewing life. It was like an anticipation of the new creation, when all evil would be overcome and God would reign in peace and love.

Some of the other psalms from this high moment of worship (96, 98, 150) focus on the fellowship of all created beings; not just humankind, but all creatures praise the Lord together. But in Psalm 47 the focus is on the nations, and almost with a contradiction. For two verses sound nationalistic, exulting in supremacy over other nations – thus verses 3 and 4:

> He has subdued peoples under us,
> and nations under our feet.
>
> He has chosen for us our heritage,
> the pride of Jacob whom he loved.

117

But as the psalm proceeds, it becomes clear that it is the rebellion of nations against God which has been subdued, and indeed transformed. The Lord is revealed as King of all the earth. His good reign, his happy kingdom, is for all nations. We recognize that when he called one people, it was for a mission to all. So now, the many peoples are together to be called 'the people of the God of Abraham'. All belong to him and so to his care and love. He is the good sovereign exalted over all. So the psalm's last verse rings out with its striking message:

> The princes of the peoples are gathered,
>   the people of the God of Abraham;
> for the shields of the earth belong to God,
>   and he is very highly exalted.

From this high point in ancient Jerusalem's worship, the little psalm and its vision pass into high moments of Christian worship. Especially the psalm brings its poetry and music to our celebration of Christ's ascension. Our Lord has indeed gone up with the shout of praise and ascended with the voice of the trumpet. Not in arrogant triumph, but through his humility, his sacrifice and rising again, he is King of all the world. Evil is brought down, and the good news calls all peoples to enter the kingdom through Jesus.

At the feast of Pentecost we celebrate the gathering of all nations as one people of the God of Abraham. The shields of the earth – all powers and principalities – belong to God. And at the feast of the Trinity, Father, Son and Holy Spirit are revealed in supreme majesty over all that exists. Yes, at these Christian feasts and their continuation in every Eucharist, the psalm inspires to the lifting up of hearts in hope and joy. We are raised above all adversities. We see already what shall be when all is accomplished. We know something already of that universal unity when the eyes of all are fixed on the ascended Lord.

O God Most High, we thank you for those moments of revelation when hope arises and passes into vision of your kingdom.
Grant us in our worship to hear already the clapping of all peoples as they rejoice to be your one great family.
Grant us to hear the trumpets that announce Christ ascended.
May we see you as King of all and sing praises, sing praises with a psalm.
For highly exalted are you, reigning in dread majesty, O Father, Son and Holy Spirit, now and for ever. Amen.

Psalm 48

Drama in church

It was all-age worship on Mothering Sunday, and the children's groups had a prominent role. Some gave a dramatic rendering of the Book of Ruth. Small children carried puppet figures which they held up on long poles. When the family of Naomi and Elimelech migrated from Bethlehem to Moab, the children bore the puppets from one side of the church to the other. A narrator was clarifying the story and came to the first great loss – there in Moab Elimelech died. The small girl holding up Elimelech promptly lowered him from view. But in the restricted space she found difficulty in tucking her long pole and its puppet out of sight. It seemed to the rapt congregation that Elimelech had made an unexpected recovery, darting up a few times and circling round. However, with the help of his relatives he was eventually laid to rest, and the drama proceeded impressively.

To some hypercritical observer the performance might have seemed an inadequate representation of the great story of Ruth. But the strange thing was that it did carry a power. Through that dramatic enactment, simple though it was, something significant was made to live and linger, something that a sermon could not have achieved.

But drama has had a part in worship from ancient times. Indeed it originated there. In Jewish worship, for thousands of years, there has been an annual re-enactment of the escape from Egypt – the Passover. In Christian worship, the very heart is the Eucharist, when the drama of the bread and wine is newly presented. And in the Psalms it is plain that other great moments in Jerusalem's worship found lively reality through sacred drama.

A remarkable example stands out in Psalm 48. Verse 9 has often been translated, 'We have *thought on* your faithful love in the midst of your temple, O God.' But the more basic meaning is better: 'We have *made a likeness* of your faithful love in the midst of your temple, O God', that is, we have depicted it in sign, in a drama.

What story of God's faithfulness could have been so depicted or dramatized in the midst of the temple? It is plainly recounted in the psalm. For, like the narrator in our all-age worship, the reciter here wants to make clear what the actions signify. It is all about an imaginary attack on

119

Jerusalem, and how the enemy was thrown down by the mere glimpse of the glory of God shining out of the city. The Lord is himself her citadel and stronghold, as the singer recounts:

> God is her citadel;
> he has shown himself to be a tower of refuge.
>
> For see, the kings assembled;
> together they swept forward.
>
> The instant they saw, they were dumbfounded;
> they were filled with terror and dismay.
>
> Quaking seized them there and then;
> writhing, as of a woman in labour.
>
> With a mighty wind from the desert,
> you broke up the galleons of war.
>
> We have both heard and seen
>   in the city of the LORD of Hosts,
>   in the city of our God:
> God has established her for ever.

Such is the story that has been shown in symbol. It has revealed how God is faithful to his promise to protect his city; as the singer says:

> We have enacted your faithful love
> in the midst of your temple, O God.
>
> As your name, O God, so also your praise
>   reaches to the ends of the earth;
> your right hand is full of justice.

The question remains for us: what do we today take from this imaginary story that was enacted in symbol so long ago? The psalm makes it plain that it was not just a local matter, a prayer for the safety of one nation's capital city. This hill of 'Zion' had an immense meaning, being described as 'the city of God', the place of his throne, from where his name shines out to the ends of the world – a city found at the centre of beauty and joy for all creatures. So the psalm begins:

> Great is the LORD and most glorious
> in the city of our God.

His holy mountain is the fairest of heights,
    the joy of all the world;
Mount Zion is the mountain of heaven,
    the city of the Great King.

To find this 'Zion' today we must begin at the humble place of our own worship. In a light of sincerity and faith and by the power of the Holy Spirit, we are led to see the fair height that towers up from that lowly place – the mountain of the throne of God, and the eternal city where he communes and rejoices with his creatures.

It is a disclosure to make us tremble, but also to give us courage. With new appreciation we look at the Zion in our worship with her towers and ramparts. With new devotion we share in the enactment of the Lord's faithful love, the everlasting drama of the bread and wine, the victory over the forces of death. Yes, walk around this Zion as the psalm says. Consider well all that is given us in the divine work done in the midst of worship. Take in the eternal might and meaning of it all. And pass on the testimony to the next generation. Such is the call of the inspired psalm-singer as he ends his chant:

Walk around Zion and encompass her,
    and count up her strong towers.

Mark well her rampart and study her citadels,
    that you may tell the next generation:

this is God, our God for ever and ever:
    it is he who shall lead us over death.

O God, the forces of pain and evil gather and sweep forward. How shall your city be saved?
The song of long ago still answers: God is her citadel, her tower of refuge.
And we too have heard and seen in your sanctuary, that you have come to the rescue. Your work lives among us as we enact your faithful love in the symbols of the bread and wine. Our joy in you will be the joy of all earth's creatures.
You are God, our God for ever and ever. You are the Lord who leads us to life beyond the shadow of death.
Great is the Lord and most glorious, in the city of our God.

Psalm 49

The costly ransom

—◆—

Rooms in Baker Street, a gaunt figure in a dressing gown, long fingers, thin and strong, playing a violin. Yes, it is Sherlock Holmes, one of the most famous figures in fiction. Keenly observant and brilliant in reasoning, he could solve mysteries of crime that baffled the stalwart officers of the law.

When grappling with the complexities of a problem, he would take up his violin. The strange music that emerged from his playing seemed to open the riddle for him. It was as though he had caught a voice from beyond. A gleam of discernment shone through the dark puzzle.

The violin and its all-important bow had not been invented in Bible times, but plucked string instruments such as the harp and lyre already had a long history. The psalmists were especially attached to their lyres, and in Psalm 49 we meet a player who, like Sherlock Holmes, saw his way through a problem by listening to the voice of his instrument. So he gains a message he wants to sing out to all peoples, to rich and poor. This is how his song begins:

> Hear this, all you peoples;
> listen, all you that dwell in the world,
>
> people of every kind,
> both rich and poor together.
>
> My mouth shall speak of wisdom,
> and the utterance of my heart shall be discernment.
>
> I will strain my ear for a parable;
> I will open my riddle with the lyre.

What was this 'riddle', this problem that beset him? Hardly a crime such as teased the mind of the legendary detective. Something broader, though bearing upon him personally. His days had come to seem 'evil'. He was oppressed by the wickedness of hostile folk all around him – 'supplanters', people who took what was his and deprived him of honour. Perhaps he was a ruler and suffered from greedy and ruthless enemies. These 'supplanters' were rich and had confidence in the abundance of their wealth.

The riddle was that in God's world such folk should prosper and be free to oppress and exploit.

Plucking his lyre, the troubled one listens as the sounds linger a moment and then pass into the beyond. Then from a higher world comes a melody that calms and enlightens. The singer's thoughts develop thus:

> Why should I fear in days of evil,
>   when the wickedness of my foes surrounds me,
> such as trust in their goods,
>   and glory in the abundance of their riches?
>
> For no one can by any means ransom himself,
>   or give to God his price.
>
> The ransom of his soul is too costly;
>   he would never have enough to pay it,
> so that he could live for ever,
>   and never see the Abyss.
>
> For one sees that the wise die also;
>   with the foolish and ignorant they perish,
>   and leave their goods to others.
>
> Their tomb is their home for ever,
>   their dwelling through all generations,
> though they made themselves owners of many estates.
>
> A person in splendour, and without understanding,
>   is like the cattle that are killed.

Such is the message the singer would have resound through the world: to the rich a warning, to the oppressed an encouragement. No one can buy themselves lasting security. No human wealth, power and pomp can defy death. The arrogant are near to doom; without their treasures, they will sink into the land of darkness. The singer adds to his warning:

> This is the way of those whose boast is in themselves,
>   the end of those that are pleased with their own mouths.
>
> They are taken like a flock to the darkness,
>   and death is their shepherd;
> and the true-hearted shall rule over them in the morning.

> Their beauty shall waste away,
> and the darkness shall be their dwelling.

But now it wonderfully appears that all this is but the foil for the vital revelation. The riddle is truly opened in verse 15:

> But God will ransom my soul;
> from the hand of the darkness he will take me.

The message is thus brought to its climax. While trust in human resources cannot buy an escape from decay and death, yet God has the power to ransom and redeem. The one who humbly trusts in him will be taken from the hand of death – will be taken up to God. So 'do not fear', sings the psalmist, sharing the comfort that has come to him:

> Do not fear if some one grows rich,
> and the glory of his house increases.
>
> For he will carry away nothing when he dies,
> nor will his glory go down with him.
>
> Though he blesses himself while he lives,
> thinking, They will praise you as you do well for yourself,
>
> yet he will enter the company of his fathers,
> who will never more see the light.
>
> A person in splendour, and without understanding,
> is like the cattle that are killed.

As we reflect on this unusual psalm we ponder both on the serious message and on the manner it was obtained. Through both the message and the manner of its coming runs the thread of humility, a quietness before God. In playing and listening to his lyre the singer must have humility. The noise of the ego must be stilled. Then the soft and hovering notes speak to the soul; a voice from heaven is received by the heart. And the message too is bound up with humility before God. Boast not of your own capacities, your possessions, your status. Be still and know that all strength belongs to God. Such a truly humble person will hear and receive that wonderful promise: 'God will ransom my soul; from the hand of the darkness he will take me.'

None can by any means ransom themselves. But you, Jesus, the Son of Man,
came to serve and to give your life as a ransom for many.

Open to me the riddle of life and death by the music of your word.
Grant that in stillness and humility I may hear your voice.
May I know that you have ransomed my soul from death, to dwell with you
in your eternal morning.

Psalm 50
Mindful of the way

—◆—

Old Burcot Lane was a familiar route for those who wanted to pick their own fruit at the farm, famous for its splendid orchards and acres of fruit bushes. The narrow, twisting lane was cut through sandstone rocks that formed walls of earthy red. On the way to the fine orchards one might think little of the humble lane. And then came the day when a 350-metre stretch of it was designated a Site of Special Scientific Interest. Geologists had shown that the rocks had very great significance. They were a peculiar formation deposited 240 million years ago among meandering rivers in the Triassic period, when the first dinosaurs and mammals appeared.

So now folk went down Old Burcot Lane more respectfully. They wondered what primeval creatures had passed this way, and, as the evening shadows lengthened, what strange ghosts might be coming round the corner. The dinosaurs were only some of the many creatures that had prepared the world for us. In spite of the millions of years, they no longer seemed so far away. Were they indeed still present in the eternal memory of their Creator? Did they still live to him? These thoughts and intuitions on the way through Old Burcot Lane seem to find an echo in Psalm 50, where the voice of God is heard declaring his bond with every animal:

All the creatures of the forest are mine,
and the beasts that roam the great mountains.

I know every bird of the hills,
and all that moves in the wild is with me.

Surprisingly, it is the voice of God that fills most of this longish psalm. For once, we have in a psalm no prayer or thanksgiving or general praise, but almost eighteen verses where God speaks to his assembled people. There is a very strong sense of his presence. He has come for this time of judgement. His glory blazes out from his sanctuary. He has words of counsel and criticism to address to his people and will not remain silent. It seems to be the great moment in worship when the covenant is re-affirmed – that bond of promise and commitment between the Lord and worshippers. A prelude in the psalm invokes attention and awe:

> The Mighty One, God, the LORD, has spoken,
> and called the world from the rising of the sun to its setting.
>
> From Zion, perfection of beauty, God shines out;
> our God has come and will not keep silence.
>
> Fire devours before him,
> and tempest rages about him.
>
> He calls the heavens above,
> and the earth, to the judgement of his people:
>
> Gather to me my faithful,
> who have sealed my covenant with sacrifice.
>
> And the heavens declare his justice,
> for truly he is the God of right.

The singer now becomes God's spokesman, bringing the divine message in the manner of a prophet. In ironical fashion the Lord in this message takes note of the sacrifice of animals. Do these people imagine they have to feed God? Should he be obliged to them for all this provision? God says:

> For all the creatures of the forest are mine . . .
>
> If I were hungry I would not tell you,
> for the world is mine, and all that fills it.
>
> Do I eat the flesh of bulls,
> or drink the blood of he-goats?

No, the Creator has no such need, and the worshippers must beware of magnifying themselves. But he commends offerings brought in thanks-giving, when worshippers make public acknowledgement of his help:

> Sacrifice to God in thanksgiving,
> and so fulfil your vows to God Most High.
>
> Then call to me in the day of trouble,
> and I will deliver you, and you shall give me glory.

In all this we discern how the speech of God is directed to those who keep the forms of worship, but slip from the true spirit of awe before him. And this is obvious also in the second part of the speech. This fastens on another part of the worship, when they recited the commandments and made responses of commitment. How can you accept these laws with your mouth, asks the Lord, yet in practice readily break them? God says:

> What do you mean by reciting my statutes
> and taking my covenant upon your mouth,
>
> when you have rejected discipline,
> and have cast my words behind you?

Vividly the Lord specifies sins committed by outwardly respectable people – sins of falsehood, harmful words, thieving and adultery. Such offenders 'forget God' – that is, in the time of temptation they do not reckon with his reality. But the Lord says:

> You that forget God, consider this,
> or I shall pluck you away, with none to deliver you.

These warning words are relevant to worshippers of every era, not least our own. Those ancient Hebrews who brought sacrifices thinking God needed them and was obligated by them; those others who gave lip service to the moral laws but in practice brushed them aside – all these types criticized in the speech of God have their counterparts today. They are indeed very common – people who in their busy self-importance or in their unchecked selfishness lose the sense of God's awesome reality. They 'forget God'. They do not truly reckon with him in his eternal majesty and in his concern for justice, truth and mercy. They do not remember his presence in and over every situation they encounter.

Too easily we slip into seeing things in the small measure of our immediate concerns and desires. We lose the sense of depth and mystery in things all about us, and so 'forget God'. Old Burcot Lane was just an awkward narrow bit on the way to the fruit farm, hardly worth a thought – until it was suddenly revealed in the immense dignity of its 240 million years and the tale of its wondrous creatures beyond our grasping. Consider this, advises our psalm; awaken to the divine glory. Be mindful of the way you must walk with the Lord. Or more exactly, in the concluding words of God's speech:

> One who sacrifices in thanksgiving gives me the glory,
> and to one mindful of the way,
> I will show the salvation of God.

127

Lord, you are present from everlasting to everlasting. Help me to hear and see.

O Mighty One, God, the Lord, you speak and call the world from the rising of the sun to its setting. From your holy hill, perfection of beauty, you shine out. Help me to hear and see.

All the creatures of the forest are yours, and the beasts that roam the great mountains. You know every bird of the hills, and all that moves in the wild is with you, Eternal One.

In thanksgiving I give you the glory. Keep me mindful of the way, ready to see your salvation.

Psalm 51
Living in God's grace

A century or two ago in old Russia, a poor man had freedom to wander about because he had lost the use of one arm in childhood. He walked great distances in Russia and Siberia to find the answer to a question that puzzled him. His question was, how to fulfil the New Testament exhortation, 'Pray without ceasing' (1 Thess. 5.17). Setting off with nothing but his Bible in his breast pocket and dry bread in his knapsack, he made pilgrimage to many holy places, putting his question to monks and counsellors. So it came about that at length he learnt to pray without ceasing through use of 'the Jesus prayer' – 'Lord Jesus Christ, have mercy upon me' (or as some use it, 'Lord Jesus Christ, Son of God, have mercy upon me, a sinner'). Reciting this with his outgoing breath thousands of times a day, he reached a state where the prayer flowed on in an uninterrupted stream, as though from its own energy. It had become the prayer of the heart, and through it he had an abiding awareness of the presence of Jesus and his grace. Eventually the pilgrim wrote an account of his wanderings and his quest. The anonymous manuscript was copied by an abbot and published in Russia. Many years later it became known and loved in an English translation as *The Way of a Pilgrim* (translated by R. M. French, 1930).

Simple and direct, it is an enthralling story and gives an example of total spiritual commitment. But some may wonder at the monotony of this way of praying. One short sentence endlessly repeated, and its thought restricted to a sinner's plea for compassion! If one is dubious about this harping upon the need for mercy and grace, one may be just as bemused by another practice in countless religious communities for most of the Christian centuries – the recital of Psalm 51 daily and at each of the seven hours of prayer. The thought of the psalm is not quite so restricted, and the expression is more varied; but it is essentially a plea for God's mercy from one who is profoundly aware of being a sinner. We must wonder if, after all, there is some vital spiritual treasure hidden in all this repetition – both of the Jesus prayer and of Psalm 51. Such a constant holding of one-self in utter need before the grace and compassion of the Lord – could this indeed prove to be a true way of living in God?

Let us look afresh at the famous psalm. What does it show about the sinner before God, and the hope that springs up in that place?

We see that the ancient Jewish scholars added a note to the heading of the psalm. Here they proposed that the original occasion of the prayer was when David was filled with remorse for a terrible sin he had committed. He had contrived the death of a faithful servant to conceal his own adultery with that good man's wife, Bathsheba. Whether or not we accept the view of this heading, the psalm appears as well adapted for anyone troubled by a particular wrongdoing. Whether such a wrongdoing is as grave as David's or relatively slight in the eyes of the world, it can have the power to blight the relationship with God, and so ruin the peace of one's soul. Someone in this situation, troubled by the memory of a particular sin, can well be led in prayer by the strong, profound words of the psalm:

> Be gracious to me, God, in your faithful love;
>   in the abundance of your compassion, blot out my offences.
>
> Wash me thoroughly from my wrongdoing,
>   and cleanse me from my sin.
>
> For well I know my offences,
>   and my sin is ever before me.

O to be so washed, to have one's heart made new, to be comforted and guided by God's Spirit! O to be close to the Lord again – as the psalm says:

> Bring back to me the joy of your salvation,
>   and uphold me with your gracious Spirit.

Sincere penitence God will not reject:

> My sacrifice, O God, is a broken spirit;
>   a heart that is broken and crushed, O God, you will not despise.

129

With such words the psalm leads on the way to release from a particular guiltiness. But what of that Christian tradition commending the psalm for regular repetition, sustaining a theme of prayer throughout our lives? In such sustained use, it will lead us before God again and again with the sense of our constant need of his grace. Before his holy being, always we shall confess ourselves sinful, not worthy of his love, often raising a barrier to it – as the psalm leads us:

> Against you, you only, have I sinned,
> and done what is evil in your eyes.

In God's presence we know that it is not just a matter of sinning on occasion, but of being sinful in our very nature. The psalmist puts it drastically:

> Truly, I was born in wickedness,
> a sinner when my mother conceived me.

What a burden that realization of inherent fault could be! But the psalm lights up the character of God in a way that fills us with hope. For the prayer rests on the abundance of his compassion, his mother-like pity and tenderness, his persevering love. The psalm leads us to call on this pity and love to help us and save us, to make us anew. So it opens to us the wonderful prospect that his grace will indeed wash us, cleanse us, re-create heart and spirit, hold us in that close communion with the Lord which is true life. Again and again through the days of our life we may say with the psalm:

> Create for me a pure heart, O God,
> and renew a steadfast spirit within me.

> Do not cast me out of your presence,
> or take your Holy Spirit from me.

And because of the Lord's abundant grace, the time of joy and praise is near for the humble soul. So we pray:

> Cause me to hear joy and gladness,
> that the bones you have broken may rejoice . . .

> Deliver me from guilt, O God, the God of my salvation,
> and my tongue shall sing of your goodness.

> O Lord, open my lips,
> and my mouth shall proclaim your praise.

Sometimes people concerned with their own guilt and forgiveness may give the impression of being rather wrapped up in themselves. But the psalm shows that this is not the true result of individual forgiveness. The singer looks forward to guiding others to learn of God and return to him. But even more remarkably, he ends by drastically enlarging his prayer to gather in 'Zion', the universal community of God. He prays:

Do good to Zion in your favour;
build up the walls of Jerusalem.

Then you will accept the offerings of fellowship,
    sacrifice burnt and whole;
    then indeed shall they offer up bulls on your altar.

Here we constantly pray that the Lord will bless, protect and renew his community. May that whole body know forgiveness and restoration of communion, and so be moved with thankfulness; not as in the ancient times to offer bulls on God's altar, but rather to thank him with that best and costliest offering – all that we have and are, to live for him alone.

So, yes, the psalm is a good prayer for us to sustain all our lives; a good prayer for us ever to confess our unworthiness and ever to trust in the Lord's forgiving love and salvation – for ourselves, for his Church and for all his world. But the last word may be given to that pilgrim in old Russia. For the Jesus prayer puts in a few words the need for us sinners to hold ourselves before the grace of God. And it adds one vital element – that all is given through the Lord Jesus Christ. Here the devotion of the psalm finds its fulfilment. In his sacrifice is given all that grace, compassion, faithful love and salvation of God. The prayer through his name finds the way from the heart to the divine heart, to enfolding in the compassion of the heart of God.

Be gracious to me, Lord, in your faithful love. In your overflowing compassion
   blot out my offences.
For I constantly tend to do wrong. My sinfulness is ever before me.
Create for me a pure heart. Do not take away from me your Holy Spirit.
Do good to your Zion, your Church. Build her again in your strength and
   blessing, till all your people offer themselves in thankfulness, to live to you
   alone, our Saviour, abundant in tender pity and enduring love.
Lord Jesus Christ, now and always be gracious to me, a sinner.

Psalm 52
Meditation on an olive tree

———◆·◆◆·———

'Where did I go wrong?' – it's a question people ask themselves when they
are conscious of some vexing failure. Things have not turned out well, and
it is not obvious why. Puzzled, they look back and wonder, 'Where did I go
wrong?' The question can also be applied somewhat differently when we
contemplate the life of someone who has done great harm. How do such
persons come to be so wedded to evil, so set on hurting others? Was there
some cause early in life? Where did they go wrong?

Such an evil person is depicted in Psalm 52 – holding great power, plotting destruction, using words of deceit deadly as a razor:

> You plot destruction, you deceiver;
> your tongue is like a whetted razor.
>
> You love evil rather than good,
> falsehood rather than true speaking.
>
> You love all words that destroy,
> and the tongue skilled in deceit.

If we wonder what was the root of this person's wickedness – 'Where did
he go wrong?' – the psalm gives a surprising answer. Not that he started
from some bitter experience, nor even that he meant to rebel against God;
but simply that, in the words of the psalm, *he did not make God his refuge.*
The depth of this error was that in practice he was trusting in something
else – his own wealth. This in effect had become his own god. So the psalm
addresses him with this warning:

> But God shall bring you yourself to ruin;
> he will snatch you and pluck you out of your tent,
> and root you out of the land of the living.
>
> Then the just will see it and fear,
> and they will laugh at him and say:
>
> See the one who did not make God his refuge,
> but trusted in the abundance of his wealth,
> and sought strength in his work of destruction.

Perhaps when we ask ourselves the question, 'Where did I go wrong?', we shall remember the unexpected diagnosis of the psalm. Have we too failed to make God our refuge? Have we comprehensively put our trust in things human, things flawed?

But the psalm would not leave us there in regret and remorse, but rather in the repentance that is a new outlook of hope, a new life with the Lord. The psalm points us to an olive tree. It is planted and carefully tended in the court of the temple, and it is a symbol of a calm, beautiful and fruitful life. As the singer has it: 'But I shall be as a green olive tree in the house of God . . .' The picture well suggests closeness to God and his gifts of peace and wholeness. But again, the psalm perhaps surprises us by taking the picture of the tree especially as a symbol of *trust*. To be like that tree is to trust in God's faithful love, thankful for his provision of life and care. We are always living in his presence and in his goodness. As the psalm says:

> But I shall be as a green olive tree in the house of God;
> I will trust in the goodness of God for ever and ever.

And as the tree grows and fruits in nearness to God's presence, so the trusting person will also be deeply blessed and will bear witness to God's name – his outreaching love:

> I will ever give you thanks for what you have done,
> and before your faithful ones I will declare
> how gracious is your name.

Visitors to the Holy Land often return with objects made from the local olive wood – a cross, a donkey or camel, a darning aid. These are reminders of that hilly land where the chief tree has always been the olive. But the olive wood is also a reminder of our Saviour. He began the last week of his earthly ministry by passing over the brow of the Mount of Olives on his way to Jerusalem, the holy city lying in the lee of the hill. After the Last Supper he went out under the night sky into the garden of Gethsemane, the 'garden of the oil-press', near the foot of the Mount of Olives. The custodians of the church we find there today think of the present gnarled olive trees as surviving, or at least descending, from the olives that watched in the night with Jesus.

But there is another link of the olive tree with Jesus. Because of its product of oil, the tree was sometimes taken as a symbol of the Messiah, the one anointed by God with the oil that made him God's Spirit-filled Servant King.

133

Putting all these thoughts together, how then do we hear the melody of this little psalm? It sounds for us an invitation to turn from the life of self-reliance, self-glory, self-sufficiency, and to join ourselves to Christ in his bond with the Father. We make the Lord our refuge. So we are to grow like that green olive tree in the house of God, and come to trust in the goodness of God for everything.

Lord, let me be still as the olive tree, receiving life from you.
I shall be as a green olive tree in the house of God; I will trust in the goodness
* of God for ever and ever.*
I will ever give you thanks for what you have done, and before your faithful
* I will declare how gracious is your name.*
O Jesus, the Anointed of the Father, guard me from the words that destroy and
* from the tongue like a whetted razor. Take me into the aura of your name,*
* that I may be still and fruitful, and ever give thanks for what you have*
* done.*
Teach me ever to make you my refuge, and always to trust in your faithful
* love.*

Psalm 53

Judgement and transformation

Sometimes the old Bible translators came to an awkward phrase, and then were given grace to make something especially memorable from it. For example, a difficult line in Job (19.20) is rendered in the New English Bible as 'I gnaw my under-lip with my teeth'; but the older translators made the line into one of our favourite sayings: 'I am escaped by the skin of my teeth.' A curious but effective saying! Another example comes from Psalm 53, a line which stays in the mind of those who recite or sing the Psalms: 'They were afraid where no fear was.' What could that mean? One woman accustomed to reciting the Psalms explained it as groundless fear – being afraid when there was no reason to fear. She added: 'like a young horse that shies at a bit of paper blowing in the wind'. We can well agree that there are often times when we have feared needlessly and, remembering the presence of our Lord, we realized we were being afraid 'where no fear was' – when there was no reason to fear. All the same, the psalm may have intended something rather different, as we shall see.

This short Psalm 53 has several points of interest. For one thing, it is essentially the same psalm as Psalm 14, though with some variations because at first handed down in a different collection. This may encourage us when, in our worship, we want to use a particular psalm but feel it right to vary it, perhaps by omitting a part, or combining it with part of another psalm.

Another striking point is that the last verse opens up hope with a splendid Hebrew phrase for the great action of God that makes all things well. It is the hope that he will 'turn the captivity' of his people, or better, 'restore them with a great restoring'. It is the great transformation when he turns the desert into his garden, when he turns death into life.

Above all, the psalm is remarkable for saying much in few lines. Not only does it give a diagnosis of the world's behaviour which remains true today; it also expresses God's determination to root out evil. And further, it voices our longing that this great salvation should soon blaze forth from his throne.

The psalm begins by finding fools everywhere – fools, because they take no account of God in their daily conduct. Not their lips, but their actions say, 'There is no God.' They think, plan and act as if he were not. These are the true fools, and there are many of them:

> God has looked down from heaven upon earth's peoples,
> to see if there is anyone acting wisely and seeking God.

> But every one of them has gone back, all alike corrupted;
> there is no one that does good, no not one.

In this grim situation the psalm brings a word of God – a threat to those who exploit and oppress, but a promise to their victims. God says:

> Are the evildoers without understanding,
> that they eat up my people as though they ate bread,
> and do not call on God?

> There shall they fear *with fear such as never was*,
> for God will scatter the bones of him that is encamped against you.

> You will put them to shame,
> for God has rejected them.

Yes, that is probably the right translation – 'There shall they fear with fear such as never was.' A most fearsome judgement is in preparation, for it has become only too evident that people everywhere have left the true God out of account. They have slipped into being gods to themselves. They adjust truth, value, morality to suit themselves. For their own ends they call light darkness and darkness light. We see much of this still today in the unscrupulous media, in business and finance, in politics. So the people of faith, humility and prayer must yearn and pray with the psalm:

> O that the salvation of Israel were given from Zion!
> When God turns the life of his people,
> > let Jacob rejoice, let Israel be merry.

Lord, warn us when our conduct says, 'There is no God.' Guard us from the folly of planning and acting without recourse to you.
Go before and follow me, and possess my heart, that all my actions shall say, 'There is a God, a Judge, a Saviour.'
O God, you look down on all earth's peoples and see their folly, their deeds of selfishness and cruelty. Bring soon your great salvation. Bring the world's great turning to life in you, that all your creatures may rejoice before you.

Psalm 54

The Infinite known in a Name

————•◆•————

A young student of theology had travelled to a northern university to visit his brother and was being introduced to the brother's slightly Bohemian friends. One of these, Daniel, was a thoughtful student of philosophy. He was humorous and politically radical. Over a cup of tea Daniel suddenly posed a teasing question to our raw theologian. 'Imagine you discover an island. The inhabitants have had no previous contact with the outside world and have not heard of God. How would you explain him to them?' Perhaps it was the suddenness of the challenge or a whiff of scepticism in the air – at any rate, the budding expert remained silent. Satisfactory words just would not come to mind. The silence seemed long, till the conversation resumed along another course. Later in life, the theological one would remember that embarrassing silence, considering what he should have said. Yet perhaps after all, the silence was a meaningful answer. We suffer more from glib talk of God than from the quiet that is eloquent of the unutterable mystery.

It is true that the Bible offers many remarkably concrete, even homely, pictures of God – our Father in heaven, shaping the world like a craftsman, sitting, marching, peering, hearing, speaking, laughing, raging, loving, grieving. But it also has ways of preserving the mystery. Often the thought is that God makes himself known to us through special manifestations such as his Word, his Glory, his Spirit, or his Name, while his infinite, utterly mysterious being still lies beyond, inaccessible to our small minds.

But it is typical of the Bible that these forms of manifestation are not put before us with any technical flourish. They are inexhaustibly pro-found, yet readily enter every mind and heart. What could seem simpler than that he told us his name, so that we could call to him in prayer? Yet we can never tell the whole of what this precious name means to us. Through the loving gift of it we can know the Unknowable, conceive of the Inconceivable, commune with the Inaccessible, the utterly Beyond.

In some of the psalms this name is seen as the saving power of God that goes out into the world to help those who have called upon it. This is what we find in the small psalm 54. The singer laments that strangers have risen against him and the ruthless seek after his soul, having no regard for God's wishes. So he asks for help:

> O God, save me *by your name*,
> and judge for me by your might . . .
>
> God is my helper;
> the Lord is the upholder of my soul.
>
> May the harm return upon those that lie in wait for me;
> in your truth put them to silence.

And when he has been saved through the Lord's name, he says, he will raise thankful praise to that name so beautiful and good:

> Freely will I sacrifice to you;
> your name will I praise, LORD, for it is gracious.
>
> For it shall deliver me from every trouble,
> and my eye shall see the downfall of my enemies.

This psalm, then, is the prayer of one who defends his soul, his very life, by calling on the holy name. The likelihood is that he is a leader defending not only himself but the whole community bound up with him. For them all he invokes that powerful name against terrifying foes that strike from hidden places. For them all he trusts in the name of the Lord who is

137

supreme helper, chief upholder of their life, faithful and true. When deliverance is given he will make thankful offerings, unstinting as the holy name is generous and gracious, ready to deliver from every trouble.

A curious thing happened to the use of God's name in Old Testament times. So strongly was the awesome divine presence felt in the name that more and more they feared to pronounce it. But how could it now be the self-giving of the utterly mysterious God? If never pronounced, how could it be the means whereby we could know his communion with us? Then in God's time came Jesus. Here now was the true form of the name above every name. With the name 'Jesus' we are enabled to call trustfully upon the infinite God; with the name 'Jesus' we are given the divine salvation. By the power of Jesus' name we defend our souls and the whole circle of God's creatures. We join the cosmic praise of this name, for it is gracious, it is God With Us. And if we were to find Daniel's island and have to speak to the native inhabitants of the inexpressible mystery of God, we could well begin with the sweet name of Jesus. With that name we could well begin, continue and end.

Lord, save me by your name and act for me by your might. Hear my supplication lifted up in the name of Jesus.

O God, you are my helper through Jesus. In him you have come to me and are the upholder of my soul.

All that I am and have I will offer to you in thankfulness for the grace of your name.

By your name I shall be delivered in every trouble. May my enemies be turned back and by your grace come to know your name.

Psalm 55

The place of peace

◆—◆—◆

Sometimes we are facing a situation from which we would gladly escape – only we know we have to stay and go through with it. Our heart may be afraid and in turmoil. O to be in some other place and time, far from antagonism and strife! But no, we cannot flee away. Who can help us?

Such an experience is vividly expressed in Psalm 55, which in the end contains some golden advice. Here we meet a leading person, probably a king. He is voicing urgent prayer to the Lord in the evening, in the morning and at noon. He implores the Lord to hear and heed his supplication. He tells him of his alarm and fear:

> I am alarmed at the voice of the enemy,
> at the clamour of the wicked . . .
>
> My heart is in turmoil within me,
> and the terrors of death have fallen upon me.
>
> Fear and trembling have come upon me,
> and a horrible dread has overwhelmed me.
>
> And I said, O that I had wings like a dove,
> that I might fly away and be at rest!
>
> Then would I flee away far off,
> and make my lodging in the wilderness.
> I would make haste to escape
> from the stormy wind and tempest.

It seems that this prayer rises in a situation of warfare. The capital city is in a tragic state. It reminds us of modern examples, when chaos has struck a previously well-ordered community or left a city at the mercy of pillagers and slaughterers. The singer in the psalm puts the evil situation before the Lord. He tells how he sees spectres of violence stalking the walls, streets and squares:

> . . . I have seen Violence and Strife in the city.
>
> Day and night they go about her walls;
> and in her midst stalk Mischief and Trouble.
>
> Ruin walks in her streets;
> Deceit and Guile linger in her square.

Whenever an old order seems to be breaking down, treachery is common. Trusted allies change sides for their own advantage. Our singer especially laments that a close ally, an intimate friend, has joined the spectres of deceit and guile:

> It was not an open enemy that reviled me,
> for then I could have borne it . . .
>
> But it was you, one like myself,
> my companion and my familiar friend.

> We took sweet counsel together;
> we walked as friends in the house of God.

Such a wound is this treachery that the singer comes back to it again later in the psalm:

> Against those at peace with him he stretched out his hands,
> and thus he defiled his covenant.

> His mouth was smoother than butter,
> but his heart was set on war.

> His words were softer than oil,
> yet they were naked blades.

The singer thus is deeply grieved by the treachery and alarmed for his city. And he earnestly prays that the enemy be divided among themselves and suddenly thrown down. His theme of trust in God as the only Saviour grows strong:

> As for me, I will cry to God,
> and the LORD indeed shall save me.

> Evening, morning and noon-day
> I will pray and make my supplication.

> And he shall hear my voice,
> and redeem my soul in peace ...

Then, like a voice from beyond, comes that golden counsel:

> O cast your burden upon the LORD,
> and he will sustain you;
> he will never let the faithful one be overthrown.

This is a counsel that is still as fresh and essential today. Here are words to recall and to follow whenever cares weigh heavily upon us – 'O cast your burden upon the LORD, and he will sustain you,' or as St Peter puts it in his letter, 'Cast all your anxiety upon him, for he cares for you' (1 Pet. 5.7).

And if, like the psalmist, we still have to go through a time of 'horrible dread', we should recall that the psalm's words of anguish come close to the ordeal of Jesus in Gethsemane. He felt this terror and dread, saying to Peter, James and John, 'My soul is sorrowful even unto death.' But at once he threw himself down and began to call out in prayer, 'Abba, Father . . .' (Mark 14.32f.). That dreadful night also brought for Jesus betrayal by his 'companion and familiar friend', whose mouth, as the psalm has it, was smoother than butter and his intention deadly as a naked blade.

This passage, and indeed all the sufferings mirrored in the Psalms, were seen by the first Christians as foreshadowing the cross. Indeed we can say that Christ gathers up all suffering into his from the beginning to the end of the world. So, when we cast our burden on the Lord, we believe that the Lord who accepts it also leads on to the resurrection and to the turning of the 'horrible dread' into his peace and joy.

And here we may find a new force in the psalmist's image of a dove. He was thinking of the rock-dove, ancestor of our strong-flying pigeons. On her long wings she could range far before returning to her home on some remote cliff in the desert. Hence the psalmist's yearning, 'O that I had wings like a dove, that I might fly away and be at rest; then would I flee away far off and make my lodging in the wilderness.' May we not believe that, as we cast our burden upon the Lord and in our fears hold fast to Jesus – may we not believe that he will send the Spirit, the holy Dove, to bear us on mighty wings to God's place of peace, leaving our fears far behind? Yes, he will bring us surely to his place of peace. Through God's grace in Christ we may pray with confidence the trusting words of the psalm: 'As for me, I will cry to God, and the LORD indeed shall save me . . . and he shall hear my voice and redeem my soul in peace.'

Lord, when my heart is in turmoil, when a horrible dread overwhelms me, when I long for wings like a dove to fly far off, then let me hear your counsel, 'Cast your burden upon me, cast all your cares on me; I will sustain you, I will care for you.'

In my time of fear, Lord, let me be carried on the wings of the Holy Spirit to your place of peace.

Hear my supplication, O God. Uphold me, for I trust in you.

Psalm 56
Tears that God treasures

Old Mrs Rigby had not been well for some time. She had no desire to see a doctor, and certainly not to get enmeshed in the processes of tests and consultations. And then she got rather worse. Her daughter Hannah looked after her with every care, but there came a day when Hannah knew she must ask the doctor to call. So she plucked up her courage and arranged for him to call that afternoon. She had to compose her thoughts. He would probably be in a hurry. How could she give him the important facts in good order and proportion, to help him come to a wise decision and not rush into some inappropriate course, if anything making things worse? What indeed were the most important things to mention from all that had happened in those days and nights of nursing? In the event, the doctor was patient and understanding. He followed her story as though he had been with her in it all. And his decision was very wise, leaving mother and daughter much happier.

Yes, it is a blessed thing when a doctor, from sympathy and experience, readily understands the story of sufferings and can take into account all those ups and downs, those fears and perplexities, that have marked the troubled days and nights.

And when we come to God to tell him of some great problem that presses upon us, can we not believe that he will readily understand our confused story – indeed already knows all the twists and turns of it that have caused us to groan and weep? Well, we are encouraged to believe so by Psalm 56. The singer here is calling to God and telling of his suffering at the hands of many enemies:

> Take pity on me, O God, for man tramples over me,
> all day long fighting and pressing upon me . . .

> All the day long they wound with words;
> their every thought is to do me harm.

But the singer also declares his trust:

> Yet in the day when I fear,
> I will put my trust in you.

> In God whose word I praise,
> in God I trust and will not fear;
> for what can flesh do to me?

He believes the Lord knows and cares deeply about all the anguish, for he says picturesquely:

> You have counted all my groans;
> my tears are laid up in your bottle.
> Are they not written in your book?

142

The comparison here is with a good steward who has stored water in skin bottles and shows how he values it by keeping a careful record in his book. So God does not lightly regard our sighs and tears. They are in his heart until the day of deliverance.

And the psalmist also finds comfort in recollection of God's 'word', making this the refrain of his song of prayer:

> In God whose word I praise,
>   in the LORD whose word I praise,
>
> in God I trust and will not fear;
>   for what can man do to me?

This 'word' from God is his promise and commitment, the light that has now shone out to us in Jesus Christ. Here is the word of God for us to praise thankfully and trust at all times, overcoming fear. What can we offer such a Saviour but our whole lives in thanksgiving?

> Gladly will I render the vows to you;
>   fully will I bring you the offerings of thanksgiving.
>
> For you will deliver my soul from death and my feet from falling,
>   to walk before God in the light of life.

O God, my tears are laid up in your bottle. I thank you that you remember every groan and treasure every tear of those who suffer.

Yet more, you share all sufferings through the groaning of the Holy Spirit and the cries and tears of Christ who takes our part.

In the day when I fear, I will put my trust in you. I praise your word and will fear no more.

Gladly will I bring you the offering of my life, you that deliver my soul from death and my feet from falling, to walk before you in the light of life.

Psalm 57

Awakening the dawn

———◆◆———

Amelia had a son, and three years later a daughter. Then she had another son, and two years later was again expecting. Confident of having a second daughter, she had chosen the name 'Dorothy' for its meaning, 'Gift of God'. However, the pattern was not maintained. She had a third son, and hastily substituted the name 'John', which she thought to have similar meaning. She wasn't too far out, but actually 'John' means 'The Lord has been gracious' – in the birth of the child. It is one of many names developed from the Hebrew verb 'to be gracious'; they are expressive of God's kindness, pity or generosity.

Such names reflect the rich experience of God's grace in the religion of the Bible. But it is difficult to hit on the ideal translation in many biblical passages about that grace. An example is the opening of Psalm 57. This is a repeated prayer which we could render, 'Be gracious to me, O God, be gracious to me.' Others have translated it, 'Be merciful unto me, O God, be merciful unto me.' Others again have, 'Take pity on me, God, take pity on me.'

The lines that follow in the psalm may help to bring us to the heart of the meaning: 'My soul takes shelter in you. In the shadow of your wings I take shelter, until the storm of ruin is passed.' It is a picture of a young bird. As a storm rages, it takes shelter under the wings of its mother. So the prayer for God's grace and pity is directed to the tender love of God, like a mother's compassion for her little ones.

The singer, as often in the Psalms, may be a king facing deadly enemies, and he looks also to the power of the heavenly King to deal with the terrible foes:

> I will call to God Most High,
> to the God who does great things for me.
>
> From heaven he will send and save me,
>   deriding those that trample upon me;
> God will send out his [angels of] faithful love and truth.
>
> I lie in the midst of lions,
> that breathe fire and are greedy for human prey;
>
> their teeth are spears and arrows,
> and their tongue a whetted sword.

Sometimes such psalms of distress end with a promise to praise God when help is given. But in the present case the singer is eager already to turn to praise. Even though the darkness has not yet lifted, he begins the song of praise that could awaken a day of salvation. Even though he is still in the midst of trouble, his heart is ready to sing of God's glory. Hear how his words of distress pass into praise:

My heart is ready, O God, my heart is ready,
that I may sing and raise a melody.

Awake, my glory, awake, harp and lyre,
that I may awaken the dawn.

I will give you thanks, Lord, among the peoples;
I will sing your praise among the nations.

For your love reaches to the heavens,
and your faithfulness to the clouds.

We notice here how in the moment of praise there is a great sense of the world's unity around God. Thus our singer can summon his own inspiration – 'Awake, my glory.' And then call his instruments to life – 'Awake, harp and lyre.' And then he calls to the angel of the dawn, that she may fly across the heavens from the east and roll back earth's coverlet of night. So he becomes one in a world of creatures united in giving thanks to God for his faithful love, which is so great as to fill every part of the cosmos. All the same, the time of suffering is not yet ended, and the singer's last words resume his earlier prayer – that God come forth in splendour and supremacy and put all things to rights:

Be exalted, O God, above the heavens,
with your glory over all the earth.

This vivid psalm has thus helped us to enter into the experience of an ancient worshipper, to enter into his night of anguished prayer and courageous praise. And we see here something of the pilgrimage of every disciple: never without trouble in this world, and sometimes in acute distress, yet always reaching for the dawn through songs of praise. Following the psalmist, we shall call up the music in our soul even before the night is ended – call up the glory of the faith within us. We shall call up the harps and lyres of hope, and summon the dawn of Christ's kingdom.

O Jesus, full of grace and truth, you have been gracious to me in giving me life and in touching my soul with the glory of faith and hope.
Be gracious to your little ones that are in the midst of foes afire with greed and cruelty. In your pity, shelter them under your wings until the storm of ruin is passed.
May my heart ever be ready with the melody of thanksgiving and praise. May I be ready for the morning when your glory will be over all the earth.

Awake, my glory of faith. Awake, my harp of hope, that I may awaken the
   dawn of the kingdom.
Be exalted, O God, above the heavens. Your name be hallowed, your will be
   done.

Psalm 58

Strong words, strong prayers

The nation's leader was popular with some, less so with others. But all
could agree that when he made a speech, he was a wizard with words. The
sentences were short, rhythmic and clear, the words well chosen. And now
and then he used a telling image, or a witty phrase that brought laughter.
Yes, eloquent speeches for such a busy man!

But then the same was true of his successor. In fact it was uncanny how
similar was his style of oratory. The explanation was near to hand. These
leaders were delivering speeches written, not by themselves, but by assis-
tants who had a talent for it. Indeed, such importance was attached to the
wording of the leader's speeches that the drafts were debated and revised
again and again. Fresh in the memory were cases when an attractive line
had turned out to be disastrous. The first moments of applause had been
succeeded by years of mockery. Some phrases had even led to riots across
the world and many deaths.

It all illustrates the power of words, which in one way or another leaders have always recognized, not least in olden times. Sometimes the ancient
peoples looked to words to have a destructive effect. With lurid incanta-
tions they sought to harm their enemies. When they made treaties, they
attached clauses that graphically spelt out the fearsome things that should
befall the one who broke the agreement. And in a few of the Psalms, the
prayers against the wicked are intensified with fearsome thoughts from
this tradition of imagery.

Psalm 58 is a case in point. It is directed against those who exercise
power with injustice and violence. Strong words are first used to address
them and characterize them in their guilt and deafness to all entreaty:

   Do you mighty ones indeed speak justly,
      do you rule earth's children fairly?

With unjust heart you act throughout the earth,
and weigh out the violence of your hands.

The wicked are estranged even from the womb;
speakers of falsehood, they have gone astray from birth.

They have venom like the venom of a snake;
they are like the deaf viper that stops its ear;

that does not heed the voice of the charmers,
for it is deaf to the skilful weaver of spells.

Are these miscreants recognizable? Are there such rulers in the world today? Are there indeed such people in various positions of power quite near to home? Weighing out, not justice, but a dominion of selfishness, all for their own class or clique, or indeed for themselves alone? Deaf to all entreaty, deaf as the horned viper, which by nature cannot hear the charmer and so is ever dangerous with its deadly poison? Do we still have in the world dominant people or classes who so ignore the needs of other creatures, that you might think they had been like that from birth?

But now the singer passes on to his sharp prayer. He has shown the evil rulers in their guiltiness, and now he calls upon God to break their power and speedily sweep them away. He knows how well entrenched these tyrannical ones are in their wealth and power, so he puts all the strength he can into the words of his prayer:

O God, break their teeth in their mouth;
the fangs of these lions, LORD, destroy.

May they dwindle as water that runs away;
may they have no strength to aim their shafts.

May they be as a snail that melts away,
or as one lost from the womb, that never saw the sun.

Before ever your pots feel the heat of the thorns,
green and blazing alike, may he whirl them away.

The 'pots' here represent the stew of evil plans which the wicked are cooking up. To boil a cauldron, people would put under it dry twigs for a quick blaze and green for a lasting heat. The prayer is that God's storm wind would whirl all the twigs away before the plans could be made ready – 'Before ever your pots feel the heat of the thorns, green and blazing alike, may he whirl them away.' With such vivid imagery, a powerful prayer is raised for God's swift and mighty action against the cruelty of those in power. And one last image is added for good measure, a gruesome one indeed. May the just and faithful people soon rejoice in victory, as the blood of the evildoers streams over the ground:

> May the just one be glad when he sees the retribution,
> and he washes his footsteps in the blood of the wicked.

A harsh image indeed, calling for an overthrow known beyond a doubt. Understandable to those who have known extremes of tyranny, but still shocking; and in some prayer books the vehement psalm has been bracketed as unsuitable for recitation or singing.

Bracketed or not, we must ponder whether there is some fruit to be had from the psalm. One thing that stands out from it is the divine hatred of the abuse of power. The psalmist's anger connects with the anger of Jesus, who thought that some oppressors would be lucky if they were only thrown into the sea with a great millstone hung on their necks – another vivid image of retribution! Another thing the psalm signals is that we should always reckon with the power of prayer. It calls us to pray with strength and passionate sincerity, in faith that the just and almighty God will draw our prayer into his work to destroy evil.

On the negative side, no doubt we should qualify that thought of rejoicing and bloodshed. The faithful will be glad at God's overthrow of evil, but should not exult in the destruction of any of God's creatures. Here we are guided by other scriptures and the example of our Lord Jesus. Our heartfelt prayer will be for the tyrant's death to sin – and new birth into the way of the kingdom.

The psalm's final verse reflects a yearning for the time of God's reign:

> . . . so that people will say, 'There is a fruit for one that is faithful;
> there is indeed a God who governs on the earth.'

It is often the case still today that the Church's message of the goodness of God fits ill with what people experience in their lives – disasters and suffering that extinguish hope. Clearly this bitterness was well known in the time of the psalm. Some were thinking, as people still do, that there was no good fruit for well-doing, no God to rule earth justly. So the psalm's prayer is for the reign of God to appear, for his name to blaze forth in holy power, for his will to be done on earth as in heaven – for the time when people will say, 'Yes, there is a harvest for faithfulness, there is a God who governs on the earth.'

So this is Psalm 58. We have found it harsh, but not without its usefulness. Certainly it has lines to be qualified. But it makes its contribution as
it declares the hatefulness of cruelty and callousness, and then leads in a
passion of prayer for the coming of God's just kingdom.

Do you wealthy ones deal justly? Do you weigh out earth's good things fairly?
Do you weigh out violence? Do you poison the earth? Do you close your
ears to every warning?
O God, break the fangs of the monsters of greed. May the flames of cruelty be
swept away by the tempest of the Holy Spirit.
May your creatures soon rejoice as the cruel and callous ones fall from power.
May we know the certainty of your victory and see the rising of your light
of justice over all the world.
Lord Jesus, help us always to pray and not to faint. May we know that your
strong voice ever joins with those who cry to the Father day and night.

Psalm 59
Songs to banish fears

There are people who claim that their dog can smile. One fine animal was
even reputed to laugh. But if there were any dispute on the point, it would
be no use citing the scripture, 'They go to and fro in the evening; they grin
like a dog and run about through the city.' It would be no use, because this
is from the old Prayer Book version of Psalm 59, where the word 'grin' had
a different meaning. It meant 'to growl' or 'howl'. So, far from being a comparison with happy dogs, the psalm's image, twice repeated, has a sinister
meaning. The dogs are wild dogs or jackals. The pack is scavenging round
the outskirts of a town at night. They are hungry and dangerous, and their
barking and howling carries into the town like cries of demons.

The psalm appears to be the king's prayer when enemy forces threaten
his city. He comes before the Lord and cries:

> Rescue me from my enemies, O God;
> set me on high above those that rise against me.
>
> Save me from the evildoers,
> and from murderous foes deliver me.

> For see, they lie in wait for my soul;
> the fierce ones band together against me.

It seems that, as darkness falls, the enemy approach the walls and shout chilling curses and disturbing propaganda:

> They gather at nightfall and growl like dogs,
> and circle about the city.

> They pour evil words from their mouths,
> and swords are in their lips.

So appeal is made to the Lord to rise up against the arrogance of the foe. May he vindicate the trust of his servant:

> But you, LORD, will laugh at them;
> you will deride the boasts of all the nations.

> O my Strength, I will watch for you,
> for you, O God, are my strong tower.

> My God will hasten to me in his faithful love;
> God will show me the downfall of my foes.

As the urgent prayer draws to its close, it depicts again the sinister threats in the night, the howls of the human jackals. The enemy's tactic was obviously very frightening. But then there arises a sound to counter it – distant still, but already mighty in effect. It is a song of trust, beginning to break with the morning into a song of thankful praise. This is the psalm's ending, with the evil sounds soon to be overcome:

> And still they gather at nightfall and growl like dogs,
> and circle about the city.

> Though they roam for something to devour,
> and howl if they are not filled,

> yet I will sing of your strength,
> and every morning praise your faithful love,

> since you have been my stronghold,
> my refuge in the day of my trouble.

> O my Strength, I will make melody to you;
> for you, O God, are my refuge, my God of faithful love.

It was in a particular time of danger that this worshipper chanted his prayer. But it is a prayer which is always timely. Always there are individuals experiencing a time of fears, of things deeply disturbing. The Church too, the city of God, endures times of fading light and circling foes, harsh and wounding voices. As we pray with the psalm, we bring our fears to the Lord. We describe them. But we also tell him of our reliance on him, our stronghold, our strength, our refuge, our God of faithful love. And the sound of the great counter-melody will grow and we ourselves begin to join in, as the hosts of God without number appear on the hills with the break of morning, and the song of praise rises over all the world.

Rescue me from my enemies, O God. From all that would hurt my soul, set me on high.

In the time of darkness, when fears raise their din, help me to call on your strength and find refuge in you.

O my Strength, I will make melody to you. For you are my strong tower, my God of faithful love.

Psalm 60

First hopes return

A faded newspaper cutting brought to life a scene from the crisis over the ownership of the Suez Canal during the summer of 1956. A photograph showed the American carrier *Intrepid* passing down the waterway. Along the bank Egyptian nurses from the Suez Canal hospital shouted angrily and waved their sandals. The newspaper explained that the sandal-waving was an old custom and the accompanying shouts meant, 'It's not mud on my shoe', or, 'Whatever you do, I couldn't care less.' Such gestures with a sandal are probably of very ancient origin, and in the Bible, too, they are connected with the ownership of land. In a colourful passage in Psalm 60 God declares that he will cast his sandal over the land of Edom, meaning he will be known as its master and owner.

In the previous line, even more quaintly, God has declared that the adjacent land of Moab will be his wash-pot; that is, Moab will be humbled and made to serve him. This image of the humble wash-bowl may have been suggested by the view looking east from the hills of Judah. The misty line of the mountains of Moab forms a rim behind the great bowl of vivid blue water that is the Dead Sea. But we may be perplexed at these picturesque sayings. God's sandals, his wash-pot, his helmet too – what does it all add up to?

Well, the psalm has begun as an agonized prayer. If we have ever experienced an earthquake in our lives – not a literal one, but a sense that our personal world has collapsed – if we have ever known such a shock, we will understand the dismay of these worshippers. The people gather before God and cry out:

> O God, you have spurned us and thrown us down;
> you were angry – O restore us anew.

> You made the earth shudder and rent it apart;
> heal its wounds, for it is shaking.

> You have filled your people with a bitter drink;
> you have given us a wine that makes us stagger.

They had thought of themselves fighting with God as their ally, even their leader. But now they were defeated. It seemed God had turned against them:

> You have made those who fear you flee,
> to escape from the reach of the bow.

> That your beloved may be delivered,
> save by your right hand and answer us.

After this call, 'Answer us', silence was perhaps kept for a while. Then the singer is inspired to report an answer, a speech of God. This may be something traditional, a poem handed down from happier times; a song of God the Warrior as he established his rule over the Holy Land, with its regions of Shechem, Sukkoth, Gilead and so on. The song is sounding anew as God's answer to his people's prayer, thus:

> God has spoken in his holiness:
> > In triumph I will portion out Shechem,
> and share out the valley of Sukkoth.

> Mine shall be Gilead and mine Manasseh;
> Ephraim shall be my helmet, and Judah my sceptre.

> But Moab shall be my wash-bowl,
> > over Edom I will throw my sandal;
> acclaim me, O land of the Philistines.

But what can the defeated people make now of this song of victory? Can they accept it as renewed promise that, in spite of their present suffering, God's purpose is unchanged? In fact their response is just to plead afresh for help, though the prayer does end on a note of confidence. The leading singer asks, 'Who can bring me to the fortress city?' – how can they scale the heights to the almost impregnable city they must conquer? How can they face such a task without God's favour?

> Have you not spurned us, O God,
> and will you no longer go out with our hosts?
>
> O grant us help against the enemy,
> for earthly help is in vain.
>
> Through God we can do mighty things;
> it is he that shall tread down our foes.

With this the psalm ends. It has revealed quite a dramatic moment – a crisis of faith. Against the people's utter dismay is set an ancient promise of God. It may sound unrealistic to them now, but they are to know that it still stands, and in God's time will be fulfilled.

There is a parable here for us. When we find the ground rent open beneath us, our world collapsed, an answer to *our* cry may also come in an old song of God, the song that is his gospel. If we listen afresh to the glowing, colourful words that we took to our hearts when we first believed, we will not think them an easy answer to the present disaster. Doubts remain, our pleading with God continues. But hold on to those old words, those great words of Christ's promises, and the sense of his sure help will grow. We shall believe again that the rough and broken territory we must traverse will be conquered and owned by him. His beloved will indeed be led up the cliffs to claim his city of peace.

O God, have you spurned us and thrown us down? The earth beneath us is torn apart. Heal its wounds, for it is shaking still.
Will you not go out with us in our battles, Lord? For earthly help is in vain.
Grant we may hear again and believe your promises from of old. In the place of our suffering may your strong presence be known, your good reign established.
Through you we can do mighty things. It is you who will tread down all adversity.

Psalm 61
At the end of your tether

A church near the town centre made great use of snappy posters to call the passing multitudes to reflection. One of these posters advised: 'When you are at the end of your tether, remember that God is at the other end.' Many were too preoccupied to notice the large board. Few who did see it gave it thought. But perhaps one or two who really were at the end of their tether took it in and were helped. Admittedly, the image of the tether had its limitations, but for a few it might have brought the realization that they were not totally alone, not totally lost – in fact, quite the reverse.

The psalms have a good stock of images for distress, but not that of being at the end of one's tether. But they have one that is even more graphic – the experience of being 'at the end of the earth'. The anguish of this state is clear from Psalm 61, which begins:

> Hear my crying, O God,
>   and listen to my prayer.
>
> From the end of the earth I call to you with fainting heart;
>   lead me up the rock that is too high for me.

In those days the earth was thought of as flat. If you felt you were at its end, its edge, it was like being on the brink of falling from the land of light and life into an underworld of darkness and death. When you prayed to God, as the psalm has it, 'from the end of the earth', you were crying to him when you were at the brink of disaster, your life in utter peril. You despair of earthly remedy. Your only hope is God. So 'with fainting heart' you call to him, 'Lead me up the rock that is too high for me.'

But what is this 'rock'? The picture is of a great rock that withstands the deadly tides. It is a place of safety with God, high above the angry waves. It is a picture of the presence of God, the home to which he draws us up in rescue and shelter and reassurance of his faithful love. As the psalm puts it:

> You shall be a shelter for me,
>   a strong tower against the foe.

> May I dwell in your tent for ever,
> and shelter in the covering of your wings.

The ancient worshippers often supported their prayer with a promise. In this psalm the king supports his plea with a promise to make music to the praise of God every day of his life. Support for his cry also comes from the prayer of his people. As he says:

> You, O God, will hear my vows;
> you will grant the request of those who fear your name.

This 'request' of the people seems to be echoed in the next verses, asking that the king's life may ever continue in God's presence:

> You will add days to the days of the king,
> that his years may continue through all generations.

> May he dwell before God for ever;
> bid faithful love and truth to guard him.

These are beautiful thoughts for the destiny of a king – ever to dwell with God, guarded by the angel-forms of God's love as promised to David. And the people could long for their king to have this blessing all the more, because in a mysterious way they had a share in his life. His life with God, they felt, would somehow embrace them all.

Such intuitions in the psalm have their fulfilment in the true king, Christ. He was 'at the end of the earth' in his suffering for us and cried to the Father 'with fainting heart'. Our sufferings are taken into his. When we are at the extremity of our strength, he is with us. As we hold to him, we are led up with him on the rock that is too high for us alone. With Christ we shall come to that shelter and strong tower, to the holy tent and the covering of the divine wings. With Christ we shall dwell there for ever, guarded by the angels of his faithful love and truth.

So the psalm comforts us greatly when our heart faints. Not here is the picture of God at the other end of a tether. But it has images of hope for us when we are 'at the end of the earth' – near to disaster or death, exhausted, beyond purely human help. In such an extremity the psalm will cry out for us, voicing the intercession of Christ and the eternal Spirit: 'O lead the way up on the rock. Grant the covering of your wings, the ministry of your angels of love.'

So, in deepest mystery, we are drawn into the life of our king, Jesus Christ. With him we pass through suffering, up to the life and peace of his eternal grace.

Hear my crying, O God. From the end of the earth I call to you with fainting heart.
Lead me up the rock of your salvation. With your Son Jesus may I dwell in the shelter of your wings. Guard me with your angels of faithful love and grace.
I will ever make music to your name and witness to your goodness day by day.

Psalm 62
The prayer of stillness

At 86, Roger was as dedicated as ever to his plants and soil. Fingers deformed by gout could not deter him. If he enjoyed anything nearly as much as his cultivating, it was long and leisurely conversation. He had many interesting stories to tell, and his friend, a little younger, had heard some of them many times. This friend would use the opportunity of an oft-repeated story to rest his mind, or perhaps to check on some detail he had not previously taken in. His approach was positive, for he himself often repeated his own recollections to his family circle – but consciously, in the hope that they would be well remembered. If he had used the language of the Bible when Roger was in full flight, he might have said to himself, 'Once has he spoken it; twice have I heard the same' – meaning, 'He has said this often.'

This turn of phrase actually occurs in Psalm 62, but here the one repeating himself often is God – 'Once has God spoken it, twice have I heard the same.' So what was the message that God had said often, wanting it to be taken to heart? The psalm gives it plainly:

Once has God spoken it,
twice have I heard the same,

that power belongs to God,
and yours, Lord, is faithful love.

Though this message sounds rather general, it had an urgent relevance in the crisis lying behind the psalm. Some weakness in the king's position has encouraged his enemies to press upon him, like attackers that see the city wall giving way under the battering rams. We hear him say to them:

How long will you assault a person, all of you intent to destroy,
as you would a leaning wall or a damaged fence?

They have taken counsel only how to thrust me from my height,
  and have delighted in falsehood;
they blessed with their mouth,
  but in their heart they cursed.

It is noticeable that nowhere in the psalm does the afflicted king actually pray or ask for anything. Rather, in humility and trust, he gathers himself to be still before the Lord. Such stillness will open the way for the action of God, which alone is decisive. So we hear these beautiful verses which are so helpful when we too need to still ourselves:

For God alone my soul waits in stillness;
from him comes my salvation.

He only is my rock and my salvation,
my stronghold, so that I shall not be utterly shaken . . .

To God alone be still, my soul;
from him comes all my hope.

He alone is my rock and my salvation,
my stronghold so that I shall not be shaken.

In God is my salvation and my glory;
my mighty rock and my refuge is God.

The task of great leaders is all the harder because they have to control not only their own fears, but also those of their people. It is the same for any person with responsibility for a family or a group. In the psalm the king well knows his people's fears. He urges them to trust. He advises them to 'pour out' before God all their anxieties. They must not be mesmerized by human pretensions and boasts. He says:

Trust in him always, O people;
pour out your heart before him, for God is our refuge.

The children of earth are but a breath, the peoples a delusion;
on the scales they all are lighter than air.

Do not trust in oppression or be deluded by plunder;
if power abounds, give it no regard.

And so to the psalm's conclusion, where the counsel of stillness and trust is undergirded by that message which God himself has spoken, once, twice, many times. It is a message we too have received so often in scripture and worship, a message we too must relate to every crisis in our life. God himself has spoken it and we must take it to heart, namely: God is just, and he is both the infinite power and the infinite love.

Whether we are public leaders or responsible only in a private circle, we will know something of the tumult that occasioned this psalm – people angry, people fearful; some aggressive and boastful, some looking for shelter, panicking, wavering. The psalm would have us pour out our fears and doubts before the Lord, and so grow into that stillness which may be the best prayer. In his mighty and loving presence, our soul becomes a still centre, full of trust; a centre from which God can bring comfort to all our circle and make the way for his deeds of salvation.

To God alone be still, my soul. From him comes all my hope.
For you alone my soul waits in stillness. From you comes my salvation.
Lord, help us to trust in you always. Let us pour out all our fears and cares
*   before you. May we find in you our rock and refuge.*
Let us not be impressed by human power and wealth. Repeat in our hearts
*   that true power belongs to you alone, and yours too is the love that never*
*   gives up.*

Psalm 63
Contemplation and action

The cottage stood at the end of a narrow lane, which then lost itself amid undulating fields. Behind the cottage the garden soon fell sharply away into a gully. The far bank rose steeply to pastures and woods. High against the sky, great oaks and beeches on the edge of the pastures looked down benignly on the garden. A brook meandered through the gully, and there were little bridges to help you follow a grass path. There were also stone steps up the banks, and the side rising towards the cottage was a mass of flowering shrubs and roses.

It was a garden conducive to contemplation, and indeed once a month it was open to any who wished to spend a few hours there in quiet meditation. In nooks and corners seats were placed for their use. A comfortable garden room, almost a cottage in itself, was also open for them, with books, kettle, coffee and cups. It was indeed a welcoming place, so quiet that you might hear nothing but the hum of insects or the call of a raven. The sheep in the pasture soothed the spirit. All was favourable for contemplation.

But no doubt, just before the open days, there would be hard work to be done to make it just right. Did the mower sometimes break down? Did the pruning of so many shrubs on the banks ever cause a back strain? Did branches from the high trees ever crash down in a storm? Was there a sick relative hundreds of miles away who suddenly needed help? Was there stress from a professional career?

Yes, in all probability the contemplative paradise would have to exist alongside toils and troubles. And often those who came to enjoy its peace had struggled to be free of care for a few hours. Sometimes it might almost seem that if the quiet garden no longer existed, that would be one less thing to worry about. But faith opposed such a thought – faith that the place of meditation and communion was a place of replenishment, a place to find guidance and grace precisely to cope with every strain and burden.

Sometimes in the psalms it emerges that the one who is there singing of a beautiful communion with God, a delightful contemplation, is a person burdened with dreadful anxieties. This is the case in Psalm 63. It seems here that the devout king has come to the Lord's sanctuary on the eve of battle. Death may be near, but his hope is that it will be the enemies of his people who fall on the battlefield, that it will be their bodies that remain on the field for the wild animals.

It is a grim glimpse of the realities of warfare, and also of the dangerous, troubled life of the Israelite kings. Apart from the ruthless enemies, the task of judging and caring for the people was an incessant burden.

The scribes who preserved the psalms have added a note in the heading of this psalm suggesting that the occasion was when David was in the wilderness of Judah. Such notes are probably deductions from words in the psalm. In the present case we should rather think of a king in a wilderness of the spirit. His thirst is not for water, but for God and his help. The dry and weary land is not the geographical wilderness, but the conditions of daily life that yield no good fruit, no rest, refreshment or joy. So the opening of his psalm can speak for us too when harsh circumstances envelop us:

O God, you are my God; eagerly I seek you;
my soul is thirsting for you.

My flesh longs for you,
as a barren and weary land that has no water.

From that wilderness of enemies and dangers, failure and pain – from that wilderness of the spirit, the psalmist has come aside to seek refreshment in a place near to God. It is a sanctuary where he will rest and pray, seeking to know God's life-giving touch and to see his light, as he eloquently says:

Therefore I seek vision of you in the sanctuary,
to see your power and your glory.

Your faithful love is better than life itself,
and my lips shall sing your praise.

So shall I bless you all my life,
and lift up my hands to your name.

My soul shall be satisfied as with the choicest fare,
and my mouth shall praise you with joyful lips,

when I remember you upon my couch,
and meditate on you in the watches of the night.

For you shall come as my strong help,
and in the shadow of your wings I will rejoice.

My soul shall cleave to you;
your right hand shall hold me fast.

The king's hope here is that in this place of close contact with God he will be enriched in spirit and made ready for the struggles that lie ahead. That wilderness will now blossom, fruit will be borne in God's cause, God's people will soon have cause to rejoice.

The psalm prompts us also, in our troubles, to come aside for a while to a special closeness with God. The expressions for communion with him are indeed strong and might seem beyond us; but through Jesus we too can be drawn into that divine embrace, we too may have vision of God's beauty and power, and the hunger and thirst of our souls may be deeply satisfied. So we shall return to the dry, harsh places with new strength and hope. We shall begin to see the victories of God.

It is surely one of the deepest sayings in the Bible when our psalmist says, 'Your faithful love is better than life itself.' Yet it seems to strain logic.

For how can that love be better than life, when without life it could not be enjoyed? Perhaps there is a strain in logic here, as the psalm strives for the utmost praise of God's wonderful love. But hidden in the great saying is the intuition of a life beyond life, a higher life with God which death cannot destroy, a life where all the pledges of his love are fulfilled.

What if we could enter and rest in the place of contemplation, and be so near to him that we knew for ourselves that his faithful love is better than life itself? Then indeed we should have risen above all dangers and distresses, and in all these things would be more than conquerors.

O God, in all the barren places and times of conflict let me find your sanctu-
ary. Replenish my exhausted soul. In your presence let me drink again the
water of life and see the light of hope.
Grant me to know your faithful love as better than life itself.
So shall I bless you all my days and lift up my hands to your name.

Psalm 64

The protecting prayer

---◆---

The village inn was centuries old. It was usually a good place for lunch, having a quiet dining room. A log fire burned in winter, and from the window you looked across the road to a neat row of cottages. On one occasion, however, the character of the room was somewhat changed by an unusual group of guests. Smartly dressed, they were seated around a table in the centre of the room, some seven or eight of them. They were well provided with briefcases, files, clipboards and mobile phones. The table also bore a large supply of coffee jugs and cups. It seemed they had been sitting there since mid-morning coffee time and had convened to discuss company business. They did not stay long after the first clients for lunch had arrived, but long enough to cause a slight unease. Their talk of sales strategy was innocent enough, but their marketing language conjured up a style verging on deceit. It was a world where words are subtly manipulated and truth obscured. No crime is committed as a rule, but a degree of deceit becomes natural, and some are certainly ruined by it.

More definitely sinister was a gathering in the room of a newspaper editor. There was no log fire, and no pretty cottages could be seen from the window. There were many steel cabinets, all of a melancholy grey. The editor was looking for ideas from his team to further his policy of damaging the government. The time seemed ripe for destroying the good name of the government's leader. Whatever ideas might be proposed – accusations of incompetence, assassination of character, malicious tales about his family – they would be projected with screaming headlines, distorted matter, spurious disclosures and unfair photography, all unremitting. And the best of it was, in the editor's eyes, that it would all be good for sales.

Across the breadth of the earth there were doubtless other gatherings being held for plotting of more deadly degree, for sudden attacks on the innocent, led by the sword of an evil tongue or the arrows of harmful words. The victims of such carefully planned attacks might well pray with these words of Psalm 64:

> Hear my voice, O God, in my prayer;
> preserve my life from dread of the enemy.

> Hide me from the plots of the cruel,
> from the gatherings of evildoers,

> who have sharpened their tongue like a sword,
> and aimed their bitter words as arrows . . .

> They search out wickedness and lay a cunning trap,
> for deep are the inward thoughts of the heart.

The psalm seems to be the prayer of the national leader, the king, as he faces the early stages of war against him. The enemies are conferring to plot his destruction. They mean to damage him first through the evil of their tongues, to wound him with poisoned words, all planned with stealth and cunning. They have no regard for the Judge in heaven. They act as though no higher power can see them and call them to account.

Anyone who is the victim of such hostility might well have a sinking heart, might well be destroyed by fear alone. But the psalmist shows a better way. Already being answered is his prayer that his life be preserved 'from *dread* of the enemy'. Fundamental is the constancy of his prayer. He has begun, 'Hear my voice, O God, in my prayer', and here the particular word used for 'prayer' (*siah*) indicates a stream of murmured or chanted sound. We imagine that his pleading psalm was kept sounding, a melody of hope set against the rumble of evil threats. Indeed, the prayer does not end without expressing the conviction that God does see and hear, and will act to protect those who shelter in him. His shafts will suddenly strike those who have aimed arrows of mischief at the innocent. Thus the psalm puts it:

> God will shoot at them with an arrow,
>   and suddenly they shall be wounded . . .
>
> And all people will fear and tell of the work of God,
>   and they will ponder what he has done.

The concluding verse foresees joy both for 'the faithful one' and also for 'all that are true of heart':

> The faithful one will rejoice in the LORD and shelter in him,
>   and all that are true of heart shall glory.

This is a picture first of the king and then of his people, rejoicing in God's goodness. It brings to mind the Christian hope of a time of justice and redemption, when Christ our King, the faithful one, will rejoice with all who are true of heart in holding to him. The recital of this little psalm can thus be for us an echo, a reverberation, of the ever-flowing prayer of Christ. He who for us endured the evil scheming and the poisoned arrows of the wicked defends us with the stream of his intercession. The dangers from the plots and tongues of the unscrupulous are indeed great, but, thanks be to God, we have a protector. The Lord Jesus will shelter us and bring us at last to his eternal joy and glory.

The ever-flowing prayer of Jesus protect me. Shelter me from the arrows of evil words. Hide me from the cunning traps of those who care nothing for your judgement. Preserve my life from dread of the enemy.
Your work of judgement is near, O God. In that time of fear and glory, may we shelter in your grace, and through your Son Jesus find rest in your compassion.

Psalm 65
The deep silence

————◆————

Amid fields clothed with sheep and lambs lay the small twelfth-century church of St Michael and All Angels. Wooded hills rose to the west, while to the east the track descended gently towards two lakes beloved of birds.

Since the farming community had dwindled, the congregation at St Michael's was less than of old, but still very loyal. Several elderly women, being hard of hearing, regularly occupied the front pews. It was probably due to them that conversation in church before the service was rather noisy. Some of them lived on their own and there was naturally a desire to make kindly enquiries and impart news, all necessarily in raised tones.

One Sunday evening, just before the worship was due to begin, the vicar, still in his black cassock, came to the front as though to make an announcement. The noise of conversation abated, and the vicar persuasively proposed that there should now be some minutes of quiet before the service began. It seemed an excellent suggestion, and the vicar, gratified, was returning to the back to prepare for his formal entrance. But almost at once, one of the women, anxious not to miss anything of importance, enquired of her neighbour in loud tones, 'What did he say?' To which came the equally forthright reply, 'I don't know. I didn't hear a word of it. I expect it was about next Saturday's organ recital. I never cared for organs myself.' And so it continued until the choir, followed by the vicar in his white surplice, swept up the aisle, signalling clearly to all that the solemn proceedings were commenced. A hush duly fell on all the congregation.

In ancient Jerusalem, though the throngs gathering for worship might be great, there were moments when all was hushed. The crowds might hear a prophet call out, as Zephaniah did, 'Be silent before the LORD God', or as Habakkuk did, 'The LORD is in his holy temple. Let all the earth keep silence before him.'

These were moments of silent awe, when the presence of God was especially felt. Sometimes this was at the moment of the offering, and this seems to be the case in Psalm 65. The psalm comes from a great assembly for the autumn festival. The nation's sins have been confessed and purged. Offerings promised in a time of trouble are now presented. There is silence, as even the music of praise dies away. After a while, a singer plucks his lyre and begins to express wonder and gratitude that God has called the worshippers and brought them so near. Thus he sings:

> Praise is hushed for you, O God, in Zion,
> and for you the vow is fulfilled, you that answer prayer.

> To you come all the children of earth, confessing wrongs;
> though our sins prevailed against us, you have purged them away.

> Happy the one you choose and bring near to dwell in your courts!
> We shall be satisfied with the goodness of your house,
> your most holy temple.

164

But let us leave that ancient gathering for a moment and visit again the church of St Michael and All Angels. Here too it is autumn, and a full congregation has gathered for a colourful celebration, the Harvest Festival. Window sills and pillars are adorned with the gold and purple of autumn flowers. The sanctuary is bedecked with fruit, vegetables, corn and loaves. The theme of this worship is thankfulness for what has been given, and also the duty of sharing earth's riches fairly across the nations. Lines from Psalm 65 are used in the anthem ruggedly rendered by the choir, and the sense conveyed is that God has crowned and blessed the year. The valleys stood so thick with corn that they seemed to laugh and sing.

Our psalm, however, originally had a different thrust. Most likely it was a prayer for the *next* agricultural round. After some six months of Palestine's regular summer drought, rains were expected. Indeed, without good winter rains the work could not start and then flourish. There would be famine and ruination, as sometimes happened. So that ancient festival in the autumn had supreme importance. God was there praised as master of the waters, giving life through the rains. The society repented of its sins and turned to God afresh in earnest prayer.

And so we find that this beautiful Psalm 65 soon passes to its main prayer. It addresses God as the one who established the living order and made the raging waters serve his purpose of life. The sacred minstrel feels the immensity and mystery of it all as he sings:

> With dread deeds in goodness you will answer us,
>> O God of our salvation,
> O hope of all the ends of the earth
>> and the sea where the Far Ones dwell,
>
> you that set fast the mountains by your might,
>> having girded on your strength,
>
> you that stilled the raging of the seas,
>> the roar of their waves and the tumult of the peoples.
>
> Those who dwell at the farthest bounds trembled at your wonders;
>> the gates of morning and evening sang your praise.

And so to the vital plea for rain, which will mean the 'crowning', the inauguration, of a bounteous year:

> O tend the earth and water her and greatly enrich her;
>> with the heavenly stream, full of water, you will prepare her corn –
>> yes, so you will prepare her.

165

Soak well her furrows and settle her ridges;
soften her with showers and bless her springing.

O crown a year of your bounty,
and let your tracks flow down with goodness.

May the pastures of the wilderness flow with your goodness,
and the hills be girded with joy.

May the fields be clothed with flocks,
and the valleys stand so thick with corn,
    that they shall laugh and sing.

So ends this song of prayer for rain – yet how much more it is than a plea for plenty! It sings of the earth with sympathy and tenderness, and sees her within a cosmic circle of worship. Her harvest garments of green and gold are garments of praise, as all that lives in her joins the song of joy in God. Beyond the earth are immense spaces and the gates of morning and evening for the sun to enter and depart. Even here the song of praise arises. Beyond earth's bounds also are mysterious waters and unimaginable beings, and even these Far Ones are turned to their Creator in hope.

And as for us, so small, so self-absorbed, how can we today find the spirit to care for the earth and pray for her in the vast cosmos? And how can our actions, with our prayers, be in harmony with the cosmic song?

If we let the psalm guide us, we will gather before the Lord, the Creator. We will confess to him the wrongs we have done and receive his forgiveness and purification. Before him still, we will offer the praise of thanksgiving, but also the praise that is silence. All our worship, especially the stillness, will be realization of his presence, his greatness, his love. Here we find true happiness – that God has called us and brought us into his presence to satisfy us with his goodness. Near to him, we are in tune with the world as God means it to be. So we rejoice in the Hope of all the ends of the earth and of the sea where the Far Ones dwell. We can join in the melody of the gates of morning and evening. We love and care for earth and all her living things – because God has brought us into his house and cleansed us and satisfied us with his goodness.

You that answer prayer, words fail to thank you.
You that bring us near, words fail to thank you.
You that purge away our sins, words fail for your goodness.
Let our silence before you be deep, and filled with knowing you.

O *merciful Creator, tend earth and soften her with showers and bless her*
  springing.
May *her fields be clothed with flocks and her valleys stand so thick with corn*
  that shall laugh and sing.
Let *not the ruthless destroy her, but let the deserts we have made flow again*
  with your goodness.

Psalm 66
The great welcome

About the middle of the twentieth century, a young Englishman began a
three-year residence in Arab Jerusalem. He was thrilled to be working for
the romantic-sounding 'Jerusalem and the East Mission'. He at once began
to try acquiring useful Arabic phrases. He had a pocket phrase-book-cum-
dictionary from 1909. This would have been excellent if he could have
more easily read its small print. How useful it would have been to roll off
the given phrases for 'This is not the horse which they showed me yesterday', or, 'Take the big trunk off the mule', or again, 'Take from the trunk the
nightshirt and slippers.' Alas, his progress was not that quick. But with one
phrase he was soon at home, for it greeted him wherever he went: *Ahlan
wa-sahlan.* This was said to mean 'Welcome!' – but more fully, 'You come
as though to your own folk and a pleasant, well-watered plain.'

So *Ahlan wa-sahlan,* the Arabic welcome, is an echo of the life of the
Bedouin, nomads who ranged over harsh desert and mountains, ever in
danger of savage attackers, fierce heat and dust, and many days without
fresh water. What a relief then to come in from 'the Empty Quarter', the
great desert, to arrive at a settlement of friendly people and recuperate in
a plain where you found springs, grass and trees! And that is the happy
welcome still evoked in the words continually in use in the Arab lands –
Ahlan wa-sahlan!

Now, there is a psalm that praises God for a divine welcome, Psalm 66.
It voices the feelings of worshippers who have been through many dangers
and hardships, but have now come to a friendly place, a well-watered plain,
a place of space and delight, a garden of life for the rescued soul. Thus it
sings:

167

> Bless our God, you peoples,
> and make the voice of his praise to be heard,
>
> who has set our soul again among the living,
> and kept our feet from stumbling . . .
>
> You [O God] brought us into the net,
> and bound us about with trouble.
>
> You let men ride over our heads,
> we went though fire and water;
> but you brought us out to a well-watered plain.

The Church has used this psalm on Easter day, relating it to Christ's resurrection. This is an ancient custom, for in some Greek and Latin manuscripts the psalm is actually headed 'Of the Resurrection'. The Old Testament people, however, sang the psalm with thoughts of the already ancient Exodus and also of some recent deliverance they had known. In the Exodus the ancestors had been led through waters and wilderness towards ease in the fertile land of promise, so the psalm calls out:

> Come and see the deeds of God,
> who in his work is terrible above the children of earth.
>
> He turned the sea into dry land,
> they crossed through the river on foot;
> come, let us rejoice in him.

And now in a recent deliverance it seemed that his ancient work of salvation was made new for them. Once more God had set their soul among the living; through fire and water he had brought them to a pleasant, fertile land. Each worshipper could echo the words of the leading singer:

> Come and hear, all you that fear God,
> and I will tell you what he has done for my soul.
>
> I cried out to him with my mouth,
> yet praise was ready under my tongue . . .
>
> Blessed be God, who has not turned aside my prayer,
> nor his faithful love from me.

As we worship today, we likewise praise God for an ancient and fundamental salvation as well as for deliverance we have known ourselves. We see our ancient salvation as the resurrection of Jesus – the act of God underlying all our existence, when our great representative was brought through the waters and wastelands of death. And springing from this we see our own present deliverance – not only our hope for when we leave this earthly life, but even now, the risen life he already gives us. On Easter day we know afresh that Christ has greeted us with his great welcome, a heavenly *Ahlan wa-sahlan*. Come in, he has said, from fears of savage enemies, come in from hunger and thirst and leanness of soul; come in from the Empty Quarter, from the empty life. Welcome as to your own family and to a well-watered plain; welcome to the fellowship of the Spirit and life by the fountains and streams of forgiveness and love! Well may we sing with the psalm, 'Bless our God who has set our soul among the living . . . I will come into your house with whole offerings . . . Come and hear, all you that fear God . . . Sing aloud to God, all the earth, sing praise to the glory of his name.'

Thus through the poetry of the psalm we acknowledge that the resurrection of Christ has become our resurrection also. A good refrain, therefore, to sing at the start and conclusion of the psalm would be: *Because Christ lives, I live also. Alleluia.*

Sing aloud to God, all the earth; sing praise to the glory of his name.
Come and see the deeds of God, who brought his people through the waters to
    freedom; and he raised again his Son Jesus, and set our soul again among
    the living.
You tried us as silver is tried. We went through fire and water, but you brought
    us to your land of springs and trees, the place of forgiveness and abundant
    life.
Blessed be God, who saw my need and heard my prayer, and saved me in his
    faithful love. Alleluia.

Psalm 67
What a mercy, what a blessing!

The days when information on radio and television was presented in restrained, impersonal tones are becoming a distant memory. The entertainment factor is dominant. The shipping forecast admittedly remains sober, but the other weather forecasts have been livened up and are presented with emotion. In sympathy with those seeking pleasure out of doors, the weather men and women lay aside their scientific training. They become antagonistic to rain. 'A thoroughly miserable morning' is forecast when plentiful rain is expected. 'A risk of showers' is cautioned against as if the clouds might spill poison. 'You might be lucky' if they pass you by. But 'beautiful', even 'glorious', are the evaluations bestowed on expected days of burning sun, and the enthusiasm is hardly dimmed by a passing reference to high pollen counts and air pollution.

This style imposed on the forecasters, shallow as it is, might be understandable. But how they would change their tune if water ceased to come from their elegant taps, if there were no water to wash in, make tea or cook with, if plants and trees died, and animals and people began to perish!

Yes, how precious, how vital is the rain. In some countries people rightly speak of it as the blessing par excellence. And when a psalm opens with a plea for God's mercy and blessing, for salvation and the light of his face, it should be no wonder that it is the need for rain that is chiefly in the singer's mind. Thus begins Psalm 67:

> God be merciful to us and bless us,
>   and make his face to shine for us,
>
> that your way may be known on earth,
>   your salvation among all nations.

It is soon evident that the psalm is a prayer for rain and growth, and in support of this plea the singer promises praise. Not just himself, nor his people alone, but all the peoples, he promises, will sing their thanks to the Creator who has made all right and just for the living world:

> Then the peoples will praise you, O God;
>   yes, all the peoples will praise you.
>
> The nations will rejoice and sing,
>   that you govern the peoples justly
>   and guide the nations on earth.

This is certainly a contrast to the forecasters' talk of 'thoroughly miserable' days of rain. For to the psalmist's mind, all the peoples can be counted on to dance and sing with joy in thanksgiving for God's keeping the world right with his rain and the consequent growth. In their thankfulness – so the singer promises – all creatures will turn afresh to 'fear' or worship God as their saviour. So the prayer comes to its climax:

> May earth give her increase;
>> may God, our God, grant us his blessing.
>
> May God give us his blessing,
>> that all the ends of the earth may fear him.

Society and attitudes have changed greatly since this psalm was first sung. In our time there is immense scientific knowledge to call on for the provision of food. There are also marvels of communication and travel, so that policies and processes, trade and distribution can be readily co-ordinated in conferences and agreements across the world. Yet all is not well. It seems that something vital is generally missing. Certainly there are terrible hindrances through greed, fear, false confidence, corruption, and ill will. Surely we still need to know that we live only by the light of God's face and are fulfilled only by the pouring down of his blessing. Surely we still need to know the times for penitence and for prayer to the Creator, and the times for thankfulness and fresh dedication to reverence and worship. In the spirit of this once much-used psalm, we need to see God's shining face in the rain and the sunshine, his blessing in the frosts and the clouds. We need to watch for his way on earth, his moving among us with mercy and guidance.

And in humility and recollection before the Creator we shall find that spirit of world unity that breathes through the psalm – when all peoples together appreciate the health and blessing of our dear earth, and all creatures together are happy in the fellowship of God.

O God, our Creator, grant us to remember that the necessities and the pleasure of life flow from your blessing. Help us to see your mercy in the rain, your shining face in the giving of earth's greening.

May the peoples learn again to see your way on earth and your salvation in all the living world. May we learn again to give thanks for the gift of life.

Grant, Lord, that we may live in reverence before your face. With all that lives in the bounds of the universe, may we fear you and joyfully sing your praise.

The blessing of the rain be on you, soft rain upon your spirit, to bring up the sweet flowers, great rain upon your spirit to wash it and leave pools where heaven shines. The blessing of the earth be on you and the wind blow with you. And the Lord bless you and make his face to shine upon you ever.

Psalm 68
Ascending with the Lord

The coverage of sport on television was benefiting from new techniques in the camera-work and replay systems. They could rerun the dramatic moments of a whole day of sport while you were still settling into your chair. For serial dramas also, the facility of replay was put to good effect. Settling down to the fourth episode, you could first see a swift reminder of the high points in the story so far – how the lovers first met, kissed or quarrelled; how some unfortunate fell down a cliff; how news came of a huge bequest from a forgotten relative in the Antipodes.

But in older times also, storytellers and poets were not without resource. The skilful bard could conjure up a swift succession of scenes to carry you along in his dramatic composition. A striking example is found in Psalm 68, which accompanied a great procession. In the thirty-five verses of the psalm there are almost as many scenes, as the singer bodies out the meaning of the procession, bringing its spiritual reality home to the hosts of pilgrim worshippers.

The ark of the covenant is being carried up the hill to its shrine in the heart of the temple. In the procession are musicians, singers and dancers and companies of tribesmen. But it is called 'the procession of God', for it is symbolic of his riding to the heights above all the universe, victorious Creator and King. He has revealed himself afresh as conqueror of chaos and death, able to give life and strength to his creatures. The singing poet brings this message home with a swift succession of scenes that display God's power and his care. As the priests lift up the ark to begin its journey, he sings thus:

> God arises and his enemies are scattered,
> and those who hate him flee before him.
>
> As smoke is driven, so they are driven;
> as wax melts in the fire, so perish the wicked
>   at the presence of God.
>
> But the faithful are glad and rejoice before God,
> making merry with songs and dances.

> O sing to God, make music to his name,
>> lift praise to him who rides the clouds;
> with his name Yah rejoice before him.

Then follow many swift glimpses of God's work. We see him as father to the fatherless, defender of widows, giving a home to the lonely, bringing out prisoners to songs of welcome. More episodes flash by. We glimpse him leading refugees through the wilderness and settling them; then pouring down rain to renew a weary land. Here he is, scattering destructive kings and armies, then giving the good tidings for women to spread in songs and dances of celebration. We see those still toiling back at home look up from the cooking pots to catch the gleam of the doves' wings – birds released from the battlefield to fly home in signal of God's victory. As the singer tells it:

> The Lord gives the word;
>> the women who bear the tidings are a mighty host.

> The kings of the armies flee, they flee,
>> and women at home will share the spoil.

> Though you have tarried among the hearth-stones,
>> see now the dove's wings covered with silver,
>>> and her feathers with green gold.

> As the Almighty scatters the kings,
>> it is like a snowstorm on Black Mountain.

Then the poet imagines the great mountains of the north looking with envy at the hill of Zion. The Lord has been content to make this humble hill his sanctuary, and the procession up her slopes signifies God's ascent up the heights of heaven. And what an ascent that is:

> The chariots of God are twice ten thousand,
>> and still thousands on thousands;
> the Lord is among them,
>> Sinai's Lord in holy splendour.

> You ascend on high, leading your captives;
>> you have received as tribute those who rebelled,
>>> that you may reign as LORD and God.

Amazing too the next flash of imagination, which shows the mighty one in his grace and redemption:

> Blessed be the Lord who daily bears our burdens,
> the God who alone is our salvation!
>
> God truly is to us the God of all salvation,
> and the LORD God is able to deliver even from death.

Swiftly then to a gruesome scene: God smites down his enemies and the flowing of their blood signals the certainty of his conquest. We must remember here that these enemies are symbols of evil, as it were cartoons of cruelty and corruption that the power of God alone can defeat. And next the view is that from the walls of the holy city, as they breathlessly watch the ascending column:

> They see your procession, O God.
> the advance of my God and King in holy splendour.
>
> The singers go before, the musicians follow after,
> in the midst of maidens playing timbrels.
>
> In your companies bless God, the Lord,
> on the way from Israel's fountain.

And as the ark is brought up to rest in its shrine, and all thoughts are on the presence of the Lord, the singer calls again and again for praise from the worshippers and from all the world:

> Sing to God, you kingdoms of the earth,
> make music in praise of the Lord,
>
> to him who rides the ancient heaven of heavens
> and utters his voice, a mighty voice.
>
> Give the glory to God, whose splendour is over Israel,
> and his glory in the clouds.
>
> God shines forth in dread majesty from his holy dwelling,
> the God of Israel who gives strength and increase to his people.
> Blessed be God!

All in all, a powerful psalm! The ceremony of procession has opened a world of meaning, and the poet-singer has helped the worshippers to enter that world – to walk in the light of God's kingdom. This was not everyday worship. It was the great climax of the yearly round, when excitement rose and hope and faith burned intensely. It can remind us of the importance of poetry, music and sacramental action in our own worship, not least in our annual festivals, The great words and melodies, the dedicated places and prayerful actions are God-given means to experience truth beyond what we could otherwise know. In alternations of movement and stillness, silence and poetry, the Lord's glory touches us and his word sounds for us.

Many facets of God's work has our psalmist made to pass before our inner eye. Of all these pictures, shall we not best remember that of God daily carrying our burdens – the Creator, conqueror of evil, enthroned above the heights of the universe, he comes humbly to us every day ready to carry the weight of our cares. Through all the scenes of his power we yet discern his lowliness and his love. So we know that the word he gave is the Lord Jesus, and the tidings he commanded are his gospel. This mighty one was in Jesus, ascending on high, leading his joyful captives, to reign for ever as Lord and God.

As God arises, the darkness is scattered. O sing to God, my heart, make music
  to his name Let me know him in his name Jesus and rejoice before him.
Lord, renew your earth, for it is weary. Guide your people away from ruthless
  deeds.
Blessed be the Lord who this day will carry my burden! Blessed be the Dove of
  the Spirit as she comes in her beauty to give us hope!
O Jesus, Word of God, you alone are my salvation. Deliver me from death and
  lead me on high in the joy of all your captives.

Psalm 69

Drowning yet hoping

The poet Stevie Smith has the knack of bringing before you the pathos of a character, perhaps of a whole life, in just a few lines. Her echoing of everyday speech gives the poems a touch of attractive humour and makes them memorable. But it is the poignant and haunting sadness which prevails.

Perhaps best known is her poem about the man who protested he was not waving, but drowning. People had always thought of him as a chap who liked larking about. Even at the end they would not hear what he tried to call out to them: not just then, but all his life he had been too far out, not waving, but drowning.

Far out, far from help, with no foothold, overwhelmed by floods – in such imagery is sometimes portrayed the figure of one estranged and deserted, alone and overcome by troubles. It is a figure that appears in the psalms, and especially Psalm 69. Here is one bowed beneath a weight of alienation and crying thus to God:

> Reproach has broken my heart;
> I am full of heaviness.

> I looked for some to have pity on me,
>> but there was no one,
> and for comforters,
>> but found none.
>
> (v. 20)

The prayer of this sufferer has begun with that image of drowning:

> Save me, O God,
> for the waters come in up to my soul.

> I sink in the mire of the great deep,
>> and have no foothold;
> I have come into the depths of the waters,
>> and the flood overwhelms me.

The psalm then unfolds as a long and moving prayer. It may have come into being as the plea of a greatly afflicted king in Jerusalem. Neighbouring rulers, it seems, accuse him of plundering their territory – it is their pretext for war. In some way even his service of the Lord and his zeal for the temple have been turned against him:

> For your sake I bear reproach,
> and shame has covered my face.

> I have become a stranger to my brothers,
> an alien to my mother's children.

> Zeal for your house has devoured me;
> the reviling of those who revile you has fallen on me.
>
> (vv. 7–9)

The psalmist is drowning in troubles and calls passionately for the Lord to act in pity, in the love he has promised his servant:

176

Save me from the mire before I sink for ever;
    may I be saved from my foes
      and from the depths of the waters.

May the water-flood not overwhelm me,
     nor the abyss swallow me up;
    may the pit not shut its mouth upon me.

Answer me, Lord, for your faithful love is gracious;
    in the greatness of your pity turn to me.

And do not hide your face from your servant,
    for I am in trouble – be quick to answer me.
                           (vv. 14–17)

In support of his prayer the sufferer promises that when God raises him up again, he will praise the name of God with a song, for this will please the Lord, he says, 'more that the sacrifice of an ox'. And even while still in his sufferings, he can look to great things beyond. The salvation of David's royal line will be a cause for universal joy:

Heaven and earth shall praise him,
    the seas and all that moves in them.
                    (v. 34)

The psalmist foresees that the holy city will be saved and the servants of God, loving his name, will abide there in peace.

So we see what a moving and rich prayer this psalm is. But there is another element in it, difficult for us, a passage of seven verses. In fearsome terms these ask for God to destroy the enemies:

Pour out your indignation upon them;
    let the heat of your anger overtake them . . .

Charge them with sin upon sin,
    and let them not receive your vindication.

Let them be wiped from the book of the living,
    and not be recorded with the just.
                  (see vv. 22–28)

Fierce words indeed, yet it is striking how the first Christians took this psalm as prophetic of Christ. It is quoted in the New Testament as showing Christ's destiny to suffer for his zeal for God's house when he cleansed the temple; his destiny also to be mocked in his suffering, and given vinegar to drink for his thirst. And that fearsome doom sought for the enemies in the psalm was found prophetic of the death of the traitor Judas.

Today the Church can further be led by the psalm to see in the figure of our Lord one who enters into the suffering of alienation – the place where none will have pity, none will understand, none will comfort, and the thirsty one is even given vinegar to drink. Jesus himself experienced that sense of drowning in troubles, sinking in mire. He stands with those who are weary with crying out. In his faithful companionship he helps them still to hope in God.

And being, as it were, *in* the psalm, he transforms the vengeful part of it. Yes, the cruel enemies deserve the judgement such as the psalm depicts. But this almighty Christ, avenger of the abused, yet prays, 'Father forgive them, for they know not what they do.' So he leads us to pray for our enemies and for the wicked in this world: beyond the doom of their wickedness may they be born anew, to become part of that universal praise with heaven and earth, the seas and all the creatures that live in them.

O Jesus, our Immanuel, God with us, it is you who are crying with the suffering: 'Save me O God, for the waters come in up to my soul; my eyes fail with looking so long for my God.'

O Lord, who bore the destiny of lonely suffering, your faithful love is gracious, your pity is great. From those full of heaviness, hearts broken by reproach, do not hide your face.

Fill us with hope and prepare in us the song of thanksgiving. Give us sure knowledge of that coming time when the heavens, the earth, the seas and all that lives in them shall rejoice in you.

Psalm 70
When we need help quickly

Henry was a young pupil at a famous boarding school. One day he had a visit from his godfather. He later confided to his mother, 'He didn't do much for my image.' The eccentric godfather had worn an old raincoat secured with string, and generally appeared the opposite of smartness and importance. In reality he was a world-renowned scholar and held a high position at Oxford. Perhaps we ourselves have known a situation like that. We have taken little note of an unimpressive person in a gathering, only to learn later that this was someone of extraordinary ability and achievement. How we misjudged!

The psalms, like people, vary in appearance. Some stand out for their beauty, with images that call out to our souls. Others are grand in size, with long sweeps of eloquent verse. And then there are some which may seem meagre by comparison, such as Psalm 70. It is short, even fragmentary. It boasts no great images or originality, indeed it seems only a rough repeat of a bit of Psalm 40. And yet its key verse may have been recited in Christian worship more often than any other verse in the Old Testament. Its value is brought out by a story from the early Christian monks.

Two young monks, Cassian and Germanus, were seeking spiritual guidance from a revered master in the Egyptian desert, Abba Isaac. They were asking him about prayer, and especially how to keep their minds set upon God without distraction. Abba Isaac urged them to be constantly reciting the verse from Psalm 70:

> O God, come quickly to save me;
> O LORD, hurry to my help.

Isaac said the bare simplicity of this verse would keep away the abundance of other thoughts. Its poverty would serve them better than the riches of grander texts. They would find it valuable in every situation, an expression of humility and of faith. 'Whatever work you do,' he said, 'whatever journey you make, do not stop reciting this verse. When sleep comes, let it find you chanting it. When you wake, let it be the first thought to come into your mind, and let it stay with you all through the day.'

Years later, when one of those young monks, Cassian, had himself become a revered elderly counsellor, he was urged to write down his memories of the teaching he had heard in the desert. Cassian's writing on prayer became standard reading in the medieval monasteries. And sure enough, the frequent gatherings of the monks for prayer throughout the day in all the monasteries always opened with the verse from Psalm 70. The Anglicans followed suit, and for many centuries the opening part of their morning and evening prayer used this verse in responsive form:

> O God, make speed to save us;
> O Lord, make haste to help us.

Congregations may have heard no instruction on such a familiar part of the service. If they reflected on it, they might well have been puzzled to begin regular daily prayers with so urgent a plea. But the monks in the desert would not think it superfluous. They had a vivid sense that demons were always on the attack. We might not put it like that, but it is a curious fact that hindrances and temptations often assail us just as we would begin a time of worship. The mind wanders, or is vexed at some detail in the proceedings. Not out of place at the outset, then, is the protective prayer, 'O God, come quickly to save me.' Abba Isaac, as we have seen, thought the prayer always valuable. When we are in distress, it is clearly appropriate. But also when things go well, we benefit from it still. For in happy times we might be in danger of forgetting our continual dependence on the Lord. We might fall into false confidence and complacency. Both in good times and bad, then, the psalm leads us to live in humility and trust, aware of our need and of the One who will help us.

The little psalm does not add much to its opening cry. It just goes on to ask that God's help be so decisive that the attackers turn and flee, leaving God's people to thank and praise him. Then the note of urgency is sounded again in the last verse:

> As for me, I am poor and needy – O God, hasten to me;
> you are my help and my deliverer – LORD, do not delay.

Many psalms urge us to wait for the Lord, and no doubt it is good to hope and trust in patience. But this psalm, so easily overlooked, encourages us also to cry to God with heartfelt urgency. With the early monks, we can take up its words to battle in prayer against the evils of the world. And against every danger that is near to us, it can lead us to seek the strong help of our Lord – not least when distractions would spoil the precious communion of worship: 'O God, make speed to save us; O Lord, make haste to help us.'

I am poor and needy – O God, hasten to me. You are my help and deliverer –
  Lord, do not delay.
May those who desire my hurt be turned back in shame. But may those who
  seek you have cause to rejoice in you.
Grant, Lord, that those who gather to worship you may be vigilant against
  temptation. Strengthen them in purity, humility and love.
Lord, hurry to my help.

Psalm 71
When strength fails

Andrew was a self-employed builder in Cornwall. Slight in stature, he was deft and agile, especially skilled in stonework. He had a pleasant manner and a kind heart. If anything, he had a tendency to undercharge, and he was not good at making his clients pay their bills. Still, he got by, and there was usually a number of irate folk waiting for him to appear, as he had said, 'directly', to put in new windows, repair the roof, or even build an extension. You would often see his wiry frame ascending a ladder with a large piece of timber, or he would wave to you as he stood on the pinnacle of a roof. If it was not a prosperous life, at least he enjoyed being his own master, free when he wished to call on his frail mother and do her shopping.

But as he himself got older, tasks he had once made light of began to seem too hard for him. Also, he could not hear well, but was impatient of hearing aids. He would smile and affirm what his clients said, but, not having understood them, would be likely to disappoint. As difficulties increased, he was glad to take work with a big firm developing old railway buildings into apartments. It was monotonous, raising wall after wall of breeze-blocks, but the money was regular. Yet at his age, how long would they keep him? His future circumstances seemed likely to be very difficult.

Andrew's situation could not be described as tragic. But he was entering a common and unwelcome experience – difficulties that mount when bodily strength begins to fail. He had a sense of being less regarded, people finding him less useful, friends being less attentive.

Sometimes in the evening Andrew liked to 'have a yarn', as he put it. He would recall times past, which might include memories of strange goings-on when he was a choirboy and 'boatboy' in the local church. He must have often sung the psalms in those days, but he did not betray recollection of verses in Psalm 71 which linked with his present situation:

> Do not cast me away in the time of age,
> or forsake me when my strength is failing . . .
>
> Do not forsake me, O God, now I am old and grey . . .

181

The psalm reflects a really serious situation for the king, perhaps David himself. As his strength fails, his enemies plot and his friends reposition themselves:

> My enemies speak against me,
> and those who lie in wait for my soul
>> take counsel together,
>
> saying, God has forsaken him;
> pursue and take him,
>> for there is none to save him.

As his prayer unfolds, the king urges upon God his lifetime of trust. At his very birth, the Lord had held him. At the peak of his career, God's miracles for him had made him to be a portent or sign, revealing to many how God works for his beloved. And he had sung songs of praise and thankful witness:

> My mouth was filled with your praise,
> and with your beauty all the day long.

And though he is now old and grey-headed, he urges that he can still fulfil a work of praise; he still has to tell the work of God to the rising generation, and speak of God's power to those who follow after. Above all, despite his distress, he holds on to hope:

> For you, LORD, are my hope,
> my trust, LORD, even from my youth . . .
>
> As for me, I will hope continually,
> and praise you more and more.

With the thought of the goodness of God, the singer's hope burns brighter. So he pledges all his remaining days to make melody of thankfulness to the Lord:

> Your goodness, O God, reaches to the heavens;
> in the great things you have done,
>> who is like you, O God?
>
> Though you have shown us great troubles and ills,
>> you will turn and revive us,
> and bring us up again from the depths of the earth . . .

Then I will thank you on the harp
   for your faithfulness, O God;
I will make melody to you on the lyre,
   O Holy One of Israel.

My lips will sing as I play to you,
and so shall my soul, which you have redeemed.

There must be many people today, growing old like our builder in
Cornwall, who could identify with that central prayer of the psalm: 'Do
not cast me away in the time of age, do not forsake me when my strength
is failing.' Younger folk, too, suffering an accident or sudden onset of
disease, know this peculiar distress of failing strength, diminished abilities.
It is acutely troubling to find that we can no longer do the tasks we were
so accustomed to doing. Our role at home or at work changes. Our self-
confidence is shaken. All the more so if the deterioration is likely to be
irreversible.

In the psalm it is striking how, in spite of the distress, the themes of
trust and hope resound. Here indeed is a prayer, in constant use for many
centuries, which leads us, yes, to turn to God and cry to him, but with a
foundation of trust and hope. It is with sure hope that we are to call to our
Lord, 'Do not stay far from me, my God; hasten to my help.' And the psalm
leads us to renew our confidence by recollecting all the wonderful things
he has done for us since our very birth, when already he held us, and then
through the years taught us and saved us.

The psalmist indeed felt that the kindness of God had so shone upon
him that he had been 'a sign to many' – through his experience others
became aware of God's goodness. We might shrink from the thought that
we had been or could become such a sign. Yet God's signs are sometimes
given in a quiet, even hidden, manner. And in our suffering, when our
strength fails and abilities diminish, we may yet unknowingly serve him as
a sign to many. He is at work in us, hidden in our patience, our trust, our
hope, our prayers, our love for others. He is present there even though we
feel failures, poor examples indeed. When we are not capable of great
deeds or words, we may still be his sign, because our hearts are open to
him. He is in us, and though we do not realize it, our mouth, as the
psalmist puts it, *is* filled with his praise and with his beauty all the day
long.

Indeed, when we are humbled in weakness, his presence is all the
stronger, his work the more fruitful. We are not growing ever more useless
– quite the contrary in God's eyes. So may he grant us to enter the hope of

the psalm and to say with our own conviction, 'Your goodness, O God, reaches to the heavens; you will turn about to comfort me; my lips will sing out, my soul also, which you have redeemed.'

Lord, my strength is failing and troubles take hold of me. But you have held
*   me since birth.*
In you I put my trust. You are my hope. Deliver me in your goodness and
*   rescue me.*
You will restore the strength of my spirit. You will revive my soul.
May my heart be so directed to your praise, that your goodness may possess
*   me and touch those who know me.*
Who is like you, O Lord? In the mystery of your work and the might of your
*   love, O Christ, who is like you?*

Psalm 72
The gold of prayer

There's a small and common word in Hebrew: *min*. Often it means 'from', but it can have other meanings and occasionally it really divides the translators. An example is the passage in Job, chapter 19, familiar as '[and though worms destroy this body,] yet *in* my flesh shall I see God'. But some prefer to take *min* here in a different sense and get, '*without* my flesh shall I see God'. Quite a difference! Another example comes in Psalm 119, verse 99, where we are usually given the startling but probably correct translation, 'I have *more* understanding than all my teachers.' Jewish tradition found this hard to swallow and preferred (with a different sense of *min*), 'I have understanding *from* all my teachers.'

Yet another example comes in the psalm we shall now be thinking about, Psalm 72, verse 15. Here we seem to have, 'They shall give him *of* the gold of Arabia.' But a better translation may be, 'They shall give him *more than* the gold of Arabia.' The thought is of the ideal king who saves the poor and needy from oppression. They thank him by giving him more than the gold of Arabia – but what could that be? What gift so precious could the poor bring? Prayers. They pray constantly for their benefactor and call down blessings upon him. This is how the whole passage now sounds:

He shall deliver the poor one who cries out,
the needy one who has no helper . . .

From falsehood and cruelty he will redeem their soul,
and their blood shall be precious in his eyes.

So they shall live,
and shall bring him more than Arabia's gold,
for they will pray for him continually,
and bless him all the day long.

As the psalm develops its picture of the ideal king, it concentrates on this defending of the poor. Some governments today have other concerns for the poor – whether their social security payments, tax credits or pensions should be raised or their housing benefits improved. But for the psalm the focus is all on the way the powerful and wealthy exploit the weak, take their land, drive out or enslave them – as still happens indeed in our world. The ideal king in the psalm is the one who stands between the poor and their oppressors. He acts against the corrupters of the legal process. He himself listens to the complaints of the poor and gives judgement in their favour. As the singer puts it:

He shall judge for the poor of the people;
he will save the children of the needy,
and crush the oppressors . . .

He will have pity on the helpless and needy,
and save the lives of the poor.

The psalm certainly differs from most modern attitudes in the ground of its hope. Today, an aspiring leader might make eloquent promises and convince people that he had in himself the right intentions, the right gifts and the right character for the high office. His coming to power would then be greeted with a wave of enthusiasm, soon to give way to a trough of disappointment. Praise for the leader is likely to be replaced fairly soon with a crescendo of grumblings, snipings, slander and abuse. But for the psalm the ideal rule is from the outset a matter for prayer. So it begins by calling on God to give *his* judgements to the new king, to make him a channel for God's own justice and good rule. Thus:

O God, give your judgements to the king,
your justice to this son of a king.

Then he will judge your people aright,
and your afflicted ones with justice.

If this prayer is granted, says the psalm, and the king becomes a true link between heaven and earth, then blessing will fall, not just on the poor, but on the very earth and all its creatures:

The mountains shall bear peace,
and the little hills goodness for the people . . .

He shall come down like rain on the crops,
like showers that water the earth . . .

Wild creatures shall kneel before him,
but his enemies shall lick the dust . . .

The corn shall be abundant on the earth and hilltops,
   its fruit heavy as on Lebanon,
and from their cities they will flourish
   as the grass of the earth.

It is a vision of the harmony of the world under God, the harmony indeed of the kingdom of God, a happy perfection that comes when the ruler is open to God, doing his will. Only the Messiah could truly fulfil such a role. Only our Lord Jesus can be such a king. We therefore recite the psalm as a prayer for his kingdom to come. May God perfect upon all creation that peace and blessing which we have begun to experience in Christ.

This is the fundamental prayer. But the psalm can also prompt us to pray more for our fallible rulers, for queens and kings, presidents and prime ministers, who too commonly receive first mindless adulation, then unfair scorn and blame. For how can they achieve any good without prayer, the continual prayer of their people? So let the psalm prompt us to pray that our rulers be channels for God's will. Let us pray that their acts of government flow from a higher justice, to crush corruption, defend the poor and the health of all the living world.

And the psalm can come yet nearer home. Are we not all of us powers and sovereigns in our own domain? Do we not all wield a power of judgement, a responsibility of rule and decision in a circle peculiarly our own? So should we not all, as members of Christ, pray to be channels of God's pity and peace? Yes, for our own work, our little rule, can also come like sweet rain on the crops and nourish God's world of peace.

Your kingdom come, O God, to save the oppressed and heal all that lives in
creation. Hasten the time of the full reign of Christ, when goodness shall
flourish and abundance of peace till the moon be no more.
We bring the fine gold of prayer for your kingdom, for our present rulers, and
for our own use of power and responsibility.
In everything may we look for your will to be done, your pity to shine through.
Blessed be the Lord who alone does wonderful things. Blessed be his glorious
name for ever, and may all the earth be filled with his glory.

Psalm 73
Coming near to God

Some friends were visiting the area where the Dead Sea Scrolls were found.
From the shore of the Dead Sea, far below sea level, you could ascend to a
natural terrace by the mouth of a ravine. There, on the terrace, you saw the
excavated remains of a kind of monastery. But rising high above that was
a mighty wall of rugged cliffs. In those formidable crags were located the
caves that had preserved the scrolls for two thousand years.

The visitors looked up in awe, and most were content to scramble about
and gaze towards the caves from far below. But one bold young man, a
keen student of the scrolls, was drawn to try to reach a cave of special
interest. At first he made good progress in his ascent, but then he became
less sure. The element of fear increased. The rocks seemed more slippery,
the route hard to choose. Once or twice he felt his steps stumbling, his feet
almost gone. It was a dangerous moment.

Then a woman's voiced sounded from below. She was shouting to him
to keep still and wait for help. By good fortune this watchful friend, a doctor working for Save the Children, was also an experienced mountaineer.
Soon she had reached him. She took hold of his right hand and began to
lead him down to safety. As his fear melted away, his steps became sure.
With immense relief he reached the easy ground, still conscious that he
had very nearly fallen to destruction.

Such precipitous places are not uncommon in and around the hilly terrain of the Holy Land. The poet of Psalm 73 clearly knew that sense of the
danger of slipping or stumbling and so falling down the rocks to destruc-

tion. He says of the wicked: 'You [God] will set them in slippery places, and make them fall to destruction. O how suddenly they will come to ruin, be overcome by terrors, and perish!' But also of himself, in a time of despair, the poet tells: 'But as for me, my feet were almost gone; my steps had all but slipped.' And the psalmist, in his time of danger, also found a rescuer. He says to God: 'But I am always with you; you take hold of my right hand. You will guide me with your counsel, and afterwards receive me in glory.'

For the singer, the high slippery place here is a picture for a spiritual danger that threatened him. What temptation could have become such an acute peril for him? He relates how he had been seized by a corrosive envy. Godless folk, arrogant and ruthless, were prospering, while he, trying to be faithful to God, had much to suffer daily. As he says:

I was envious of the proud;
I saw the prosperity of the wicked . . .

The common sufferings are not for them;
they are not smitten like other folk.

Therefore pride is their necklace,
and cruelty covers them like a garment . . .

Did I then cleanse my heart in vain,
and wash my hands in innocence?

All the day long have I been stricken,
and every morning chastened anew.

The psalmist tells how the injustice made him bitter in heart, consumed by a grief within. He was near to speaking out against God. It was like being on a mountainside where his feet had almost gone, his steps had well-nigh slipped. How then did his rescuer reach him? First, he was restrained by a sense of loyalty to his fellow believers. Here was a spiritual fellowship which strengthened him in the crisis. As he says:

But if I had said, I will speak thus,
I should have betrayed the company of your children.

But still he was deeply troubled – until he came to the sanctuary, the place of communion and inspiration. He relates:

When I thought to understand this,
it seemed too hard for me,

until I came into the sanctuary of God,
and then I discerned their end.

For you will set them in slippery places,
and make them fall to destruction.

O how suddenly they will come to ruin,
be overcome by terrors, and perish!

It seems, then, that in the holy place and the time of worship God came to the psalmist and gave him light. So he saw that the wicked, scornful of God, had nothing of real value. Their apparent prosperity was hollow; suddenly they would come to ruin. But the faithful, beset by many sufferings, yet had incomparable treasure. God held them by the hand and would never forsake them. With renewed faith the psalmist sings to God:

But I am always with you;
you keep hold of my right hand.

You will guide me with your counsel,
and afterwards receive me in glory . . .

My flesh and my heart shall fail,
but God is the rock of my heart
and my portion for ever.

You will probably agree that the psalmist describes a world we still know. It is a world which causes much perplexity in the life of faith. All around us we see injustice, the success of the godless, the unchecked power of greed and oppression. Inevitable too is the experience of the body's decline in sickness and in the infirmities of growing old. There is the temptation still to take the bitter way, turn from God, go far from him, even to worship false goals. And still today the psalm insists that in God alone is our satisfaction and our eternal happiness. The only good is to draw near to him, shelter in him and live as his witness. The psalm's conclusion still has force:

Those who go far from you shall perish;
you will silence those who forsake you for false gods.

But it is good for me to draw near to God;
in the LORD God I will make my shelter,
that I may tell of all your works.

The psalm indeed is much treasured, for it beautifully witnesses that true life and contentment consist in being close to God. It witnesses also to the value of the fellowship of worship. In time of doubt and bitterness, Christ's disciples support each other. An individual may lose sight of heaven's light for a while, but is steadied by feelings of respect and loyalty towards the fellowship. Prompted by such feelings, the troubled person comes again to the place of worship and may be granted insight – a new perspective.

On the dangerous mountainside the rescuer has come. We have waited in stillness, and now he has come and taken our hand. He guides us with his counsel. There is nothing we could have, in heaven or earth, as wonderful as his nearness. And though our heart and body fail, he is the rock of our heart and our portion for ever.

Lord, purify my heart that I may know you in your goodness.

In time of bitterness and despair, let me not betray the company of your children, but rather be strengthened by their fellowship.

Ever and again may I come into your sanctuary and know that you are near me.

Keep hold of my right hand and guide me with your counsel. Make my steps firm on the path to your eternal glory.

O Jesus, whom have I in heaven but you? And on earth there is none that I desire beside you.

Psalm 74
Why does God not intervene?

————◆•◆————

We may have often heard readings from the Old Testament about how God made the world. Yet we might find it difficult to remember the details and the order. Perhaps if we, as a group, were to pool our recollections, we would get quite a lot of material together. One of us might recall the Spirit of God hovering over the waters. Another might contribute how 'God saw that it was good' at the end of each day's work. The day when God rested would certainly come to mind. And most of us would recall the Man set in the garden and the Woman made from his rib. And then the serpent . . . yes, between us we would probably gather up quite a story.

But would anyone have contributed the recollection that God as a warrior king slew monsters in the midst of the earth? Would anyone have remembered that at creation he crushed the seven heads of Leviathan? Or that he was careful to build up edges round the ends of the earth? Probably not. For the fact is that only part of the Old Testament's lore of creation is well known. There was actually quite a variety of it. The poets presented the creation in different ways, for they were not concerned with science as we know it. The various traditions took shape to throw light from different angles on life as it continues, life under God.

In one great psalm that recounts the creation, Psalm 74, the singer is primarily beseeching God about a disaster caused by invaders. Why is God not striking them down? Why has he withdrawn his mighty hand and kept it at rest in his bosom? In the course of his prayer, the singer unfolds an account of creation which he hopes may bring God once more to do mighty deeds and once more master the forces of chaos. Just hear how passionately the singer complains, and then calls up the mighty blows of the world's beginning:

> How long, O God, shall the adversary taunt,
> and the enemy revile your name?

> Why have you withdrawn your hand,
> and held back your right hand in your bosom?

> O God, my King of ancient time,
> who did deeds of salvation in the midst of the earth,

> it was you that cleft the sea by your power,
> you that broke the dragons' heads on the waters.

> You alone crushed the heads of Leviathan;
> you gave him as food for creatures of the desert.

> It was you that cleft fountain and torrent,
> you that dried up ever-flowing rivers.

> From you came day, from you the night;
> you alone established the sun and all the lights of heaven.

> It was you that set up all the edges of the earth,
> you that fashioned both summer and winter.

> Remember, Lord, how the enemy derides,
> how a foolish people scorns your name.

And the singer concludes with urgent appeal:

> Arise, O God, take up your own cause;
> remember how the fool reviles you all day long.

> Do not forget the voice of your enemies,
> the din of your foes that ascends continually.

Imagine the plight of the worshippers who first pleaded with God in this psalm. They are gathered on the temple hill, but the holy place is utterly ruined. The invaders have come in like woodmen swinging axes. They have stripped away all the precious work in gold, ivory and fine woods. Then they demolished and burnt the temple to the ground. Death's caves, says the psalmist, are filled with the victims of violence.

The singer puts it to the Lord that it is his own house and his own people that have suffered. This house was the dwelling of God's 'name' – a form of his presence, the giving of his very self. And yet the enemy has roared in triumph and stripped and plundered without let or hindrance. God has kept his hand in his bosom. He has allowed it all. In a sense, the psalmist reckons, he has used it to express anger against his people.

It all happened two and a half thousand years ago. Yet similar things still happen today. Good things and people are ruthlessly destroyed, and God does not prevent it. A whole people, worshipping God, is slaughtered. A politician is building peace, but then is murdered. Beautiful creatures in the wild are wiped out. Locally, too, a school is burned down. A boy steals a car and runs down a mother and children on the pavement. A man of wisdom and kindness dies early of cancer. Yes, across the world and close to home, evil is done and it seems that God's hand remains at rest in his bosom. And now, as then, we may see no explanatory sign or hear word of just when things will change.

But though the ancient people said in the psalm that they had no sign and no prophet who could see through the darkness, we know now that help was near. For it was from around this time of disaster that great prophets arose – Jeremiah, Ezekiel and the author of Isaiah 53 and its vision of the Man of Sorrows. And perhaps when we too feel utterly perplexed, a light is not far away, a lamp to guide us through the darkness.

Surely we shall find the God-given lamp when we meditate on the passion of our Lord Jesus. Here above all was the 'name', the self-giving of God apparently left at the mercy of the wicked. Here was his dove abandoned to wild beasts. The mighty hand of the Creator was apparently held back, inactive. But in reality that hand won the mightier victory, the triumph of love. Christ gathers all the world's sufferings into that great work of transformation. In his time, all will be seen bathed in the light of his resurrection. As the night is his, so is the day. Beyond the sun and all the lights of heaven will shine on all the light of the risen Christ.

From ancient days, O Lord, your people have known times of forsakenness and the ruin of the good and holy. Grant us to perceive that you suffer with us, and for us. So strengthen us in faith to trust that the great resurrection is prepared, and the transformation made sure for the time according to your will.

You who divided the sea by your power and gave us from the cross the fountain of life, have mercy upon your suffering ones.

Rise, O Sun of hope, and shine on all the dark places of the earth. Lord, have mercy. Christ, have mercy. Lord, have mercy.

Psalm 75

Pillars of worship

—◆—◆—◆—

Cars multiplied. People were darting about as never before. The social effects of this mobility included the loss of many smaller shops and an increase in crime. Another effect, not so often discussed, was the way worshippers would seek out churches. The faithful began to range considerable distances to select a style of worship and fellowship to suit their preferences. This practice has had advantages and drawbacks. But wherever the balance may lie, it will be good if, from time to time, we reconsider what gives validity and truth to services of worship – something at a deeper level than personal preference.

These thoughts have been prompted by a few simple words that open Psalm 75:

We give you thanks, O God, we give you thanks,
    for your name is near,
        and your wonderful works are told.

Simple words – but what does that really mean, 'for your name is near'? Behind the words lies awareness that the infinite God is beyond our searching, utterly mysterious. But in his grace he has made himself known to us, to the extent that we can love and serve him and call to him in prayer. All this is enfolded in his name. When he gave his name, he could be met as Father, Lord and Saviour. Calling on this name, his people could commune with him and ask him into their lives to guide and protect.

They came to think of the name as specially present in the sanctuary. This meant that here God gave himself in communion and responded to prayer. As the people gathered in his name and poured out their hearts before him, his name was 'near' – his presence was strongly known. So the worshippers there became very close to the One who, but for his compassion, would be far beyond all their knowing.

Another feature of worship is also touched on in the psalm's opening when it says: 'Your wonderful works are told.' In the assembly of worshippers it was customary to recount the marvellous deeds of God. This included his work as Creator, founding and caring for all the living world; also his work as Saviour, defending the humble who trust in him. The past was recalled in order that the same power of God should fill the present. Like the use of God's name, so this recounting of God's works was a means of finding and knowing God. As his deeds of power and love were told, his character was conveyed, his presence made strong over all the gathering.

And our verse also includes a third feature of the worship – 'We give you thanks, O God, we give you thanks.' In the songs of praise and thanksgiving, the worshippers acknowledge the presence and self-giving of God. They affirm their trust and, as they praise, they take the wonderful work of God to themselves.

Thus this simple verse has mentioned three mighty pillars of worship. And they are still found in great cathedrals or in the humblest room where disciples gather to worship in spirit and in truth. Recalling these pillars, they are: first, that *we call on the name of God*, given us now as Jesus; second, that *we tell of his deeds* as we sing and testify; and third, that *we give thanks*, immersing ourselves in his grace as we praise him.

These fundamentals of worship mentioned in the psalm come to take on special Christian forms, not least in Holy Communion, the Eucharist or Thanksgiving. And there will be many variations in the resources and emphases which the churches bring to their acts of worship. But we must ever recall the fundamentals. So we shall value with profound gratitude and humility every opportunity we have to be with a group who together call on his name, tell his deeds and respond with thankful praise.

But as we survey these bastions of worship, some may be disappointed that we have not mentioned the sermon. On this, however, the main part of the psalm does have something to convey. For the psalm quickly moves to its main concern – admittedly not a sermon, but certainly a message from God. In a time of international wrongdoing, God sends assurance to the worshippers that at the right moment he will put right the world's order. God says:

> I will seize the time appointed,
>   and I myself will judge with justice.
> The earth shakes, with all that dwell in her,
>   yet I will set right her pillars.

The singer then expounds this basic message. There is rebuke of human arrogance and those who would promote themselves:

> Do not lift your horn on high,
>   or speak with an insolent neck.
>
> For neither from the east nor from the west,
>   nor yet from the south comes exaltation.
>
> But God alone is the judge;
>   he puts down one and raises up another.

And the singer vividly warns of the danger that the wicked are courting:

> For in the hand of the LORD there is a cup,
>   and its wine is foaming and fully mixed.
> When he pours from it, all the wicked of the earth
>   shall drink it down to the very last drop.

In our time, people who can voice a word direct from God are few, but a sermon will usually be based on an inspired word of scripture. Preachers will hope that their own words may carry truth from God. The psalm certainly reminds us that in worship the speaking is not all to be from the human side. In one way or another there is a word to be heard from God.

Father, we thank you that out of infinite mystery you have come to us in your name – the revelation of your love in Jesus.

O Jesus, when two or three are met together to call upon your name, you are in our midst. Your name is near and your wonderful works are told. Your blessing passes among us.

Renew in us the spirit of worship, that we may tremble and rejoice at your presence. In stillness may we discern your words of judgement and of promise. May we go forth to live our days in the melody of your praise.

Psalm 76
The power of a name

—◆◆◆—

Times were becoming hard for booksellers. Had people become less appreciative of books? Or was it that authors had deteriorated? Was the trade looking for bigger returns than of old? Whatever the cause, the situation was reached where the shop windows and interiors were filled with pseudo-books, volumes purporting to be by celebrities. Sports personalities, pop stars, butlers, criminals, who might not on their own be capable of writing two good sentences together, here laid out their adventures and philosophies with the aid of a ghost writer. And each work would be there in quantity, for brisk sales were expected, making large profits for all concerned. A dismal spectacle for anyone who loved real books!

Yet it was all a testimony to the power of a name. For one cause or another, these dubious authors had become well known to millions across the world, their names a household word. Their books might never be read right through. No matter. They sold briskly on the strength of the great name.

Now there is a psalm which seems to begin with the thought of a great name – Psalm 76. The name in this case is that of God himself. As the old Prayer Book renders it: 'In Jewry is God known; his name is great in Israel.' Admittedly, the Bible has long been a bestseller, but on closer inspection the psalm is not speaking of a general fame or a name that is a household word. Rather it speaks of a powerful *action* of God, God breaking upon the earthly scene with a mighty judgement and salvation. The psalm declares that 'God has made himself known in Judah' – he has come out of his hidden mystery in no uncertain manner. That 'his name is great in Israel' means here that his people have witnessed the explosive power of his self-revelation in his name.

But what is the psalm referring to? What has happened? Some great historical event, perhaps, when invaders suddenly turned tail? We could then compare astonishing events in modern wars, turning points where all-conquering foes suddenly met their ruin.

Yet it may be better to understand the event as something imaginary and symbolic, a dramatic element in the sacred festival, a kind of sacrament. It would represent the protecting love of God, focused in a dramatic scene.

Mention is made of 'Salem' – that is, Jerusalem or Zion, the holy place of worship and communion. The message is that God ever keeps this sacred place from the attacks of the wicked. Only it is put dramatically, as a story. It is imagined how armies came with swords and flaming arrows. But when God appeared in radiance and uttered his mighty word, they all fell, powerless and still:

> There [in Zion] he has broken the flaming arrows,
> shield, sword and line of battle.

> In brightness you appeared,
> glorious from the hills of prey.

> The mighty ones were plundered and slept their sleep,
> and none of the men of war could find their hands.

> At your thunderous word, O God of Jacob,
> both chariot and horse fell still.

> In your dread majesty you appeared,
> and who could stand before your face in the time of your wrath?

> You sounded doom from heaven;
> earth trembled and was still,

> when God arose for judgement,
> to save all the poor of the earth.

Perhaps the psalm will strike us now as over-optimistic. In our world today, in many countries, we scarcely see such justice of God, but rather destructive conflict, vengeful rage, ruthless pride. But the psalmist knew well of such horrors. And still he rounds off his positive message with further confident affirmations. Truly, he says, the raging of the peoples will be turned into thankful praise, and 'the remnant of their rage' God will 'gird on' – that is, he will take the humbled peoples to himself as his ornament of beauty and delight. For he will have cut down the pride of the despoilers and revealed his fearsome glory to bring a new order of peace.

It must often have been almost impossible to accept such assurance and promise. Armies did come and Jerusalem was destroyed. Down to our own day, the pride of evil leaders has often run amok. The good and holy things and the people trusting in God have often been destroyed by the flaming arrows. Yet the psalm has reached us through a long succession of worshippers who experienced such ravages. We must hear with respect its testimony to the supremacy of God, who in his faithfulness will save all the meek of the earth. We wonder how the psalmist came to his vision. Has he seen what *will* be when the kingdom comes? Has he divined the inner meaning of the cross and resurrection? Has he been nourished in his faith by particular experiences of God's care in this troubled world, such as we too may have had?

Something of all these thoughts may be true. But certainly we can sing his song of faith in harmony with Christian convictions. When we pray 'Hallowed be thy name' we are asking that God should glorify his name, that he should manifest it with all the impact of his holy power. We are asking him speedily to make himself known, shattering the pride of wickedness. Yes, with the Lord's prayer we are daily asking in effect that the vision of this psalm be fulfilled. May the eternal reality of God's great name swallow up all the sufferings of this present age. May all the earth, may all creation, be filled with the mighty knowledge of God as the waters cover the sea.

> Grant, Lord, that in the high moments of our worship we may see the certainty of your work, when you make great your holy name, stun the warmongers, and save all the poor of the earth.
> We bless you for the beauty of your appearing in Christ and for the glory of his resurrection.
> Renew the faith of your worshippers that you will complete this mighty revelation, turning the world's ragings into songs of praise.

Psalm 77

Strenuous praying

Janet was a mild and kindly soul. You might then be surprised to learn that every Tuesday afternoon she put on a neat coat and hat and walked to a gathering of warriors. To be exact, the name of the group was 'the Prayer Warriors'. It consisted of some eight women and three men. They would sit around the table in the dining room of one of their homes. The person whose turn had come to lead would mention special concerns for that week. After an interval of quiet and a reading from the Bible, they bowed their heads. They prayed aloud as each felt moved. In due time the leader brought the prayers to a close. Thoughts now turned to tea and biscuits, which were soon conjured up. Conversation blossomed, until the warriors had to disperse. Janet was soon home, happy that a good purpose had been accomplished.

Next door lived old Jeremy. In his own way, he also interceded. He would sometimes take the church's prayer list in his hand as he meditated in his armchair. He couldn't always put a face to the names, so he was not always as moved by their plight as he should have been. Occasionally, indeed, he dozed off. Still, his intentions were good.

Now, in Psalm 77 intercession appears as an altogether more strenuous and passionate matter, admittedly in some time of acute disaster. The singer chants his prayer on behalf of the people, and he describes the agony of the praying in order to emphasize the urgency of the situation. He tells how his cry to God is loud. And it goes on through night and day, with hand outstretched imploringly and spirit agitated. Times of silence come when words fail and eyes stare helplessly. This is how the singer describes it:

> With my voice I cry to God,
> with all my voice, that he may hear me.
>
> In the day of my trouble I seek the Lord;
> by night my hand is stretched out and does not tire,
>   and my soul refuses to be comforted.
>
> I think upon God and I groan;
> I ponder, and my spirit faints.
>
> My eyelids are held open;
> I am so stricken that I cannot speak.

Then the singer tells of his thoughts and how he has agonized over the situation, wondering whether God has finally put away all his pity and faithfulness:

> I consider the days of old,
> and remember the years of long ago.
>
> I commune with my heart in the night;
> I ponder, and search my spirit.
>
> Will the Lord be for ever spurning,
> will he not again show favour?

> Has his faithful love ceased for ever,
>   and his promise come to an end for all generations?

Such thoughts are leading to the edge and must be countered. What can the intercessor say now to call forth the compassion of God, which, deep down, he knows still endures? He turns to the story of past salvation:

> But I say, This shall be my entreaty:
>   to recite the deeds of the right hand of God Most High.

> I will celebrate the acts of the LORD;
>   I will recall your wonders from of old.

The old story of salvation told how God parted the waters to make a path for the people escaping slavery. The singer describes the violence of the chaotic waters, and how God mastered them. God passed through the mighty waters, his footsteps unseen. So he reached his people and led them to safety like a flock, through the hand of Moses and Aaron.

At this point the singer suddenly ceases. Not a word more. We imagine a silence, when hearts yearn for the Saviour to come in the same way now. O that he would now pass mysteriously through this sea of troubles, and take his beloved by the hand to safety!

For the modern Christian the psalm is a reminder of how strenuous is the task of intercession when it is fully shouldered. Sympathy, true sharing with the sufferer, is itself demanding, even painful, and the burden may have to be carried night and day. Earnestness is still needed. The body adds its own language to the vocal entreaties, and not only the hands that stretch towards heaven. Yes, intercession is still a very hard task.

But the psalm also shows us where the burden can finally be rested. For we intercede on the strength of what our Lord has done. Reading the Bible calls all that grace and salvation of old into the present. Celebrating Holy Communion again brings Christ's salvation into our own lives. Our prayers are 'through Jesus Christ, our Lord'. They draw strength from what Jesus has done.

So let the psalm prompt us to combine our entreaties with recalling how our Saviour freed us from bondage, how he comes to us through the surge of troubles and leads us by the hand to safety. And so often, still, his footsteps through those waters will not be known. How he will come, when he will come, we may not know. Often, indeed, people are saved and they do not realize that it was he who did it. But may we who have prayed through Jesus Christ, may we above all, be ready to give him thanks. Thus

we shall add our story to the testimony of the ages, the witness and thanksgiving to our mighty and faithful Saviour.

*Of old, O God, your way was in the sea, your paths through the troubled
waters, and your footsteps were not known. Come now through the sea of
our troubles and lead us to your land of peace.*

*Lord, as the gospel story shines ever new upon us, may we receive it deep in
our spirit. So we shall know that your faithful love has not ceased and your
promises stand firm for ever.*

*Your way, O God, is in holy splendour. Yet also it is often hidden in mystery.
What god is so great as you, our Lord – Father, Son and Holy Spirit?*

Psalm 78
Eyes fixed on the Lord

A large part of a violinist's skill is in the handling of the bow. To have a
good bow is as important as to have a good violin – a bow finely made
from well-chosen wood, and in good condition, straight and true. No less
in archery, the archer depends on a good bow, resilient and true. Great vio-
linists and skilled archers alike insist on such perfection in their imple-
ments. But it is harder to be themselves so true. Just as the poet who weaves
words to perfection sometimes fails lamentably to live a beautiful life, so
the good violinist may live out wretched music, and the good archer may
sadly miss the target of human existence.

In Psalm 78 we hear of renowned archers in the ancient world who
in their own conduct 'started aside like a bow not true'. The psalmist is
singing a long, poetic sermon to the great assembly of pilgrims in
Jerusalem. He is inspired to unlock lessons from the past. He meditates on
the fickleness of God's people and the persevering grace of the Lord. The
archers he mentions are the tribe of Ephraim. They lived in the beautiful
centre of the Holy Land and for centuries were the leading tribe. But the
time came when they were defeated by the Philistines, their temple at
Shiloh destroyed, and the ark of the Lord captured – the ark that was
believed to carry the glory and presence of God. How could such a thing
have happened? The singer recalls the defeat of the once valiant Ephraim:

> The children of Ephraim, best equipped of bowmen,
> yet turned back on the day of battle.
>
> For they had not kept God's covenant,
> and refused to walk in his laws;
>
> They forgot his deeds,
> and the wonders he had shown them.
>
> (vv. 9–11)

This is the heart of the matter for the singer, that 'they forgot his deeds'. He tells how, through the generations, whenever the people lost the sense of wonder and thankfulness for all God had done for them, they grew apart from him, lost their faith and trust, and were easily led astray into evil ways. It came to the point where, as the singer puts it:

> They tested and defied the Most High God,
> and did not keep his testimonies.
>
> They turned back and fell away like their ancestors,
> starting aside like a bow not true.
>
> (vv. 56–57)

And so the enemy was able to triumph. The state and its religious structure collapsed:

> God forsook his dwelling in Shiloh,
> the tent where he dwelt among humankind.
>
> He gave his glory into captivity,
> and his beauty into the enemy's hand.
>
> He delivered his people to the sword,
> and dealt angrily with his heritage.
>
> (vv. 60–62)

And the singer recounts how the Lord yet persevered in his good purpose. He called David from the tribe of Judah and made Jerusalem the new centre of worship, with the ark restored. The builder of the new temple is said to be, not Solomon, but the Lord himself:

> And he built his sanctuary like the heavens,
> and like the earth which he founded for ever.
>
> (v. 69)

So the psalm ends after all with a happy picture. Here is God's temple linking earth and heaven. Here is the Lord's minister, David, anointed to care for the people 'according to the wholeness of his heart' – whole towards God – 'and with the wise skills of his hands'.

At the opening of his song, the psalmist has said that he offers 'mysteries' and a 'parable', and it seems to us that in truth his song foreshadows the Christian revelation. As God let his ark, vessel of his glory, fall into the hands of the Philistines, so Jesus was left in the hands of his captors. As God restored the ark and built for it his new temple, so he raised Jesus again to heavenly life and glory. As the temple linked heaven and earth, so Jesus became the way to life in God. As God appointed David to shepherd his people, so he made Jesus our good shepherd, leading us daily in the path of life, with loving hands and perfect wisdom.

Yes, the psalmist has seen into the depths of God's love – how he perseveres to save, forgives and in the end triumphs. And there is an earnest message for us in the psalm: when your eyes are only on your own desires, you drift away from the Lord. You lose the sense of his wonderful grace and you wander down paths that lead nowhere. So we are urged to remember, and hand on the remembrance; remember how the Lord came to save us, remember how he has given us water from the rock and bread from heaven. So let our eyes be set on our Saviour, our Shepherd, on Christ our Lord.

Enable us, Lord, to hear the singer's parable and the mysteries he pours forth
  from of old. May we apply to ourselves his counsel of remembrance.
May we not forget your deeds and commandments. May we remember, and
  put our trust in you. May our spirits keep faith with you.
In our wilderness also you will open rocks and give drink as from the deeps.
  In our wilderness you will give us the bread of heaven.
May my heart ever be fixed on you, my Rock and my Redeemer.

Psalm 79
Returning good for evil

In the Book of Psalms there are 150 compositions, with quite a variety of themes. It's not surprising that in church worship or private prayers we often make selections. We pick one or more psalms out of the book to suit the occasion.

But there has also been a tradition of reciting the psalms in their given order. What a world of experience that is! What struggles of anguish and faith, what alternations of light and darkness! Quite often the sequence takes you from proclaiming God's good rule to lamenting a terrible, unjust situation. The contrast can be breathtaking.

This is the case when we reach Psalm 79. The preceding psalm has just told us that God has 'built his sanctuary like the heavens and like the earth, which he has founded for ever', and, moreover, he has provided a king to shepherd his people with care and skill. What a contrast now to hear Psalm 79 at once cry out to the Lord that his temple and people have been devastated:

> O God, the nations have come into your heritage;
> they have defiled your holy temple,
>> and made Jerusalem a heap of stones.

> They have given the bodies of your servants
>> to be food for the birds of heaven,
> the flesh of your faithful to the wild beasts of the earth.

> They have shed their blood like water all around Jerusalem,
> and there was no one to bury them.

The singer does not doubt the power of God. Rather, he assumes that God is angry with his people. So the appeal is to his pity:

> Do not remember against us the sins of former times;
> let your compassion hurry to meet us, for we are brought very
>> low . . .

> O let the groaning of the prisoner come before you;
> by the might of your arm save those condemned to die.

And the singer urges the Lord to repay the neighbouring states for gloating at the downfall of the Lord's temple and people. The passionate request runs thus:

> Return to our neighbours sevenfold into their bosom
> the taunts with which they have taunted you, O Lord.

> But we, who are your people and the sheep of your pasture,
> will give you thanks for ever,
>> and tell of your praise to all generations.

204

We can understand the emotion driving this prayer, but how could we endorse such a request – that God repay the mockers 'sevenfold into their bosom'?

In ancient times, justice was supposed to be on a par with the offence – an eye for an eye, but no more! But sometimes a command was given exceptional force by carrying the sanction of a sevenfold penalty, a threat of getting back seven times the harm you had caused.

By contrast, the number seven was sometimes used in picturing exceptional kindness. How good if you forgave your adversary seven times! And our Lord extended it to 'seventy times seven', so much did he value the forgiving heart. How then could his followers be at home with this psalm that prays for a sevenfold reprisal on the malicious neighbours?

Well, the early monks were great reciters of all the psalms, and they were guided in their understanding by the fifth-century commentary of Cassiodorus, a devout Roman governor. Most monasteries had a copy of his work. He would have us turn this repayment of 'sevenfold' into the sevenfold gift of the Spirit. (It is in the Greek and Latin Bibles that the spirit-gifts in Isaiah 11 can be counted as seven, against the six of the Hebrew Bible.) We pray then for our adversaries that God will bring upon them the sevenfold spirit prophesied in Isaiah 11, the spirit of wisdom, understanding and the fear of the Lord. Even for those full of hate and evil intent we pray that the Spirit fill them with a better counsel, with knowledge of God and reverence. God grant us, with them, to be raised by the sevenfold power of the Spirit into his kingdom of love. With such prayer we find the way from the psalms of desolation to the psalms of praise, from the overpowering horror of ruin and slaughter to invincible knowledge of God's new creation.

O God, in many places still your temple is defiled and your city made into heaps of stones. The blood of your servants is shed like water. The wicked mock your laws and lay waste your dwelling place.
Remember not our former sins. Let your compassion hurry to meet us, for we are brought very low.
Turn the hearts of the pitiless. Return into their bosom the sevenfold power of your Spirit to convert them to fear of you in wisdom and good counsel, that none shall hurt or destroy in all your holy mountain.
May we, with them, give you thanks for ever and praise you to all generations.

Psalm 80
The light of the face of God

Suddenly there dawned the Age of Information. While there were still things you could not find out, the quantity, the variety, the speed of information was amazing. Some were aroused to a new interest in history, especially family history. They found they could gain sudden disclosures of family settings and occupations. It was noticeable, however, that the story of one's ancestry became more complicated as one moved back. Two grandfathers and two grandmothers could be coped with. Four great-grandfathers and four great-grandmothers began to stretch the mind. Really formidable was the tally of fathers and mothers producing the tenth generation – one thousand and twenty-four. And to produce the twentieth generation, only five centuries ago, the mothers and fathers would number, according to one bemused researcher, one million, forty-eight thousand, five hundred and seventy-six.

It was much simpler for the ancient Hebrews. In those days you had only one ancestor to count at each rung of the generation ladder, however far back you climbed. This was because only the father was reckoned with – so just one at every stage: your father, his father, his father, and so on. Much simpler.

Of course, leaving the mothers out of the reckoning will not do for a balanced account of heredity. But the simplicity of the Hebrew scheme led them to think readily of a people as the 'seed' of one remote ancestor. They could even think of the ancestor and people as one – the ancestor still lived in his descendants. Thus 'Israel' was a name of the ancestor Jacob, but it could also mean his descendants, the people 'Israel'. The people could thus readily be seen as one body, one mega-person.

This is what we find rather prominently at the beginning of Psalm 80. Here there is mention of the ancestor Israel, his son Joseph, Joseph's brother Benjamin, and Joseph's sons Ephraim and Manasseh. But the singer is chiefly thinking of the peoples descended from them, tribes that have come to a time of terrible suffering. This is how he begins his prayer for them:

> Hear, O Shepherd of Israel,
> you that led Joseph like a flock.

> You that are enthroned above the cherubim,
> shine out before Ephraim, Benjamin and Manasseh.

> Stir up your mighty strength,
> and come to our salvation.

The tribes mentioned here had been the strong centre of God's people. The singer refers to them just by the name of their ancestor. So we feel the unity of each tribe – a people as one body. But later comes another vivid expression of their common life, the people of God as his vine. This 'vine' God brought from Egypt and planted it in the Holy Land. It grew well under his care, but now . . . well, this is how the singer puts it:

> You took out a vine from Egypt;
> you drove out nations and planted it again.

> You made room about it,
> and when it had taken root, it filled the land.

> The hills were covered with its shade;
> and its boughs were like the cedars of God.

> It stretched out its branches to the sea,
> and its tendrils to the river.

> Then why have you broken down its walls,
> so that all who go by pluck off its grapes?

> The wild boar from the forest roots it up,
> and all the beasts of the field devour it . . .

> It is cut down and burnt in the fire;
> they perish at the rebuke of your face.

The vine was very characteristic of the Holy Land, a big part of their economy. They knew all about the labour and care of it, nursing it to develop its branches, tendrils and fruit. A shocking and pathetic sight to them would be a vineyard abandoned and ruined. But this very disaster, mourns the singer, has happened to God's vine, Israel. Yes, there was a time of his care, a time of health and growth. But now God's people are desolate, trampled and ruined by invaders.

In our day, alas, there are peoples who suffer a similar experience. And more than peoples. For we are learning more and more to see humans as part of the web of all life. Slowly we are waking up to the unity of our life with that of all creatures. Yes, not just the Church, but all creation is like one vine, one living system, drawing up one life from God. In many places we see the walls of this living order broken down and ravagers at work. We but think of the precious remnants of the rain forests and of the last habitats of the wild creatures. We but think of countries ravaged by decades of senseless wars. So, with the words of this psalm, from all the depths of our soul, we can implore God's protection of the Church, of the peoples, and of the creatures of earth and sea, O so vulnerable:

> O God of Hosts, return again;
> look down from heaven and see.
>
> Care for this your vine,
>   and guard what your right hand has planted,
> for the sake of the son you made so strong for yourself.

We notice there a special feature of this psalm. Twice it speaks of one at God's right hand, the 'son' or 'son of man' that he made so strong for himself. The singer meant the king whom God had appointed and enabled to rule for him in the power of the Spirit. As the years passed, the figure of the Messiah seemed to shine ever more through these words, and Christians found here Christ. Our prayer then becomes that God will save his ravaged creatures through Christ and for the sake of Christ, who came because God so loved the world.

And now we find new force in the psalm's refrain verse that three times asks God to let his face shine upon us, that we might be saved. For Christ is indeed the face of God and the light of his salvation. Similarly, St Paul says (2 Cor. 4.6), the light of the knowledge of the glory of God is given in the face of Jesus Christ.

The end of the psalm puts another great thought before us. When Christ's light shines upon us, bringing us a foretaste of the salvation of all the world, we are to devote our new life to him. In this commitment we pray with the psalm:

> LORD, God of hosts, restore us again;
> let your face shine upon us, that we may be saved.
>
> And so we shall not go back from you;
> let us live, that we may proclaim your name.

O God, kind shepherd and king supreme over all creation, look with pity on the ravaged ones. Stir up your mighty strength and come to save them.

*By your work, Lord, the great vine of life was planted and nourished. See how
it suffers in the fires of greed and cruelty. Care for your vine, for the sake of
your Son, Jesus.*
*Through him restore. Through him let your face shine upon your world in
salvation.*
May we abide in him. Let us live, that we may proclaim your name.

Psalm 81

I hear what you say, Lord . . .

It's a source of wonder how suddenly a word or phrase becomes fashionable. Those who speak for government or companies or other public bodies
suddenly with one accord become so wedded to a word or turn of phrase
that their speech would seem defective without it. Such a fashionable
notion is that of hearing or listening. A government makes a great thing
of staging meetings throughout the land in order to 'hear' the people's
views. A bank claims it is 'the listening bank', hearing what its customers
want. Really ominous is the common phrase 'I hear what you say' – the
next word is likely to be 'but'. Alas, a lot of this fashionable 'hearing'
belongs to a style of *seeming* sympathetic and receptive, while in reality
pushing through one's own agenda regardless.

Now there is a lively psalm, Psalm 81, where God looks for his people to
'hear' – but in a way that will really affect their conduct. God says:

> Hear, my people, and I will admonish you;
> O Israel, if you would but listen to me . . .

> If only my people would now listen to me,
> if Israel would but walk in my ways.

Clearly, it would be no use the people saying 'I hear what you say, Lord',
and then ignoring his wishes.

The matter is presented rather dramatically in the psalm. Pilgrims mass
in the temple court for the worship decreed by God long ago. The moment
has come when the ceremonies acclaim him with music of praise. The
singer calls:

209

Sing aloud to God our Strength;
   with joyful praise greet the God of Jacob.

Make melody and sound the drums;
   sweet lyres, together with the harps.

And the fullest weight of fanfares on the ram's horn trumpets joins in the greeting of God the King. It is clearly a momentous occasion, this time of his presence.

Then quietness and awe. The singer now tells of his inspiration. He has heard a mysterious voice, the divine voice. So he sings out the very words of God, recalling how God freed his people from slavery:

I released their back from the burden;
   their hands went free from the basket.

And God continues, 'In that oppression you called to me' – '*you* called'! Yes, those hands that went free from the basket loaded with the tyrant's bricks, those hands were yours! Centuries have melted away. It is you, my present worshippers, who have been set free from slavery. It is you who must hear your Saviour's claim on you:

When oppressed, you called to me and I delivered you . . .

Hear, O my people, and I will admonish you;
   O Israel, if you would but listen to me!

There shall be no strange god among you;
   you shall not bow down to any alien god.

Thus the challenge to 'hear' came through to the worshippers of the psalmist's day. But was it to be another case of 'I hear what you say, but . . .'? Or was it a true hearing-and-responding, a hearing that became a walking in God's ways? Would these 'hearers' now live daily in keen awareness that he was Lord and God?

The challenge comes on through the psalm to us. We are now the ones God calls to listen. *We* are to hear with all our hearts the call of God to turn from false worship and to live every day alive to him, in joy and with a willing spirit.

In the time of worship, Lord, you come into our midst. We greet you with awe and joy.
We listen for your word. Give us sensitive hearts to hear your rebuke and your promise.

May our listening be renewed commitment. In hearing you, may we turn
from false desires to a walking with you.
Make us ready to receive your wonderful gifts. May our spirits be freed from
old tyrannies, and fed with honey from the rock that is Christ.

Psalm 82

A crime that shakes earth's foundations

How are governments to be judged? How do you assess the performance of rulers? Various tests could be applied. Have they reduced the national debt? Has the Stock Exchange recorded better share values? Are exports balancing imports? Have they cut red tape? Have they won a war or established a peace? Have they reduced crime? Have they improved hospitals, schools and railways? There could be many such tests of good government, some of them complicated to apply.

In the short Psalm 82 God himself judges rulers, and his yardstick is remarkably simple. His report is terse. His conclusion is drastic. God addresses the rulers in question and assesses them as follows:

> How long will you govern unjustly,
> and show favour to the wicked?

> You were to rule for the weak and orphan,
> defend the right of the humble and needy,

> rescue the weak and poor,
> deliver them from the hand of the wicked.

> They have no knowledge or wisdom;
> they go about in darkness, while earth's foundations shake.

Now, in some nations today, politicians are tempted not to be too concerned for the poor and precarious folk who might have little effect on elections. Even if these people vote, they are easily swayed by unscrupulous propaganda. So their needs are little regarded. But God's speech in the psalm expresses a different view. Because the exploiters are given favours and the weak left in their power, he says, the very foundations of the world are shaking.

Who are the rulers that God is addressing, and where does his grand assize take place? Well, it is a visionary scene. The singer is a kind of prophet. He will have been pondering the evil conduct of the nations, and wondering what God will do about it. And now an answer has come to him in the form of a vision. He sees God standing in an assembly in heaven, a gathering of all his servants, including angels with charge of nations. It is these heavenly powers that he finds guilty of favouring the wicked and not protecting the poor. No doubt human rulers on earth are guilty too, but for our psalmist the evil stretches beyond human greed and cruelty. He supposes the just God must have delegated rule to lesser beings in heaven, who are now found to have failed in their duty. God accuses, then condemns them. They are to fall and die, as would any doomed tyrant on earth. Such is the psalmist's vision, and he responds with a short but fervent prayer:

> Arise, O God, and govern the earth,
> for you shall take all nations as your possession.

Thus he beseeches the Lord to grasp all the nations in his own hand, to be directly the 'Lord of every nation', and so establish the order of his perfect rule. It is a prayer like that of Jesus – 'Thy kingdom come, thy will be done.'

We may well feel that the thought-world of the psalmist differs from ours. Divine assemblies and angel-princes over nations probably do not bulk large in our faith, though connecting with visions in the New Testament's Book of Revelation.

Even so, the psalm declares something that will always be of vital importance. For it declares that injustice and exploitation are not ignored by the sovereign Creator. They are abominable to him. He will certainly rectify all that is amiss. His infinite power and wisdom are committed to the cause of kindness, where each cherishes the weaker creatures in their power. The widow and the orphan, the poor and the alien, and all the vulnerable ones they represent, these will in God's appointed hour be exalted and their oppressors thrown down. No more than the psalmist can we satisfactorily explain present injustices, yet we can follow his visionary conviction that God will secure the triumph of right and love. And we follow the psalmist also in praying that God should soon take possession of all hearts and govern a universe perfect in peace and good will. It is our fervent prayer, and, with Christ, our daily prayer.

Lord, move those in authority to pity and tenderness for the weak and defenceless.

*I myself have power. For you, O God, have given me power to show kindness
and extend the hand of care and compassion. Help me to beware of com-
plicity in some cruel oppression. Guard me from ignoring the cries of any
of your creatures in my field of action or influence.*
*Raise up your power and come among us, and with great might save all that
are cruelly treated.*
*From the psalmist's vision may we gain encouragement in the struggle against
oppression. May we see that your decision has gone out against the ruthless, and that you will surely found your kingdom of compassionate love
between nations and individuals and all beings that you have made.*

Psalm 83

Powerful prayer against evil

Imagine you are riding your horse near the Syrian border. The wind is
rising. Suddenly, with rushing sound, thousands of round objects come
rolling and bounding across your path. Your horse rears and shies. A
dangerous moment!

But what are these round objects? They come from large wild plants of
the thistle family, growing in abundance in the wilderness. After flowering,
the big heads of the plant fold, dry up and break off – light, tufty wheels
that dart along, chased by the wind.

Calming your horse, you resume your journey. But alas, a worse fright
befalls you. For as your path ascends a scrubby hillside, you hear a distant
crackling and smell smoke. You know you must ride for your life. The
many months of summer drought have made the thorns and scrub like
tinder, and now a fire is racing madly before the tempestuous autumn
wind.

Scenes such as we have imagined are in the mind of the psalmist of
Psalm 83. He draws on them to sharpen his prayer against enemies that are
conspiring against his country. May God drive them away as the wind
drives the thistle-wheels or the forest flames: 'O my God,' he cries,

> O my God, make them like rolling thistle-balls,
> like chaff before the wind.

As fire that blazes through the forest,
as flame that devours the mountains,

so drive them with your tempest,
and rout them with your storm.

The psalm is unusual in giving particulars of the threat to the nation. Ten peoples are named as having formed a coalition to wipe out the Israelite kingdom. The league of enemies includes neighbours on the north and south, the east and west, and yet others behind them – a wide ring of hostility. The moving force behind the coalition is the plan of the great world power of the time, Assyria (modern Iraq). It suits Assyria for the moment to use its allies and satellites to spread the cost of the proposed war. The diplomatic journeys as the coalition takes shape are no secret, being intended to frighten the Israelites.

So in Jerusalem the worshippers call upon their God, as the leader raises this urgent prayer:

O God, do not be still;
do not be silent or at rest, O God.

For see, your enemies make tumult,
and those who hate you lift their heads.

Against your people they plan with cunning;
they scheme together against your treasured ones.

Come, they say, let us finish them as a nation,
that the name of Israel be remembered no more.

As the prayer against the encircling danger continues, it gathers force with use of comparisons, and first, historical ones: may God overthrow the foe as he did in the nation's early days, when he routed mighty kings and the great host of invaders from the desert. And then come comparisons from nature: let the conspirators flee, as when the storm wind drives the thistle-heads or the forest flames – 'so drive them with your tempest and rout them with your storm'.

Such forceful prayers with vivid comparisons belonged to a traditional way of praying to repulse enemies. We are probably used to milder prayers. But it may be right to pray with all the force of our souls when we encounter great wickedness. Against those who devise evil and press others to share in it, encircling and destroying God's 'treasured ones', against such a coalition of evil we may well pray for the Holy Spirit to storm upon them and drive them back.

But the psalm itself also introduces a positive note: in defeat and humiliation may the enemy come to repentance and to a knowledge of God's glory. Thus:

> Fill their faces with shame,
> that they may seek your name, O LORD . . .

> And they shall know that you, whose name is the LORD,
> are alone the Most High over all the earth.

This positive note in the psalm's prayer encourages us to work through to a positive meaning also in those images for the rout of the enemy. For after all, the rolling thistle-heads are not dead remnants being swept to annihilation. They are clusters of seeds, from which can spring new and abundant life. Similarly, the forest fire is not all a tale of destruction. Through the flames, thorns and strangling growth are cleared. Space and light are restored to plants that were being choked. Thus the psalm can lead us to pray strongly that the tempest of the Spirit may drive the evildoers from their purposes, but we ask that in the end the Spirit-storm may prepare the way for their new life pleasing to God.

The New Testament specially encourages such a prayer, for it connects the images of rushing wind and fire with repentance and new life. Matthew and Luke report John the Baptist as announcing that one will come after him who will baptize with the Holy Spirit and with fire. John is here pointing to the saving work of Christ which will lead the penitent from darkness to light, from death to new life. So we may well take up the psalm to pray against evil, and still ask that the evildoers may with ourselves be swept by the wind and fire of the Spirit into Christ's kingdom, to find new life in his peace and love.

O God, your enemies make tumult and scheme together against your treasured ones. Do not be still. Do not be silent or at rest, O God.

Make them like thistle-wheels before the wind. As fire that blazes through the forest, so drive them with your tempest.

Upon the corrupters and the harmers bring the wind and fire of the Holy Spirit, to baptize them from the death of sin to the life of Christ.

Psalm 84

The swallow that nested near God

It is a heart-warming thing to win the trust of wild creatures. As Simon's cat grew older and more sedate, he felt able to encourage the birds in his garden. He soon got to know the regulars, from the small wrens, tits and robins to the neat collared doves, plump wood pigeons and majestic ravens, and he gave them all names. The most trusting was Thora, a song thrush. She had introduced herself in cold weather, and despite being often chased by the blackbirds, she soon established a routine. She would signal at the kitchen window and Simon would go out with currants, which she would take from his hand. More cautious were the ravens, which usually kept to the lofty trees. But their distinctive cries made them easy to keep track of, and from the first break of dawn. It was always a thrill if they ventured to come down on the small space of grass.

The ways of birds are observed and admired in several parts of the Bible. The note of trust and contentment sounds in a psalm well known to choristers, Psalm 84. The familiar words of the anthem from the psalm run: 'Yea, the sparrow hath found her an house, and the swallow a nest where she may lay her young: even thy altars, O LORD of hosts, my King and my God.' Beautiful – yet it may be that the point of this description of birds is often missed. The singer is expressing the feelings of pilgrims who have come to Jerusalem for the great annual festival. When still far from the temple, they hungered for that nearness to God and thirsted for the living water of his presence: 'My soul longed and fainted for the courts of the LORD; my heart and my flesh cried out for the living God.' But now, the singer continues, the bird has found her home. The bird is their soul. Just as the swallow nests in peace and contentment in the temple walls, so the pilgrim's soul has found her true home near to the altars of God. The singer expresses this joy of nearness to the living God on behalf of all the pilgrims as he sings:

> How lovely is your dwelling,
> almighty LORD of Hosts!

> My soul longed and fainted for the courts of the LORD;
> my heart and my flesh cried out for the living God.

216

But now the bird has found her home,
    the swallow her nest,
where she may lay her young near your altars,
    Lord of Hosts, my King and my God.

Happy are those who dwell in your house,
    for they are ever praising you.

'Those who dwell in your house' – here the singer thinks of the priests and other temple staff who can stay constantly in that place of blessing. But then he goes on to describe the special blessing of the pilgrims, those who have had to travel to Jerusalem and can only stay a few days. While they were still planning, then beginning their journey, God's grace was already touching them and strengthening them, because of their purpose. And as they passed through parched places, their faithful footsteps brought promise of good rains and growth. All this is captured in the psalm:

Happy those whose strength comes from you,
    for the ascent to your house is in their heart.

Passing through the driest valley,
    they make it a place of springs,
and the autumn rain will cover it with blessings.

They will go from strength to strength,
    until they see the God of Gods in Zion.

But now the singer has an earnest request to make of God. It is perhaps the main point in the psalm. He asks for blessing on the king, the shepherd and protector given by God. The belief was that through this ruler the blessing would pass to all the community. So the prayer is made thus:

Lord God of Hosts, hear my prayer;
    give heed, O God of Jacob.

Look with favour on our shield, O God;
    regard the face of your Anointed.

Then the singer supports his prayer and concludes his psalm with further praise. He is thankful again for the place of meeting with God, the Lord who gives his worshippers light and life:

Better indeed a day in your courts,
    than any thousand I could choose.

Better to touch but the threshold of the house of my God,
than to abide in the tents of wickedness.

For the LORD is both sun and shield,
   giving grace and glory;
the LORD will not withhold good
   from those who walk in truth.

Almighty LORD of Hosts,
happy the one who trusts in you.

It is a well-loved psalm and not difficult to connect with our own experience of God. In the first place, the psalm leads us in wonder at the gift of communion with the Creator and thankfulness for the place of that communion. How lovely the place and time of finding him afresh in worship! We find him as our sun and shield, the Saviour who will not withhold good as we trust him with all our heart.

And then the psalm helps us to see our life on earth as a pilgrimage, a journey to the house of God, a journey home. At the outset of the life-journey, that goal seems far, far away. One might easily take no thought for it or lose the sense of it. But what a blessing there is for those who keep that goal in mind and heart, going along life's path with the aim of travelling ever closer to God! At once God begins to strengthen their spirit, and all along their way he takes them 'from strength to strength' as they grow in the riches of his grace. It is not an easy path. Much of it is through hard, dry country, seemingly fruitless. But for the places where they tread, the water of life is promised, good things of the Lord are prepared. These pilgrims carry blessing on their way, God's touch of life. In his own time he will reap a harvest there. And when they reach their goal, what happiness! The last ascent is made. The soul finds her home by the altars of God. The Lord is found and known in the fullness of his grace and beauty, the Lord our sun and shield, who withholds none of his goodness from the pilgrim who has truly longed for him.

The psalm has one more link to our own experience. For when the singer prays God to regard the face of his Anointed, he foreshadows our reliance on Christ. Jesus is now our king and shepherd, our shield against all evil. All our prayer is in his name. May God look on us as found in him. May the love of the Father for the Son be upon us also, as we are joined to Christ.

This concluding thought indeed embraces all that the psalm has suggested to us. For it is through Christ that we gain the joy of communion with God. And it is through Christ that we make the pilgrimage – through him day by day we tread the hard journey of life, in deepening grace, in rising hope. Through Christ we come into the nearness of the almighty God and find with full contentment our eternal home.

How lovely is your dwelling, O Lord of Hosts! How good to dwell with you, our sun and shield!

But now, Lord, the way of my pilgrimage is long. I pass through desert places. My heart and my flesh cry out for you. Hear my prayer and help me, for the sake of your Anointed, Jesus Christ.

Give me strength day by day. Keep my heart set upon the ascent to your house.

May I discern your messages in the ways of birds and in the changing skies. On the deserts where my feet have trodden give sweet rain and the gathering of a harvest for you.

O Lord of Hosts, my King and my God, grant me the happiness of trusting in you.

Psalm 85

The messenger of hope

Winter had been long and bleak. The ground was hard and dead, the skies shrouded in mist and cloud. But at last the season turned. There came a day when the sun shone warmly. Light showers fell briefly to clear the air and wash the earth. Birds tried out their new songs. Aconites, snowdrops and fresh grass livened the feet of the trees. You sensed a springing in the earth, responding to the kindness of the skies.

People in Bible times also felt there could be an answering of one part of nature to another. They sensed a fruitful communion of earth, skies and growing things. They saw it as begun by the word of God, sending out his powers of right order and faithful love – his mercy and truth.

Prophets pictured such a harmonious communion when they brought messages of hope during hard times. So spoke Hosea (2.21–22), and so sang the prophetic voice in Psalm 85. This psalm singer is especially poetical. He sees the Creator's powers embodied in angels, who look to each other and run to embrace and kiss each other. In effect, his vision is a promise of harmony in nature, a time when God will bless.

But the psalm has begun as a prayer from a desperate situation. There have been years of drought and famine. The singer pleads with God by recollecting how in times gone by he transformed such evil situations:

> LORD, you once showed favour to your land,
> and restored the life of Jacob.
>
> You forgave the offence of your people,
> and covered all their sins.
>
> You took away all your indignation,
> and turned back from the heat of your wrath.

And so the prayer rises that God would grant such a transformation now, bringing new life and joy to the suffering earth and famished people:

> Restore us again, O God of our salvation,
> and let your anger cease from us.
>
> Will you for ever be angry with us,
> will you stretch out your wrath for evermore?
>
> Will you not turn again and revive us,
> that your people may rejoice in you?
>
> Show us your faithful love, O LORD,
> and give us your salvation.

After this earnest plea, we imagine, a pause ensued – a time of listening. Then the singer reports the Lord's response. It is a message of *shalom*; all will be right. This is how the singer reports it:

> I will hear what the LORD God speaks:
>   truly, he speaks peace (*shalom*)
> for his people, the folk of his covenant –
>   only let them not turn back to folly.
>
> Even now his salvation is near to those who fear him,
>   that glory may dwell in our land.

And the singer recounts a vision that filled out the message. The grace of the Lord appeared in angelic forms of love, faithfulness and right order. These angelic figures are seen in happy communion. They hasten to embrace and kiss. They respond to each other from heaven and from earth. They make the way ready for the coming of the Lord to save and bless:

Love and truth have met together;
right and peace have kissed each other.

Truth springs up from the earth,
and right looks down from heaven.

The LORD shall indeed give blessing,
and our land shall give her produce.

Right goes on before him,
and prepares the way for his steps.

Yes, a poetic vision indeed. But is it one we could share today? We would probably not see the light of hope in just that form. Yet still, thank God, we have people who in very dark days can convey a similar hope. They radiate it in their words and, even more significantly, in their conduct and in their very being. These are true saints of God. In times of pain and hardship they can speak and live as though all that matters is love and faithfulness, truth and goodness. Even now in a suffering world, in a corrupt world, they know – though not knowing it in so many words – they know that truth will spring up from the earth and right look down from heaven, love and peace will kiss each other, and glory dwell in our earth. They perceive the world as suffused with the goodness of God. Beyond the darkness they see his light. As mothers, brothers, nurses, teachers, salesmen, engineers – in many walks of life – they already mediate the power of his love in their hope and faith. They are with the angels that prepare the way for his steps, as he comes to save and restore.

And yet this is a calling for all who love the Lord. In the hard times, we are to pray from the depths, holding up to God the sufferings of the world with faith that recalls his former deeds of salvation. And we are to be with those who listen for what the Lord God will speak. We are to be ready to carry his word on our lips and in our lives. We are the ones called to embody his *shalom*, his promise to make all right.

Through Christ, the psalmist's vision will fill our hearts with the light of hope. In our Lord Jesus we see already the embracing of love and truth, we see the glory of God on earth and the healing for all things. Here, in Jesus, is the bright hope which is our witness and our life.

Lord, the wonder of your salvation is told in the Gospel. The times of your healing and forgiveness are remembered in praise.
Restore us again, O God of our salvation. Turn again and revive us. Show us your faithful love that your people may rejoice in you.

I hear what you answer. I hear you speak peace. Sustain me with hope, that I
may ever see in Christ the coming of your love and truth, the kiss of earth
and heaven, your glory in our land.
May I ever be a messenger of your peace.

Psalm 86
A very great gift to ask for

It's not so common to see people knitting as it used to be. Once upon a time there were many formidable female knitters. They filled every moment possible with the snip and click of their knitting needles. They ventured on intricate designs and shapes, inspired by all the women's magazines. There were also a few men who were good at the art. One became a celebrity on television and a leader of fashion, famed for his use of colour. Another was a bishop, who knitted his way through many a long meeting of a church synod.

Well, to knit is to weave together, to unite. The word is used memorably in Psalm 86 in the translation of the old Book of Common Prayer, verse 11: 'Teach me thy way, O LORD, and I will walk in thy truth; O knit my heart unto thee, that I may fear thy name.' 'Knit my heart unto thee' – that is beautiful, but a plainer translation gives: 'Unify my heart to fear your name.'

It's a prayer to be made single-minded and wholehearted towards God. There are so many cares, so many interests, so many desires, so many fears that divide and diminish our attention. O for a single mind, a heart composed, to be ever awake to the Lord! But we need not just sigh for it. The psalm leads us to *pray* for it, a prayer that will surely be answered:

Teach me, LORD, your way, that I may walk in your truth;
compose my heart to fear your name.

With such words we ask that the Lord himself will act to unify, to knit together our hearts, that we may love and attend to him constantly and sincerely. So we will be taught by him and our steps will find and follow the best way, the way of his faithful care.

Now, in the psalm, this prayer to be made whole towards God is not made from a tranquil place and time. Indeed, the singer tells of being 'in the lowest pit' and of facing 'the horde of the terrible'. It is in such a time of distress that he is calling to the Lord in simple and familiar words:

> Have pity on me, Lord,
> for all day long I call to you.
>
> Gladden the soul of your servant,
> for to you, Lord, I lift up my soul.
>
> For you, Lord, are good and forgiving,
> abounding in faithful love to all who call out to you . . .
>
> In the day of my distress I call to you,
> for you will answer me.

Then the singer supports his prayer with thoughts of the greatness of this saviour God:

> For you are great and do wonderful things;
> yes, you alone are God.

It is at this point that prayer is made for the heart knit together, the heart composed to fear God and walk in his truth. The singer might have just promised a wholehearted devotion. But instead, in humility, he prays God to teach him and mould him so. The promise is meant all the same. Yes, if God will enable him, he will indeed live wholly for the Lord. If he is saved, he will always testify to it:

> I will thank you with all my heart, O LORD my God,
> and glorify your name for ever,
>
> that your love is great upon me,
> and that you have delivered me from the lowest pit.

Our singer ends by asking that the Lord may give a sign of his favour, a sign that will make the enemies ashamed of their hostility. We can well understand this. In our own times of distress, how glad we are to see some token of God's love, some assurance that he will not forsake us. Such a sign may come in some circumstance, something said or done. But always we can be comforted by the supreme sign, the sign of the cross. It tells us plainly that the Lord is with us in the lowest pit of suffering. It assures us that the Lord will raise us again, raise us to live and rejoice in the abundance of his faithful love.

Lord, hear my prayer and have pity on me. Gladden me again, for to you I lift up my soul.

You are good and forgiving, plenteous in faithful love to all who call out to you.

Teach me your way, that I may walk in the strength of your love. Knit my heart into one consciousness of you, the only God, the faithful, the compassionate.

Give me a sign to strengthen me. Tell me again that your love is strong upon me, and you will deliver me from the lowest pit.

Psalm 87
A reality beyond all imagining

Among the beautiful old properties around London you may see, in Chiswick, an elegant Georgian residence called Syon House. It is set in spacious grounds, with ample lawns, gardens and woods. You can readily picture there the life of an aristocratic family in the eighteenth century.

But how much more the imagination perceives when history and archaeology get to work! Vast and awe-inspiring buildings then rise high above the Georgian house, and the whole site pulsates with the life of a large medieval community.

The immense reality which had once been visible began to yield its secrets suddenly, when a well-equipped team of archaeologists moved in for three days of televised exploration. Not far beneath the lawns were quickly found the bases of pillars and walls. Their spacing pointed to a monastic church on the grandest scale. Nearby, the team uncovered evidence of other buildings that would be needed for a large organization of nuns and monks. Here, in short, had stood a magnificent abbey of the order of St Bridget, built through the pious patronage of King Henry VI – only to be destroyed in the sixteenth century by Henry VIII. The splendour of the church can be envisaged by comparison with other works of Henry VI, such as the great chapels of King's College, Cambridge, and of Eton College.

If you meditated on the new discoveries, you could look afresh at Syon House and its lawns, and in the mind's eye see the medieval marvels towering above it. You might even hear the chanting of psalms and see the ordered life of a multitude of robed figures at work and at worship.

One of the psalms they might be singing is in fact all about Syon (or, as usually spelt, Zion). It is Psalm 87, only seven verses long, but with a mighty theme. For the ancient people, Zion was the temple, holy hill and city of Jerusalem. For Christians it links with the Church. But whether we see Zion as the holy city or as the Church, the psalm shows us an immense meaning that towers above and beyond what we have first seen.

The greater vision is given us in few words. The singer first tells of the Lord's supreme love for Zion, and how he built her on 'the holy mountains' – divine heights that reach into heaven:

> On the holy mountains is the city he founded;
> the LORD loves the gates of Zion above all the dwellings of Jacob.

The singer goes on to call Zion 'the city of God'. He has a word of God to deliver, a word about her destiny. It's a word heavy with meaning and promise. God has spoken and said:

> I enrol Egypt and Babylon as those who know me;
> Philistia and Tyre with Ethiopia, each as born there.

Then the singer, like a prophet, draws out the meaning of the word and the vision:

> Yes, of Zion it shall be said, Each one was born in her,
> whom the Most High has established.
>
> The LORD shall record, as he writes up the peoples,
> each one as born there.

And what a vision this is! The Lord is seen writing up his register of those who know him, his book of life. Recording where they were born, he's writing down whole peoples as natives of Zion, born in her – whole peoples that were considered foreigners, and even enemies of Jerusalem. Finally, all these peoples are seen gathering to worship in Zion, singing and dancing God's praise together. They testify that they have found new life in this holy Zion, as though in Paradise:

> And as they dance, they shall sing:
> All my fresh springs are in you.

We are left wondering. How could this ancient singer have been able to see beyond the little institutions of his day, beyond the human failings and the bitter enmities – see beyond to such a vision of reconciliation and universal love? It must be that he belonged to a tradition inspired by communion with God as Creator. This was the Creator in whose hands the world ever remains. This was the God who would achieve his purpose of a universe perfect in beauty and love.

The singer relates that God's mighty creative word has been spoken. The Christian joy is that this Word became flesh in Jesus, and he has gathered us as the first fruits of his kingdom. When we look with the natural eye at the Church, we may not readily see her greatness. But the eye of faith sees a mighty meaning towering up to heaven. It sees the Church as she is destined to be. She is the City of God in all the beauty of divine love binding all creatures. None is counted foreign, none an enemy. She is a garden of life nourished by springs of salvation. The multitudes who live in her are glad indeed of their new life in this Zion, this new world, and as they dance they sing to her: 'All my fresh springs are in you.' God help us so to see his Church today, and to be filled with thankfulness and joy in her.

Lord, you have founded your City, your Zion, your Church, on the holy mountains. You love her very gates. You have spoken that she shall be your kingdom of reconciliation and new life.

Readily I see the gathering of those with whom I worship. I see the building, I see the fellowship. It is good to be in this place, to join in prayer and praise, hear your word, receive the bread and wine of communion and the commission to witness.

But have I seen only a small part? Do I see the meaning that towers to the heavens? Let the Spirit show me outlines of Zion's mighty mysteries – the body of Christ, the kingdom of God, the new creation.

May I know that you will overcome all the world's enmities and gather all into your Church, to dance and sing by the fountains of your eternal life.

Psalm 88

Never parted from the hold of his hand

————◆◆————

There is a beautiful story about Jesus and a twelve-year-old girl – the daughter of Jairus. She was at the point of death. Jesus was called to her, but was delayed on the way by another needy person. When at last he arrived, the girl was being mourned as dead. People were beside themselves, and with the wailing crowd (as Matthew tells us) were professional flute-players – an old custom in mourning for the dead. Jesus had them all leave, and he went in where the girl lay. He took her hand and spoke to her. In Mark's Gospel there is a precious recollection of the actual words, still in the Aramaic language: *Talitha cumi*, 'Little girl, arise'. And so it was. The girl got up and was able to walk. Soon she was enjoying the meal which Jesus had told them to give her.

One of the interesting details in the story is that reference to flute-players. It seems that in the hour of grief their music could express something beyond words, a sorrow too great for words. We find something of the kind in Bach's *St Matthew Passion*. It has passages where the singer falls silent, and the depths of our Lord's suffering are contemplated in the wordless music of the instruments.

Now, it so happens that some psalms have a heading that asks for an accompaniment of flutes. One of these psalms is especially sorrowful – Psalm 88. One can well imagine interludes between the verses where flutes pierced depths and heights, seeking meaning in the pain, calling on the mercy of heaven. Such mourning flutes would well support the psalmist's prayer, as he feels he is already in the realm of the dead, and very near to being finally enclosed in it. Thus he prays:

> LORD, God of my salvation,
> I cry day and night towards you.
>
> May my prayer come into your presence;
> turn your ear towards my crying.
>
> For my soul is full of torments,
> and my life has come to the land of death.
>
> I am counted with those gone down into the pit;
> I am like one whose strength has departed.
>
> My couch is among the dead,
>   with the slain that dwell in the tomb,
> whom you remember no more,
>   and they are cut off from the help of your hand.
>
> You have set me in the lowest pit,
>   in a place of darkness in the mighty deeps.

Whatever the nature of the affliction – perhaps an extreme illness – the sufferer has, as it were, descended into the land of death, and will be gone for ever if the Lord does not act soon. We can understand the sufferer's sensations and emotions. But what are we to make of his thought that those finally gone into the land of death are cut off from God's hand, remembered by him no more? This was a sad perspective common in Old Testament times, though a more hopeful view was to develop. At all events, the psalm expresses something which is always valid – horror at the thought of being cut off from God. We ourselves can get an intuition of that horror when, through one cause or another, we have lost sight of God's reality and have felt cut off from our Creator, the source of all beauty, truth and love. Thanks be to God that we are not left in that cold and dismal place. Again and again, he seeks and saves us.

And even this dark psalm can help us in deeply troubled times. From beginning to end it is prayer, reaching for God even from so deep a valley. Each of its three parts utters the name of God in its first line, the name that God revealed so that his people could call upon him in every need – the name which our English Bibles give as 'Lord'. Yes, the psalm leads the cry of someone wholly turned to the Lord, claiming his promise of mercy and salvation: 'Lord, God of my salvation, I cry day and night towards you.'

From early times the Church heard in the psalm the voice of Christ on the cross, and so found an immense meaning. It became the plea of sufferers throughout all time, as gathered up by the Man of Sorrows who represents them all. He prays for every soul that is full of torments, for everyone imprisoned, for everyone forsaken, for the one whose strength has ebbed away, for the one who has fallen into the land without memory, for all that are swept over by the tides of fear and horror. Our Lord Jesus is beside all these sufferers. He shares their pain. He cries out for them.

And his prayer is heard. The victory over suffering and death is won. To the heart of the sufferer the Risen One speaks: 'Fear not. Though you walk in the valley of the shadow of death, yet fear no evil. For I am with you. Your hand also I take, and to you also I shall say, Little one, arise.'

Lord, God of my salvation, I cry to you day and night. My soul is full of torments, and my life has come to the land of death. I am imprisoned and cannot go free. My eyes fail through all my trouble. Loved ones and friends you have put far from me. My best companion is now the darkness.
I stretch out my hands to you, Lord, God of my salvation. In the watches of the night, hear the prayer beyond words. In the melodies that have no

words, hear the anguish. *In the hour of the cross, give faith in the Rising Again.*

Psalm 89

When darkness hides God's faithfulness

Some things are so moving that they can hardly be related in public without a catch in the throat and a pause to recover composure. Such stories are often to do with faithfulness. How some person, or indeed some animal, proved faithful can make a deeply touching tale. What makes it so moving may well be connected with conflict or hardship. The faithfulness shone out when all seemed lost. The setting of trouble and danger enhances the touching beauty of the faithful conduct.

There is a very popular hymn, 'Great is thy faithfulness'. But here (at least in the form generally in use) there is no cloud or shadow. All is bright from beginning to end. The hymn praises God for unvarying compassion, mercy and love – a faithfulness that is just great in guidance, forgiveness and countless blessings. The chorus summarizes the simple testimony: 'Great is thy faithfulness, Lord, unto me.'

That is all very positive, but more true to experience may be the changing colours of Psalm 89. This begins brightly enough:

> I will sing always of the loving deeds of the LORD;
> with my mouth I will make known your faithfulness
>   throughout all generations.

We might think that the psalm, like the hymn, is set to praise God's faithfulness without any note of tragedy. And so it seems for a long while – for no less than 37 verses. The singer tells of the pledge which the faithful God gave David and his descendants. He tells also of God's powerful work as Creator and ruler in the heavens. In all this mighty work God shows faithfulness:

> Right and justice are the foundation of your throne;
> faithful love and truth go before your face.

How happy then the people who worship this God! In the holy ceremonies they see his glory and the beauty of his face. So they are replenished and made able to 'walk' with him – to go about their daily lives with the light of his favour upon them:

> Happy the people who know the praises of your glory,
> and walk, O LORD, in the light of your face.
>
> With your name they rejoice all the day long,
> and are exalted by your goodness.
>
> From your beauty alone they have strength,
> and by your grace you lift up our horn.

After this general praise, the singer recounts in detail the commitment God made to David. He tells how God sent a prophetic message to the king, declaring how he had chosen him and anointed him with holy power. In that message he promised that David would overcome enemies and be supreme also over other kings, as God was supreme in heaven. God's love would ever support him, even as his life flowed down through his descendants:

> My faithfulness and love shall be with him;
> and through my name shall his horn be exalted.
>
> And I will set his hand upon the sea,
> yes, his right hand upon the rivers.
>
> He shall cry to me, You are my father,
> my God and the rock of my salvation.

The message had further declared that if David's descendants did not keep their side of the covenant, they would be punished; but still the commitment to David would stand:

> By my holiness I have sworn once for all,
> that I will not prove false to David.
>
> His seed shall endure for ever,
> and his throne as the sun before me.

And so the psalm finally arrives at its last section, which proves to be in sharpest contradiction to all that has gone before. We now realize that all the singer's praise of God's faithfulness and all the recounting of his promise to David have been leading up to a great cry from catastrophe, from a situation belying God's faithfulness and belying his promise. The singer can now be recognized as an heir of David, defeated and brought near to death, his throne hurled down to the dust, his country ruined. He remonstrates with God, 'You have spurned and rejected your Anointed, you have despised the covenant of your servant, you have defiled his crown in the dust.' And the lament of God's royal servant concludes:

> Where, LORD, are your loving deeds of old,
> which you pledged to David by your faithfulness?

> Remember, LORD, how your servant is mocked,
> and how I carry in my bosom all the many peoples,

> while your enemies mock, O LORD,
> while they mock the footsteps of your Anointed.

And so this great prayer of lament comes to an end. It has held up to God the traditional praise of his faithfulness, only to put beside it the terrible situation which contradicts it. Remarkably, the prayer asks nothing of the Lord except that he should 'remember', or we might say, take to heart. Surely, if God took to heart the frailty of his anointed king and the mockery of the enemies, he would intervene!

Just what had brought David's throne to this plight we cannot tell. But near to the time of Christ the psalm was taken to refer to the expected saviour, the Messiah. The enemies were said to be mocking him because his footsteps were so slow – he was so slow to come and restore David's glory.

Then the Church in her turn applied the psalm to Christ the Messiah. It was made a 'proper psalm' – appointed – for Christmas Day. With this use the good news is given that God *has* remembered. He has acted according to his faithful promise. In the child Jesus he brings the fulfilment of David's destiny, he brings the eternal kingdom. God has indeed kept faith.

But the psalm on Christmas Day also brings home to us a grave truth: just as the people of old knew a great humiliation and suffering, a heavy shadow of contradiction falling across God's promise, so it will be in the new era. We shall know and proclaim God's faithfulness in Christ, the Messiah, but crucifixion and resurrection still stand together. For the Church, Christ's body, the holy fellowship of the Spirit – for the Church there will still be humiliation, desolation, mockery. Through the time of suffering there will still have to be tenacious trust, such as was shown in the old Jewish tradition when they added that noble verse at the end of the psalm:

> Blessed be the LORD for ever,
> amen and amen.

With this verse the Lord is praised still in the time of suffering; indeed, trust in his faithfulness is affirmed twice over – 'amen and amen'. And on Christmas Day and every day Christians may take up this double amen. For the faithful light shining in Christ we bless the Lord. For the faithful light even when hidden in the thick darkness of suffering, again we bless the Lord. In the fifteenth century Thomas à Kempis put it well: 'Lord, if thou willest that I should be in the light, blessed be thou. If thou willest that I should be in darkness, again blessed be thou.' Yet we believe that through the faithfulness of our Father and the Lord Jesus Christ, the last word will be light.

I will sing always of the loving deeds of the Lord and with my mouth make known your faithfulness.
For the coming of the greater David, the Saviour Christ, and for his dying and rising which have opened for me the door of life, I will sing always of your faithfulness, O God.
In the days of trouble and in the shadow of death, I will sing of your faithfulness, O God, and bless your name, amen and amen.

Psalm 90

Morning glory

Sometimes kind friends give you plants they can spare from the abundance of their own gardens. It is evident from those gardens that the plants you've been given should turn out splendidly. But alas, you don't have the right place for them. The plants fail, and you hope your friend will not remember to enquire how they have fared.

There was a couple who were rather spasmodic gardeners and often found themselves in this predicament. In particular, they had failed to benefit from gifts of morning glory. But one year, taking the hint from a famous garden in Cornwall, they kept the plants in pots inside the open porch over the front door. The result was delightful. Every morning they would rush to open the front door and see how many flowers had opened.

There might be nearly thirty light blue trumpets, vibrant against the white walls and door. But as the day declined, so the flowers would droop and wither. Their time was over. And now the plants must gather strength to bring out a new generation for the morrow. The words of the psalm came to mind: 'In the morning they grow up like the grass, early they blossom and flourish; by evening they droop and wither away.'

That's a great psalm, Psalm 90. It's echoed in favourite hymns such as 'O God, our help in ages past'. Not that the psalm is dealing with morning-glory flowers. It's for a suffering people that the singer has come before God. He would move the Lord to take pity on such quickly passing creatures. If they live to be seventy or even eighty, it is all but a flicker in the eternity of God's reality:

> Before the mountains were born, or earth and world brought forth,
> from everlasting and for ever you are God.

And by contrast, how quickly God calls us back to the dust from which we come:

> You turn man back to dust
> and say, Return, O children of earth.
>
> A thousand years in your eyes are but as yesterday;
> they pass like a watch in the night.
>
> You carry them away as though but a dream.
> In the morning they grow up like the grass,
>
> early they blossom and flourish;
> by evening they droop and wither away.

And even the little time humans have is spent in folly, toil and trouble. If they would keep in mind how soon their time is over, they would not want to waste it – perhaps they would gain wisdom through reverence for God's reality:

> Who knows the power of your anger,
> and your wrath, as you should be feared?
>
> So teach us to number our days,
> that we may harvest a heart of wisdom.

And so the singer gathers up his prayer for his people. May this night of suffering be followed by a morning bright with God's faithful love.

Through the forgiveness of God, through his pitying and faithful heart, may these short lives yet be filled with joy, beauty and fruitful work:

> Turn us again, LORD. O how long?
> Have pity on your servants.
>
> Satisfy us in the morning with your faithful love,
> that we may sing and rejoice through all our days . . .
>
> Let your work be revealed to your servants,
> and your glory be over their children.
>
> May the beauty of the LORD our God be upon us;
> and prosper the work of our hands for us,
>   O prosper the work of our hands.

From those last words we gather that the work of their hands has *not* prospered. There will have been years of shortage, years of starvation. They admit their faults. They have gone away from God, their creator and provider. So all their hope is in his forgiveness, compassion and faithful love. Even so, we might think they ask little – only to have some good years to make up for the sorrowful years. Beyond that, they expect only to return to the dust.

How can Christians today link with such an outlook? We can certainly learn from those ancient worshippers to put all our hope of joy in God. In his compassion and faithfulness alone must we hope for happiness and lives fulfilled. And like the people of the psalm, we can 'harvest a heart of wisdom' only through recollecting our littleness before the immensity and infinity of God.

But it was not given to the people of the psalm to see through the darkness of death. Still, they entrusted to us the precious key – the faithful love of God. In due time, through the resurrection of Jesus, it opened the mystery. It was seen that the Faithful One will never abandon us. His love holds on to us and takes us up into the eternal life of Christ.

So, before every Easter morning, and in all our nights and darknesses, we can pray the prayer of our psalm with all the richness that was hidden within it: 'O satisfy us in the morning with your faithful love.' With this prayer we ask him to bring us through the present time of hardship to the eternal joy that welcomes us in Jesus Christ our Saviour. In him is the morning glory that will never die.

Lord, help us to realize every day that we pass briefly on earth before your eternal face. Before the mountains were born or the worlds brought forth,

from everlasting and for ever you are God; but our time on earth is like the
flower that passes in a day.
Through this humility let us harvest wisdom. May we centre all our desire
and all our trust in you.
May we awaken to the morning of your faithful love in Christ. In him, our
risen and eternal Lord, may we sing and rejoice for ever.

Psalm 91

In the shadow of the cross

All over the world, mothers have sung lullabies to their children to lull
them to sleep. But the cradle songs passed down from ancient societies
have a deep and earnest quality. They aim, not just to induce sleep, but to
call up spiritual power to protect the child. These songs are a kind of
charm – and the word 'charm' indeed comes from the Latin *carmen*, meaning 'a song'.

Sometimes the words of a charm were not sung, but written on something that might be fixed on a door or hung round the neck or wrist. They
were meant as a protection against harmful things thought to stalk about
in the night or to strike like an arrow by day – diseases, accidents, ill wishes.
From ancient temples in Egypt come such charms, written on small paper
scrolls made from the papyrus plant of the marshes. Pilgrims would buy
them at the temples and wear them to ward off danger. The words of the
charms were taken from the blessings spoken over the Egyptian kings, and
the common folk hoped the protection would work for them also.

There is a colourful psalm which at first glance looks a bit like those
paper charms of ancient Egypt – Psalm 91. It promises protection from the
fowler's trap and from the word that destroys. It wards off the terror of
the night and the arrow that flies in the day, the pestilence that walks in the
darkness and the plague that destroys at noon. It even promises that in
rough places you will not strike your foot against a stone, but be carried
clear as if borne on the hands of angels. Some scholars have even wondered whether it was like the case of those papyrus charms from Egypt –
words of protection originally spoken over the king being used in the
psalm to benefit ordinary worshippers.

But when we take the psalm as a whole, we see that it goes well beyond the bounds of a charm. The protection it speaks of is for one who lives extremely close to God Most High and utterly trusts in him. The promises, we might say, are for the one who is in the bosom of the Father, or as the opening words have it:

> You that sit in the shelter of the Most High,
> and nest in the shadow of the Almighty,
>
> saying to the LORD, My refuge and my strength,
> my God, in whom I put my trust –
>
> he shall deliver you from the fowler's trap
> and from the word that destroys.
>
> He will cover you with his pinions,
>   and you will shelter under his wings;
> his faithfulness will be your shield and rampart.

Clearly, these are no random assurances, offering luck such as people still try to grab for themselves when they have a mascot for a car or for a football team. The promises in the psalm respond to an extraordinary love and trust. God says at the end of the psalm:

> Because he loves me, I will deliver him;
> I will set him on high, because he knows my name.
>
> When he calls to me, I will answer him and be with him in danger;
> I will deliver and glorify him.
>
> With days unending I will satisfy him,
> and fill him with my salvation.

Originally the psalm will indeed have been meant for the king, 'the Lord's Anointed'. It was expressing an ideal, and nearer the time of Jesus was justifiably taken to speak of the hoped-for saviour king, the Messiah. For Jesus, however, the promises of the psalm were not to be taken shallowly. His work was not to unfold in easy triumph. The story of his temptation has the tempter using our psalm – why not prove yourself to all by jumping from the pinnacle of the temple? For God will command his angels to bear you up, so that you shall not strike your foot against a stone. Jesus knew that would be a false way, without real trust. He also knew that his way of closeness to the Father in genuine trust would be a way of vulnerability, and so of suffering to the death. All that loving protection pictured by the psalm was to be hidden in a terrible mystery, to shine forth only beyond the cross.

And what a challenge this is for us as followers of Christ! United to him, we can take the glowing words of the psalm to ourselves. With him we nestle in the shadow of the Almighty, who covers us with his pinions and shelters us under his wings. Through him we know the divine faithfulness that is our shield and rampart, warding off the arrows of terror and violence. We too are carried by angels over many a stony place. When we call on God, he is with us to deliver us.

But for us, too, these promises are not to be taken shallowly. Their truth will sometimes be hidden. Our love of God and our trust are proved in patience and in hope that reaches beyond the crosses of this world. It will often seem too hard a way for us. It is only possible in the grace of Christ. With him beside us, we too can stand against temptation, in the face of those enigmas and contradictions that hide the protecting love of God. His hand in ours, we can follow the lantern through the darkness. Then at last we too will be satisfied, filled with God's salvation.

Almighty Lord, you are my refuge and my strength, my God in whom I put my trust, my Saviour to whom I give my love.
Grant me the faith to know your love and care even in suffering. May I not fear the terrors of the night, the arrows of sickness, or the word of malice.
In all danger and adversity may I know that your protection overshadows me and will bring me to the fullness of your salvation in the Lord Jesus Christ.

Psalm 92

What is good?

We all want something good. But ideas of what is good vary widely. Many think it would be good to gain wealth and possessions – often called 'goods'. Some seek good in fitness and health, some in exotic travel. For some, all the good they want is bound up in the care and enjoyment of family. Others concentrate on the good of education or the acquisition of a skill. Some pursue the arts. Some find good the excitement of watching sports. And some think it good to award themselves 'a really good time' of heavy drinking or eating. Yes, there are many views of what is good.

One view is put forward with conviction by a psalm – Psalm 92, which begins, 'It is good to . . . '. How will it continue? Not likely with commendation of having great cars, clothes or luxury holidays. Not likely with garden make-overs, banquets or binges. No, the psalm commends as really good something we haven't even mentioned yet, and it does so like this:

> It is good to give thanks to the LORD,
> and to make music to your name, O God Most High,
>
> to tell of your love early in the morning
> and your faithfulness in the watches of the night,
>
> with the ten strings of the harp
> and the music that sounds from the lyre.

Yes, this psalm-singer has a firm conviction about what he has found good. He says it is good – a sweet and worthwhile thing – to thank the Lord. It will be a witness, a testimony to all who may hear. But above all, such thanksgiving is a communion with God. As we thank him, we move out of the self-enclosed prison we tend to live in. We break the bands of a human-centred world. Our thankfulness turns us to God and we realize afresh how great and merciful he is. We rejoice in him. No wonder it is good to give thanks to the Lord! In such thanks, we are opening ourselves to the bright, warm sun of his grace.

The singer describes a giving of thanks which is done in music. His chanted song is accompanied by harp and lyre. Now the great value put on music in the psalms is again connected with communion. Music is taken to be a God-given means of bearing thoughts to and from heaven. Our psalmist mentions especially the offering of his music in the watches of the night and early in the morning. He is thinking no doubt of music in the temple during vigils in the night and at sunrise. But we can relate his words to the deep experiences of life underlying the ceremonies of worship. Through the night of suffering it is good to sing of the faithfulness of God. And how good then to rejoice in the daybreak of salvation, to raise the music of thanksgiving when the love of God is revealed!

The singer knows well that this daybreak often seems a long time in coming. He knows that many people mistake the mystery of God's working and come to ignore his reality:

> How great are your works, O LORD!
> Your thoughts are very deep.

> A senseless person does not perceive,
> the fool does not consider.

It becomes clearer now that the singer is probably the king, and has been newly strengthened by God's spirit. Vividly he says:

> High as the horn of the wild ox
> you have lifted up my horn;
> I am anointed with flowing oil.

> My eye has seen the flight of my foes;
> my ears have heard the rout of the wicked who rose against me.

The thankful psalm now moves to an end by picturing further how God blesses his faithful servants. They are like noble trees, such as those well-tended in the courts of the temple:

> The just shall flourish as the palm tree,
> and shall grow mighty like a cedar in Lebanon.

> Well planted in the house of the LORD,
> they shall flourish in the courts of our God.

These servants of God have a strength that is all of grace, given in a life of communion with God. Even in old age, when natural strength ebbs low, they still bear fruit for him, especially as witnesses to him; as the psalm puts it:

> When old, they still bear fruit;
> they are healthy and full of life,

> to proclaim that the LORD is true,
> my Rock, in whom there is no wrong.

Yes, this is a psalm of strong images and brave confidence. Is it perhaps soaring above our own experience? In our times of 'night' and weakness, we may not see the positive words as suiting ourselves. Hardly for us the exhilaration of the wild ox raising his horn, or of the king freshly anointed and filled with the Spirit. Hardly for us the comparison with majestic and fruitful trees. Words not for us – especially if we suffer from bad health or the limitations of advancing years.

But here we may be mistaken. There is a great strength and fruitfulness which we can enter through the work of the Lord Jesus. He is the one above all that God has anointed – God's 'Messiah', meaning 'Anointed One'. The horn raised on high becomes a sign of his resurrection. He knew the mystery of God's work – work so often hidden. The majestic tree, ever fruitful, represents the power that goes out from his cross to scatter the enemies of good.

As we trust in him and live in him, he gives us the strength and joyful spirit to be his witnesses. May the music of our souls sound out our thanks. In all that we are, may we declare that he is true, our Rock in whom there is no wrong. Such a life of thanksgiving we shall indeed find good, good beyond compare.

Your thoughts, Lord, are very deep. Often we do not perceive your work. We lose faith that you are preparing our salvation.

Cause me to rejoice in your work. Help me to know your faithfulness in the hour of darkness. When morning breaks, may I be ready to tell of your faithful love. Through all my life may I make music of thankfulness.

As you raised high your Anointed, the Lord Jesus, so raise your servants who trust in him. In every phase of life, and to the end, may we bear fruit, as we witness that you are true God and faithful Saviour.

It is good to give you thanks, O Lord.

Psalm 93

King of all creation

From the radio came an unmistakable singing voice, deep and rich. The song, from years ago, was 'Ol' Man River'. Every word was clear, as Ol' Man River was described and his life compared with that of the slaves on the plantations along the banks. Not for him the heavy toil and the short life soon forgotten. He must know a lot, but don't say nothing. He just keeps rolling along.

The song had caught that ancient way of seeing nature in personal form. The great river was seen as a person, with an endearing name and an impressive personality. This way of thinking is sometimes reflected in the Psalms – valleys that laugh and sing, rivers that turn and flee, mountains that skip like lambs. It stands out in the short but powerful Psalm 93. Here again we meet great waters with names and personalities. They are rivers and wild waves of the sea that lift up roaring voices and rear in foaming pride. The singer's voice was probably not so rich and deep, but his thought is certainly profound. He is picturing the convulsions when the world was created, and he imagines a battle. He sees the wild waters as forces of chaos, trying to rule the world with desolation and horror. But God, the Creator, mastered them and made them serve his purpose of life and beauty. The battle is pictured in an old poetic style:

> The rivers lifted, O Lord,
>> then lifted the rivers their voice,
> the rivers lifted up their din.

> More than the thunders of their Majesties the Waters,
>> their Lordships the Breakers of the Sea,
> more glorious was the Lord on high.

So the victory was won. And with still fewer words the singer evokes the ordered, beautiful world resulting from God's mastery of chaos. The word of God, with strong commands, shapes the living order. From the majestic presence of God, from his heavenly temple, stream his rays of life and beauty. Yes, all is of that Word and holy Presence, so the singer just says:

> Your commands are very sure;
> holiness adorns your house, O Lord, for evermore.

And now, as the faithful worshippers are caught in the timeless moment, the beginning of the Creator's kingdom shines upon them. They are filled with hope for the new year of nature's growth. And beyond that grew a hope for the healing of history, when swords would become ploughshares and all creatures be at peace.

Yes, so many layers of meaning – the beginning, the present and the end! All has been caught in the opening words of the psalm, where the Creator appears victorious:

> The Lord is king!
>> He has robed himself in majesty;
> he has robed himself,
>> yes, girded himself with glory.

> So the world is established;
> it shall not be overthrown.

> Your throne was established of old;
> you are from everlasting.

A thrilling psalm indeed, for all its brevity. But with its ancient tones and pictures, how can it lead the thoughts and experience of people today?

Well, above all, it sets our mind on the Creator rather than on the world itself. We might have thought of the creation as something done long ago, or as a world now lying wholly in human hands and desires. But the psalm would bring us face to face with the Creator, radiant in supreme power and will for life and goodness. And still, in *our* worship, in moments of depth and intensity, he confronts us as he did the people of the psalm. He fills us also with faith and hope. He is the Creator who mastered chaos. He is more than equal to the upsurges of evil in our times. The corrupters and wreckers will not prevail. We can trust in his will and power to complete his kingdom.

Now, when Christ preached on earth, his message also centred on the reign of God, the Lord as king. And as disciples of Christ, we can readily hear his gospel echoing in the psalm. In Christ the creator-word became flesh. In him appears the new creation. In him we find the victory over the wild forces of destruction and death. In our faith and worship he appears before us, radiant in majesty, beauty and love. From his presence in world and Church the holy light streams out. He is King, he is Lord. His commands are sure. His holy power will not fail to make all things right.

O Christ, you have ascended. You are King, and the true world will not be overthrown.

Like angry waters, troubles rear and surge. Earth trembles with the din of arrogance and ill will. But you are supreme and we trust in your kingdom.

Keep us, we pray, in the radiance of your presence, attentive to your commands, and filled with the joy of your new creation.

Psalm 94

Quiet in days of trouble

———◆◆◆———

A national newspaper once ran a cartoon strip in which one of the characters was a clergyman, a somewhat amusing figure. When he made a remark, the 'balloon' proceeding from his lips sometimes contained only the chapter and verse of a Bible reference. Thousands of readers must have been getting down their Bibles more often than usual. In one episode of the serial, someone dropped a heavy object on the clergyman's foot. As he looked heavenwards, his balloon simply read: 'Psalms 94.1'. Diligent readers turned up the passage and found the words of the injured party: 'O LORD God to whom vengeance belongeth, thou God to whom vengeance belongeth, show thyself!'

An understandable reaction in the circumstances. And who knows, perhaps there was somewhere a reader who forgot the newspaper for a while and read on into the psalm. If so, the humorous moment would be succeeded by graver thoughts, easily matching the front pages of the newspaper, pages that featured atrocities committed by an evil government.

The psalm indeed throbs with the sufferings of the common people and calls urgently on God to come out of his apparent inactivity. Will he not heed the wrongs and make them rebound on the perpetrators?

> Rise up, judge of the earth;
> turn back the deeds of the proud upon themselves.
>
> How long shall the wicked, O LORD,
> how long shall the wicked triumph?
>
> How long shall they pour out words of arrogance,
> how long shall the evildoers boast?
>
> It is your people, LORD, they crush,
> and your heritage they afflict.

And the singer puts it sharply to God that this evil is an affront to his own rule of the world. Kings were supposed to take care of otherwise unprotected people, such as widows, orphans and resident aliens. So God, the king of all, must surely not overlook the present suffering. Surely he will not let the wicked think he does not see their cruelties!

The singer then goes on to remonstrate with the wrongdoers and to encourage the suffering people. God who made the ear, he says, surely can hear the cries of the oppressed. He who made the eye can see the wrongs that are done. Yes, he sees and knows, and he will not fail his people. The government of the world will turn again to justice.

With such thoughts the singer warns and comforts, and all the while the pressure is on God to vindicate these words of trust. As the prayer-song moves to its end, the trustful statements take on a personal warmth:

> If the LORD were not my help,
> my soul would soon dwell in the land of silence.

And if I say, My foothold is gone,
your faithful love, O LORD, shall hold me up.

In the multitude of cares within me,
your comfort will gladden my soul.

So the psalm ends in confidence that God will not support the throne of wickedness that condemns the innocent to death. The corrupt rulers will find their deeds rebound upon themselves. With that, the singer finishes his appeal to 'the God of vengeance'.

It should not be difficult for us to understand the passion that drives this prayer. Even when we enjoy peace and security, we are kept aware of other places beset by cruel injustice, pillage and slaughter. So the psalm can still lead the prayers of those who would call on God to avenge the wrong-doings and take the part of the oppressed. The desired retribution is to be the justice of *God*, not human revenge. The psalm even leaves open the possibility that the oppressor might come to a better mind. 'Consider,' the singer urges, 'consider, O foolish ones; when will you understand?' Their evil deeds will rebound on them, but who can say what the end will be in the hands of the eternal, infinite and merciful God? Meanwhile, the heart of the psalm's prayer remains as the always relevant call for the mighty work of God, which alone can turn the government of the nations to justice.

And in the multitude of our troubles, says the psalm to us, in all the agonies of today, God's comfort will gladden our soul. Even in our days of tragedy and pain, he can give us tranquillity and trust.

Here it is helpful to remember how the Church has heard the voice of Christ in such psalms of strong prayer. Christians have heard in them the echo of the intercessions Christ ever raises. In his earthly ministry he was passionately concerned at the abuse of the little ones and asked, 'Shall not God avenge?' (Luke 18.7–8). So in our psalm we may well hear something of his prayers for the vengeance that will make the cruelties rebound. His prayer will succeed. From Christ also we may ask and receive without delay the gift of a quiet heart, confident in his faithful love.

O God, how long shall the evil ones triumph? They pour out words of arro-gance. Their hearts are closed to your will. They ruin your heritage and crush those in their power. O Lord God of vengeance, blaze out in majesty! Give to the sufferers the comfort of your Spirit. May they have quietness of heart and confidence in your justice.

*Through the prayer of Christ we have faith. Through him we know that you
   will not fail your little ones or forsake your heritage.*
*O Jesus, you are my stronghold and the rock of my trust. Your faithful love will
   hold me up.*

Psalm 95
Today

---◆◆◆---

Night and day – how they shape our existence! How strange it would be
without this alternation, this letting go and taking up again of our consciousness, this constant measuring out and parcelling up of our time!
Admittedly, when night falls, the effect is not as decisive as it used to be
before the development of powerful artificial lighting. More activity continues through the night than used to be the case. But still the division of
existence into night and day remains a fact of incalculable importance.

One benefit immediately comes to mind – the opportunity of the new
day. The night brings cessation, stillness, a letting go of work and worries.
With the new day comes a fresh start. The challenges of the day can be
taken up with new resolve and new strength.

And often there is a new surge of hope. Could this be the day when a
lingering problem is solved? Could this be the day when a corner is turned
and a new vista opens before us? O that today we could find the right
opportunity and take it! 'O that today' – that is an echo of an oft-recited
psalm, Psalm 95 ('the Venite'). For this psalm the opportunity of the new
day is something of the utmost importance, something on which all our
happiness will depend. On this day we are to enter before the face of our
Creator, kneel before him and worship. And then comes the great 'O that
today':

> O that today you would hear his voice,
> and not harden your hearts.

When the psalm was first composed, this day of opportunity was a high
day in the annual festival. It was to pilgrims gathered from all over the land
that the singer called, inviting them to follow the great procession into the
temple court:

Come, let us sing out to the LORD;
let us acclaim the rock of our salvation.

Let us come before his face with thanksgiving;
let us acclaim him with psalms of praise . . .

Come, let us worship and bow down;
let us kneel before the LORD our maker.

For he is our God,
and we are the people of his pasture,
    the flock tended by his hand.

We imagine the pilgrim-worshippers now in orderly rows in the spacious court before the temple. After the excitement of the praises, they were to be still, heedful of the message God would speak through the prophet-singer. God says:

Do not harden your hearts as at Meribah ['Place of Dispute'],
on that day at Massah ['Place of Testing'] in the wilderness.

And the speech of God goes on to recall how the ancestors had hardened their hearts in the journey through the wilderness. They were not trusting God. Impatient in their desires, they were always ready to grumble. In closing God out of their hearts, they closed themselves out of the pleasant land God had prepared for them. And the singer comes to an abrupt end with the vow that God made: 'They shall not enter into my rest.'

A stern ending to God's message! The present worshippers must be careful not to harden their hearts, or they too, like the ancestors, will not be allowed into God's pleasant land, the happy life with him.

So we see that in the early use of the psalm that was a challenging moment in the yearly festival. 'This day' was a day of great opportunity before the face of God, a day of decision and life-or-death consequences. Then the Church, from early in Christian times, appointed the psalm for use every day – *every* day! So now Christians were called on every day to enter before God's face with thanksgiving. Every day we are to kneel before him, vividly aware of his presence, his awesome reality, our Creator, King and Shepherd. And it is always 'today' that we must hear his warning not to harden our hearts, lest we be shut out from his pleasant land and left in the wasteland of our own desires and discontents.

Let us then gladly accept the psalm's invitation. Let us take the opportunity of every new day to come before God's face with thanksgiving, and acknowledge that he is our God and we are the flock cared for by his hand.

Let our hearts be warm towards him, eager for his guidance, patient, trusting and thankful. So shall we this day hear his voice and enter into his rest.

Lord God, in your hands are the depths of the earth and the peaks of the mountains. The depths and heights of all existence are in your hand, in your good power.
This very day I come before your face with thanksgiving. I kneel before you, my maker and my shepherd-guide.
Speak, Lord, and enable me to hear, to receive deep in my soul your healing and guiding words. Let me be open to your counsel. May I trust in your provision. Guide me through the wilderness to enter into your rest, the land of life and delight in your presence.

Psalm 96

A new song

A publisher's guide to authors advised them to beware of using the words 'new' and 'recent'. The thought was that, with the passing of time, such words would become inappropriate. It was good advice, although an ancient college not far from this publisher was still managing very well with the name 'New College'. And the same publisher had for centuries done well from publishing a work called 'The New Testament'. It is noticeable, moreover, how popular the word 'new' remains in the marketing of all sorts of products. It's like a banner of promise and excitement.

In the field of music the appeal of the new has become less certain. For much of the twentieth century, new compositions were likely to be discordant and unmelodious, and they had to be slipped into concert programmes with something old to sugar the pill. But there had been a time when such as Bach and Haydn were expected to be for ever providing something new, and they did so, amid general excitement and delight. And even in the twentieth century, new music was sometimes warmly requested for great occasions, such as the royal coronations where new anthems and marches added much to the fresh joy of the ceremonies. For the new reign it seemed important to have a new song.

This must have been a longstanding conviction, for we find it already in Psalm 96. 'Sing to the Lord a new song,' cries the singer, '. . . proclaim among the nations, The Lord is now king!'

This proclamation of the Lord's new reign, along with its new song, takes us to the high point in the Old Testament's year of worship. The ceremonies at the temple stirred the hearts of a vast concourse of pilgrims. It all signified that the Lord had come with power. The psalm declares him glorious in his splendour and majesty, radiant in power and beauty. The 'new song' was a rapturous greeting of this new presence. It was also a message to all the world, that with his new reign had dawned the salvation of all creation. So the psalm begins:

> Sing to the LORD a new song;
> sing to the LORD, all the earth.
>
> Sing to the LORD, bless his name;
> tell the tidings of his salvation from day to day.
>
> Declare his glory among the nations,
> his marvellous deeds among all peoples.

The 'new song' declares that the Lord has shown himself to be far above all other powers:

> For great is the LORD and very glorious,
> terrible in majesty over all the gods.
>
> For the gods of the peoples are feeble,
> and it was the LORD who made the heavens.

Nowadays, of course, there are no longer national gods as the psalmist knew them – the official gods of surrounding nations. But we do have nations that in effect worship what they take to be the sources of their prosperity – economic, natural and cultural resources which give them wealth. The psalmist's message for today would be that while all these powers and resources may serve the Lord, he alone is God. He is supreme and is able to dispose of all as he wishes. He alone is to be worshipped.

> Give to the LORD, O clans of the peoples,
> give to the LORD the glory and the power,
>
> give to the LORD the glory of his name;
> take up your offerings and come into his courts.

> Bow down to the LORD in the beauty of his holiness;
> dance at his presence, all the earth.

When the singer says, 'Dance at his presence, all the earth', he thinks both of earth herself and all creatures that live on her. The Lord is the Creator, and his reign means his ordering and life-giving work for all that he has made. Not just for human beings, but for all creatures is this celebration of the reign or kingdom of God:

> Let the heavens be merry and earth rejoice,
> let the sea thunder and all that it holds,
>
> let the highland exult and all that is on it,
> the very trees of the forest sing out in joy
>
> before the LORD, for he has come;
> he has come to rule the earth.

But what is this new reign of God? How could it be new when the psalm was first sung, and new still when the psalm has been repeated down to the present day? Was this one of those unwise uses of the word 'new' which the publisher warned about?

Hardly so. For it seems that in biblical times there was at the height of worship an element of rapture, an experience freed from the ordinary bond of time. We may ourselves have had such a time-transcending experience even in daily life. There was, for example, the case of a person recently bereaved. He was listening to Beethoven's choral symphony on the radio. Towards the end, in the 'Ode to Joy', the music takes on a dancing rhythm. This listener began to see, in his mind's eye, many people ascending a mountain. They were emerging from swirling mist and nearing the summit. As they recognized each other in the clearer air, they were laughing and their step grew lighter. The listener understood that they were ascending the mountain of God and leaving behind the mists of death. The vision pulsated with the bounding rhythm of the music. The listener was quite transported into the scene, joining in the recognitions, living in it all with tears of joy.

Anyone who has had such an experience beyond time will appreciate the rapture of the pilgrims at Jerusalem's temple. The framework of worship throughout the year strongly governed their minds. There were no 'media' to distract them. When the great festival came round, they lived in its story wholeheartedly with tears and laughter.

Now, our psalm belonged to that great moment in the ceremonies when the cry went out that the Lord had come. He had come in glory to begin a reign of justice over all the world: 'Proclaim among the nations,' cries the singer, 'The LORD is king! He has come to rule the earth . . . in justice and . . . faithfulness.'

It was indeed a scene above time. It resounded with the music both of the first creation and of the great end when all should be perfected. The worshippers had ascended the sacred mountain to be in God's presence. And now they lived in the fresh joy of the world's creation, but also anticipated the richer joy of the fulfilment, when the sufferings and conflicts would be turned into God's peace.

But how can such a psalm relate to our worship today? In the Christian context the psalm is heard to proclaim the new reign of God through Christ – Christ the Alpha and Omega, the one at the beginning and end of all meaning. His good reign takes up the gladness and hope of the first creation. His reign is the fulfilment, the final perfection. And in Christian worship still we proclaim the great NOW of his kingdom. In the preaching and sacraments and in the movement of the holy seasons, the time of his suffering, rising and ascending comes new upon us, the time above time. The words of the psalm come to fullest meaning. The work of the Lord – the Lord himself – is present to us: 'He has come! Proclaim among the nations, The LORD is king! Let the heavens be merry and earth rejoice! Let the sea thunder and all that it holds. Let the highland exult and all that is in it, the very trees of the forest sing out in joy before the LORD, for he has come, he has come to rule the earth in justice and the peoples in his faithfulness.'

So, most eloquently, the psalm expresses for us the eternal truth that again and again is present to us in worship and colours our daily lives with its joyful assurance. Through this revelation of the Lord's new reign, we can bear the troubles of this age with courage and hope. They are passing and fading. Already we see his glory. His reign is begun and will soon be all in all.

As we hear your gospel anew, Lord, let us sing. Our souls shall sing to you in
*   thankfulness, wonder and praise. We shall sing because you are come. You*
*   are present in victory and faithfulness. Even now the new song can be*
*   heard, with the dance of the earth and the thunder of the sea, the chorus of*
*   all your creatures for your praise and glory.*
Glory to the Father who is terrible in majesty above all the gods of the
*   peoples. Glory to the Son who is ascended and reigns over all. Glory to*

the Spirit who is the presence and the beauty of holiness. Glory be to the one God, Creator and King for ever.

Psalm 97

Sowing the seeds of the morning

Early one April, the postman began to bring greetings for Easter. Most cards carried scenes of spring flowers, lambs, chicks and ducklings. One card, homemade, was rather different. It came from a hermit in North Wales and carried a photograph she had taken from the front door of her tumble-down cottage. Most of the lower half of the picture was just black, but peeping out above this darkness was the rim of the rising sun. This tip of brilliant gold was still confined within a band of luminous purple cloud. Above that was a small sea of pale blue sky with island clouds of gold-edged purple. At the top of the picture lingered another mass of darkness, but here you saw signs of a golden radiance pressing through from within. In short, the picture had caught that moment at dawn when the might of the sun is still mostly hidden, but every onlooker must be aware of the concealed fire which is so near to breaking through.

We may find a parable here for the vision of God sometimes described in the Bible. An example comes in Psalm 97, one of a series of psalms from the climax of the great festival in ancient Jerusalem. A vision has seized the worshippers – God come with glory to begin a new reign! But the glory is described as hidden:

> The LORD is king! Let earth rejoice,
> and the hosts of islands dance for joy.
>
> Cloud and thick darkness are all around him;
> right and justice are the foundation of his throne.

The singer goes on to tell of the divine fire and lightning, but this is his way of imagining how God routed his foes on the way to the present scene. In storm and fire, the Lord brought all the world's powers into subjection:

> Fire went before him,
> and burnt up his foes on every side.

His lightnings lit up the world;
earth trembled at the sight . . .

All who served idols were ashamed,
   all who sang the praises of mere nothings;
the gods themselves bowed low before him . . .

Truly, LORD, you are the Most High above all the earth;
   you are highly exalted over all the gods.

So now he is present to his people gathered before the temple. Though his fire and light are hidden in thick cloud, his nearness is strongly felt. How can the worshippers endure the awesome presence? The singer re-assures them of the Lord's love, his care for all who turn from evil:

The LORD loves those who hate evil;
he keeps the souls of his faithful ones,
   and delivers them from the hand of the wicked.

Light is sown for the one who is just,
and joy for the true of heart.

'Light is *sown*' – a surprising yet beautiful expression! Some ancient sources indeed have a different word, giving 'Light is *risen*'. But our Hebrew text can be accepted with its 'Light is sown'. The thought may be of that moment in the dawn when gleams of light are scattered from the central point to touch hilltops and clouds with flecks of gold. There was such a 'sowing' and scattering of morning light in our hermit's picture. But that picture, with its dark masses above and below, suggests a further meaning of the light that is 'sown'. For this light is first concealed before it comes out in all its beauty, just as seed is hidden in the dark of earth before it rises in bright green life and flowering.

And here again is a parable of the kingdom of God. The gospel pro-claims that the Lord is king. Victorious over evil, he has established the world of true life and goodness. Against that gospel weighs the continuing experience of violence, disease, evil and death – a heavy mass indeed that still hides the victor's full glory. But in Christ the sun has made its coming known. Assurance is given that the light of salvation has been sown, and the new life will be revealed in all its beauty and joy.

The ending of the psalm calls us to let the joy of God's revelation con-tinue to resound in a life of worship and prayer. 'Rejoice', it calls,

Rejoice, you right-hearted, in the LORD,
   and give thanks with the remembrance of his holy name.

'His holy name' – as it happens, the order to which the hermit in North Wales belongs is the Community of the Holy Name. In harmony with the psalm, this community prompts us to live in thanksgiving for the name of Jesus – for his presence and revelation. The holy name, after all, is at the heart of God's making himself known to us, a God who walks with us, ever responsive to our prayers. So let us indeed give thanks with our hermit friend, with her community, with all who ever have shared the psalm's faith and joy. With all these, let us give thanks for God's revelation in Jesus. Let us give thanks for the light that is sown, and for the glory that will at last break through all the clouds of sorrow.

Lord, help me to reject evil. Form in me a heart that is true and pleasing to you.

Grant that I may live in the gospel of your kingdom, knowing the glory of your salvation that is already rising through the dark clouds of this passing age.

May I live in thankfulness for the name of Jesus, speaking it in my heart in constant prayer and praise.

Psalm 98
The world that God so loved

Do you sometimes yearn to go back to a place you knew long ago? We may think of a hillside, a brook, a particular tree. How we would love to see and know them once more, to be a part of that beloved landscape once again! But not so often, if at all, do we think that place longs for us, misses us, would recognize us if we returned. Yet in the Bible there is sometimes an indication that a landscape or a place knows its inhabitants and feels for them. There's an example in the Book of Job (7.10): someone who dies and departs to the land of death, says Job, will never come again to his home on earth. The place where he lived will know him no more. It's as though that familiar place is bereaved. It misses him, even mourns him.

It's a thought that a modern priest-poet has taken up – John O'Donohue of Conamara, where Irish mountains look out to the Atlantic ocean. Is it possible, he asks, that a place loves those who live in it? Could your land feel your presence and be glad of your care for it? Has it waited long ages for the appreciation of your eyes, for your words, for your friendship?

How good it is when the sensitive souls of poets, artists and musicians lead us and encourage us in feelings of fellowship with earth, air, waters and all that lives in them! And how good it is to find that the Psalms – the sacred poetry and music of scripture – know well this sense of fellowship! They link it to the high moment of worship, when all that exists is seen as turned to the Creator in love and adoration.

In such a high moment of worship lives the singer of Psalm 98. How easily he passes from the instruments and voices of the human congregation to the voices of sea and mountains! All are one in this thankful praise of God:

> Acclaim the LORD, all the earth;
> break into singing and make music.
>
> Make melody with the lyre,
> with the lyre and the voice of song.
>
> With trumpets and the voice of the horn,
> sound praise before the LORD the King.
>
> Let the sea thunder and all that fills it,
> the round earth and all its creatures.
>
> Let the rivers clap their hands,
> the mountains also join the praise.

No doubt in this vast circle of praise the humans are doing their best with their little voices, instruments and dancing limbs. But what a voice rises from the deep waters, what clapping from the dashing waves, what dancing from the trees and grasses and all their host of creatures!

And all are seen as one congregation – one Church, we might say – which willingly responds to the call to praise their Creator. It is all a contrast to the feeling you get in some churches today, a feeling of being shut away from the good earth, the waters, the animals, as though Christ's salvation were only for humans. But in Cornwall, land of Celtic tradition, you will sometimes see a stone cross set on a hill, open to the elements and wild things. Round the head of the cross there may be a circle, suggestive of the sun and so of the light of the resurrection shining through the crucifixion. Such crosses marked places where Christians gathered for worship, before a church building could be raised. It would be a good place for the worshippers to sing our psalm, centring their faith on the salvation won in

Christ's death and resurrection, but readily embracing in that faith the earth with her rocks and green things, the sea quite close, the gulls and larks, and so many other kinds of God's creatures. Yes, by the ancient cross on the hill would be a good place to hear the reason the psalm gives for its call for universal praise – it is because the Lord the Saviour is present. He 'has come to rule the earth', to begin his reign of right and goodness, having won salvation from all harms and sorrows.

Actually, our psalm has had a special use in Christian services. A common pattern of worship has a reading from the Old Testament, and later a reading from the New Testament. Between the two readings the Magnificat has been sung – Mary's song of thanksgiving makes a bridge between the old covenant and the new. But sometimes, instead of the Magnificat, our psalm has been sung, and in that position between the two testaments its depth of meaning is revealed. Through the psalm's opening words now shines the marvel of the salvation won by Christ for his people and for all creation:

> Sing to the LORD a new song, for he has done marvellous things;
> his own right hand and his holy arm
>> have wrought salvation for him.

> The LORD has made known his salvation;
> before the eyes of the nations he has shown his justice.

> He has remembered his love and faithfulness to the house of Israel;
> all the ends of the earth have seen the salvation of our God.

The patterns of Christian services will vary with circumstances, but we can always hear the gospel resounding in such psalms. The one truth shines through the scriptures old and new, the truth that flows from God's ancient purpose and his eternal reality.

But what are we to make of the psalm's ending, its joy in the perfect reign of God? This last verse is giving the reason for the great call to praise: the Lord is present, 'he has come to rule the earth; he will rule the world with right and the peoples with his justice'. Still today, there has to be a lot of hope in such a statement. Sorrow and injustice still abound in the world. Yet even now there is a reality of the kingdom that we can rejoice in. Above all, there is the presence of Christ. He has come, and through the Holy Spirit is ever with us. We begin to know now that good order and beauty that abound in the presence of God.

If it were not so, how sad the world! How wretched if power and reality lay only in the hands of humans, with their addiction to greed and cruelty, deception and selfishness! But no, we believe the kingdom is the Lord's, and in Christ he has come and is present. Still he reigns in a mystery, a hiddenness. But to those who receive him he opens the beauties of his kingdom – his truth, his forgiveness, his love, his assurance of the triumph of good.

So yes, 'let the rivers clap their hands and the mountains also join the praise'. Let us live already in the universal circle of love and thankfulness to God. For in Christ he has come, he has come to rule the world. His justice and goodness, the enduring realities of his cosmic kingdom, are open before us, already sending their light through all our existence.

Lord Jesus, you have come and brought salvation, and the people of your
Church rejoice – but also the sea, the sky and earth and all that live in
them. For your salvation is for all creation. Your reign is the shining of your
beauty and goodness into every part of the living order.
May my heart join the melody of praise. May my soul rise in the thankful love
of the universe to you, divine Word through whom all has been created.
Let ocean thunder and rivers clap their hands. Let mountains and valleys
echo with thanksgiving. For Christ reigns in goodness and grace now and
for ever, in the unity of Father, Son and Holy Spirit. Amen and amen.

Psalm 99
Trembling before God

Looking back over the years, the old people in the congregation could see quite a change in the style of sermons. For one thing, the pulpit had been abandoned. Sermons were no longer spoken from on high, but from ground level. Then again, the preacher was provided with a microphone – fine when working well. But perhaps the main difference was a change from one-way to two-way traffic. There was an input from the congregation, as the preacher asked them their views. So it was no great surprise when, for a series of sermons on 'doubt', they were asked to write in about their religious doubts and difficulties. This idea proved almost too fertile. Several preachers were kept busy for months trying to answer the problems raised. One of the sermons had to address a clutch of difficulties raised about the Old Testament. There were specific questions, such as the old chestnut, 'Who did Adam's sons marry?' And then there were broader issues, such as, 'Why does God in the Old Testament seem so different from the New Testament's God of love?' This latter question had been posed by a gentle girl in the youth group, and the preacher wondered to herself if she was not typical of a generation brought up with so much stress on the kind and friendly side of God that they had no sense of awe in his presence, no place for fear and trembling. In her sermon she tried to show that the compassion and enduring love of God are well recognized in the Old Testament, but still with awe and dread before his holiness. The preacher felt she had not coped very well with this question.

Some weeks later she happened to be reading Psalm 99, and there in the space of a few verses she found vivid expression of what she had been groping to say. The psalm unfolds from the great proclamation: 'The Lord is king!' It is the moment in the annual festival when the ceremonies have symbolized the ascension of God in triumph to his throne. His presence shines out from his temple. His new reign will be a glorious blessing – but will include judgement and decisions of fateful consequences. It is a time for praise – yes, but also for trembling. So this is how the psalm begins:

> The Lord is king! The peoples tremble;
> he has taken his seat above the cherubim,
>   the earth is shaking.
>
> The Lord is great in Zion,
> and high above all peoples.
>
> They give praise to your name,
> for it is great and awesome. Holy is he!

'Holy is he' – three times this refrain will sound. As the people bow to the ground, the cry acknowledges that this Lord who is now present is the only true God – powerful, mysterious, exalted, beyond all compare. Then the psalm declares that he is the one who establishes right order, just rule; he loves and commands it. Through kings and priests he has set it in his people. At this time of new year he will renew it – but the worshippers may wonder in fear if there will have to be a purging judgement, a holy fire upon all their corruptions. Again they bow low before the footstool of the king of all creation, and again the cry is raised, 'Holy is he!'

But now the psalm introduces the thought of the mercy of God. For how could sinful mortals come before him, how could they live in his presence, except for his compassion and forgiveness? The thought is not put brashly. Rather there is quiet recollection of God's grace of old that responded to the prayers of the leaders he had raised up:

> Moses and Aaron, chief of his priests,
>   and Samuel, chief of those that call on his name,
> these would call to the LORD, and he would answer them.

> From the pillar of cloud he spoke to them;
>   they kept his testimonies and the statutes that he gave them.

> O LORD our God, you answered them;
>   a forgiving God you were to them, pardoning their offences.

Nothing is said here directly of the present worshippers and their hope of answered prayer, pity and forgiveness. In the awe of this moment, they cannot venture to ask directly, but only recall the ancient mercy. The prayer that it may be so again remains wordless. And so the psalm ends in further praise. For the third time they bow down and acknowledge that he alone is God, the heart of all truth and reality:

> Lift high the praise of the LORD our God;
>   bow low before his holy hill. Holy indeed is the LORD our God!

Yes, that is a great message that comes through to us from the Old Testament. Doubts and difficulties we may find in abundance as we read these ancient records and try to relate them to our world. But here is a word we always need to hear and receive: 'Holy is he!' In deepest reverence we must acknowledge him and bow low before him. Then we shall know the wonder that he, the Holy One, yet receives us in love. Beyond a Moses, Aaron and Samuel there has appeared the figure of Jesus, and as he makes intercession for us, we too may know the forgiving God who pardons our offences and renews our life before him. But the psalmist would have us remember the wonder of it, as we fall in praise before the throne of the almighty and eternal God – 'Holy is he!'

Almighty God, your kingdom has dawned upon us in your Son Jesus. In all the might and majesty of your revelation, we are yet given one strong to call upon your name and plead for our forgiveness.
Through him we give thanks for your pity and your pardon, and we ask that you will always keep us in the sense of your holy and eternal being, to live before you in awe and wonder all our days.
Glory to God, so great and merciful; the Father, Son and Holy Spirit, from everlasting to everlasting. Amen.

Psalm 100

The life that is dance

In a Cornish village the Sunday morning service proceeded at a steady pace. A long hymn from the nineteenth century was followed by another long one from the eighteenth century. To a city person it all seemed rather grave. But a bright shaft came through with the next hymn, Sidney Carter's 'Lord of the Dance'. Though the music was still rendered in subdued fashion, the words were vibrant. Creation was seen as the Lord's dance. His earthly ministry was seen as still his dancing. Even on that Friday when the skies turned black, the Lord yet danced. They cut him down, but he rose up high, he the dance that will never die. And always he calls us to dance, wherever we may be. In sorrowful times as in good times, he will lead us in the dance, he the eternal Lord of the Dance.

After the service, a few friends happened to be talking of this hymn. What was this call to dance? One woman, ever quick, suggested it was for children. But others made more considered suggestions. To live as though dancing, some thought, meant holding on to God's joy. It meant living for him with commitment of body and soul. It meant living with beauty, and in a measured harmony with God's world. You dance sometimes as an individual, and sometimes in a company. And always this our dance of life follows the lead of Jesus, the Lord of the Dance. It is part of the whole created order, which dances with movement of beauty and joy for God.

Then one of the friends noticed a connection with a favourite psalm, Psalm 100:

> Acclaim the LORD, all the earth;
> worship the LORD with dancing,
> come before him with shouts of joy.

It is the psalm known as 'the Jubilate', familiar as 'O be joyful in the Lord, all ye lands'. It has often been sung in church after the New Testament reading, a joyful response to the story of the Lord's work. It is indeed all about our response to his goodness. The dancing movement and cries of joy answer the revelation of God, the only true God, who has made us and cared for us:

> Know that the LORD alone is God;
> he made us and we are his,
>> his people and the flock of his pasture.

As worshippers, we are to pass through the holy gates into his presence, with song and movement expressing thankfulness for all he has done. The call sounds out again:

> Enter his gates with thanksgiving,
>> his courts with praise;
> give thanks to him and bless his name.

> For the LORD is good, his love endures for ever,
> and his faithfulness throughout all generations.

When the psalm was first sung, this passing through his gates meant a great moment in the annual festival. The pilgrims entered the temple courts in joyful procession. They were dancing and raising their voices in thanksgiving and praise. But what was done on such a great day of worship caught a meaning for the whole of life. Because of this great day, the pilgrims would know God's invitation every day – to enter his gates, worship him with dancing, bless his name with every movement of their life, because of his love and his faithfulness, because of the triumph of his goodness.

And the little psalm of only four verses drops in another mighty thought. This joyful, thankful worship offered by God's people, his beloved flock, is on behalf of all creatures. In its full width, the psalm's call is to 'all the earth' – that is, the world and all its teeming life. All God's creatures are called to the dance of thankfulness before his face. We his people are to begin the dance in worship and in daily living, until the whole world knows again that he alone is God, maker and carer of all, their spring of love and faithfulness.

O God, you have come to us in the name of Jesus and opened the gates into your presence. Lead us to enter and to dance in response to your love and faithfulness.
May all the movement of our life be towards you in commitment and thanksgiving, in beauty and in harmony with all your creation.
Lord Jesus, lead us ever in the joyful dance of life.

Psalm 101

The depth of a ceremony

———◆◆———

It seems to be a fairly common situation: there comes an invitation to a wedding or a baptism – and all the concern is what to wear! A new hat will be needed, and probably also an entire new outfit. The driver in the family is just as anxious about routes and parking. In short, such incidental details so seize the attention that there is little energy left to reflect on the profound meaning of the ceremony itself.

Yet how deep is the significance of such ceremonies at the turning points of life! The experience and faith of thousands of generations are gathered and focused there. Solemn promises are matched by divine gifts. A new life beckons. Yes, a pity to be distracted by concern for new hats and handbags or for parking spaces.

Reflection on the rich meaning of such observances can well be extended to one of the psalms – Psalm 101. Here the ritual is not for a wedding or baptism, but for a vital stage in the life of the king. Either he is being installed at the beginning of his reign, or his reign is being renewed, perhaps at the new year. The ceremony opens up the deep meaning of his calling. He must make pledges, as he hopes for God's help. His destiny and the well-being of his people are in the balance. Heart and spirit must be set sincerely upon this solemn action.

The ceremony has a dramatic character. The king is being tested. He appears forlorn, longing for God to come to him. Before that can happen, he has to make a solemn vow to reign justly and faithfully. So his prayer and vow take the most intense form – the musical chant of a psalm:

> Of faithful love and justice I will sing,
> making music to you, O Lord.
>
> My song shall be of the way that is pure –
> O when will you come to me?

And now the king's vow unfolds. He promises to live and work with faithful love and justice, and then spells this out in ten particulars. He is thinking especially of his life within the palace, which is the centre for his private life, but also for the government of the country. As regards his own example, he promises that both his heart and his actions will be wholly given to the Lord:

> I will walk in purity of heart
> within the walls of my house.
>
> I will not set before my eyes
> a counsel that is evil.
>
> I will abhor the deeds of unfaithfulness;
> they shall not cling to me.

Then he promises to work only through honest, true-hearted ministers. Not easy, for there was always the pressure on rulers to favour rich and powerful people, even though they might be corrupt. He vows to have no truck with such:

> A crooked heart shall depart from me;
> I will not know a wicked person.
>
> One who slanders another in secret
> I will quickly put to silence.
>
> Arrogant eyes and a greedy heart –
> I will not suffer them.
>
> My eyes shall be on the faithful in the earth,
> that they should dwell with me.
>
> One that walks in the way that is pure
> shall come and be my servant.
>
> There shall not dwell within my house
> one that practises deceit.
>
> One who utters falsehood
> shall not stand before my eyes.

What a standard for government! The top person pledged to God in purity of heart and conduct; requiring the same dedication in all who serve in the government; keeping clear of people of greed, arrogance and deception!

The king now rounds off his vow with a promise to work for justice every day. As the sun rose every day like an emblem of justice, pure and all-seeing, so a king was supposed to hear the complaints of his subjects, holding session early every morning. He was to be available especially to the poor who had no other defender. So he sings:

> Morning by morning I will silence
> all the wicked of the earth,
>
> to banish from the city of the LORD
> all those who practise evil.

Thus the king has ended his vow by promising to be daily such a rising sun of justice, lighting up the evil deeds of oppression and fraud, bringing relief to all who were ill-treated.

Now all this ideal of government could have been put to the king in a sermon. But no, it was conveyed in dramatic ceremony, a kind of sacrament. The king had to experience what it would be like if God withdrew from him, what a horrible desert of a life is left when our corruptions drive away the Holy Spirit. With full soul he had to chant his plea to God: I will sing of faithful love and justice, Lord – I will pledge myself to hold to them. O when will you come to me? Do not delay, O my Saviour! Such was the force of his prayer.

We may imagine that his psalm was followed by a sign of God's acceptance, such as robing or anointing. Where sincere promise had been made, the divine power embraced and sustained. Grace was given for the otherwise impossible task.

The psalm surely speaks to societies today, as they struggle with the deceptions and greed that cling to political office – the slanders, treacheries, ambition and corruption that penetrate and cling to the centres of power. The psalm declares to modern rulers that only through dedication to God's standards can his blessing be retained. Only with the faithful and just ruler will the Lord of all destinies be present. And without that presence, all will turn to ashes.

A solemn message for rulers. But also for each of us in the little kingdoms where we have responsibility. In our own domains of rule and care, we are to pledge ourselves again and again, morning by morning, to faithful love and justice, to honesty and kindness, that the Lord may come to us and abide with us – that he may work through us with all his fruitfulness.

Have mercy on our rulers, O God, king of all. Come to them. By your Spirit,
teach them to love justice and faithfulness, purity and humility.
Give them strength to overcome the corrupters and the ruthless.
Lord Jesus, cleanse and renew me in love, that I may ever dwell with you and
be a servant in your kingdom.

Psalm 102
Praying in sympathy

A little town in Cornwall is blessed with a pleasant pool. A stream winds through beds of reeds and yellow irises to cascade into the large pool, where many kinds of water birds nest and swim. Many a delivery man, builder or sales representative seems to have time to drive in close to the water and sit contentedly watching the birds. Two swans on a little island were very popular. But when one died, people saw how grief reduced its mate to a pitiful condition. But it was not unusual. It is well known that animals may grieve to death when they lose a mate or indeed a friend or a master.

Some people too have a special gift of sympathy. You hardly dare tell them of a pain you may have, as you might see them suffer even worse than yourself. But when it comes to praying for others, sympathy is surely a necessary gift. It's easy enough to say, 'I'll remember you in my prayers', or, 'Say a prayer for me.' Yet the task is not a light one. The true intercessor enters into the suffering that is held up to God for his mercy.

There's a striking example in Psalm 102. The singer chants an urgent prayer of intercession. The distress of all the community is concentrated into this one praying figure. The holy city and all her people are gathered into his soul. He feels the suffering of all. It seems that Jerusalem, Zion, lies in ruins and many of her people are captives. It is a bitter tragedy for a city that God once chose as the place of his presence on earth, the sanctuary from which his name and glory were to shine out to all nations.

The singer begins by pleading for a hearing. Though God now seems to be distant, may he hear and quickly answer:

> LORD, hear my prayer,
> and let my crying come before you.

> Do not hide your face from me
> in the day of my distress.

Then the singer seeks to move God by describing his distress. It is the pain of one who has entered deeply into the tragedy of the beloved city:

> My days are consumed in smoke;
> my bones burn as in a furnace . . .

264

I am weary from the noise of my groaning,
and my bones cleave to my skin.

I am become like an owl of the wilderness,
like the owl that haunts the ruins . . .

My days are like a shadow that declines,
and I wither away like grass.

Against this picture of a weakness near to death, the singer sets the greatness and majesty of God. He is the everlasting Creator and king. When earth and heaven perish, it will be for him just like the wearing out of a garment that can easily be changed. Surely he has appointed the time when his pity will come to Zion, building her again, setting free the prisoners?

And so the singer's faith reaches out to that future time when testimony will be raised to the goodness of the Lord and the nations will gather to join in Zion's thankful worship. Thus he sings:

You will arise and have pity on Zion;
it is time to have pity on her,
surely the appointed time has come.

For your servants love her very stones,
and feel compassion for her dust.

Then the nations shall see the name of the LORD,
and all the kings of the earth your glory,

when the LORD shall have built up Zion
and shown himself in his glory.

We see here how the intercession passes between the two contrasting realities. There is the suffering of the broken city, embodied in the one who prays, and over against that is the eternal majesty of God, reached for in praise. It is as though the praying person, through depth of sympathy, would be a bridge between the earthly suffering and the divine pity.

We may find a parable for this bridging work of prayer, a parable in the work of a great artist. In front of a university library, on a green and spacious campus, stands *Ancestor I*, a bronze sculpture by Barbara Hepworth. The massive figure consists of four sections stacked one upon another, and each weighing about half a ton. The sections are suggestive of head, torso, hips and legs. They also suggest forms in nature and the prehistoric stone monuments that are part of the west Cornish landscape. Thus the dedicated sculptor moved between the human and its ancient home in nature. Describing her feeling for the rolling countryside, she used these remarkable words: 'I, the sculptor, am the landscape.' She, representative of the human, through artistic sympathy, was one also with the ancient stones and hills and waters. In the outpouring of her soul-filled work, she served as a bridge.

And likewise in our psalm, the intercessor comes forward with the sufferings of Zion in his own soul and reaches out to God in prayer and praise. He becomes a bridge between the human tragedy and the divine pity.

But can we follow the sculptor's words right through and say that the intercessor *is* the divine pity? Hardly – until we hear in the psalm the praying of Christ. In Christ we see the one who is from among us, our representative with the sympathy to enter the depths of earthly suffering. But also in him we see the compassion and love of God. He is the bridge. By his supreme prayer of sympathy, he calls the divine pity into the troubled body of Zion – into the suffering Church, into the fallen world.

The gifts and callings for the work of prayer differ from person to person. May God make us all intercessors to the degree that he wills. May he give us grace to stand in our own fashion on a watchtower of prayer for our afflicted friends, for the wounds of the Church, for the sufferings of the world. May he gather up our prayers into the intercessions of Christ and the groanings of the Holy Spirit, until it be told out that the Lord has looked down from his holy height,

> to hear the groaning of the prisoner,
> to set free those condemned to death,
>
> that the name of the Lord be told in Zion,
> and his praise in Jerusalem,
>
> when the peoples are gathered together,
> and the kings, to serve the Lord.

I watch and am like the bird that sits alone on the rooftops. In quietness and solitude, Lord, I would feel for the sorrowful. I would stand with those who have no earthly helper.

I call down for them your pity and loving-kindness. I bring them to your feet, Lord Jesus, that you may embrace and comfort and heal.

The story of your mercy shall be told in Zion. Your name, fountain of pity and love, shall be proclaimed in your Church and among all your creatures for ever.

Psalm 103
A soul that soars on high

———•◆•———

What wonderful things are the feathers of a bird! Protecting from cold and wet, achieving the miracle of flight, making beautiful patterns of colour, and regrowing seasonally in a manner to suit the particular bird's way of life! In the time of moulting, as old feathers are pushed out and lost, a bird may hide away. It may have a ragged and pathetic appearance. Its flight may be less sure, and danger is more acute. That is a time to survive and wait for renewal. But when the new plumage is duly grown, warmth, power of flight and beauty are restored.

In the wilderness and desert around the Holy Land live great-winged birds such as eagles and griffon vultures. Desert folk, minding goats, sheep and camels, would know when these birds were troubled by moulting, just as we notice the plight of our local birds. And then they would wonder at a bird's renewed vitality as, with feathers replaced and wings and tail restored, it mounted high on the currents of warm air, dived and tumbled, or floated effortlessly over great distances.

To the biblical poets, such renewal of the great bird's life and strength was a parable – an image of the renewal worked in us by God's grace. In Psalm 103, this parable of moulting rounds off a list of the good things the Lord does for our soul. These are God's gracious acts which enable us to rise again from dejection or weakness, rise on the breath of God's Spirit with fresh joy in living:

> Bless the Lord, O my soul,
> and all that is within me, bless his holy name.
>
> Bless the Lord, O my soul,
> and do not forget all he does for you,
>
> forgiving all your wrongdoing,
> healing all your sicknesses,
>
> redeeming your life from death's hold,
> encircling you with faithful love and compassion,
>
> satisfying you daily with good things,
> so that your youth is renewed as an eagle's.

The singer has given a list of God's mercies where surely all of us can recognize something of our own experience. Daily we are nourished in body and soul. From many a sickness we have been healed, and sometimes delivered from the shadow of death. Time and time again we have been forgiven for wrongdoing. Have we not known ourselves encircled by his compassion and persevering love?

As the singer develops these thoughts, he dwells on a grace that especially renews us and raises us to the heights, the grace of forgiveness:

> Compassionate and gracious is the LORD,
> patient and plenteous in faithful love.

> He will not always be contending,
> nor for ever be displeased.

> He has not dealt with us according to our sins,
> nor rewarded us according to our offences.

> For as the heavens are high above the earth,
> so great is his love over those who fear him.

> As far as the east is from the west,
> so far has he removed our sins from us.

> As a father has compassion on his children,
> so the LORD has compassion on those who fear him.

So the concluding call goes out: to this God of such compassion and understanding, a father to all his creatures, to him let there be thankful praise from all the universe:

> Bless the LORD, you his angels,
> you mighty ones who do his bidding
>   and obey the voice of his word.

> Bless the LORD, all his hosts,
> you servants who do his pleasure.

> Bless the LORD, all that he has made, in all places of his dominion;
> bless the LORD, O you my soul.

Bless, bless, bless – seven times the singer uses this particular word in his calls for praise of the heavenly king and father. It means here a kind of praise overflowing with thankfulness, warm and heartfelt. And we notice that while the singer calls on all in heaven and all on earth so to bless the

268

Lord, his last call, like his first, is directed to his own soul: 'Bless the LORD, O you my soul.'

Do we suffer from smallness of vision? Are our concerns petty, our sympathies narrow? It is a common complaint. But this beautiful and enthusiastic psalm offers a key to a wide country and spacious sky of the spirit. In our *soul*, our true inner being, let us consider the mercies of God, especially his forgiveness of our sins. Then let our souls bless the Lord, turning to him in joyful gratitude and new dedication. With that disposition of our soul, a golden key, we shall find a wide world of hearts and voices turned to God. We shall be in sympathy, in love, with all creation. We shall rise above pettiness, rise on the currents of God's spirit-wind and range joyfully through the vastnesses of his dominion. Yes, the soul forgiven and turned thankfully to God has already entered the kingdom of God. Our soul has part in his new creation.

Lord, we are frail and pass soon from the earth. But your faithful love is from of old and for ever.

Grant that, in fear of you, aware in every moment that you are Lord, I may find your faithful love.

Let the truest, deepest depth of me bless you. May every fibre of my being thank you for forgiving me, healing, redeeming, encircling me with your tender love, and filling me daily with good things.

May my soul bless you, that you renew her like the birds that rise again through the skies.

Lord and king of all, you are compassionate and patient. Your love reaches high over all the earth.

Bless the Lord, O my soul, and do not forget all he does for you.

Psalm 104

The way to love of the world

It seemed a good thing that some of the demand for electricity should be met by wind-power – clean, free and for ever self-renewing. However, a dispute arose when it was proposed to put hundreds of the tall wind-turbines on top of hills in what had hitherto been a beautiful natural scene far from the constructions of human beings. Both parties to the dispute made a good case. The argument brought to mind the way humans have hitherto generally helped themselves to the earth's resources without any consideration except for present profit. Here is gold or coal or clay or peat or tin or oil – let's rip it out. Here are forests – let's exploit them to extinction. Here is a river – let it service our industries and take our poison and waste. Here is a fine mountain or lake – should be good for tourism. It was a pervasive attitude. Only human advantage really counted.

Quite different is the view in a great psalm which surveys the manifold creations of God, Psalm 104. Here the poet does tell of some of nature's products which are God's provision for humanity, but they are mentioned well down the list. Other creatures are considered first. And even before them we hear of the great and mysterious elements which are first thought of in their direct usefulness to God. The light is the garment he wraps around himself, a garment of heavenly glory. He has spread the skies as his curtain. The clouds are his chariot, the winds his winged steeds. Storms and lightnings are his servants.

Then the poet's thoughts move from these high mysteries down to the earth. He marvels at the springs and brooks which God sends among the hills – for the benefit of the wild animals: 'They give drink to every creature of the field; the wild asses quench their thirst.' He thinks of the thickets that grow in the flood-beds of these streams, and he sees them as provided for birds, which give voice among the branches. In the rain he sees God replenishing the earth and making grass to grow for animals, and fruits and corn for humans to harvest.

Then the poet comes to the great trees such as cedars and firs. He makes no reference to the use of the straight trunks even in ancient times for grand building projects. What comes to his mind is that the Lord himself planted such mighty trees and so gave homes to certain kinds of birds, such as the stork. As for the high mountains, their usefulness is for the nimble wild goats, while the rocky crags and cliffs serve as refuge for the rock-badgers (hyraxes) with their tenacious feet. Again, the usefulness of the night is as the time for the beasts of the forest, such as lions, to come out. Daytime is noted as the time for human work. But the poet's thought quickly returns to the multitude of God's creatures, and so on to the vast world of sea creatures, where ships have a modest part:

> How many are your works, O Lord,
>   and all of them done with wisdom!
> The earth is filled with your creatures.

> Yonder is the sea, great and wide,
>> and there move creatures beyond number, both small and great.

The singer thinks of all these creatures not as useful to humankind, not in relation to human beings and their desires, but in relation to God. They are in the close bond of his care:

> These all look to you
>> to give them their food at the proper time.

> When you give it them, they gather it;
>> you open your hand and they are filled with good.

And it is God's enjoyment of the creatures that is mentioned, not human enjoyment:

> May the glory of the LORD be for evermore,
>> and the LORD ever rejoice in his works.

Thus our psalm gives a perspective on the earth and her creatures very different from that of the dominant outlook in most of human history. Not only has humankind grabbed at resources in disregard of the species; the animals themselves have been treated as there only to be exploited or eliminated. How far indeed from St Basil's admirable prayer: 'May we see that they do not live for us alone, but for themselves and for you, and that they love the sweetness of life.' Assertive humans have been like very selfish children who consider everything only in the light of their own desires.

The poet-singer, indeed, does not end his beautiful survey of God's creation without thinking of the human wickedness that troubles the earth. So in his last verse he prays: 'Let sinners be taken from the earth, and the wicked be no more.' This prompts us to the thought that, as we grow in love for earth and her creatures, we must pray strongly against the wickedness that would devastate them.

But perhaps the greatest treasure of the psalm is that it shows us the way to a loving and reverent relation to all creation. This way appears in the identical opening and closing words: 'Bless the LORD, O my soul.' We are to live in thankful adoration of the Creator. Such is the call, and it is to be heard and heeded in the first place by each of us in our own soul. I, in the depth of my own being, am ever to bless the Lord, the Creator, and so shall I find a deeper love of all that he has made.

Then how good it will be for the air and waters, for the earth and her manifold creatures, when all humankind loves the Creator and can sing with the psalm:

271

I will sing to the LORD as long as I live;
I will make music to my God while I have my being;

So shall my song be sweet to him,
while I rejoice in the LORD . . .

Bless the LORD, O you my soul.

O Lord my God, let me know your glory, you that wrap yourself in light as in
  a garment and ride on the wings of the wind.
Let me see your care for wild creatures in the brooks that run among the hills,
  in the trees and in the rocky heights.
Let me see your wisdom in the setting of the sun and in his rising, in the great
  width of the sea and the leaping of her creatures.
When you hide your face, all are troubled. We die and return to our clay.
O send out your Spirit and create us anew. So may we live in your new king-
  dom of blessing and love.

Psalm 105
The name that gives delight

A woman used to recall that her late husband, a man of some dignity, would nevertheless blossom into song when shaving. He would usually render a song of Schubert in a rather distorted English version: 'I'd love to carve her name on every tree.' He sang it with the enthusiasm of a young lover thrilled at every mention of his girl's name, and working up to the climax, 'Thine is my heart; thine is my heart and shall be so for ever.' It was a good song for working up a lather.

Certainly, many have known the haunting music of a name when they fall in love. In one word the name seems to call up the identity and character of the beloved. In that treasured word the person seems present and close. The young lover wants to proclaim the name, and is amazed that everybody is not falling down and worshipping that wonderful person.

There's something similar here to the experience of coming to love the Lord. The psalms sometimes call on the worshippers to rejoice at his presence, to give thanks for his goodness, to declare his name and sing songs of delight in him. We find a good example in Psalm 105:

Give thanks to the LORD and proclaim his name;
make known his deeds among the peoples.

Sing to him, make music to him;
make songs of all his marvellous works.

Rejoice in the praise of his holy name;
let the heart of those that seek the LORD be merry.

As the lover is always hoping and seeking to meet the beloved, and constantly recalls the beloved's actions and virtues, so the psalm calls to the lovers of God:

Seek the LORD and his strength;
seek his face for evermore.

Recall the wonders he has done,
his marvels and the judgements of his mouth.

And young lovers seem to have such a lot of time just to be together, or write long letters, or sit thinking of all the other has said and done. They think it time well spent. Similarly, the worshippers in our psalm have lots of time to rest before the face of the Lord. Without haste, they recall at length the story of his faithfulness.

It is a story that runs all through the generations from Abraham to themselves. They recollect that even 'when they were small in number, few indeed and strangers in the land', even then he was mindful of his promise. So he guided and protected them, and prepared for the time when they would have a land and a home where they could live before him according to his teachings. There were times of suffering, but these were the gateway to blessings. Thus Joseph's great mission began when he was sold as a slave: 'They afflicted his feet with shackles; his neck was ringed with iron.' So the word of the Lord tested him, until he marvellously was raised to become ruler of the greatest country, Egypt. Later, the Hebrews were hated and oppressed, but the Lord was still faithful: 'He brought his people out with silver and gold, and there was not one among their tribes that stumbled.' Through many a hazard and obstacle he led them, and at last gave them a place to live in communion with him and 'faithfully keep his laws'.

Here the psalm brings its long story to a close. It has been a story of God's grace and faithfulness, and in the singing of it the worshippers have immersed themselves in that faithful love. They have sought and found the Lord afresh. The song of testimony has made them see anew the reality

273

of the Saviour. They have proclaimed and praised his holy name, and so known him close in power and blessing.

When Christians today would seek the Lord by recalling the story of his faithfulness as they have known it, they can still begin with Abraham. But they will especially remember the promise that in him all the nations would be blessed. They will recall the adventures of Joseph and the lesson of the testing he had to go through before he was exalted. But above all, Christians will remember the sufferings of Jesus before the joy of his resurrection. And they will give thanks that in him they have found a promised land where they can live in constant knowledge of God, a country watered by the spring of eternal life and lit by the sun of his grace. Here in Jesus is the place where we can live to do God's will, enabled by his forgiveness and the renewing gifts of the Holy Spirit. What a story of salvation and faithfulness we have to tell! What cause to give thanks to the Lord, proclaim his name and make known his deeds!' What reason to sing to him, make music to him and make songs of all his marvellous works! Let us ever respond to the psalm's call and rejoice in the praise of his holy name, and with a merry heart seek the Lord and his strength, seek his face for evermore. For Jesus is our beloved. His name is beautiful, and his presence is our delight and our very life.

Lord, fill us with joy in your name as we tell of the marvels of your grace and faithfulness.
Grant us wisdom and devotion in seeking you.
Bring us already into that promised land where we may live constantly in fellowship with you and see the beauty of your face.

Psalm 106
The lesson of history

In days gone by, the subjects taught in school had a clear-cut, straightforward appearance. None more so than the one called just 'History'. Your timetable would tell you when you would have lessons in History. Your examination certificate might say you had passed in History. You might even go on and take a degree in History.

But that clear-cut package called 'History' was something of an illusion, as grew obvious in an era when school syllabuses were constantly being questioned and revised. Information was multiplying in every field. Societies became ever more diverse through waves of immigration. In the competition for teaching time, History seemed too big, and getting bigger every day. What parts of it were important for today's students? And there was the problem of interpretation. How could aspects and facts be selected and presented fairly, and not as propaganda? Only dictatorships had confident answers. They defined the subject to promote themselves. They wrote the textbooks and controlled the teachers. Even in less regimented countries, the teachers of History tended to talk up national heroes and victories. Most nations, it seemed, could look back at a line of victorious generals and brilliant inventors. If one could put it all together in one world-view, it would seem that there were not nearly enough defeats to correspond to the victories, while many inventions must have been made in different countries several times over, all about the same time!

Now, the Bible contains quite a lot of history. Indeed the Old Testament is sometimes credited with having pioneered historical writing. But surprisingly, the ancestors and rulers were often remembered for their failures. An example is the long recital of history in Psalm 106. This recital aims to show how the fathers 'did wrong and acted wickedly' – quite a difference from our modern national histories! Another difference is that the conduct of the fathers is assessed *in relation to God*. Forget about wealth and empire. Were they responsive to God? Were they faithful to him? That's all that matters to the singer of this long psalm.

He begins with the Exodus, the classic time of God's miraculous help. Already the ancestors were unworthy. As the singer relates:

> In Egypt they did not consider your wonders,
>   or remember the greatness of your faithful love,
> but defied the Most High at the Sea of Reeds.

Even if they were impressed at first by their deliverance, it was not for long. The singer tells: 'Very soon they forgot his works; they would not wait for his counsel.' Then, passing through the wilderness, they gave way to cravings and jealousies: 'They forgot God their Saviour', and worshipped other gods. They did not believe God's promise to bring them to a pleasant land and murmured in discontent. When, in spite of all, the people entered the fertile land, they learnt more worship of idols and sacrificed children.

And so the singer unfolds his view of history, reaching at last the tragedy of national defeat and exile, the long humiliation out of which this psalm arises. But the condemnation of the ancestors is not made with a sense of superiority, as though to say, 'We would not do such things.' On the contrary, the singer expressly says at the outset,

> We have sinned with our fathers;
> we have done wrong and acted wickedly.

The old sins are still with us, the singer means to say. Still we do not keep in mind the wonderful and faithful deeds of God. Still we give way to cravings and are moved by jealousy. Still we put worthless idols in place of God's glory. We too disbelieve God's promises. We too shed innocent blood. So the psalmist speaks for his people and leads them in confession and penitence.

But can he also lead modern people, our generation? As we heed him, we begin to see in our history much worshipping of false values, sins of our ancestors which we continue. For still we 'forget God', not having him in the centre of our hearts and motivations. We too yield to cravings, to greed, to shallow fashions, even to shedding innocent blood. We have much to confess and repent of.

The psalmist has one supreme lesson of history to guide us with – the invincible quality of God's love. The psalm keeps returning to the crucial theme: in pity and faithfulness God persevered with the former generations, and so he does with us. Our penitence is to be begun and completed in thankful praise, a holding fast to the God in whom alone the world can truly live and hope and be glad. So the opening and closing calls of the psalm ring out to us in our generation:

> Alleluia. Give thanks to the LORD, for he is good;
> his faithfulness is for ever.

> Who can express the mighty deeds of the LORD,
> or tell out all his praise?

'Save us, O LORD our God . . . to give thanks to your holy name and glory in your praise. Blessed be the LORD . . . from everlasting to everlasting, and let all the people say, Amen, alleluia.'

Almighty God, we who come together to worship you and give thanks for your faithful love, we listen to the story of generations who forgot you. And we confess that this sin continues in us. Our mind is not set on your deeds and your goodness. Our daily living does not flow from trust in you and from fear and love of you.

But we thank you for the long story of your persistent love and pity and miracles of renewal.

Happy those who treasure what is right and do what is just, according to your will and through your grace in Jesus.

Remember me, Lord, in the time of your favour to your people and world. Though I have forgotten you, remember me, Lord. Though I have been brought low by wrongdoing, raise me again. May I see the happiness of your new world and rejoice in the gladness of your new creation, through Jesus Christ my Saviour.

Psalm 107
The surge of thankfulness

There was a neighbour who always had time for a chat. He would soon bring in memories of his boyhood eighty-odd years ago in South Wales. Though he was now somewhat detached from church life, a lot of his recollections concerned characters and episodes in church and chapel. He would recall the rising fervour of the Welsh sermons in the chapels and the colourful testimonies which were given by repentant sinners. The old neighbour had a twinkle in his eye as he recalled, without disrespect, how graphically the former unrepentant ways were depicted. And here he was touching on a possible problem in the practice of testimonies. They tended to follow a conventional pattern, applauded by the converted, but unconvincing to others.

Yet testimony is valued and recommended in the psalms. Repeatedly so in Psalm 107, which urges: 'Let the redeemed of the Lord declare . . . Let them tell of his deeds with songs of joy . . . Let them exalt him in the assembly of the people, and praise him in the session of the elders.' This long and vivid psalm indeed centres on experience of God's saving power and the consequent duty of thanksgiving and testimony. It brings home its message by getting us to imagine four dramatic examples of danger and deliverance.

The first case is of travellers lost in a desert:

Some lost their way in the wastes of the wilderness,
and could find no path to a settlement.

We see them faint with hunger and thirst. They cry to the Lord, their only hope. He hears their prayer and saves them. And now they are to give thanks to him who 'satisfies the longing soul and fills the hungry soul with goodness'.

The second picture is of people suffering a dreadful imprisonment. They sit 'in darkness and the shadow of death, bound fast in misery and iron'. They have come to this prison because in some way they have despised the counsel of God. But their sincere prayer is heard. The Saviour comes to them, shattering the prison doors of bronze and breaking through the bars of iron. These rescued ones too must 'thank the LORD for his faithful love and his wonders for the children of earth'.

The third misfortune is severe illness, which in this case was brought on by a foolish way of living. These sufferers could not eat and were close to death. But the Lord heard their prayer and 'sent his word to heal them'. Now they must bring offerings and thanksgivings. They must tell of their deliverance with songs of joy.

The fourth case is that of seafarers caught in a tempest, a fearful experience in those ancient ships:

> They went up to the heavens and down again to the depths;
> their soul melted away in their peril.
>
> They reeled and staggered like a drunkard,
> and all their wisdom was confused.

But the Lord answered their cry and stilled his waves. What relief to come safely into the haven! And now, insists the singer, now they must thank God for the wonders of his faithful love. They must praise him at the temple, where they make pilgrimage to bring the offerings they promised.

These four examples of rescue vividly catch the joy of the transformation and the surge of thankfulness towards the Saviour. Not least are we thankful if it has been a case where we fell low through our own folly. We have known the mercy of our Saviour. He has come to our help despite our failings. So the psalm leads us to thankful acknowledgement in the gathering of worshippers. As it says: 'Give thanks to the LORD for he is good; his faithfulness is for ever . . . So let the redeemed of the LORD declare.'

And yet, as the old Welsh neighbour observed, difficulties can creep into the practice of testimony. There may be a temptation to boast of one's own piety. There may be insensitivity to the fate of those who cried to the Lord and yet perished, or continue still in a long ordeal. Yes, there are noble sufferers, like Job, who might find the psalm's presentation glib. And then again, we sometimes experience a depth of mercy, a wonder of transformation, which we can hardly convey to close friends, let alone to a wider public.

But there need not be anxiety on this score. The psalmist himself concludes on the note of pondering, deeply considering, discerning. The last verse runs:

> Whoever is wise will ponder these things,
> and discern the faithful deeds of the LORD.

And after all, what pleases the Saviour above all is the heart truly turned to him in responding love, truly rededicated. Over and above all formal testimony is the music of a life given to him in deepest thankfulness. This is the natural testimony of a heart reborn in love. Such a song of praise will carry far its message, and carry it with conviction.

Father, help us to pray in faith.
When we lose our way in a wilderness, prompt our cry to you.
When we are bound fast in misery, move us to earnest prayer.
In sickness, help us to call out to you.
From the stormy waves, hear our cry.
Sometimes our lives are flooded with the light of your love, and our hearts marvel and rejoice at your goodness to us. But we also know times of perplexity, when the meaning of great changes is hidden. Help us then to ponder until we discern your good working.
In light and in darkness, help us to thank you with the offering of our lives. Help us to recount your goodness with every movement of our being.

Psalm 108

Sun, arise!

It's an old story. A violin has been found in the attic. The long-neglected instrument is dusted and tuned, and a few notes are attempted. The sound is poor – no Stradivarius here. Disappointing. But someone perseveres. With more playing, the violin seems to awake from a long sleep and find its true voice. Such instruments are responsive to atmosphere and benefit also from the vibrations made by playing. But whatever the factors involved, a violin or cello seems to be deadened by disuse and to need sympathetic awakening before sounding in full beauty.

In Bible times the stringed instruments were not yet played with a bow, but were plucked. The psalm-singers especially mention their lyres and harps. In Psalm 108, the singer seems to be in the sanctuary even before night is ended. He is ready to offer praise and prayer at first light. He has companions with him, also ready with their lyres and harps. He calls to all the instruments to awake, to be ready for the music of praise. Thus he begins:

> My heart is ready, O God,
> that I may sing and make melody with all my soul.

> Awake, harp and lyre,
> that I may awaken the dawn.

It's a beautiful thought. As though the singer and musicians, opening their morning praise, would also wake the angel of dawn, that she may fly from the east to roll back from earth the coverlet of night. Moreover, the song of thankful praise is to be heard across all the world:

> I will give you thanks, LORD, among the peoples;
> I will sing your praise among the nations.

> For your love reaches over the heavens,
> and your faithfulness to the clouds.

Wide thoughts indeed! Is this a case of a poet enjoying the luxury of exaggeration, as some modern poets might do? Surely there is something deeper here. The singer, being in the temple of the Lord, considers himself on the threshold of heaven. Of all earth's 'thin' places, transparent to the other world, Jerusalem's temple was felt to be the thinnest. The presence of God was near and powerful. Those who served the Lord in that place felt that they were at the heart of the universe, assisting in the alternations of darkness and dawn, the world's resting and awakening. From such a place the call could indeed go out to all nations and to all creatures. To all, then, this singer testifies that the faithful love of God fills every part of the living order.

We might think that such a song of praise arises from a very happy situation. But not so. For the song quickly turns into a prayer, a cry from need. May God arise in power to save a suffering people: 'That your beloved may be delivered, save by your right hand and answer us.' It becomes apparent that the nation is in great trouble. There is war between the neighbouring peoples, and Jerusalem's forces have suffered defeat.

The next words, however, carry a reassurance from God, echoing the poetry of the nation's early years:

> God has spoken in his holiness:
>> In triumph will I portion out Shechem,
> and share out the valley of Sukkoth.

The message means that in both main parts of the territory, west and east of the River Jordan, the victory of God will be seen. And it is further promised that God's people will be his instruments in the victory, while he will make the adversaries submit. It is a colourful passage, speaking of God's helmet and sceptre, his washbowl and his sandal. But it amounts to an assurance of peace and honour, with adversity overcome.

It was hard to accept the glowing words, and the singer renewed the prayer. How can he scale the great rocks that defend the enemy's fortress? 'Have you not spurned us, O God?' he asks. 'Will you not go out with our hosts?' And the conclusion of his prayer affirms that only through God can they overcome the foe:

> O grant us help against the enemy,
> for earthly help is in vain.

> Through God we can do mighty things;
> it is he that will tread down our foes.

In the vivid language of this psalm there is much food for meditation. For one thing, we reflect on the rise and fall of nations – now the crown or sceptre of God, and now the mere washbowl. As you look towards Moab from Jerusalem, you see the dry hills tumbling down and down to a great rift. There lies the long, bright blue lake of the Dead Sea. Above the water rises a rim of misty mountains, the mountains of Moab. The noble sight has been interpreted scornfully in the psalm: in God's kingdom this once proud people will be, not God's crown or sceptre, but his washbasin. But even in humiliation, it is a service of God, a destiny with him. Yes, whether the nation, the Church, or we as individuals are high or low, tasting glory or humiliation, it will be enough that we are of service in the kingdom of God.

And in time of setbacks, failure and distress, the psalm leads us to come to the 'thin' place, where the Presence is near through the name of Jesus. In the time of darkness we must be there, ready to waken the music of our soul to praise God, ready to waken the dawn, that angel of prayer who rolls back the night. And still the answer comes and remains. God has spoken in his holiness, his invincible majesty: his kingdom comes, his peace and blessing will prevail.

Lord, while the night is still about me, my heart is ready, that I may sing praise to you with all my soul.
I will awaken the harp of my heart to give you thanks. I will call the wide world to awake to your beauty, your glory and your faithful love.
But how high the rocks on our way to you! How shall your Church rise to conquer the strong cities of evil?
Earthly help is in vain. But through you we can do mighty things. Be exalted, O God, in the revelation of your glory. Save by your right hand and answer us.

Psalm 109

The last words of the betrayed

The cross of Christ is sometimes spoken of as a 'tree'. And the thought may be not of dead wood, but of a living tree, ready to break out again in the beauty of growth and fruit. Its destiny is as a tree to benefit many. It is a tree beyond all trees, the cosmic tree of life, its fruits and shelter saving all creation.

This thought of the cross becoming again the green tree of life is used in a striking poem of Edwin Muir, 'The Transfiguration'. He pictures the time when Christ comes again and the tormented wood is cured and lives again in the green garden of Eden. And he couples with this another great transformation. The traitor Judas, who had brought a curse of damnation upon himself, takes a long journey back to his time of innocence, becoming again a child at his mother's knee. So, through the divine mercy, the betrayal at last is undone, never again to be done. Through the cross, the ancient curse of damnation has been lifted.

And a heavy curse it was. Its weight is indicated in the New Testament with a quotation from Psalm 109. Centuries before the ministry of Jesus, this psalm portrayed a traitor and the doom that was to hang over his head. Then, in a gathering of early Christians, St Peter preaches and declares that in this psalm the Holy Spirit has foretold the treachery of Judas, and how he will be replaced among the twelve disciples – fulfilling the psalm's words, 'His office let another take' (v. 8; Acts 1.20).

Now this is only one of a number of psalms which the New Testament links with its account of Christ's Passion. Even the words of Jesus on the cross draw from the Psalms. These links with the Psalms signal that the terrible events have a deep meaning in God's eternal purpose – his salvation through his Messiah.

Of course, when Psalm 109 was first chanted as an earnest prayer to God, it spoke from a crisis then raging. A king, it seems, was presenting himself to the Lord as 'helpless and poor', his heart wounded with grief, his knees weak with fasting. He poured out to the Lord how all his efforts to make peace had been abused by relentless foes:

> Do not be silent, O God of my praise,
> for a mouth of wickedness and treachery
>   they have opened wide against me.

> They have spoken against me with a tongue of falsehood;
> with words of hate they have surrounded me,
>   and made war against me without cause.

> In return for my goodwill they have set themselves against me,
> even though I prayed for them.

> Thus they have rewarded me evil for good,
> and hatred for my goodwill.

The sufferer went on to pray that judgement might fall on the chief traitor. Let no prayer of his be heard, and let the curse of destruction fall on any continuance of his life in descendants:

> Let his children be fatherless
> and his wife become a widow . . .

> Let the creditor seize all that he has,
> and strangers plunder his labour . . .

> Let his line come soon to an end,
> his name be blotted out in the next generation . . .

> He loved cursing . . .
>   so let it be as the garment he wraps around himself,
>   like the sash that he wears continually.

With such words was the traitor's doom prepared. For himself, the sufferer's hope was in the pity and faithfulness of his Lord:

> I have become for them one to be mocked;
> those that look upon me shake their heads in scorn.
>
> Help me, O LORD my God;
> save me according to your faithful love.

The psalm's bitterness is understandable. But its prayer is a difficult one for Christians to make their own. No wonder some prayer books put brackets round the vehement verses, suggesting they be omitted in recitation. Some translations seem to help by making those verses words of the enemy against the psalmist – but it's a strained and unlikely theory.

We do best to follow the lead of the New Testament. An incident in history has come to speak as prophecy. It has become a poetry of revelation. It illuminates the betrayal of Jesus the Messiah and the terrible consequences for the perpetrators.

But once the psalm is taken up into the story of our Lord's sufferings, we know that these consequences are not the end. Yes, the treachery is there, reflecting the treachery of all of us. Yes, the traitor is engulfed in misery, as are we all through our sins. But now the royal sufferer, the Messiah, our Lord Jesus Christ, has a yet more powerful prayer concerning the traitors and sinners. Out of the unutterable depths of the divine love he prays: 'Father, forgive them.'

With this prayer, the Messiah's eternal intercession, comes hope for all – though all have part in the treachery, callousness and cruelty, the arrogance and greed that struck him down. The psalm came to be the revelation of the betrayal of the divine Friend and the selling of our souls for ruthless gain. The revelation shows the misery that then enshrouds our life. But once the link was made with Jesus, it pointed beyond the misery and death, allowing the vision of the green tree and the innocence restored.

So, in the psalm's words, we may well 'give great thanks to the Lord', and 'praise him among the multitudes'. For not only does he stand faithfully 'at the right hand of the needy one', but also has come to save traitors and sinners of every kind. In the mystery of eternity, with his 'Father, forgive them' he will make all again to be well.

Lord Jesus, help us to hear from the psalm that our words and deeds of ill will
*   come back to harm ourselves.*
Help us to follow your way in not returning evil for evil.

Lead us into the depths of your prayer, when you, the betrayed one, Love
crucified, ask the Father to forgive your persecutors.
Help me, O Lord my God. Save me according to your faithful love.

Psalm 110

Drinking from the brook by the way

Dixit, dixit Dominus – forceful words well set to music by Handel. It was one of the pieces he composed for the Duke of Chandos, whose palace was near Edgware, Middlesex. The words are the beginning of Psalm 110, more familiar to us as 'The LORD said to my Lord'.

It is recorded that Jesus set a puzzle from these words for his opponents: if the Messiah was, as they said, the son of David, how was it that David, prophesying in the psalm, could address him as 'my lord'? We read that 'no one was able to answer him a word, neither dared anyone from that day on ask him any more questions' (Matt. 22.41f.).

That David wrote the psalm was the common opinion of the time, which Jesus did not see fit to challenge. But if we more generally connect the psalm with the enthronement ceremonies for the kings of David's line, these opening words are less puzzling. As the new king takes the throne, it seems that a prophet, a kind of inspired bard, addresses him with this psalm. He begins with a word from God, a message which calls the king to sit and reign with God:

> A word of the LORD for my lord: Sit at my right hand,
> till I make your enemies a stool for your feet.

After this direct message, the prophetic singer describes God's grace for the king. This will mean power over adversaries, and indeed a new life in close relation to God. Already this day, new life has been given, a kind of new birth. These are the prophet's words:

> The LORD shall extend the sceptre of your power from Zion,
> so that you rule in the midst of your enemies.
>
> Royal grace is with you on this day of your birth
>   in holy majesty from the womb of dawn;
> upon you is the dew of your new life.

285

That new birth is a marvel and a mystery. It was perhaps signified by baptism at dawn in the sacred spring below Jerusalem.

And the inspired singer has yet more gifts of God to announce. The new ruler will be both king and high priest, in the pattern of an ancient king of Jerusalem called Melchizedek. It is an especially solemn appointment, for God swears never to take it back. Furthermore, with God beside him, this royal priest and warrior will be God's agent of judgement on all nations: 'The LORD at your right hand will smite down kings in the day of his wrath. In full majesty he will judge among the nations, smiting heads across the wide earth.'

The conclusion of the psalm brings another vivid picture, which again puzzles us somewhat:

> He who drinks from the brook by the way
> shall therefore lift high his head.

This, again, is less puzzling if we connect it with the royal ceremonies. We may imagine that the king was given a cup of water from the holy fountain in symbol of strength given by God – strength to accomplish his great mission. Thus the king, following the way of his destiny, will be replenished by divine life, and so at last, after many trials, be uplifted in glory.

The prophet's words were weighty indeed. But centuries passed, and there came an era when there were no more kings of David's line. Understanding of the psalm now focused entirely on thought of the royal saviour who was to come, the Messiah. This was the general understanding when Jesus discussed the psalm, and it was fairly based on the visionary character of the original utterance. The psalmist had indeed seen deep into the purposes of God.

A vision of the Messiah, then – but our immediate reaction may be that this picture of a conquering king does not fit Jesus. Yet we must then take account of the fact that the New Testament applies this psalm to Jesus more frequently than any other psalm. How can this be? It is because the first Christians took the psalm to disclose the glory of the *risen* Christ. Again and again in the New Testament, the psalm's words 'Sit at my right hand' are linked to Christ's resurrection. The risen Christ ascends to sit at his Father's right hand, a unique closeness for the One who hears the Father's very thoughts and carries out his will. In the power of the Father he will conquer all the forces of evil.

And when the psalm tells of a day of birth 'in holy majesty from the womb of the dawn' and with the dew of new life, Christians think of the sonship of Christ. What was shown in Bethlehem, then in the baptism in the Jordan, and again at the transfiguration – this is now shown more gloriously in the resurrection and the ascension to the very throne of the Father.

The first Christians also found the psalm eloquent of the priesthood of Christ. In him is fulfilled God's statement in the psalm: 'You are a priest for ever, after the order of Melchizedek.' Far beyond all kings, priests and prophets, Christ is appointed supreme mediator, the One who brings us to the Father, overcoming our sins, gaining us access, praying for us with all the power that the Father has bestowed on him. And Christians also found in the psalm reference to Christ's part in the last judgement, at the side of the Father who in full majesty smites down the leaders of evil.

But the psalm's last word has brought to mind that way of pain which Christ trod for our sakes: 'He who drinks from the brook by the way . . .' He drank of the cup of suffering on the cross, but it proved to be the water of eternal life. So his head was raised high and he sits for ever at the Father's right hand.

Dixit, dixit Dominus . . . yes, let Handel's anthem ring out: 'The Lord said unto my lord . . .' Let the testimony of all who know Christ ring out. The Lord has sworn and will not go back. Christ is appointed the eternal High Priest, the King, the Son, and through him the holy dawn will become the full light of the new creation.

Almighty God, strengthen us in the certainty of your word: evil will be overcome, your work in Christ will be accomplished.

Jesus your Son is eternal king and priest. He reigns with you and makes atonement for the sins of the world. May we ever be upheld by his prayer and his blessing.

Lord Jesus, give us grace to follow you. In all our sufferings may we so drink of the brook of your eternal life that you raise our heads in the joy of your kingdom.

Lord, the darkness is still heavy upon the world. As your kingdom dawns, bestow on me the light and dew of birth into eternal life with you.

Psalm 111
The essence of wisdom

There are people who are clever, but not wise. In some things expert, in general they are foolish. Evidently, expertise and wisdom are not the same thing.

There's a fine poem in the Bible that speaks of this distinction. It is tucked away in the Book of Job as chapter 28. The poem depicts the expertise of those who search for copper, silver, gold and precious stones such as onyx, coral, crystal and lapis lazuli. In remote places they drive shafts deep into the earth. They hang in darkness far beneath the feet of travellers. They know how to split rocks and divert streams. How clever are human beings, and how bold and ingenious in pursuit of wealth! But one thing they cannot find or possess: the wisdom of the Creator. And the poem ends with counsel from the Creator: though man can never grasp the divine wisdom, there is a wisdom, an understanding which he can embrace –

> The fear of the Lord, that is wisdom;
> to depart from evil is understanding.

Now a similar thought is expressed at the end of Psalm 111:

> The fear of the Lord is the beginning of wisdom;
> a good understanding have those who live by it.

'The beginning of wisdom' – or perhaps 'the essence of wisdom', for the Hebrew word can mean either 'the beginning' or 'the chief part'. The psalm is teaching that, if you live in the fear of the Lord, you have a good understanding. You have a wisdom that gives purpose and beauty to your life.

But what is meant by 'the fear of the Lord'? It's a favourite expression in the Bible. We might say it means to know God *as God*, to be alive and awake to his awesome reality. So the fear of God is an awareness that affects all our thoughts and all our actions. His reality, his will, has become the chief factor for us at every turn. And this, the psalm teaches, is the essence of wisdom.

But that is the ending of the psalm. It will surely be helpful to note the thoughts that lead up to it. Perhaps these will show us how to grow in such fear of the Lord. The psalm is one of those 'alphabetic' psalms, its lines beginning with successive letters of the Hebrew alphabet. This tends to give each statement a weight of its own, but nevertheless our poet has held to a connecting thread of thought. At the outset we find ourselves in a gathering for worship, for the psalm begins:

> Alleluia!
> I will thank the LORD with all my heart,
> among true-hearted friends and in the congregation.

This thankful worship may be in a small circle ('among true-hearted friends') or it may be in the full assembly ('in the congregation'). But whether with few companions or with many, the individual must still contribute sincere devotion: 'I will thank the LORD with all my heart.'

The thankfulness is for the deeds of God – his wonderful work for life and salvation:

> Great are the deeds of the LORD,
> sought out by all who delight in him.

The deeds are 'sought out' as the worshippers learn about them, study and reflect on them, letting their minds dwell on them with delight. They are especially the deeds which saved his people and gave them life before his face. He revealed himself, he bound the people in a bond or covenant with himself, and he gave them a place to live faithfully by his teachings. Here the singer specifies one particular commandment – would we have guessed it? It is the commandment to 'remember':

> He appointed a remembrance of his wonders;
> the LORD is gracious and compassionate.

Those ancient deeds of God in Egypt, on Mount Sinai, in the wilderness and crossing the Jordan – those great acts to shape a worshipping people were to be recited and taught to every generation. It was not for the sake of historical record or cultural identity. It was to lead succeeding generations into direct knowledge of God as saviour and guide. Through the remembrance, the salvation was made present. The Lord's presence was known. As the psalm puts it: they were to know that 'holy and awesome is his name'.

And so we see where the psalm's thread has brought us. It started with the gathering for worship with few or with many, and with a thankful heart. Then came delight in seeking out or studying his deeds and his purposes. Then was mentioned the solemn commemoration of his saving and shaping his people, bringing awe of finding him anew in his power and presence. And so the psalm's thread reached the conversion of our self-will and self-sufficiency to the fear of the Lord. This is an awareness that will light up our whole soul – such fear of the Lord that is the beginning, the essence and the crown of wisdom. Here is a light to live by. Here is the spring of a life of worship, praise, and constant delight in our God.

I will thank you, Lord, with all my heart, when I worship in a circle of true-hearted friends and in the congregation.
Grant that I have delight in dwelling upon your deeds of creation and salvation.
In the ceremony of the bread and wine, which you have appointed, may the deeds and the presence of Christ possess me. Give me sustenance in the way of life with you.
May I ever fear you, remembering your power above all powers, your guidance above all earthly wisdom, your love above all earthly delights.
Glory to the Father, who has sent salvation to his world.
Glory to the Son, who gives us the bread and wine of the new covenant in remembrance of his Passion.
Glory to the Holy Spirit, the Spirit of understanding and fear of the Lord.

Psalm 112

A treasure found in the vestry

There's many a thing you may find in a church vestry. One day an old book came to light. It was a massive altar book, beautifully bound and printed. Alas, on some pages it was spoilt by drippings from wax candles. Yet hardly 'spoilt'. On reflection, the wax blobs and stains seemed especially precious. They took you to moments of solemn worship many years ago. Indeed, they preserved moments from the climax of the Christian year. For the wax-strewn pages were precisely those that bore the prayers and praises offered up as the vigil of Easter Eve passed into the day of the resurrection. All lights in the church had been extinguished in preparation for the bringing in of the newly kindled flame of Easter. From that flame, with careful ceremony, the candlelight was gradually spread to the altar and the whole church. No wonder wax fell on the great prayer book, for the chanting of its vital words was maintained while the darkness was receding.

The candles, beautiful in themselves, had deep meaning. They represented the light of Christ who had risen from the darkness of death. Happy were those baptized at this time – an ancient custom. In sign of their new life, they were each given a candle lit from the Easter flame.

And here was an old book revealing such thrilling scenes. It breathed the spirit of faith and awe, a poetry of worship. But it no longer suited the current manner of worship and had been laid aside and forgotten. But in spite of great change in style, the lines of faith continued strongly in that church. And it was still the practice, whatever the season, to present a lighted candle to the baptized person or godparent in sign of the risen life. The candle was given with the words: 'You have received the light of Christ. Walk in this light all the days of your life.' And all the congregation added: 'Shine as a light in the world, to the glory of God the Father.'

This simple action well marked out the Christian way. From the flame of Christ's light, his disciples bring light into the world's darkness. They carry a candle lit from the Easter flame. Drawing from the risen life of Christ, they live in kindness, purity and faithfulness. They reflect the gracious qualities of their Lord. The light in their hearts and faces and hands has come from God's own light.

Now, this is a truth prepared in the poetry of the Psalms. An example comes in Psalm 112. This starts suitably with praise of the Lord. Then it portrays a person happy in knowing God and so reflecting his light:

Alleluia!
Happy the one who fears the LORD,
and greatly delights in his commandments . . .

He will rise in the darkness as a light for the true of heart,
gracious, compassionate and just.

It's an alphabetic psalm. Its statements begin with successive letters of the Hebrew alphabet. This conveys a sense of fundamental truth, the elements of true living. From worship of the Lord, the psalm says, comes blessing. The person attentive to God grows in the divine qualities of grace and kindness, becoming a light of hope that rises in the world's darkness.

And this life drawn from God is indeed a happy one: 'Happy the one who fears the LORD . . . How happy the one who lends in kindness . . . and gives freely to the poor!' There is a wealth here, enough to share and to give. But it is a happiness which is ready to face and overcome tragedy. The

291

light has to shine in darkness. Courage and faith have to be ready against evil tidings. And there are troubles, adversaries, such as always assail a person true to God.

The psalm strongly contrasts the passing nature of evil with the lasting inheritance of the life in communion with God. 'The hope of the wicked will perish', while those who fear the Lord 'will remain in everlasting remembrance'; they will have a blessing that stands for ever.

Here again, the teaching of the psalm finds fulfilment in Christ. The soul that shines with the light of Christ is lit by his resurrection. Such a person does not fear tidings even of death. As the old wax-stained altar book explained, it was through the darkness that they brought in the Easter flame, to spread the light of Christ which is eternal life.

Grant me, Almighty God, the happiness of fearing you and delighting in your commandments.

Enrich me with the wealth of the Spirit, the blessing that overflows and abides for ever. Make my heart steadfast, ever trusting in you.

Light my candle with the light of the risen Christ. May I rise in the world's darkness as a light of pity and goodwill, a light of hope and encouragement, a light of faith and love.

Psalm 113

God revealed in humility

The water of the great lake is fresh and clean and, like the air above it, is pleasantly warm. This is the Sea of Galilee, where you can imagine the stories of Jesus with confidence – the small towns by the shore, the boats, the wild places, the storm and the calm.

Another such region where you can confidently picture Jesus with his disciples is the Mount of Olives. The ancient path still leads from Bethany over the top of the mount, then steeply down to pass by the garden of Gethsemane, across the Kidron Valley, and up again into Jerusalem. In the last days of his earthly life, Jesus was staying with his friends in Bethany. He came along and down that path daily to teach in Jerusalem, and climbed back up to Bethany every night. How close we feel to him if we are fortunate enough to tread the stony path, see the great views of the wilderness to the east and of Jerusalem below, and pass among the ancient olive trees of Gethsemane!

But it is not only places which can bring home past events. The Gospels offer many a detail which can seize an alert imagination. Sometimes, for example, there is a word or phrase preserved in the actual language of Jesus, an echo of his own voice which would not die away – *Amen, amen*, 'Surely, surely'; *Ephphatha*, 'Be opened'; and best of all, *Talitha cumi*, 'Little girl, arise.' And not so often noticed is the clue which can help us to hear Jesus sing. It is recorded that when they had finished that last supper together, Jesus and the disciples sang a hymn and went out on to the Mount of Olives. What was this hymn-singing?

An ancient Jewish custom bodies out the scene for us, and may well enable us to hear the actual words sung. When a family gathered for the Passover meal, remembering the salvation of the Exodus, it was customary to sing a group of praising psalms, Psalms 113–118. They would sing two before the meal and the rest after it. This was very likely the nature of the singing at the Last Supper. In that tense situation, the words of these psalms would carry a huge depth of meaning, prophetic of a new time of salvation and of the way that Jesus must take.

We hear this prophetic power already in the first of the group, the beautiful little Psalm 113. It begins with a threefold call to bless and praise the name of the Lord – God as he gives and reveals himself:

Alleluia!
Praise, you servants of the LORD,
O praise the name of the LORD.

May the name of the LORD be blessed,
from now and for evermore.

From the rising of the sun to its setting,
may the name of the LORD be praised.

The rest of the psalm brings one main thought: wonder that this God so high above all should come down in humility to the rescue of the lowly and despised:

High above all nations is the LORD,
and his glory is above the heavens.

Who is like the LORD our God,
that has his throne so high,

yet humbles himself to behold
the things of heaven and earth,

taking up the poor from the dust,
lifting the destitute from the ash-heap,

making them sit with princes,
with the princes of his people;

giving peace to the barren wife,
making her a joyful mother of children?
Alleluia!

So the psalm which began with such stress on 'the name of the Lord', the form in which he is known, now illustrates the way he comes and shows himself. See, he has come down to the town's garbage heap, where the outcasts scavenge for scraps to keep themselves alive and seek warmth among the ashes. He has taken them up in his arms and restored them to honour and plenty. And see again, he has noted a childless wife, miserable and despised in that society. He has comforted her and made her happy in her home, a joyful mother.

These are but some examples of the way individuals may experience God's grace beyond words. But what a resonance for Christ's followers then and ever since! For he who is the expression of God's heart, the very name of his love, has humbled himself to come down from on high, down to the lowliest. He let himself be made poor and despised. He gave all to show pity to the lonely and lost. He has taken them up and restored their souls in the glory of his love and fellowship.

Yes, praised be the name of God that is expressed in Jesus. May this name of our God be blessed from now and for evermore. From the rising of the sun to its setting, may the name of our Lord be blessed.

Lord Jesus, we remember how you took the bread and broke it and blessed your Father in heaven. We remember how you took the cup and gave thanks and praise. With your disciples you sang the psalms of praise and prophecy. You went out on to the Mount of Olives strong in trust, steadfast in your mission.

Strengthen us also in the bond of trust. Give us courage to be faithful to our mission.

We bless the name of the Lord most high, who has humbled himself to take up the poor from the dust.

Psalm 114

Our journey through the wilderness

Cars and aeroplanes, television, computers, mobile phones, nuclear energy – such commonplaces of life today do not seem to hinder us from identifying with the ancient people who wandered for forty years in the wilderness. Some of our most-sung hymns picture our modern struggles and doubts as like the hardships in those old wilderness stories. And as we sing the hymns, we hope for the same mercy and power of God that are described in those stories.

Take 'Guide me, O thou great Jehovah'. We ourselves ask here to be fed with the bread of heaven, and to drink from the crystal fountain flowing from the rock. We would be guided through our life by the fiery cloudy pillar, until at life's end we reach the verge of Jordan. We ask to be landed safe on the other side by the Saviour whose name is 'Death of Death' and 'Hell's Destruction'.

That is a great Welsh hymn by William Williams. Also much sung is the poem of the American, Love Maria Willis, which we know as 'Father, hear the prayer we offer'. She shows the spirit of those vigorous, pioneering women of the nineteenth century. She prays, not for ease, not to be ever in green pastures, but to tread rejoicingly the steep and rugged pathway. She would not rest idly beside still waters, but rather smite the living fountains from the rocks along her way.

The popularity of these hymns shows how well the ancient stories catch the inner meaning of experience in any time, place and culture – the hopes, the doubts, the getting lost and being found, the danger, the hunger, the marvel of satisfaction, the awesome last barrier, the beckoning of a life beyond. But above all, the hymns are loved and sung because, as we take to ourselves these images of need, we can experience the Lord in his same power to save.

Actually, these wilderness stories have been used like this for thousands of years. There is a psalm, so short, yet so dramatic, which shows how the ancient people too recalled the stories in order to come face to face with the Saviour they told of. It's Psalm 114, which begins at once in story form. It is relating in a very imaginative way how the ancestors were delivered in the Exodus. It goes thus:

When Israel came out of Egypt,
the house of Jacob from a people strange in speech,

Judah became his sanctuary,
Israel the heart of his dominion.

The sea but looked and fled,
the Jordan ran back in its course.

The mountains skipped like rams,
the hills like lambs and kids.

We see that just one feature of the years in Egypt is mentioned – the language, which seemed so strange to the Hebrew tribesmen. There was quite an African character to the Egyptian language, but no doubt it was hearing it from the mouth of harsh gang-masters and police that made it seem so un-homely, so horrible. The people miraculously escaped, but only to face the danger and hardships of the desert. And a new and awesome destiny had come upon them. As the psalm puts it, God possessed them; in them he made his sanctuary, the place of his holy presence and power. They became central to his work on earth. Though they were but a tribal people, the Creator of all was in them, working for all. The natural world was aware of him and responded to his presence. So the psalm-poet tells how the waters fled before him to leave a way for the fugitives. The mountains trembled at his coming. In their alarm, says the poet, they skipped like lambs and kids.

That is already vivid enough to help us see it. But the singer goes a step further. He actually calls out to the fleeing waters, the jumping hills and the quivering earth. He calls out to them as if it is all happening now:

What ails you, O sea, that you flee away,
and Jordan that you run back,

you mountains that you skip like rams,
you hills like lambs and kids?

Tremble, O earth, at the presence of the Lord,
at the presence of the God of Jacob,

who turns hard rock into a pool of water,
flint-stone into a springing well.

A brilliant psalm! So long ago it had the pattern we still follow in our hymns and Eucharists. A few imaginative recollections of the ancient salvation unite us with the same grace of God. We are included in his mighty deed, his setting free and leading on the way of hope. His presence is with us. It is our lives also that are filled with his vocation and mission, our life made meaningful with divine purpose. The holy and almighty One is present before us. And still he is ready to turn the flinty rock into a springing well. The very place of our sufferings and failures he will transform into the place of new life.

Mrs Love Maria Willis wrote of her eagerness to leave behind the still waters. She would rather smite the living fountains from the rocks along her way. True, the human arm of Moses smote the rock in the ancient story, but it was the command and power of God that gave the miracle. So let us be led by the psalm above all to know the Saviour's work and presence, and to believe in his transforming power.

Indeed, the gospel story tells us more of the living water – it is the water of eternal life that flows from the hard rock of Christ's sufferings. In prayer and worship we find that story present and including us. May we have faith that whatever rocks lie in our way, our Lord, ever with us, can turn them into a pool of water. For us too, he will make the flint-stone into a springing well.

Tremble, my soul, at the presence of the Lord. Where will he lead me? What is the rock he will turn for me into a well of life?
Lord, I do not know the way. Lead me by the light and fire of your Holy Spirit. Help me in my fears and hungers. Strong deliverer, be thou still my strength and shield.

Psalm 115
The gods that cannot deliver

'To wander is the miller's joy, to wander, to wander.' It was not a select choir that sang these immortal words, but the entire 400-strong junior school. The dynamic music master directed from the piano, where he hammered out the rhythm of the mill-wheels on the long-suffering keys.

It was the practice at that traditional school to render several such songs en masse at the annual prize-giving day. Their next piece, equally earnest, introduced a sacred note: 'Non nobis, Domine' – 'Not unto us, O Lord'. This was based on Psalm 115: 'Not unto us, O LORD, not unto us, but unto thy name give the glory.' It seemed a good choice for prize-giving day. Let no one bask in glory; all is of God. A similar sense was found in the psalm by King Henry V after the battle of Agincourt. He ordered all to kneel as this verse was sung. In Shakespeare's play, Henry says of the victory, 'Take it, God, for it is none but thine . . . Let there be sung Non Nobis and Te Deum.'

A celebration of victory – yes, the psalm's opening words seem to belong to such an occasion. But read on a line or two, and we find that the opposite is the case. This is in fact a time of defeat:

> Not to us, LORD, not to us, but to your name give glory,
> for the sake of your faithful love and truth.

> Why should the nations scoff
> and say, Where now is their God?

It was in times of suffering that the nation would protest in that fashion. 'See,' they would say to God, 'the nations round about are mocking you, saying "What a fine protector this people has! What sort of a god is that?" So, Lord, you must act for the sake of your own honour. Not for *our* glory, but for your own you must help us. Act for the reputation of your faithfulness and power.'

Our psalm does not keep harping on like that. It goes on to build up the force of its prayer by expressing faith. Defiantly, it declares the Lord's supremacy above all gods and idols:

> Our God, he is in heaven;
> whatever he wills, he does.

> Their idols are but silver and gold,
> the work of human hands.

> They have a mouth, but cannot speak;
> eyes they have, but cannot see.

> They have ears, but cannot hear;
> a nose they have, but cannot smell.

> They have hands, but cannot feel;
>   feet they have, but cannot walk;
> they make no murmur with their throat.

Those that make them will grow like them,
and so will all who trust in them.

In this brave defiance there sounds a message still relevant today. As the community of faith seems to grow weaker, the derisive 'Where now is your God?' may not be uttered in so many words. but it is the thought underlying much of today's culture. Faith can still be defiant. The idols of today – wealth, luxury, pleasure, power, prestige – such idols give promise of happiness, but how they disappoint! These gods of silver and gold also have a mouth, but cannot speak truth. They have ears, but cannot hear for their own clamour. They have hands, but no just feelings. Those who propagate them grow like them, becoming callous to the best qualities of the human heart, insensitive to truth and kindness. And the same fate threatens those who trust in them. Their lives are in danger of becoming shallow, emptied of all deep joy.

The psalm urges us to give trust rather to the Lord. Through the time of pain and failure, hold on to him in trust, and he will be seen again to give blessing. With this counsel different voices seem to sound in the psalm, as one part of the worshipping fellowship encourages another:

O Israel, trust in the LORD.
He is their help and their shield.

O house of Aaron, trust in the LORD.
He is their help and their shield.

You that fear the LORD, trust in the LORD.
He is their help and their shield.

The LORD will remember us, that he may bless.

The psalm rounds off its appeal to God by promising praise. When he restores their life on this good earth, they will for ever give thanks, for, the singer says:

It is not the dead who praise the LORD,
not those gone down into silence.

It is we who will praise the LORD,
from now and for evermore. Alleluia!

We may think it a childlike simplicity as the singer here hints that, if they are to praise the Lord, he must keep them alive and strong to do it. But there is depth in the childlike thought as it grows into the realization that true life *is* praise of God. The only true and lasting joy is the enjoyment of God our Creator and Saviour.

How different the outlook of so many today, worshipping the gods made by human hands, the idols that disappoint. In weakness, humiliation and hardship our psalm defiantly raises its banner, beginning and ending with its theme of 'Not unto us' but to the Lord be all worship, praise and thanksgiving; in him alone be our trust. For such a life, blessing will appear again. Those who trust in him will grow to be like him. In faithful love and goodness they will find true life, the blessing that endures for ever.

Children of God, trust in him. Whatever he wills, he does.
Trust in him, and not in the work of human hands. Even in suffering trust in him, for he is our help and our shield. He will remember us that he may bless us.
Lord, on this good earth that you have entrusted to us, let us know true life as we give you glory. We will trust and praise you, now and for ever.

Psalm 116

Some aspects of love

———•▸◂•———

Such a small word for so great a thing – 'love'! Such a small word to summarize the Bible and our understanding of God – 'love'! Such a small and homely word for what makes life worth living – 'love'!

Love has many aspects. Sometimes we know it as the cause of our actions. We do something out of love. Likewise it is said of God: because of his great love for the world, he gave his beloved Son. Jesus too calls for action because of love, out of love: 'If you love me, keep my commandments'; 'If you love me, feed my sheep.'

Another aspect of love is that it may be quickened by gratitude. We respond with love to someone who has done us a great kindness. Our hearts respond to someone who has rescued us from misery. We are filled with love and the desire to do something in return. It's the same with regard to God: 'We love, because he first loved us.'

One other feature of true love we may mention: it endures. Often it is said of God, 'His love is for ever.' And in the story of Jesus washing his disciples' feet it is said: 'Having loved his own in the world, he loved them to the end.'

But where is this meditation on love leading? The fact is that there's a psalm which begins simply: 'I love.' This is Psalm 116, probably one of those sung by Jesus and the others at the Last Supper. A plain translation of the opening gives: 'I love, for the LORD has heard the voice of my pleading.' So here we have a case of love welling up in response to a great deliverance, one from near death. The opening verses may be rendered thus:

> I am moved with love,
> for the LORD has heard the voice of my pleading.
>
> He turned his ear to me
> on the day that I cried out.
>
> The deadly cords entwined me;
> death's messengers of pain took hold of me,
>   by grief and anguish I was seized.
>
> Then I called on the name of the LORD;
> truly our God is full of compassion.
>
> The LORD watches over the simple;
> I was wretched, and he saved me.

So the singer calls to his soul to return to a happy rest, comforted by the abundant kindness and compassion of God. 'How can I make return', the singer asks, 'How can I make return to the LORD for all the goodness he has poured on me?' In his gratitude he has a renewed desire to serve the Lord. 'I am your servant,' he says, adding 'the son of your handmaid' – that is, like a servant born in the household, a lifelong servant, especially loyal.

His dedication comes to a focus in the ceremony of fulfilling vows, the promises he made when he was in trouble. Before all the assembly of worshippers at the temple, he 'will raise the cup of salvation and proclaim the name of the LORD'. It is the ceremony of thanksgiving and testimony, bearing witness to all the people that the deliverance is owed to the Lord. And he declares that the Lord holds all his servants precious and never thinks lightly of their sufferings and death: 'Costly in the eyes of the LORD is the death of his faithful ones.'

Now, do we remember falling in love? It sometimes happens that when we fall in love a whole new world is lit up for us. We see more beauty in the trees and flowers. We love the birds and animals. We awake to poetry. We become kinder to everyone. We live in the Spirit and know his gifts of love, joy and peace. Our love is then not a narrow preoccupation with one person, but a new sensitivity to all. Perhaps that is why our psalm begins, not 'I love the Lord', but simply, 'I love.' The singer is newly possessed by love. He is filled with love, a love that springs of course from gratitude to his Saviour, but which gives new eyes of love for all God's world.

Do we have to wait till we too are saved from near death before we can enter into this psalm? Surely, if we know Christ has died to save us and has brought us from death to true life, surely then we can say after the psalm: 'I love, I am filled with love. What can I do in return for all his goodness to me? I will raise the cup of salvation. At the celebration of the Lord's Supper I will bring to focus all my gratitude and dedication to his service. In daily living I will proclaim his name and bear witness to his abundant kindness. I love, because he first loved me. And I shall love him to the end.'

Lord, let me love, let me be filled with love, for you have saved me.
You have loosed my bonds, and I will walk before you in the new land of life.
I will love all that you have made. I love, through my love for you.
In the gathering of worshippers, mindful of your sacrifice, I will eat the bread
and raise the cup, and sing the song of thanksgiving.

Psalm 117

When few words are needed

Ireland's rugby team was having a great season. After one remarkable victory, the award for Man of the Match was given to the man who was by far the smallest in the team. In spite of his smallness he had made an outstanding contribution. But no – it would be better to say, not *in spite of*, but *because of* his smallness. Playing in his particular position, he needed to be especially agile and deft. Extra bulk or height would have been a disadvantage.

Now, among the psalms there is one so small that it has often been mistakenly tacked on to a neighbouring psalm. But it really is a separate psalm, though only two verses long. This is Psalm 117, and St Paul recognized its importance, quoting it in his great letter to the Romans. Yes, in the team of psalms it makes an outstanding contribution in spite of its smallness. But again, we should rather say, *because of* its smallness.

Actually, the psalm has in miniature the customary shape of a Hebrew hymn. The singer issues a call to praise, and then gives a reason:

> Praise the LORD, all nations;
> sing praise to him, all peoples.
>
> For his faithful love rises mightily over us,
> and the truth of the LORD endures for ever.

And that is all. That is the whole psalm! It's striking that the singer's call is to 'all nations' and 'all peoples'. He thinks of the congregation, the present circle of worshippers, as made up of all earth's peoples! Not just the folk obviously present in the temple, nor even the whole house of his own nation, but all nations, all peoples! For this singer, they are all one family, one great entity. When he gives the reason for such praise, he just speaks of God's goodness to 'us'. He assumes all have the experience of the Lord's 'faithful love' and 'truth'. These two Hebrew words are connected with covenants and pledges. They are commonly used for God's commitment to Abraham, David or the chosen people. But they are also used of God's commitment to all his creatures, and the psalms are strong on this point. This *universal* love is what our little psalm seizes on. And it does so without complication, without palaver. So directly, so naturally, it lives in the vision of the worldwide family, rejoicing together in the committed, enduring love of the Lord. What was revealed to one nation – God as 'the Lord', his covenanted love and truth, the life of devotion and praise – all this is taken simply as the inheritance of all.

No wonder that St Paul quotes the psalm as he wrestles with the question of Israel's vocation and God's love for all nations. The great apostle rests all on God's purpose in Christ. From among the people made close to God emerges Jesus, the Creator-Word made flesh, and the calling of the one people is fulfilled in the salvation of all. Christ, says St Paul, confirms the promises given to the fathers, and now it is for all nations to glorify God for his mercy – that is, his faithful love and truth.

Let us, then, heirs of this universal faith, join in the praise of our Lord. Let us direct all our love and obedience and thankfulness to him. For over us his faithful love rises mightily. It fills the world, and the world to come. It embraces and blesses all existence. And his truth, his faithfulness, is for ever. Whatever befalls us in this passing world, in life, in death, in the great Beyond, his goodness and grace remain and hold us in Christ's salvation for ever. *Sing praises to him, all peoples!*

*Help us, Lord, to enter into the simplicity of faith. When words become few
and arguments die away, grant us to rest in the love which is everywhere
and for ever – your faithful love given to us and to all creatures in Jesus
Christ, the Way, the Truth and the Life.*
Help all nations to live for your glory and praise.
(An ancient prayer:) *Almighty God, praised by the mouth of all nations, we
pray you to enlarge our soul with your truth and make strong your mercy
upon us.*

Psalm 118

The day that the Lord has made

Can we think of a day in our life that was supremely wonderful and joyful? Perhaps it was a day when a child was born. Or perhaps it was a day
when a long illness was correctly diagnosed and the way opened to recovery. Perhaps it was a day when someone lost was found again. Or it may
have been a day when a first appointment ended a long and penurious
struggle to begin a career. Perhaps it was a day when a refugee found a
home and a new life. There are many and various possibilities for our
supreme day, a day we might think was made in heaven.

In Psalm 118 the worshippers are celebrating such a day, and they have
no doubt of heaven's part in it. They sing:

> This has come from the LORD;
> it is marvellous in our eyes.

> This is the day that the LORD has made;
> we will be glad and rejoice in it.

Looking again at our own wonderful day, when we ourselves were
flooded with joy, we may well see that it contained a big element of relief.
Because previous days had been so hard, this day was all the more wonderful. And such is the case in the psalm. The singer at the centre of the
rejoicing tells of much previous struggle and pain. It seems that he is a
king, and he felt that all nations were attacking him, like angry bees or
fierce flames:

From the grip of distress I called to the LORD;
the LORD answered me and set me in a wide place . . .

All nations surrounded me;
with the name of the LORD I drove them back.

They surrounded me like bees,
    they blazed like fire among thorns;
with the name of the LORD I drove them back.

Yes, the joy was in the transformation – from death to life, from rejection
to honour:

The stone which the builders rejected
has become the head of the corner.

What was this victory that the Lord had given? Why were all nations
attacking? It may well be that this was no event of history. We know that
the psalm had its place in the chief festival of the year, and there are signs
that the victory it celebrated was symbolic. Those festivals had a poetic and
dramatic character. The processions and other ceremonies encapsulated
God's grace to a trusting king and people. They were signs, sacraments,
that brought knowledge of God, powerful experience of him.

Certainly, many verses in the psalm give glimpses of the great procession, up through the temple gates, into the wide court where the column
passed with dancing step around the great altar. The air resounded with
the calls and responses of joy. The scene was festive with all the green
branches of palm, myrtle and willow carried by the worshippers:

Give thanks to the LORD, for he is good;
his faithfulness is for ever . . .

It is better to take refuge in the LORD
than to put your trust in mortals . . .

O the sound of singing and salvation
that rises from the tents of the just . . .

Open to me the gates of salvation;
I will enter to give thanks to the LORD . . .

Come, LORD, give salvation;
come, LORD, give prosperity.

Blessed be he that comes in the name of the LORD;
we bless you all from the house of the LORD.

The LORD is God and has given us light;
　with green boughs link the dance
　　up to the horns of the altar.

The psalm is one of the most quoted in the New Testament. No wonder, for its thoughts and scenes seem vividly prophetic of the gospel story. For one thing, it is a thanksgiving, a kind of 'eucharist', for it begins and ends in thankfulness for the love of God that is for ever faithful. The worshippers in the psalm are uplifted with joy through the action of God, a salvation that has come through one person. Here was one who carried in his heart the fate of all. He was the target of the evil forces. He was tested in suffering and peril. Death thought to claim him for ever. But through trust and prayer he won through. The Lord's right hand did mighty things and raised up the trusting one. Now he ascends and passes through the gate of the Lord. Only for the one that is just and true will these everlasting doors open. For him they open, and give entry also for all he brings with him. All enter into the holy presence, embraced by God's blessing and salvation. In dance and song they celebrate the day of heavenly light, the day the Lord has made, the day when the stone the builders rejected has become the chief cornerstone.

How readily we take this psalm to ourselves as a prophecy fulfilled in Christ! With him, we too trust in the time of peril, hard testing from the hand of God. We trust and call upon his name. Then with him still, we are brought up the steep path into God's light. This, the day of our own deliverance, is the day that the Lord has made. It is a day of new birth, of new health, the day when the lost is found, the fulfilling life begun, the day the wanderer finds a new home. Feet dance for God, heart and lips sing for him. For God in Christ has brought us into his day that will never end.

With you beside me, Lord, I will not fear.
It is better to trust in you than in all the wealth and pretensions of human
　beings.
You have given me new life that I may recount your deeds of grace and mercy.
　You have made for me this day and given me its light.
You are my Lord, and always I will thank you for your faithful love.

Psalm 119
Sweeter than honey

It's a word you won't find in the Bible – 'sugar'. Our Lord speaks of salt and mustard, mint, dill, cumin and leaven, but never of sugar. The biblical people were without the sugar we use so lavishly from sugar cane and sugar beet. As a result, they were keenly appreciative of the sweetness of honey – chiefly, it seems, that of wild bees. To their taste it was exquisite.

To express delight in God's word or teaching, they thought of honey. To recite the holy words with throat and tongue and lips seemed even more delightful than to taste that marvellous sweetness of honey. So says the singer of Psalm 119:

> How sweet your sayings to my tongue,
> sweeter than honey to my mouth!
> (v. 103)

But many other ways does this singer find to express appreciation of the Lord's teachings. For example, he compares them to old treasure you might be excited to stumble upon:

> I rejoice over your word
> as one who finds great spoil.
> (v. 162)

Here there is the excitement of discovering a worth and a beauty you had not suspected.

Then again, the singer compares the sacred words to songs that cheer and encourage on a long journey. We must imagine pilgrims resting for the night at an inn, reviving their spirits with songs of faith:

> Your statutes have become melodies for me,
> my songs in the house of my pilgrimage.
> (v. 54)

Another comparison that he uses for God's word is that of a lamp. Not a great light such as we might have from our powerful batteries or plugs. Only the flame of a wick that draws up oil. A humble light in a great circle of darkness, but welcome indeed:

> Your word is a lantern to my feet,
> and a light upon my path.
>
> (v. 105)

These are but a few examples of the praise of God's word in this long psalm, God's word known in his teachings and counsels. In fact almost all the 176 verses refer to the Lord's word in such a loving fashion. Why should this be? What is the purpose of this unique psalm? The singer gives us the answer as he prays:

> Consider how I love your precepts;
> give me life, LORD, in your faithful love.
>
> (v. 159)

The prayer is that the Lord should take into consideration this love for his word, and so come to the rescue. Here then is a person praying from extreme suffering, and commending his prayer with constant avowals of love for God's word, the word known in law and commandments, counsels and encouragements. So sweet and precious, so rich in life and light, because it is the outgoing of God's wisdom and mercy and love. Surely, hopes the psalmist, surely God will respond to one who so loves his words of guidance and promise.

Yes, the prayer rises from some terrible situation. The singer declares that his soul cleaves to the dust and melts away in tears of sorrow. Arrogant people have dug pits for him. They persecute him falsely and have almost made an end of him on earth. He has become 'like a bottle in the smoke' – a skin bottle stored in the rafters and so grimy from smoke, an image for the miserable condition of mourners. Then again, he is like a lost and starving animal:

> I have gone astray like a sheep that is lost;
> O seek your servant, for I do not forget your commandments.
>
> (v. 176)

With great tenacity, then, this sufferer prays that the Lord would seek him in his lostness and breathe new life into him. 'See, Lord,' he says in effect so many times, 'see how I love your word.' The love is so deep, surpassing all else, because in the holy words and teachings he finds the Lord himself. No wonder they hold for him such marvel and inexpressible beauty:

> Though sorrow and anguish have found me,
> your commandments are my delight.

> I open my mouth and gasp,
> as I long for your commandments.
>
> (vv. 143, 131)

And he is ever eager to find more of this holy treasure:

> Uncover my eyes that I may see
> the wonders of your law.
>
> (v. 18)

The singer does not go far from these few basic thoughts. With slight variations he repeats them again and again. For each letter of the Hebrew alphabet in turn there are eight verses beginning with that letter, and there are eight different words for the Lord's teaching rotated again and again, though in varying order. With this pattern, great length, and restricted range of thought, the psalm is indeed peculiar. But while a famous German scholar (B. Duhm) judged it to be terrible poetry, Christians from early times found it to be 'a paradise of all fruits'. In fact it was the treasured daily food of prayer for countless Christians down the centuries, especially in the monasteries. This was because they linked the word of God so loved by the psalmist with the revelation of Christ. The psalm thus led them to pray for God's breath of life in the name of Christ. They commended their prayer through the love of Jesus, the Word of the Father.

And we too may be bold to pray the psalm through love of him, this Jesus whom we trust and praise and would know and obey more and more. So the simple but unfathomable words of this great psalm will sustain our prayer through Christ, whether we pray for ourselves or for others in need. And all the time we are blessed by being held in communion, touched by the delight of remaining before the face of God.

O God, for all whose souls cleave to the dust and melt away for sorrow, let my cry come to you through Jesus, your Word and your Son.

O Christ, you are the very Word of the Father, the expression of his creating power and love. You are the Way and the Truth, speaking to us in commandments and counsels, teachings and promises.

You are my delight and my treasure, my lantern, my shepherd, my fountain of life. You are my song in the house of my earthly pilgrimage.

O God, before the break of morning I cry to you, and I wait in hope for your word.

Psalm 120

He is our peace

'Well, I can't be in two places at once!' So we say with some irritation when beset by unreasonable demands. But there is a psalm – Psalm 120 – where it would seem someone *is* claiming to be in two places at once. Traditional translation has: 'Woe is me that I sojourn in Meshech, that I dwell among the tents of Kedar.' It is generally thought that Meshech was in the Caucasus, while Kedar was hundreds of miles away in the Arabian desert. Puzzling!

A likely solution is that the singer is using proverb-like expressions. The peoples of Meshech and Kedar were probably proverbial for vengeful savagery. We might more clearly then translate:

> Pity me, that I am like a stranger in Meshech,
> or like one who must dwell among the tents of Kedar.

The singer is lamenting to God, telling him of the trouble he is in. He relates how he tries to make peace with his aggressive enemies, but is only rebuffed with threat of war:

> Too long my soul has dwelt
> with the enemies of peace.
>
> I am for peace, but when I speak of it,
> their mind is only for war.

The singer has begun by declaring that he is turning to the Lord in a time of distress, but still with hope:

> To the LORD I cry in my distress,
> and surely he will answer me.

Then the prayer begins with the holy name that we render 'LORD'. In giving the name, God invited the prayers of sufferers. He is eager for them to call upon him in their troubles. The present trouble is described as an attack through damaging words:

> LORD, deliver my soul from lying lips
> and from the deceitful tongue.

Such verbal attacks are often lamented in the psalms, hostile words like sharp or flaming arrows. They may be the prelude to open war, and in themselves they are already deadly. Carrying falsehood and distortion, they are designed especially to damage a leader by spreading hatred, confusion and discontent. So, in his prayer, the singer looks for the justice of God to fall upon these archers of evil words. He warns the evil tongue that it will be requited with arrows of judgement from the hand of God:

> What shall he give you, and what more besides,
> O you deceitful tongue?

> The sharp arrows of a mighty one,
> and burning shafts of broom.

It's a picture of fire not easily put out, for broom or juniper brands were noted for retaining heat.

In our own society, we are alas accustomed to the ruthless use of words. Most obvious is the verbal warfare between political parties. As elections approach, arrows of deceit and distortion fill the air – and at other times also. Flames of misrepresentation and hatred destroy good causes and good leaders. The art of appealing to the worst in people is practised skilfully and cold-bloodedly. Those who have lived through full-scale war itself know how thoroughly the weapons of words are deployed. Things may have been worse in the psalmist's time, inasmuch as society was less educated and more tribal. But on the other hand, our modern inventions bestow terrible powers for the spreading of falsehood and the manipulation and control of minds.

But our psalm arises not only from the distress caused by false words. The singer is very grieved that his overtures of peace are met only with hatred and violence. 'I am for peace,' he says, 'but when I speak of it, their mind is only for war.' We can well understand this, for in our time also, peacemaking is a dangerous business. Good individuals have been murdered when they carried the banner of peace, and indeed were near to achieving reconciliation.

Jesus especially blessed the peacemakers. He could hardly value them more than when he says, 'Blessed are the peacemakers, for they shall be called the children of God.' He knew fully the sorrow of representing God's peace, only to be answered with hatred and death. Christians have indeed seen the psalm as prophetic of him. Through him we gain courage to offer peace, to represent peace, in spite of all hostility. With him we will suffer for peace. But with him also, we will trust that in the end the peace of God will prevail.

And, thanks be to God, that peace, here and there, already breaks through. A Japanese woman reached out the hand of peace to those who had suffered in Japanese prisoner-of-war camps. Bitter still, decades after those appalling cruelties, the elderly survivors were minded to rebuff her with contempt. But their hatred, understandable as it was, weighed as a harmful burden on themselves, and she felt she must persevere. Those who, however reluctantly, accepted her invitation to visit Japan, were shown the face of kindness. One old veteran told of his ill temper persisting as he was treated as an honoured guest. Still vexed, he went with the family to feed the fish. But on the way, the miracle happened. The woman's little daughter took his hand and smiled up at him, and his heart melted. The lake, the fish and the birds now seemed to him perfectly beautiful. And still today, as he speaks of the little girl, his voice breaks and his eyes fill with tears. For in that blessed moment, a great weight of implacable hatred was lifted from his soul. Yes, blessed are the peacemakers, who by the Holy Spirit persevere for divine peace. Truly, they shall be called the children of God.

Lord, deliver my soul from lying lips and from the deceitful tongue, whether they would destroy me or poison my mind against others.
Grant that I be rooted in your truth and guarded by the purity of your word.
In the pattern of Jesus, let me be a person of peace, and never discouraged. In all distress, help me to raise my cry to you, and know that you will answer me.

Psalm 121

The message on the doorpost

An autumn day broke over Primrose Lane. Reluctantly, it seemed, the daylight grew stronger and the rain eased off. Here and there, people began to emerge from their front doors. Young folk, swinging satchels, lurched towards the school bus. A woman in a smart black suit hurried into her car for a day of accountancy. Over the road another woman stumbled towards her car for a day of nursing. A dapper man checked that his car was gleaming and fit to represent the company. By now they were emerging all along the lane, intent on the day's tasks. Most seemed tense or worried. Not surprisingly, for many were the pressures of modern life, and no one knew what the day held in store for good or ill.

But there was one man who came out in a rather different manner. He rested his hand on a small object fixed to the frame of the front door. As he paused for a few seconds, his lips moved gently. Then he set off at a steady pace up the road to the railway station. If you saw this man on his return in the evening, you would notice the same unusual behaviour. Reaching his front door, he would again put his hand on the object fixed to the doorpost, and pause awhile before letting himself in.

What was it all about? The object on the doorpost was a small metal cylinder containing a rolled-up parchment. Written on the parchment were two passages from Deuteronomy (6.4–9; 11.13–21), including these words: 'The LORD is our God, the LORD alone. And you shall love the LORD your God with all your heart and with all your soul and with all your might. And these words shall be upon your heart, and you shall talk of them when you sit in your house, and when you walk by the way, and when you lie down, and when you rise up. And you shall write them on the doorposts of your house.'

Our friend in Primrose Lane was following a Jewish custom thousands of years old. As he touched the cylinder on the doorpost, he recited the verse from Psalm 121: 'The LORD will guard your going out and your coming in from now and for evermore.' Thus he laid hold of the promise of the Lord's protection as he went out upon his day's business. And when coming back in, he gratefully acknowledged the day's protection and gathered it again to take into his house.

'The LORD will guard your going out and your coming in from now and for evermore' – this is the end of the well-loved Psalm 121, summing up repeated assurances of the Lord's protection for his trusting ones. Those promises are eloquent:

> He will not let your foot be tripped;
> he who guards you will not slumber.
>
> See, the guardian of Israel
> will neither slumber nor sleep.
>
> The LORD himself will guard you,
> the LORD at your right hand will be your shade.
>
> By day the sun shall not strike you,
> nor shall the moon by night.

The LORD will guard you from all evil;
he himself will guard your soul.

We may wonder here at the lack of conditions. There is no 'He will guard you if . . .' But the memorable opening lines of the psalm do show how from our side there must be trust:

I lift up my eyes to the hills;
O from where shall my help come?

My help will come from the LORD,
the maker of heaven and earth.

It is as though we look up to the hills from a valley of troubles, wondering where help is to come from. Then we affirm from a believing heart: 'My help will come from the LORD. He alone is my helper, the Creator, the only LORD. In him alone is my trust.' Yes, to such a heart, to such a faith, the great promises of protection are made.

But even then, will no harm indeed ever strike us? Many times we experience wonderful instances of his protection. Yet we must expect to suffer on earth. Was not our Lord Jesus, so strong in faith, struck down, and all the faithful martyrs after him? Truly, there is a mystery in this promised watchfulness and caring of God our protector. But if our going out and our coming in is with the love of God in our hearts, we may be sure that in the end no harm will triumph over us. In God's eternity, his 'evermore', the secret of his loving care will be revealed. We shall know that in his faithfulness he has guarded our soul from all evil. He has truly guarded our going out and our coming in for evermore.

That neighbour who paused to touch the box on his doorpost and say the psalm verse – he was connecting with a great tradition of faith. It was a simple act of body and soul. But it would be no surprise to learn that it lifted stress from his soul and nourished him in the peace of God. Might we do something similar?

Lord, possess our hearts and minds, so that in all our goings out and comings in we are mindful of you and take to ourselves your promise of protection.
When we lift up our eyes to the hills in longing for your help, may we hear your promise to guard us from all evil.
Let me rest in the shadow of your wings, from now and for evermore.

Psalm 122

Praying with love for Jerusalem

Even in our era of traffic and concrete, the names of some cities have retained a touch of romance. We sometimes hear nostalgic songs about New York or Copenhagen, Vienna or, most of all, Paris. A tear has even been raised for 'dear old London town'. Some cities do have fine centres, monuments or parks. But seen as a whole, from boundary to boundary, the modern city is not a thing of beauty. The characteristic that comes readily to mind is sprawl. Compared with cities of old, our cities are vast areas, sprawling monsters ever greedy to swallow more fields and woodlands.

Cities are often mentioned in the Bible, but they were nothing like the cities of our time. Relatively small, they were usually built of stone and lay snugly over a hill, surrounded with fortified walls. There was no scope for random development. With the need for defence against invaders and for access to water, and sometimes with the dominance of temple and palace, all was thought through and unified.

For many centuries Jerusalem was such a city, built on a small but steep hill that had the advantage of a gushing spring at its base. Then King Solomon extended the city to the higher hill on the north side, where he had room for a splendid temple and palace. But still all was knit together, circled by its wide wall. It would be a thrilling sight for the many thousands of pilgrims bound for the annual festival, as they approached over the ring of higher hills. And what an experience soon to find themselves in the great fellowship of worshippers within the holy gates! Their feelings are caught by the singer of Psalm 122, from the moment when a party of pilgrims prepared to leave their village, to the time when their feet stood in the temple courts:

I was glad when they said to me,
We will go to the house of the LORD.

And now our feet are standing
within your gates, O Jerusalem –

Jerusalem, you that are built
as a city bound in fellowship.

Here the singer appreciates that the compactly built, unified city suits the unity and fellowship of the worshippers. Architecture and mood go together. The buildings suit the soul. They lift the spirit. It was especially important for Jerusalem. For this was a tribal people with a history of tribal feuding. But Jerusalem, 'built as a city bound in fellowship', brought the tribes together in unity before the Lord. As the singer says:

> Here the tribes ascend, the tribes of the LORD . . .
> to give thanks to the name of the LORD.

> And here stand thrones for justice,
> the thrones of the house of David.

Yes, it was the centre for all the tribes to gather and worship, but it was also the centre of justice. There the kings of David's line had the duty of upholding God's laws and hearing the complaints of the poor. What a great role for a little city! What a great ideal for this city to fulfil: the centre where the name of the Lord is praised and God's living order is upheld! And the singer knows what a lot is at stake and what the dangers are. With great emphasis he calls on the worshippers to pray for Jerusalem with all their love and earnestness, to pray that God's blessing and peace ever abound in her:

> O pray for the peace of Jerusalem;
> may blessing abound on those who love you.

> Peace be within your walls,
> tranquillity within your palaces.

> For the sake of my brothers and companions,
> I will pray down peace upon you.

> For the sake of the house of the LORD our God,
> I will seek good for you.

The psalm has a direct message for us: 'Pray for the peace of Jerusalem.' For this central city and for the peoples of the Holy Land there is an urgent need to pray, to ask the Lord with all our hearts for their blessing, justice and peace. And beyond the physical Jerusalem there is the city of God, the Church that enfolds us in our faith and worship. For this spiritual Jerusalem too we must pray down blessing. God has made her a place of meeting, a joining of soul to soul and of Creator to creatures, the place of the fellowship of the Holy Spirit. He has made her a place of reconciliation and a fountain that quickens the living order. He has made her the very heart of gladness, blessing and peace.

But she is clothed in humility and vulnerability. She suffers the anger of chaotic forces and the wounding of sin. So pray for her, and ask for her the renewal of peace and tranquillity. Pray down the Lord's blessings upon her, and in this proof of your love for her you will yourself be blessed.

Lord, may glad desire ever bring us to your house.
When our feet stand within your gates, help us to discern the meaning. May
*   we know the binding of love between all who are turned to you.*
Help us to know the place of your justice and hear your rulings on our daily
*   life, that we may live in accord with the living way of your creation.*
Lord, hear our prayer for the peace of Jerusalem.

Psalm 123
The mercy of God

There are fashions in first names. A name which has not been in use for ages, if at all, suddenly reappears in strength. Suddenly the young all seem to be called Joshua or Olivia, Ethan or Emily. But some names maintain a steady popularity – such as John or Anne. Such names have not only long continued common; they have also appeared in numerous variations. 'John', for example, appears also as Ian, Shane, Hans, Giovanni, Juan, Jack or Jock – the list seems endless. The family of 'Anne' includes Hannah, Anita, Nancy, Jane, Jean, Joan, Janet, Joanna and Jessie. What is the root of all these names in the family of John and Anne? It is the Hebrew word for 'grace' or 'to be gracious'. 'John' means 'The Lord has been gracious'. It is the mother's exclamation of gratitude to God when she has given birth. So all through the world, wherever one of this great family of names is used, there is testimony to the grace of God, testimony that we live only through his compassion and kindness, his mercy, his grace.

One of the best known and most used Christian sentences begins with the word 'grace'. It's the end of St Paul's second letter to the Christians in Corinth: 'The grace of the Lord Jesus Christ, and the love of God, and the fellowship of the Holy Spirit be with you all.' It's a mighty prayer and will repay much meditation. It is striking that 'the love of God' takes second place. We may imagine that Paul has let the prayer flow readily from his heart. So he begins with the beginning of the distinctive Christian experience, when we become aware of 'the grace of the Lord Jesus Christ'. Through that lowly, most beautiful gate we come to 'the love of God', not as in second place, but in the centre, the heart of all things. We are led into it by the grace of Christ, and then kept and nourished in it by 'the fellowship of the Holy Spirit'. As we meditate further, we see that each part of the prayer is in the others. It is one great blessing upon us, God's grace, love and fellowship, through Father, Son and Holy Spirit.

But what really is 'grace'? Surely, we think here of Christ's good will, kindness and compassion, all the more wonderful because shown to us so unworthy. In his grace he reached out to us and suffered to save us and bring us new life. But already in Old Testament times there was knowledge of God's grace – his pity, kindness, mercy. The psalms often pray that the Lord will be gracious, taking pity on his suffering people. In one example, the leading singer speaks of his eyes that look up imploringly to the King of heaven, yearning for his grace. This is Psalm 123, which begins thus:

> To you I lift up my eyes,
> you that sit enthroned in the heavens.
>
> As the eyes of servants look to their master's hand,
> as the eyes of a maid to the hand of her mistress,
>
> so our eyes look to the LORD our God,
> until he take pity on us.

Just as servants in those days were dependent on the kindness of their masters, so these worshippers acknowledge that only the commands and gifts of God the King can meet their need. The singer is praying for a people oppressed and scorned. Their soul is bitter that they have suffered so long at the hands of arrogant foes who are prosperous and callous. So the prayer rises:

> Have pity on us, LORD, have pity on us,
> for we have had more than enough of derision.
>
> Our soul is filled with the scorn of those at ease,
> with the derision of the proud.

'Have pity on us, LORD', they pray repeatedly – have compassion, have mercy, be gracious, let your grace be upon us. This prayer has echoed constantly in Christian worship and devotion. It is the *Kurie eleison* that is the heart of all our supplication: 'Lord, have mercy; Christ, have mercy; Lord, have mercy. Lord Jesus Christ, have mercy upon me.'

With such a prayer we lift our eyes to heaven in hope and in confidence through our Lord Jesus Christ. But if our soul is bitter at the scorn of those who fare better than us, we have to let Christ's grace overcome our bitterness. For his grace can not only deliver us from trouble, but also remake us in the likeness of God's love. Then our soul is filled, not with the scorn of those at ease, not with bitterness and envy, but with the Holy Spirit, who brings communion and fellowship with God.

Yes, let the Johns and Janes, the Annes and Ians, the Joans and Giovannis be glad of the grace of God hidden in their names. Let all the humble be led by the grace of the Lord Jesus Christ into the love of God, and remain there for ever through the fellowship of the Holy Spirit. Amen.

King of heaven, we lift our eyes and our prayer to you: Have mercy, Lord. In pity act for all your little ones that suffer under the cruel and callous.
All living things, Lord, hang upon your kindness and goodness. Kurie eleison, Lord, have mercy.
The grace of the Lord Jesus Christ call us out of darkness and out of emptiness.
The love of God fill our souls.
The fellowship of the Holy Spirit keep us in the divine communion, now and evermore.

Psalm 124

If the Lord had not been with us

Imagine you are in mountainous country. You are a few thousand feet above sea level. As you scramble up the track, there is little to see but arid slopes, rocks and boulders. There may be danger from snakes or robbers, but the last thing you fear is flooding. And yet the peril is real. Higher in the mountains, winter storms may already have broken. Water could be cascading down parched gullies and gathering into the ravine that you are ascending. A huge wall of water may rush round a bend and hurtle down at you so suddenly, so fast, that you have little chance of escaping. It's as well we are only imagining it. But deaths through such mountain floods are not uncommon in the Holy Land. The danger was known to the psalmists, as we see in Psalm 124:

> If the Lord had not been with us,
> let Israel now say,
>
> if the Lord had not been with us,
> when men rose up against us,
>
> then they would have swallowed us alive,
> when their anger burned against us;
>
> then the waters would have drowned us,
> and the flood gone over our soul;
>
> right over our soul would have swept
> the proud and raging waters.

Is the singer looking back through history and acknowledging God's grace and protection? Or does he refer to some recent deliverance? We can't be sure, but certainly the psalm is an emphatic testimony to the Lord's help in time of peril. And it seems especially designed for all the people to join in. The first line has a swinging lilt in the Hebrew. It's followed by a call for everyone to join in. Then the first line is repeated and the psalm gets fully under way. Yes, this is a testimony which all the assembly are glad to sing, so conscious they are of perils God has saved them from.

After that comparison with the mountain storm-flood, the picture of peril changes – it becomes the jaws of a monster, then a cunning trap to catch a bird. The people indeed had been trapped, but, they say, the Lord broke the snare and set them free. So they bless him, and bless the name he gave them to use to call for his help:

> Blessed be the Lord,
> who has not given us up for a prey to their teeth.
>
> Our soul escaped as a bird from the snare of the fowler;
> the snare was broken and we went free.
>
> Our help is in the name of the Lord,
> the maker of heaven and earth.

Now, how do we relate to that dramatic testimony from the pilgrims gathered so long ago in Jerusalem? Recently, at the request of a magazine editor, an elderly man was writing some reminiscences of years gone by. He found it hard to recall the events in their proper sequence and in full detail. Things that were said and done floated back into his mind, but often they were like isolated points of light emerging from a mist. One impression, however, grew upon him more and more – wonder at the perils he had been in without realizing it at the time. He wondered what prayers had been said for him, what angels had been sent to guard him. For indeed there had been times when a storm-flood of troubles might have swept him away. There had been times when he might have been lured into a trap. But the divine hand had saved him – the Name of the Lord that works through prayers and unrecognized angels.

And it is good for all of us, individuals or nations, to pause and reflect on the dangers we have been saved from. Perhaps people today are inclined to attribute their escape to luck or chance. But it is a wonderful thing when our eyes are opened to see that God has saved us – saved us no doubt for a purpose, for new dedication to his service. It is wonderful and uplifting, joyful and inspiring, to be able to say, 'Blessed be the LORD who has not let me be a prey to their teeth. My help is in the name of the LORD, the maker of heaven and earth.'

It is a reminder, too, of how misguided we are to face dangers or adversities without calling upon his name. Are we that confident in our own strength and wisdom? Or has our sense of God's reality so weakened? Let us hear again the testimony of the psalm, and of people today who have known the marvel of God's help, his response to those who call on his name.

A widow who had faithfully brought up a family in spite of poverty was arguing with her son about religion. She would not normally have said anything about it or about her own hardships either. But he, with all the advantage of education, was holding forth, and his confident dismissal of faith goaded her into a sudden exclamation. With wide eyes she exclaimed, 'How do you think I could have managed all these years without the help of God?' The young man and the others present were struck to silence. The unexpected words, bursting from the heart, gave them much to ponder.

Our psalm leads all the faithful in such testimony. When we truly discern the way we have come, we shall think less of our own strength, or luck or chance, and rather say, 'If the LORD had not been with me, the waters would have drowned me. But blessed be the LORD who has not given me up. My help is ever in the name of the LORD, the maker of heaven and earth.'

O God, our Creator and Saviour, help us to search our heart and discern how you have safely brought us to this day.

We thank you for coming to us in the name of Jesus, the name through which we can call upon your help in every trouble. Through our Lord Jesus Christ we pray that you will save us from danger that may rush upon us, and from the traps that would lure and seize us.

Blessed be the Lord who has not given us up for a prey to their teeth, but has broken the snare and set us free. Now and evermore our help is in the name of the Lord.

Psalm 125

Prayer against corruption

It was a book to haunt the imagination – James Hilton's *Lost Horizon*. He told of a Buddhist monastery hidden and protected by the mountains in Tibet. It was Shangri La, a paradisal place on which rested a timeless peace. There even death had little chance to intrude, as the monks lived to astonishing ages.

One of the psalms seems set to picture Jerusalem as a kind of Shangri La. This is Psalm 125, which begins: 'Mount Zion shall not be overthrown, but stands for ever. Jerusalem has mountains round about her, and so the LORD is round about his people, now and for evermore.' The concluding thought is of a people sheltered by peace. So here we have a holy city, a place of peace and protected by mountains round about. It is the community of those who trust in the Lord. They are secure within the ring of his protection.

It's an idyllic picture the psalm begins to unfold – but only to contrast it with a sad reality. For the little psalm turns out to be an urgent prayer from a difficult situation. We might compare the situation in occupied countries in the Second World War. When the Nazis took control of a country, they made use of the former administration. So rapidly were they increasing their empire that they needed to use the former officials and administrators, while taking care that their own control was absolute. The result was that some of the subjugated people entered willingly into the Nazi ways and zealously carried out their cruel policies. Others, of better character, found that they could hardly keep clear of the evil, and in some measure were defiled by it.

The people of the psalm are likewise suffering under an evil regime, which the singer calls 'the sceptre of wickedness'. Some of the people have already turned to crooked ways. But even others of better character, the good people, are under pressure to stretch out their hand to wrong.

So the singer leads prayer for God's help. He gives force and urgency to his prayer by weaving in strands of those old promises and hope – that Jerusalem would be protected, that the trusting ones would never be overthrown. Surely God will not allow this evil dominion to rest and remain on his people, causing such a falling away from faith and goodness! So the prayer rises, weaving its contrast of faith and present suffering. All is covered in a few lines:

> Those who trust in the LORD are like Mount Zion,
> which shall not be overthrown, but stands for ever.
>
> Jerusalem has mountains round about her,
> and so the LORD is round about his people, now and for evermore.
>
> The sceptre of wickedness shall not rest on the portion of the just,
> lest even the just stretch out their hands to wrong.
>
> Do good, LORD, to those who are good,
> to those who are true of heart.
>
> Those who turn to crooked ways
>   the LORD will lead off with the evildoers;
> peace be over Israel.

History was to give little scope to such peace. Again and again the divine protection around Mount Zion was obscured by the smoke and fire of war and oppression. And sometimes the sceptre of wickedness held sway over the society in a less dramatic fashion.

Perhaps now is such a time for many countries in the modern era. Some suffer corruption under tyranny or anarchy. In affluent countries, people are eased into selfish and crooked ways through luxury and the encouragement of greed and instant gratification. From the psalm we should learn rather to trust in the Lord and to pray against the corrupting power. In the fellowship of the Holy Spirit we are then strengthened to share the vision of Christ and his saints and the people of the psalms. We see through to the divine protection which does not yet eliminate suffering or temptation, but in the end, in God's time, will be seen in all its power and marvel. Those who trusted in the Lord will be found to stand as surely as God's holy mountain. The psalm prompts us here and now to pray for that time of vindication and for deliverance from corruption. With Christ himself we pray, *Thy kingdom come . . . lead us not into temptation but deliver us from evil.* With courage and faith we must ever pray that his peace rest over his people and over all his creation.

Father, the sceptre of wickedness rules over many peoples at this time.
  Persecution falls on those who are good and true of heart. Over much of the earth an evil regime of greed and godlessness holds power and incessantly pours its doctrines into the minds of young and old.
Lord, do not let these sceptres of wickedness rest and remain upon your world.
  Come quickly to take away the destroyers and corrupters.
Strengthen us against temptation to do wrong.
Peace be over all your creatures, which you have made in wisdom and love.

Psalm 126
Tears over a bag of seed

In education today young people seem to have great choice of subjects. Those offering the various subjects strive to make them seem attractive and enjoyable. Against this trend, however, is the fact that some of the greatest treasures of education can only be attained by way of a long and difficult apprenticeship. Take languages, for example. There is much grammatical spadework to be done before one can benefit from the great cultures and literatures of foreign peoples, ancient or modern. Or again, take music. The early years of study in music are not without pleasure, but what a lot of discipline and determination is needed to reach real competence on an instrument or in the art of composition! For so many great subjects we could say that only those who sow in tears will reap in joy.

  And there we have done it – we have quoted a psalm, the hauntingly beautiful Psalm 126. This is how it ends:

  Those who sow with tears
    shall reap with songs of joy.

> One who goes out bitterly weeping, bearing the bag of seed,
> shall come in singing for joy, bearing the harvest sheaves.

The psalmist himself is not thinking of education. His concern is with a period of national hardship. His parable from nature will encourage the people to hold on to their faith. From time immemorial sowing the seed had seemed like a burial. Some older peoples in that area, indeed, carried out customs of mourning as they sowed. Certainly, all that was done in cultivation was done in hope and earnest prayer. In due course came the sprouting and fruiting, and so at last the joy of harvest. So nature gave her parable of hope and fulfilment, tears of faithfulness turning at last to laughter of thankfulness.

While that is the end of the psalm, the beginning is just as picturesque. The singer builds up his plea to God by recalling happy years gone by. Those were times when neighbouring peoples were awed to see how the Lord had blessed his people. Thus the psalm begins:

> When the LORD restored the life of Zion,
> we were like those who dream.

> Then our mouth was filled with laughter,
> and our tongue with songs of joy.

> Then they said among the nations,
> The LORD has done great things for them.

> The LORD indeed did great things for us,
> and how we then rejoiced!

In all this recollection the singer is preparing for his great plea. He has shown his belief that only the Lord could give such happiness, and he has implied the consideration that great praise would rise to the Lord, even from foreign nations, if he would again restore his people in happiness. And now comes his plea, a prayer for new life. An old translation rendered it memorably: 'Turn our captivity, O LORD, as the rivers in the south.' We may better give the sense thus:

> Restore, O LORD, our life again,
> as you revive the brooks in the wilderness.

The singer here draws a picture from nature in the southern wilderness, the Negev. Through a long summer the area is dried up. The channels cut by winter's water flowing from higher hills are now just parched gullies. But when a new round of winter rain pours down them, they turn into ribbons of green, their banks bright with grass and wild flowers. It is a transformation from death to life, and for such a transformation in their own circumstances the people pray: 'Restore, O LORD, our life, as you revive the brooks in the wilderness.'

The psalm does not disclose to us what kind of death lay over the people, but it may well have been a series of bad seasons, with drought bringing starvation and bondage. So they pray for a great turning, a merciful action of God that will bring back the joy of true life. It would be like that remembered time when once he had restored their life so wonderfully that they thought they must be dreaming. In those former days their mouths were filled with laughter and their tongues with songs of praise. O that such days would come again! And so the prayer rises passionately, 'Restore, O LORD, our life again, as you revive the brooks in the wilderness.'

In our day we often hear of plans to 'regenerate' communities. It usually involves rebuilding and also attracting new businesses which will give employment. Not only communities, however, need regeneration. For individuals also there may be a need for a great turning, a drastic change from an arid, heavy-hearted existence to a new life of beauty and laughter, a mouth filled with songs of praise.

The psalm leads us to the thought that such a great turning or transformation comes only from the hand of God. It is he who is able to do great things for us. To him we must cry with all our heart and in him we must trust. But the inspiring comparisons made by the psalm bring us also the thought of our bond with nature – the sowing and the reaping, the rain that turns hard earth into a place of flowers and green life. Our happiness in new life from God's hand will be the greater if we respect the harmony of his creation. Let us love and care for the earth and the life-giving waters, the seed and the growth, and all the living creatures made by God's hand and word. Let us pray and care for them as for ourselves. Then we and all the earth will be as those that dream, as together we laugh and praise our Creator.

Turn our captivity, O Lord, as the rivers in the south. Deliver us from the death-way of sin and restore us by your living water. By your Spirit fill our mouth with laughter and our tongues with songs of thanksgiving. O Lord, restore our life as you restore the gullies in the wilderness.

Help us to persevere in prayer and faithful service, believing that as we sow in tears, we shall in your time reap with songs of joy.

We praise you, Lord, that again and again the seed has been sown with weeping, but the harvest sheaves have been brought in with joy.

Psalm 127

Achievement and anxiety

In a leafy suburb, the residents were having a time of prosperity. They had lots of money to spend, and one of the outlets for their wealth was building. It seemed as if every other house was having an extension built or a new driveway laid. Some houses had even been knocked down to make way for grander ones. The massive vehicles and machinery of the modern builder's art were everywhere to be seen, virtually part of the landscape. A profitable time indeed for house-builders!

Another line of business doing well from all this activity was home security. All these fine buildings needed careful guarding. Indeed, the wealthy residents were more anxious about the property than their predecessors had been, especially as it was now fashionable to be away a lot of the time on holidays and breaks. Watchdogs and Neighbourhood Watch schemes were not enough to put their minds at rest. So a brisk business was done in security systems, and the song of the birds was often drowned by the piercing sound of alarms, usually having gone off by mistake and generally ignored.

One day, however, for those with ears to hear, a relevant counsel was given in the neighbourhood church. A psalm was sung – Psalm 127 – and its message was blunt:

> If the LORD does not build the house,
> its builders toil on it in vain.
>
> If the LORD does not guard the city,
> its guard is wakeful all in vain.

It is striking that the singer does not advise us just to seek the Lord's help or guidance in our building or guarding. He goes further. All is in vain, he says, if the Lord does not actually himself build the house or guard the city. How can this be, that God should act so directly? Well, we have to be so humble and open to God that he works through us. In humility and attention to him, we become a channel of his peace and of his work. But we are up against the anxious, untrusting tendency in our hearts, so the singer continues:

> In vain you rise up early
> and go so late to your rest,
>
> eating the bread of anxious toil,
> for he gives to his beloved in sleep.

This was a counsel our Lord was to develop so beautifully, as he pointed to the wild birds and flowers and God's care of them. It is also a theme used memorably in the French poetry of Charles Péguy (1873–1914). Péguy, in his poem 'The mystery of the Holy Innocents', imagines God speaking to the night, his 'daughter of the silver cloak'. God praises her as the only one who can bring comfort to anxious man, who can't leave off his calculating, his ever worrying, his thoughts that rattle round in his head like seeds in a pumpkin. Péguy imagines that, as night brought an end to the terrible day of Calvary and soothed God's own mourning, so she comes every evening to the least of us. She comes and wraps us in her mantle of silence and shadow, lifting away the racking anxiety of the day. The one who stubbornly resists, calculating still as though the world would stop without him, such a one does not please God. 'The one who pleases me', says God, 'is the one who rests in my arms like a laughing baby.' It sees the world in its mother's eyes, and only there.

The French poet here comes close to our psalm's counsel. To let the Lord build the house or guard the premises, the psalm teaches, we must put away that over-anxious spirit, restless from early morning to late at night, 'eating the bread of anxious toil'. We must put things into God's hand, for he who made us and upholds the universe, he can give to his beloved even as they sleep.

But now the singer goes further with the thought of what the Lord gives:

> See, children are a heritage bestowed by the LORD;
> the fruit of the womb is given by him.

And the singer extols the benefit of that strong family given by God. He imagines them 'in the gate', the arena where legal disputes were tried. The interests of such a family would not be easily trampled on. 'They shall not be put to shame when they speak with adversaries in the gate.'

That's a vivid glimpse of the old society. But what is the message of these verses for today, in circumstances so different? First, that in matters of family we should think of the Lord's action – his gift, his blessing, his guarding, his purpose. In this again, the counsel is to trust and not to be harried by anxiety.

And further, as we learn from early Jewish teachers, the 'children' given by the Lord can include all whom we may influence and love. We may be literally childless, but God may have given us a huge family of those we care for, pray for, influence. The childless may in God's time be astonished to see how many such children he has blessed them with.

Yes, for those folk in the leafy suburb there was plenty in the psalm for them to think about. It speaks of a wealth such folk could miss through preoccupation with their own efforts, plans and desires. It is the wealth of trust in the Lord, that openness to him which lets his Spirit work through us to build the house, guard the city, create a family. People may suppose we have been hard-working, but we shall know that all is given us as our spirits rest in his arms.

Lord Jesus, you have taught us to consider the ravens and the raiment of the wild flowers. You teach us to trust in the Father's goodness for our bread, clothing and shelter. Help us so to rest in you that you can work through us.

Grant us to be humble and open towards you, so that you can enter in and do your good and beautiful work through our hands.

May we know the strength of belonging to the great family of those who love you.

Psalm 128

A beneficial fear

—◆◆◆—

Happiness and fear don't usually go together. We expect rather that happiness would begin when fear ended. But Psalm 128 pictures another situation and begins quite emphatically:

> Happy is everyone who fears the LORD
> and ever walks in his ways.

Here is a singer confident that great happiness comes to everyone who *fears the Lord* and *walks in his ways* – two biblical expressions closely connected. To 'fear the Lord' is to know him truly as God, to recognize him as the greatest reality, infinite in power and goodness. If we fear the Lord, we know his claim upon us and his grace supporting us. We know him before us and with us in every place and in every time. If we fear the Lord, we must surely be humble, no longer god to ourselves.

And further, as the psalm says, we 'walk in his ways' – the movement of our life, the daily actions as we come and go, our long-term aims and direction, all is in company with him, a walking with him. His ways are marked out for us by his teachings, especially the counsels and commandments of Jesus, his laws of trusting and showing kindness, praying and giving thanks, loving God and our neighbour. Walking in such ways, alive to God, we find the happiness which the psalm celebrates.

People visiting the Holy Land are sometimes shocked by the dryness of the hills. It is not a lush green landscape such as is found in Ireland or Britain. But like many hilly lands around the Mediterranean, it has a special glory in its orchards of olive and fig trees and its terraces of vines, pleasant indeed under bright skies. The psalm-singer now draws some comparisons from the vines and olives that were such a big part of the people's life. That was a life where a good family of children was much prized. When there was talk of happiness, the people thought not only of good crops and flocks, but also of a household of lively children. So the singer puts his promise of happiness like this:

> You will eat indeed the labour of your hands;
> happiness and blessing will be yours.
>
> Your wife will be like a fruitful vine within your house;
> your children like olive plants round about your table.
>
> See, this will be the blessing
> for one who fears the LORD.

The conclusion of the psalm develops this blessing upon the fearers of the Lord. It's like a strong prayer that they may be healthy and fruitful, see the holy city abide in peace, and live to see peace upon their children's children:

> The LORD bless you from Zion,
> so that you see Jerusalem happy all the days of your life,
>
> and see your children's children.
> Peace be over Israel.

The psalm, then, gives us a good insight into that life of long ago, with its vines and olives and many children. But we probably feel that the blessings held out by the psalm do not quite fit our circumstances. As regards eating the labour of our hands, well, we wouldn't care to rely on what we can grow in our gardens. Then we *would* lose weight! And as for children round the table like numerous lively olive plants round the old trunk – just think of the problems of getting them to and from school and kitting them up with soccer-club shirts, computers and mountain bikes! The mind boggles. To say nothing of the wife safe within the house!

But underlying the ever-changing circumstances, there are constants. We would still wish that our labours provide for the needs of our family, to feed, clothe and house them. We would still wish for a happy home, a place of love and respect. And we must still care for the well-being of the wider community, knowing our dependence on others and our responsibilities to them. And we must ever seek the peace of our Zion, the Church, with the handing on of its treasure from generation to generation.

So, after all, the blessing spoken in this psalm has deep meaning still for us. As we fear the Lord and walk in his ways, we too shall have lives that are fruitful and happy. The Lord will bless us from the Zion that is his Church. He will grant us to see the glory of his new creation, his kingdom of eternal peace.

Lord, grant me the happiness of fearing you. Help me ever to know your presence and power, and ever to live in the ways of your commandments and fellowship.
Deliver me from barren thoughts and deeds.
May the fruits of the Spirit grow in me through fear of the Lord.
May love, joy and peace abound in your Church from generation to generation.

Psalm 129

Furrows of suffering and hope of healing

A householder was vexed at how often the doorbell rang, and there at the door would be someone offering to attend to her roof for a very modest price ('to start with', she thought to herself). Eventually she began to take an interest in the appearance of the roof and chimney from the road. Was there something that was attracting the attention of all these kindly entrepreneurs? Sure enough, there was. For one thing, a young elder tree was growing out of the side of the chimney. Several green plants were sprouting up from the end of the gutter. A number of roof tiles were hosting clumps of moss. No doubt it was all harmless, she thought, but it was rather an invitation to the odd-job men, and she had better do something about it.

As it happens, greenery sprouting on housetops was something well known to the people of the Bible. Their houses usually had one storey and a flat roof. To keep out the heavy winter rain, the roof of beams, rafters and brushwood was surmounted with a layer of earth and then one of clay. On such a traditional house today you can still see the little rollers kept on the roof to use after the first autumn rain, sealing up cracks made in the months of unbroken sunshine. After good rain, the covering on the roof would soon green over. Even corn seeds would have arrived there and would grow rapidly in the warmer but still showery days. But there was no hope of a useful crop. Before it could mature, it all perished in the summer drought, the burning sun, and the withering winds that periodically blew in from the great deserts. The rooftop growth had not the depth to survive.

This suggested a parable for the fate of evildoers. Cruel ones might seem at first to flourish. They sprang up boldly. But in God's season, his enemies would wither, being rooted in shallow soil and without supply from the true source of life. No harvest for them.

The parable is used in Psalm 129. The singer begins by reflecting on all the cruelties the people have suffered. But then he declares that God will put an end to those who so attack his 'Zion', the heart of his kingdom. The singer affirms:

> All the enemies of Zion
> shall be confounded and turned back.
>
> They shall be as the grass on the housetops
> which withers before it can grow up,
>
> so that no reaper can fill his hand,
> nor a binder of sheaves his bosom,
>
> and none that go by say, The blessing of the LORD be on you;
> we bless you in the name of the LORD.

The singer knows what a harvest should be like. The reaper would fill his hand, grasping a thick bunch of stalks to cut with his sickle and then drop for the binder to pick up. The binder gathered the cut stalks in the fold of his garment over his chest, until he had enough to tie into a sheaf.

But from the growth that sprang up so boldly from the housetops there was not enough yield to give a harvester even one handful to cut, nothing for a binder to gather in his bosom. And so it will be for the enemies of God's kingdom. They spring up bold and brazen. But by the time of God's harvest, all will have withered. Here will be no harvesting where passers-by in courtesy ask the Lord to give the workers strength, and the harvesters in responding courtesy ask a blessing for the passers-by. There is no such happy harvest-time for the destroyers. Their lives bear no good fruit.

Not just these last lines of the psalm, but the whole of it is picturesque, mirroring the country life of old Palestine. At the outset the psalm invites the great assembly of worshippers at the festival to join in and sing of the many times when invaders have ravaged the land, breaking and tearing as farmers break and plough up the earth:

> Many a time they have afflicted me from my youth up,
> let Israel now say,

> Many a time they have afflicted me,
> but they have not prevailed against me.

> Over my back the ploughers ploughed,
> and made their furrows long.

> But the LORD is good and has cut in pieces
> the cords of the wicked ones.

Yes, invaders ploughed over them cruelly, but the Lord cut the cords that drew those vicious ploughs. He put an end to the ravages. He saved his people – and so he will do again and bring the forces of evil to nothingness.

But how does the little psalm resound in our world today? Certainly there is still much cruel ploughing on the back of God's earth and people, no end of hate and destruction. Yet to us the psalm brings the voice of those who have suffered cruel attacks again and again, but still acknowledge God as their Saviour and rest all their hope in him. This voice affirms that the life of enmity to God's cause is barren, without harvest, without blessing.

We accept this witness as we enter into the psalm, understanding 'Zion' as the heart of God's kingdom, embodied in the Church. Here we find the happy harvest and the mutual exchange of prayer and blessing in the fellowship of the Holy Spirit. Here we see the world's sufferings and scars gathered up in the Passion of Christ and so transfigured in the harvest of his resurrection. Through him all the enemies of the good kingdom will be turned back. The Lord is good, and his blessing will be established on all his creatures for ever.

O God, with the people of the psalm we bear witness to many cruel assaults, but also to your goodness and acts of deliverance.

Grant that the enemies of your kingdom may see that their way leads only to a withering of all that is good. May they long for the better way, where words of kindness and acts of blessing are exchanged.

In all our sufferings give us courage to believe that through Christ we shall reap the fruits of the Spirit, and in him our sorrow will be turned into joy.

Psalm 130

The cry from the depths

A teacher of creative writing used to exhort her students to grip the reader with the very first sentence. We may think it hard to do better than Jane Austen at the beginning of her great novel *Pride and Prejudice*. This is her first sentence: 'It is a truth universally acknowledged, that a single man in possession of a good fortune must be in want of a wife.' Incomparable Jane, with her humorous irony, has here launched us well into her story.

In a very different setting, the authors of the Psalms also knew the value of a gripping first line. Their compositions were often quite short and made up in part of traditional thoughts and expressions. Not for them the striving for originality that we find in modern 'creative writing'. But they did endeavour to seize the attention of God – to please him with a new song of praise or to move him with an urgent cry of need. So almost every psalm works some fresh beauty into its traditional language. And those we remember best are those which *begin* strikingly. Such a one is Psalm 42: 'As a hind pants for rills of water, so pants my soul for you, O God.' Or again, Psalm 121: 'I lift up my eyes to the hills – O from where shall my help come?' And how strong the first line of Psalm 19: 'The heavens are telling the glory of God.' How impressive Psalm 23: 'With the LORD as my shepherd, I shall not be in want.'

We could make quite a list of such fine opening verses. But there is one psalm where, in the Hebrew, all the force of the beginning is concentrated in the opening word which we translate 'Out of the depths'. This is Psalm 130, which opens thus:

Out of the depths, Lord, I call to you;
O Lord, listen to my voice.

There are many kinds of 'depths', some good. We can speak of depths of meaning and depths of love. There are depths of mystery and depths of truth. But in our psalm the depths are depths of trouble. Hebrew poets often spoke of the waters of chaos. They thought of waves of trouble and destruction that were sweeping the sufferer into the very jaws of the underworld, imagined as the land of darkness and death. In the depths of these chaotic waters, the sufferers were almost overwhelmed, almost gone. Their cry to the Lord was the cry from the very edge.

Our psalm then, with its first Hebrew word, begins with a most urgent cry for help, 'Out of the depths, Lord, I call to you.' It appears that the singer is the representative voice of a great national assembly. He appeals to the Lord to listen to the cry: 'May your ears be attentive to the voice of my supplications.' What the nature of the trouble is, we cannot be sure. Possibly the occasion is a 'day of atonement' when the people brought to focus all their wrongdoing of the preceding year, acknowledging it as a heavy shackle that was keeping them from true life and happiness. Certainly the prayer is for the forgiving mercy of God. The people yearn for that forgiveness to break upon them like a new dawn:

If you, Lord, retained offences,
who then, O Lord, could stand?

But with you there is forgiveness,
so that you may be feared.

I wait for the Lord, my soul is waiting,
and for his word I hope.

My soul looks for the Lord more than watchmen for the morning,
yes, more than watchmen for the morning.

The watchmen keep vigil in the darkness – yes, and it seems likely that the worshippers too are watching through the night. But not just for the daybreak are they watching, like watchmen in the city, or the priests posted on the temple walls ready to signal the moment for the morning offerings. No, the worshippers are looking for a daybreak of salvation, when the Lord will announce forgiveness of their sins and liberation from their troubles. Their plea to the Lord stresses how they wait for him in hope and trust, wholly committed to him as their only saviour. Without his forgiveness, the singer says, no one could endure. No one would be left to 'fear' the Lord, that is, to worship him.

Such is the plea of trust and hope, and it is sustained also in the closing verses. Here the singer turns to the assembly with the same trustful thoughts:

> O Israel, wait for the LORD;
> for with the LORD there is faithful love,
>   and with him is plenteous redemption,
>
> and he will redeem Israel
> from the bonds of all his sins.

'Wait for the LORD' – but what a concentration of waiting is meant! The eyes of the heart are set towards him, the Lord so plenteous in faithful love and the redemptive power that frees us and renews us.

It is this concentration of hope and faith that we can chiefly learn from the psalm. How far the modern mind is from such single-heartedness! There is so much to distract and to dissipate our attention. But when we come into the depths of trouble, when the waters of chaos begin to over-whelm us, how we need to find that concentration of faith! The psalm then leads us to call to the Lord with full sincerity, and to centre all our hope and trust and longing in him, the Faithful One, full of pity and redeeming love. Against the depths of our trouble we must trust in the depths of his goodness. O the depth of his wisdom and the height of his faithfulness! As the old hymn has it, 'O the deep, deep love of Jesus!' On that we must fix our inner eye, watching more than watchmen for the morning, waiting in sure hope that the night will end and the sun of healing and blessing will rise upon us.

Out of the depths, Lord, I call to you.
Out of the depths, Lord, multitudes cry to you.
May the Spirit lift our prayer beyond all the din of the world's chaos. Father, may the prayer of the love of Jesus reach your heart of compassion and forgiveness.
In the depths and in the darkness, I wait for your word and I look for your light.

With you is faithful love and redemption, and you will set your world free
   from the long and heavy chains of all its sins.
O the deep, deep love of Jesus that finds me and lifts me up to you!

Psalm 131

A prayer that doesn't ask for anything

It was a pleasant family gathering. The time had come to move into the
adjoining room where sandwiches, cakes and trifle had been set out invit-
ingly on the table. Anticipation rose. The moment had almost come – if
only Auntie could bring her speech to a full stop. Instinctively they all
began to move towards the alluring table.

And then the dreadful truth dawned. During the slight delay, the four-
year-old boy had busied himself in shaking salt and pepper liberally over
all the food. Lovers of trifle were especially aghast. The lad had meant well.
It was just another application of his restless energy. Like many other children about that time, he was said to be 'hyperactive'. Cause and cure were
disputed, but it was a fact that soon after his mother changed his drink he
became a model of tranquillity.

Some years later, another little boy known to the family also suffered
from a perpetual fever of energy. Only now, the restlessness was termed
'attention deficit syndrome'. All the same, they thought it best to hide the
salt and pepper. He was forever on the rampage. When he came to visit,
how the house shook as he ran up and down the stairs! Fortunately, as the
years went by, he too became calmer.

Whatever it was, some factor in modern life seemed to have made this
restless condition particularly common. But mothers in Bible times did
not have it altogether easy. They did not speak of attention deficit syndrome or even of hyperactivity. But they well knew of their children passing through a disturbed and querulous period. This occurred at the time
of weaning from breastfeeding, usually done as late as the age of two or
three. As the children made this transition, they would be distressed and
restless. They would struggle and cry in frustration. They would need a lot
of soothing and calming till at last they could rest peacefully on their
mothers.

This common situation of olden times is reflected in a small psalm, Psalm 131. The singer tells the Lord how he has made the transition from protest and indignation to a state of quiet trust. As a mother weans her child, he says, so he has calmed his soul. This is how he puts it:

> LORD, my heart is not haughty, nor my eyes set high;
> I do not vex myself with great things
>   or matters too marvellous for me.
>
> But I have quieted and stilled my soul
>   as a weaned child upon its mother;
> like a weaned child is my soul upon me.

It may seem quaint that he should work on his own soul until it rests, as it were, in his arms. But we sometimes do something similar as we exhort or becalm ourselves.

But why should we have a psalm about an individual who has quietened his soul? Well, the little song has one more verse, and here the singer turns to the great assembly of worshippers and exhorts them to come to a similar state of mind:

> O Israel, hope in the LORD,
> from now and for evermore.

This last verse is the goal of the psalm. The singer has meant all along to lead his people in a turning to the Lord in quiet faith. He wants them to move on from grand outpourings of prayer and protest over present troubles, move on to rest quietly in the arms of the Lord.

The singer has the same message for us also. 'There is much you cannot understand', he tells us. 'In vain you ask why, why, why. Now is the time to place it all in the hands of the Lord. Trust in him, hope in him who knows all your needs. Be still as a comforted child. Calm your soul and rest at peace on him. Yes, hope in the Lord, from now and for evermore.'

Father take from my heart the discontent of haughty pride and ambition.
*   Give me a humble, simple spirit in your presence.*
The things too great and marvellous for me I entrust to you.
I put aside my restlessness. I quieten my soul. I hope in you from now and for
*   evermore.*
May all your people learn again to be still and rest upon you in trust.

Psalm 132
Finding a place for the Lord

If you entered a humble cottage in old Russia, your attention would probably be attracted by the corner of the living room. On a small shelf fitted across the corner would stand a holy painting with a little lamp burning before it. The picture might show the face of our Lord or of Mary his mother. It helped the family to sense the presence of God and to live day by day in prayer and trust. They would not care to live in a house, however grand, where a place had not been found for the Lord.

Going well back into Old Testament times, we read a story of King David finding a place for the Lord. He had taken possession of an ancient city called Jerusalem and made it the centre of his kingdom. He recovered the ark of the Lord from long neglect and made a sanctuary for it in Jerusalem. This ark was a portable chest, rich in meaning as the symbol of the covenant that bound all the tribes to each other and to the Lord. Even more, it was used as a sign of the presence or 'glory' of God.

Accounts of how David brought this ark into Jerusalem are given in the history books of Samuel and Chronicles. It was a tremendous occasion, a festal procession with many musicians, and the king himself danced energetically before the ark. But one significant detail is not given in these histories. We learn of it only from Psalm 132. The psalm alone shows us how David made it an absolute priority to 'find a place for the Lord'. The facts come in this opening prayer:

> LORD, remember in David's favour
> all the hardship he endured;
>
> how he swore an oath to the LORD,
> and made a vow to the Mighty One of Jacob:
>
> I will not enter the dwelling of my house,
> nor get up into my bed,
>
> I will not grant sleep to my eyes
> or slumber to my eyelids,
>
> until I find a place for the LORD,
> a dwelling for the Mighty One of Jacob.

How come that only a psalm has preserved this detail of the story? We probably owe its preservation to a custom in worship at Jerusalem. Year by year in the great pilgrimage festival in the autumn, the ceremonies symbolized the foundations of life. God's acts for his world and people were remembered and experienced anew. Included was the renewal of the sanctuary as centre of God's presence, and the psalm shows how for this they re-enacted David's procession with the ark. The current king would have gone before the ark and, like David, refused to sleep until the sanctuary was reached and the place had been found for the Lord. The psalm was sung during the procession and echoed the voices of David's men long ago as they recovered the ark from neglect and set out with it to the place where they would kneel before it. And all through this commemorative procession, the psalm sustains prayer that God will recall David's devoted service and so look favourably on his descendant, the present king and his people. 'Arise, Lord', they sing,

> Arise, O LORD, to your resting place,
> you and the ark of your glory.
>
> May your priests be clothed with salvation,
> and your faithful sing for joy.
>
> For the sake of David your servant,
> do not turn away the face of your Anointed.

Then the psalm brings God's answer to the prayer. As David had sworn before all else to find a place for the Lord, so God has sworn to bless his descendants and his people. The place David had found – it now appears – was what God had already purposed. The singer puts it thus:

> For the LORD has chosen Zion;
> he has desired her for his dwelling.
>
> This shall be my resting place for ever;
> here shall I dwell, for I have desired her.
>
> I will abundantly bless her provision;
> her poor I will satisfy with bread.
>
> Her priests I will clothe with salvation,
> and her faithful shall sing for joy.
>
> There I will make a horn spring up for David;
> I will keep a lamp burning for my Anointed.

Wonderful promises. But in the course of history, great trials and tribu-
lations were to follow. The psalm itself has long outlasted the sanctuary,
the ark, and the kings of old Jerusalem. What then of God's promise of
the 'horn' meaning victory for David, and the 'lamp' meaning life for his
descendants? What of the 'bread' that would feed humble people, and the
garments of salvation that would clothe the servants of the Lord?

To guide us here, the New Testament puts forward its own little psalm.
St Luke gives it in his first chapter. Here God is praised that in Jesus he has
raised up the horn of salvation in the house of his servant David. Also that
he has sent Jesus as the Dayspring from on high to give light to those who
sit in darkness.

Christians continue to recall before God that greater David, our Lord
Jesus, who gave absolute priority to his Father's cause, whatever hardship
it entailed. And we pray the Father ever to bless us for the sake of what
Jesus accomplished. Through him, now and for ever, God's oath is fulfilled.
The humble are clothed with salvation and fed with the bread of life. They
are led by Jesus into the most holy place, the presence of the Father. And a
sign of that place is given wherever they 'find a place for the Lord' – in
church, in their homes and in their hearts.

*We thank you, Father, for the places and symbols that disclose to us the self-
sacrifice of Jesus, that opens the way into your presence.*
Every day may we bow low before the throne of your glory and mercy.
Satisfy us, poor as we are, with the bread and the wine of eternal life.
Keep the lamp of faith ever burning in the place we have found for you.
*O Jesus, Dayspring from on high, give light to those who sit in darkness and
in the shadow of death.*

Psalm 133

Where the grace of God flows down

Many a man ponders whether or not to grow a beard. Will it enhance his
appearance? Might it add weight to his personality? It might save time and
keep the throat warm. No doubt there would be some disadvantages. All
in all, a difficult decision, which in the end is probably made by the woman
in his life.

The history of beards is patchy. The ancient Egyptians were remarkably clean-shaven, likewise usually the Romans. In Russia, Peter the Great took against beards. He put a tax on them, and was liable to cut them off if he came across them. On the other hand, we read that among the Jews, Turks and Persians the beard has long been a sign of manly dignity, while Muslims have commonly sworn by the beard of the Prophet.

Also in support of beards we should count the psalms – if we are to judge by the little Psalm 133. This particularly notes that when Aaron, the first high priest, was anointed to his office, the precious oil that was poured over his head ran down onto his beard and then on to the collar of his garments. In such cases a good long beard, like old age itself, was valued and venerated. It spoke of experience and wisdom in the ways of the Lord.

Everything in the psalm's picture is highly symbolic. The pouring out of the oil is thought of as the action of God, who here gives to his chosen minister something of his own holy power and blessing. Given liberally, it flows over the beard, which stands for the whole person. Then it flows down over the priestly robe which bears the names of the twelve tribes. This means that through his Anointed, God has touched his whole people with blessing and has consecrated them to his service.

But the psalm is not yet done with the thought of a beard. It is found again, though less obviously, in the next verse. Just as the holy oil ran off the beard of the venerable high priest, the psalm says, so life-giving dew runs off the great Mount Hermon. But where is the beard in this picture?

Well, in Palestine and Syria today you hear the mountain called Jebel esh-Sheikh, the mountain of the sheikh or elder. This huge massif, over nine thousand feet high, is likened to a venerable elder because its summit remains white with snow even through the summer, and the snow also straggles down the mountain folds like a great white beard. This aspect of Mount Hermon seems to have guided the psalmist as he sings first of the holy oil flowing off the beard of Aaron, and then of the quickening dew running down the breast of Mount Hermon, the venerable Old Man towering above the Holy Land. Both pictures speak of blessing poured down by God to give life and healing. But where in the life of God's people can such blessing be found? The need for healing and reviving is great. Where can we look for God's copious ointment and dew?

The psalm gives but one answer, and a mighty thought it is. It is like the thought of Christ's prayer in the Gospel of John, chapter 17, 'that they may be one'. The psalm-singer is looking at the vast and orderly assembly of pilgrims ('brethren') keeping festival in the open courts of the temple. How beautiful, he thinks, is this fellowship in God's presence! Their common purpose, to worship God, begets a love that is fruitful for God, a love that is true life. So he sings:

> See, how good and how pleasant it is
> when pilgrims dwell together as one!
>
> It is like the precious ointment on the head,
> that ran down upon the beard,
>
> ran down upon the beard of Aaron,
> and on to the collar of his garments,
>
> as though the dew of Hermon
> ran down on the hills of Zion.
>
> For there the Lord has commanded the blessing,
> even life for evermore.

And still today, when we are as one in love of the Lord, we receive and carry out to the world a wondrous blessing. God's holy and healing ointment will flow to all we hold in our hearts. His dew of life will run out to the arid places. 'Holy Father,' Christ prays, 'sanctify them in your truth, that they may all be one, as you are in me and I in you. Then the world will believe that you have sent me.'

We thank you, Father, for the bond of love that unites all who sincerely worship you. We thank you that in our pilgrimage we are strengthened by the fellowship of the Holy Spirit.

We praise you for the oil of consecration and healing that flows from your Anointed, Jesus the Messiah. We give thanks for the dew that gives life to all who are united in you and runs on to the earth's dry places.

See, how good and how pleasant it is when pilgrims dwell together as one! There the Lord has commanded the blessing, even life for evermore.

Psalm 134

The dazzling darkness

Are you good at climbing steps? One way of practising is to visit great museums and libraries, as their front entrances are so often set above imposing flights of steps. It's a style that follows that of ancient temples, which were built on high terraces and entered by an ascent of many steps.

The idea of ascending steps to reach a high ideal is nowadays applied quite widely. The step-by-step ascent is often the only way to accomplish a daunting task. Many people learning music take exams for 'Grade One', 'Grade Two', eventually to reach the dizzy heights of final 'Grade Eight' – and 'grade', from Latin *gradus*, means 'step'. The student climbs by grades, 'gradually' – that is, by steps.

Now it so happens that there is a run of fifteen psalms that are each headed 'A song of the steps' (sometimes translated 'A song of ascents'). A Jewish tradition thinks of these psalms as having been sung on a flight of fifteen steps in the temple area, though there are other theories about this unique psalm heading. The psalms in question are Psalms 120–134, and early Christian teachers thought of them as a gradual ascent to the presence of God. The last step in the ascent would be Psalm 134, and sure enough, we find the worshippers here raising their hands before the Holy of Holies, the inner shrine that signified the dread presence of the Creator. We notice also that it is night-time as the singer calls the worshippers to praise and thank the Lord:

> Come, bless the LORD, all you servants of the LORD,
> who wait at night in the house of the LORD.
>
> Lift up your hands towards the holy presence,
> and truly bless the LORD.

To this call comes a response from the congregation, wishing a blessing for the singer:

> The LORD who made heaven and earth
> give you blessing out of Zion.

And that is the end! It's one of those very short psalms that leaves us plenty to reflect on – especially if we think of those ascending steps, bringing us here to the last step, right before the most holy shrine, the very presence of God.

Near we may be, but the psalm has us, not bathed in glorious light, but attending upon our Lord *in darkness*. It is a darkness which puts away our sight of earthly things. For a while we are freed from attachments to what is not God. We are prepared to be with the One who is beyond all we can see or say or imagine. There is pain in this night, for our hearts have been set on the world.

But as we wait upon the Lord and bless him and lift our hands to him in love and thankfulness, that darkness of bereavement is suffused by a mysterious light of heaven. Some have called it a 'dazzling darkness'. Still in the earthly night, our spirits are touched by the dark radiance of the Holy Spirit. He comes to our poverty and humility, to our trust and our love. The Lord who made heaven and earth gives us blessing out of Zion.

The little song has indeed shown us much about that last step before the Holy of Holies, about the waiting in the night in the house of the Lord, the night that is better than this world's brightness. But it adds another deep thought. Though the ascent has sometimes seemed lonely and has needed individual courage, the pilgrim was not alone. For this psalm on the last step, it is a fellowship of worshippers who stand together in the night. One has encouraged the others to bless the Lord. Blessings have been spoken in response. The golden chains of prayer and loving wishes and shared faith have supported and guided each member of the family of God. Thanks be to God for the fellowship of the Holy Spirit, whereby his creatures are led up to the place of eternal life in his presence!

In the communion of the Holy Spirit we climb the steps of faith.

On the last step we stand together and lift our hands to the all-holy presence.

It is night and we no longer see the things of this world. We lift our hands and we bless you, Lord, for creation and for redemption, for life through your Word, for your love given to us in Jesus Christ.

It is night, yet the night is not darkness with you. In our emptiness we know your fullness, in our poverty your riches, in our night your beauty.

O Lord, Creator of all, send out your blessing from the Zion of Calvary. Send it upon our companions in faith. Send it upon all your world. Send it upon me.

Psalm 135

A particular personal treasure

A scholar in retirement was trying to reduced the clutter on his shelves. He had *some* success in diminishing the number of books, papers and pamphlets, but you still could not say he was clutter-free. It seemed a never-ending struggle, and he resolved to redouble his efforts.

But one object on the shelves would always be sacrosanct. It was a nineteenth-century writing box made of mahogany with brass inlay round the lock and corners, and it opened to form a useful writing surface. It must have been in the family some hundred and fifty years. But it had no great value, being of a common type and anyway in need of repair. What made it a particular personal treasure was the accumulation within – letters, cards and photographs that he had chosen to keep there because of some dear association with events or people in his life. Not least, there were letters from the young woman who was to become his wife. Yes, the old writing box and its contents had become a dear possession he would never part with.

For such a personal treasure the Hebrews had a word. It's found eight times in the Bible – *segullah*. Usually it refers to the Lord's people as his *segullah*, his special treasure, chosen and kept by him for ever. We find it, for example, in a psalm of ringing praise, Psalm 135. The people here is seen as one body called after its ancestor whose name was 'Jacob' and later 'Israel'. The psalm leads praise of the Lord for his gracious choice:

> Alleluia! O praise the name of the Lord;
> praise it, you servants of the Lord,
>
> you that wait in the house of the Lord,
> in the courts of the house of our God.
>
> Praise the Lord, for the Lord is good;
> make music to his name, for it is sweet.
>
> For the Lord has chosen Jacob for himself,
> Israel for his dear possession.

'His dear possession', *segullah* – what encouragement the word contained for those worshippers! You are the Lord's special treasure, it said. You are his very own that he will never abandon.

But deeper consideration showed that with the Lord's choice went also a bestowal of responsibility. Already in these opening verses the responsibility is there. These treasured worshippers are the Lord's 'servants'. They 'stand' or 'wait' in his house, watching and listening for his commands. They hold themselves ready to please and obey him. It is clear, too, that they have to lead his praise. They must 'praise the Lord, for he is good'. They must 'make music to his name, for it is sweet'. And of course, such praises sung in the house of the Lord are to be simply the expression of hearts that truly love God and value him above all. The praise signals their desire that every pulse of their being should be for him, for love of him, for his glory.

Yes, it turns out that to be the Lord's *segullah*, his special treasure, is to show a responding love, a total dedication. So much appears in the opening part of our psalm, which then rolls on with typical cries of praise. The leading singer throws in his personal testimony: 'Truly I know that the LORD is great; our Lord is above all gods.' The Lord, he says, is able to do whatever he wills in heaven and earth, in the seas and in the great deeps. See how he brings up clouds from the ends of the earth, and how he makes lightnings with the rain and leads the winds out of his stores. Nor are the nations able to live without him or escape his will. Remember how he acted with dread wonders upon ancient Egypt, that mighty empire, and brought the Hebrews out from cruel bondage there. Indeed, says the singer, this Lord is the only real God. What the peoples worship cannot save or create. The Lord alone is the Eternal One who hears and saves:

> Your name, LORD, is everlasting,
> and shall be called upon throughout all generations.

And the psalm ends with a great call for all who fear the Lord to bless him – to praise him with thankful hearts till his sanctuary resounds: 'You that fear the LORD, bless the LORD. Blessed from Zion be the LORD, who dwells in Jerusalem. Alleluia!'

Thus the psalm leads the people in their calling as the Lord's special possession. It leads them in standing ready for his service and in offering the life of praise and thanksgiving. Moses would have been happy with the psalm, for it was related that he heard God's voice on Mount Sinai promising the people, 'If you will obey my voice and keep my covenant, you shall be to me a special treasure from among all peoples . . . you shall be a kingdom of priests, a holy nation' (Exod. 19.6). Like priests, they would serve between God and his world, praying, blessing, mediating knowledge.

Christians believe that through Jesus Christ this calling has passed to his Church, gathered from all nations. As St Peter tells the Church in his first letter: 'You are a chosen race, a royal priesthood, a holy nation, a people for his treasured possession, that you may show forth the glorious deeds of him who called you out of darkness into his marvellous light' (1 Pet. 2.9).

So there is the story of God's *segullah*, his special treasure. We might have said it had a fine ending in St Peter's letter, but it's a story that still goes on. We have received it through Moses, through the psalm and through Peter, but it continues in our lives and the Church today. We have become part of that *segullah* which God keeps for ever. We are to rejoice that God, Creator and King of all, specially treasures us. But in our happiness we are to thank him and live to please him, especially by showing his goodness to all the world.

We wait before you, almighty Lord, and we give thanks for your goodness and the beauty of your name given in Jesus.
You bring up the clouds from the ends of the earth, and rain and storms from out of your store-houses. You guide and judge the nations.
Through Jesus you have brought us close to your heart. May we always serve and bless you with the music of fervent praise and thanksgiving.

Psalm 136

Songs that inspire

Two brothers worked in music-hall and concert parties. They liked to compose songs, and usually one brother wrote the words and the other set them to music. On one occasion, when the wordsmith heard the tune his brother had just composed, he cried 'Piffle!' To which the musical one replied, 'Good, it will suit your words then.' They had a good laugh and put the song aside.

But soon after, they were pressed to enter a competition for the best marching song. Having nothing else ready, they submitted the disdained composition. It won, and soon it was adopted by top entertainers. It was the time of the First World War, and before long all our armies were marching to the little song. Even the enemy forces took up the tune.

You may have guessed what it was – 'Pack up your troubles in your old kit-bag and smile, smile, smile'. Its instant success was due to its suitability for singing on the long, long marches which the soldiers of those days had to make. The strong and easy rhythm, the simple tune and cheerful words, all lifted the spirits of the marchers, lightened their step and sustained them on many a long and painful route.

But the power of a song to inspire a group in a hard task has long been known. Especially effective, from time immemorial, has been the responsive work-song, still to be heard in Asia and Africa. The solo leader addresses calls to the others, and each time they reply with lively rhythm.

The leader develops his or her part with verve and variety, while the group repeat their refrain without change. If you have ever witnessed such work-songs – maybe when a ship was unloaded at an East African port, or when a car was hauled back up to a mountain road in Jordan – if you have ever seen and heard a team of workers chanting to each other, you will have been struck by their happiness and their making light of a heavy task.

The same style of responsive work-song was used in the great task of praising the Lord in the temple courts of ancient Jerusalem. The leader of the hymn would call out, not to the Lord, but to the throng of pilgrims as if they were a great work team. He would bid them praise God, and then he would develop his call by giving reasons, mentioning examples of God's power and goodness. The mass of worshippers would keep responding to his calls with a constant refrain. Not surprisingly, such refrains are only written here and there in the psalms as we have them. But in one of the Dead Sea Scrolls the refrain is written out fully for every verse of Psalm 145. And in our own Bibles, the refrain is fully preserved in Psalm 136, where, for the second half of every verse, we find the rhythmic response: *ki le'olam ḥasdo*, 'His faithfulness is for ever'. Such faithfulness here means a committed love, a constant good will that doesn't let you down. Such reliable love was especially valued if it was maintained towards a family through several generations, or towards a tribe through centuries. But our psalm knows the deep truth that God is faithful *for ever*. How the psalm hammers away at this wonderful theme! You must imagine the great throng of worshippers uniting in the rhythmic cry with shining eyes and clapping hands, responding to every line of the lead singer: *ki le'olam ḥasdo*, 'His faithfulness is for ever':

> Give thanks to the LORD, for he is good;
> *his faithfulness is for ever.*
>
> Give thanks to the God of gods;
> *his faithfulness is for ever.*
>
> Give thanks to the Lord of lords,
> *his faithfulness is for ever,*
>
> to the One who alone does great wonders,
> *his faithfulness is for ever,*
>
> who by wisdom made the heavens,
> *his faithfulness is for ever,*

who laid out the earth upon the waters,
his faithfulness is for ever,

who made the great lights above,
his faithfulness is for ever,

the sun to rule the day,
his faithfulness is for ever,

the moon and the stars to rule the night,
his faithfulness is for ever . . .

It may be that as we ponder this psalm we may feel that the unvarying refrain doesn't quite suit every verse. The beginning fits fine: 'Give thanks to the LORD for he is good, *his faithfulness is for ever*.' But what about '[the LORD] who by wisdom made the heavens, *his faithfulness is for ever*'? To whom was he being faithful when he first created the world? And a little later in the psalm, traditional translations may give us a surprise: 'He smote the firstborn of Egypt, *for his mercy endures for ever*; he swept Pharaoh and his host into the Sea of Reeds, *for his mercy endures for ever*.'

In fact, these surprises are invitations to meditate further. So we come to see that the faithfulness of God is essential to his creation. He never makes things and then, as it were, turns away. His creating initiates dynamic, living realities. He remains ever with them and in them, energizing and guiding according to his purpose. And all he does with them is in faithfulness.

Nor does he leave the nations to get on with an existence of their own. His Spirit again is there, energizing and guiding. The psalm recalls how within history he chose a family for particular service and made promises to them. When they were enslaved in Egypt he acted against the obstinacy of that great power. He struck the country with plagues and their pursuing army with a tidal wave – all in faithfulness to the family of Abraham. Aptly then, the psalm says still, 'His faithfulness is for ever'. But the conclusion rests again on the universal love of God:

[he] who gives to all creatures their food,
his faithfulness is for ever.

O give thanks to the God of heaven,
his faithfulness is for ever.

And so the sacred work-song comes to its end. Another great task of praise and thanksgiving is done. How does it relate to our first thoughts about 'Pack up your troubles' and the singing teams of labourers in Asia and Africa? Those were songs for hard toil, giving unity and strength in many a heavy task. And really, the work of praise and thanksgiving is also a hard task. The calls and responses of song are needed there too, one pilgrim encouraging another, all in a spirit of unity. The praise is a hard task, for there are many times when the faithfulness of God is hidden from us. Tragic events seem to contradict our faith. And always the selfish human world is pulling us away from love of God, trying to blot out our consciousness of the wonderful Creator and Saviour who wants us to set our heart on him in every moment and situation.

So, yes, we must be glad of faith's work-songs, the shared melodies of love for God and his Christ. And not just actual singing, valuable as that is. But all the shared melody of prayer and love, all the calling and answering in kindness, all the standing together in suffering. In a hundred ways, in the power and fellowship of the Holy Spirit, we shall call to each other and rejoice in God's faithfulness. And so, together, we shall walk the long hard way and lift the burdens with joyful hearts and undying hope.

Lord, you have created all in faithfulness. You remain with everything you have made, that your goodness shall be fulfilled in all.

We thank you for your faithful love, which is not for a day or a thousand years, but for ever.

We thank you that your creative wisdom has come to us in Christ, and with him is given your grace and truth and everlasting faithfulness.

With him, in the power of the Holy Spirit, we watch and pray for the saving of all creatures that are enslaved and oppressed. In all places of torment we pray for the revelation of your faithful love.

Psalm 137

An old memory and a fresh commitment

You can learn much about great events of history – the dates, the battles, upheavals of population, names of leaders and so on. But you may need to hear of some personal story, perhaps just one little incident, if you are to feel the reality of it all. When an old soldier recollected how, on Christmas

Day 1914, mysteriously, warfare ceased and men mingled in friendship with their enemies for a few hours, the personal memory brought home the pathos of that trench warfare.

And what a weird glimpse of the reality of the Holocaust was given by the memory of a teenager's shoes! She had thought the shoes too plain and had fixed bright bobbles on them. She was wearing them when she was taken to the Auschwitz death-camp. The woman registering the new arrivals noticed the shoes and asked to have them. So a conversation arose, and when it emerged that the teenager was a music student, the woman was able to save her life by putting her forward for the camp's orchestra. Then the girl's sister arrived in a later batch of prisoners and recognized the shoes now worn by the receptionist. Anxious enquiry led again to conversation and to an assignment that saved her life also. That tiny detail of the bobbles on the way to the gas chambers – a personal glimpse that brings home the strange horror of that place and time.

In the sixth century before Christ, the kingdom of Jerusalem twice rebelled against the domination of the Babylonian empire. The outcome was the destruction of Jerusalem and its temple and the deporting and resettling of the skilled classes in distant Babylonia, southern Iraq. One of the psalms, Psalm 137, begins with a recollection that gives a sudden glimpse into that sweep of history. In a world without photography, recordings or journalists, this recollection of one moment paints the scene and voices the passions:

> By the rivers of Babylon we sat and wept aloud,
> when we remembered Zion.
>
> On the trees along the banks
> we hung our lyres unused.
>
> Our captors asked us there for a song,
>   those who had despoiled us, for music of joy:
> Sing us one of the songs of Zion.
>
> How should we sing the songs of the LORD
> on the soil of a foreign land?

Since that remembered moment a good while had passed. The psalm was being sung after the end of the exile. Now back in a still ruinous Jerusalem, the worshippers are commemorating the tragic day of the temple's destruction. The singer has recollected that incident beside the rivers of Babylon to show how through thick and thin they stayed loyal to the holy place. They remembered Zion with love and sympathy. How different even the landscape was in Babylon! Flat country lay around a great river with many streams and canals, waterways lined by poplar trees similar to willows. They had sat down by the waters to remember Zion with prayer and ceremonies of mourning. The psalm-singers had carried their lyres as their most precious possession all the long march from Jerusalem, many hundreds of miles. And now the lyres were hung silent on the branches of the poplars, a sign of deep mourning. Their captors mockingly asked for cheerful music, songs indeed from Zion's festivals, praising her beauty and blessing. Impossible. They could not sing in that place and time those songs of God.

Following his recollection of that scene, the singer reaffirms his commitment to the Lord's city. He sets Jerusalem above all other joys. If his loyalty ever fails, may his playing hands fall limp and his singing tongue go dumb:

> If I forget you, O Jerusalem,
> may my right hand forget its powers.
>
> May my tongue cleave to the roof of my mouth,
> if I do not exalt Jerusalem above my highest joy.

What a passionate loyalty! And it now flows on into a prayer for judgement on the destroyers of Jerusalem. May the Lord not forget their treacherous and ruthless deeds. The singer's concluding words evoke a vivid and terrible scene. As the Babylonian conquerors killed the small children of Jerusalem, God bless those who would repay them in kind, killing their little ones in their turn.

The desire for revenge is understandable. It is commonly to be met with in our time. But it cannot lead our prayers. The Church recognized this and usually took the words in a different sense – 'Babylon' was a symbol for evil, and her 'children' to be destroyed were our evil thoughts.

But perhaps we can best take the passage to remind us how vengeance breeds vengeance, a cycle of hate. And so we give thanks for all who have interposed and broken such cycles by doing good to enemies, wishing well to persecutors, overcoming evil with the prayers and actions of love. To this end, the prophet Jeremiah sent a word of God in a letter to these very exiles in Babylon: 'Seek the peace of the city (Babylon) whither I have caused you to be carried away captive and pray to the Lord for her' (Jer. 29.7). Likewise the Book of Proverbs taught: 'If your enemy be hungry, give him bread to eat' (Prov. 25.21). And best of all, Jesus insists against any other tradition: 'Love your enemies and pray for those who persecute you' (Matt. 5.44).

So, in the Spirit of Jesus, we must stand back from the vengeful conclusion of this psalm and let the better teachings come flooding into our minds. Yet from this passionate psalm we can still learn to love God's Church above our chief joy. This home where we learn of God, meet God, grow in God – yes, we will love and work for this our Zion, setting her above all worldly pleasure and wealth.

If I forget you, Jerusalem of the Spirit, shall not my life turn barren?

Thanks be to you, Lord Jesus, that you appointed apostles, preachers, pastors and sacraments, and with your presence formed a spiritual home for all nations. And here you draw us into worship and nourish us with the springs of your eternal life.

Help me ever to remember and serve your holy Church for your sake, and in her time of humiliation to love her and pray for her all the more.

Psalm 138

Angels in the choir

In many churches and cathedrals it is usual for the choir to be divided in two halves facing each other. This suits the shape of the building, but also helps the music. The singers can watch each other's lips and take their cue from an appointed chorister, while the sound itself is distributed to best effect.

Such dividing of choirs in fact goes back to time immemorial. One of the great preachers of the early Church, St John Chrysostom ('the Golden-mouthed'), said something of interest on such a choir. He was preaching on Psalm 138, which in the Greek version begins: 'I will give you thanks, Lord, with all my heart; I will sing psalms to you facing the angels.' The good bishop explained this by imagining a great choir praising God. It is divided in two. On one side are the angels in heaven, and, facing them, the singers on earth. They watch each other and strive to match each other, and their voices blend and ring through the cosmos.

This interpretation shows the great ideal of worship among the early Christians. In the holy time and place, communing with God, you are united with all who praise him in heaven and earth. It was an ideal already strong in the Psalms. In Psalm 138 itself, however, a single person sings, and we may think of King David or one of his descendants. He is conscious that he makes his music of praise before the dwellers in heaven. The boundary of heaven and earth fades in worship. He appears to be standing in the court before the temple itself, accompanied by his musicians. And so he sings:

> With all my heart, LORD, I will give you thanks;
> I will make music to you before all heaven.
>
> I will bow down towards your holy temple,
> and will give thanks to your name,
>
> because of your faithful love and truth;
> for you have glorified your word above all your name.
>
> In the day that I called, you answered me;
> you exalted me, with glory in my soul.

The singer thinks of his praise as testimony, which in a mysterious way carries across the earth and brings to others the impulse to faith. He imagines other kings coming to know the Lord and join in his worship:

> All the kings of the earth shall thank you, LORD,
> when they have heard the words of your mouth.
>
> And they shall sing in the ways of the LORD,
> that great is the glory of the LORD.
>
> For though the LORD is high, he watches over the lowly,
> and well he knows the proud from afar.

The singer clearly knows that there must be humility in true praise. You give the glory to God, away from yourself. Whether in great people or small, the Lord desires the humble heart, 'and well he knows the proud from afar'.

We might be tempted to think that songs of praise and thanksgiving are fine when we are prospering. Then we have a lot to give thanks for. But our psalm seems to be one of those that praise God even in suffering. For its closing words, though full of trust, speak of furious enemies and a great need of God's faithful love. The last words indeed may be the climax and goal of the psalm:

> Though I walk in the midst of trouble,
> you will keep my life against the fury of my foes.

The LORD will accomplish his will for me.
O LORD, your faithfulness is for ever;
  do not forsake the work of your hands.

Here at the end, then, the singer makes his appeal. Knowing that God has created him and has a purpose in him, he relies on God's commitment and faithful love: 'Do not forsake the work of your hands.'

Thanksgiving in suffering, thanksgiving linked with urgent prayer – is this not a good pattern for us? We must think so when we consider the example of our Lord Jesus, especially at the Last Supper. That last meal, on the brink of his arrest and condemnation, we repeat as he commanded, and we call it the Eucharist – the Thanksgiving. For there he broke bread and gave thanks, and shared the wine as his blood was to be shed. In a time of fear and peril he gave thanks and praise, and he held to a trust like the psalmist's: 'Though I walk in the midst of trouble, you will keep my life from the fury of my foes . . . The LORD will accomplish his will for me.'

In the Eucharist, then, let us grow into this pattern, and let us ever be refreshed by the words of this psalm. And let us keep also the precious knowledge that in our praises we join the cosmic choir. Who knows where our testimony will blow, seeds on the wind that can become trees of beauty for the Lord?

With all my heart, Lord, I will give you thanks and make music to you before the dwellers in heaven. Kings and peoples shall thank you, Lord, as they hear your promises and receive your healing.

O King, exalted above all, grant me a lowly heart, that you may be pleased to come to me.

Guard me, my Saviour, in the midst of trouble, and accomplish your will for me.

Psalm 139

The encompassing Spirit

In some houses you may still see a warning notice on a wall. It can be a work of art, beautifully stitched and framed. Or it may take the form of a tile or a plaque. It warns you that God will hear every word you say and know the thoughts you think. He is the unseen guest at every meal. It is a salutary reminder, even if it seems rather threatening.

But God's knowledge of the heart and of every thought and action can hardly ever have been expressed as radically as in Psalm 139, which begins:

> LORD, you search me and know me.
> You know my sitting and my rising;
>> you discern my thought long before.
>
> You know well my journeying and my halting,
> and are acquainted with all my paths.
>
> For there is not a word on my tongue,
> but you, LORD, know it all together.
>
> Behind and before you enclose me,
> and lay your hand upon me.

Yet as the psalm progresses, we find that this line of meditation is not dominated by threat and fear. God is certainly understood to be supreme judge and the psalmist expects to be examined for any wrongdoing, any 'hurtful way'. But more and more he speaks of wonder at God's creating him and being ever with him and about him:

> Such knowledge is too wonderful for me,
> so high that I cannot grasp it.
>
> Where shall I go from your Spirit,
> or where shall I flee your face?
>
> If I climb up into heaven, you are there;
> if I make my bed in the depths beneath, you are there also.
>
> If I take the wings of the dawn,
> and dwell in the farthest sea,
>
> even there your hand shall lead me,
> and your right hand shall hold me.

This worshipper, we see, has a lively sense of God's power to be present everywhere and to know everything. But more than this, he is aware that God knows him intimately as only his Creator could, and likewise cares for him. We all have some idea of how an artist or an author is involved with his or her creation; and we know the bond of a mother with the child she has carried and nurtured. Beyond even these deepest feelings of human creativity, the psalmist contemplates the purposing, caring Creator who

wove and fashioned him in the womb, and was at work for him even
before that:

> It was you that created my inmost parts;
> you wove me in my mother's womb.
>
> I thank you that I am fearfully and wonderfully made;
> marvellous are your works, my soul knows well.
>
> My frame was not hidden from you when I was made in secret,
> and wrought in the depths of the earth.
>
> Your eyes saw my form yet unfinished;
> already my parts were all written in your book,
>
> as day by day they were fashioned,
> when not one of them was ready.

Modern science traces the long, long story of our origin before our formation in the womb, and we hear much of genes and DNA. More mysteriously, our psalmist speaks of his origin in the depths of the earth, a secret
fashioning beyond the womb known only to God. And in God's heart,
already then, there were thoughts for him, caring thoughts and purposes.
And even if I could know and count them all, he says, I could not com-
prehend the sheer fact of you my Creator, ever with me:

> How many are your thoughts for me, O God;
> O how great is the sum of them!
>
> If I count them, they are more in number that the sand;
> if I reached the end, I would still have you.

These thoughts of wonder and adoration are expressed in beautiful
poetry, and the verses are naturally much loved. But what follows sounds
harsh, and the word 'hate' sounds repeatedly. We should understand this
'hate' as meaning practical opposition to evil, but even so, the passage may
still sound over-zealous:

> O that you would slay the wicked, O God;
> O that the murderous would go away from me!
>
> For they speak of you with wicked purpose;
> against you they raise their voice for evil.
>
> Those who oppose you, LORD, do I not oppose,
> and those who rise against you, do I not abhor?

> I oppose them utterly;
> they have become enemies also for me.

This prayer follows the tradition of the anointed kings who were responsible for upholding God's order and were themselves the targets of murderous enemies. The singer is appealing to God by stressing that he has utterly opposed such cruel ones, God's own enemies. He has had no part in their evil schemes.

And now we see better the nature of the entire psalm. The singer is a leader in mortal danger. He has drawn close to God to seek his help, and he knows that his motives must be pure and acceptable to God. So he has meditated on the all-seeing judgement of God, asked for help and now concludes:

> Search me, O God, and know my heart;
> try me and know my thoughts.
>
> See if there is any hurtful way in me,
> and lead me in the everlasting way.

Now if we think again of those warning notices on people's walls – God can hear everything you say, see everything you do, know what you are thinking – if we compare such notices with our psalm, the basic difference is one of purpose. The notices address you. A well-meaning teacher is warning you. But the psalm, from start to finish in all 24 verses, addresses God. It is a prayer for God's help. The praying person is so aware of the enfolding presence of God that his words take on the note, not of fear or anxiety, but of worship and adoration. Being in danger from murderous enemies, he is glad of the presence and penetrating knowledge of the Lord. God will know the rights of the case, and there is only wonderful comfort in the recollection of his surrounding presence, his embrace, his good purpose and care from the day of his birth and long before that. Beyond all passing troubles and conflicts, his wonderful Creator will stay with him and about him and will guide him safely on the everlasting way, a path of communion with God for ever.

But can we take up such a prayer? Dare we invite God's scrutiny of our hearts and all our lives? How gladly we must turn to Christ, who will bring us into the way that is first repentance and forgiveness, then new birth in loving harmony with God – the way of communion that is eternal life. Through Christ we can gladly pray that the murderous ones also die to sin and find new life in him. Through Christ we wonder and rejoice at the multitude of God's thoughts for us. We see the love that has no bounds, and we say with the psalm, 'Such knowledge is too wonderful for me, so high that I cannot grasp it.'

O God, all-seeing Judge, grant me ever the grace of repentance, forgiveness and new life in your Spirit. Lord have mercy upon me.
Let me ever rejoice in your encompassing Spirit and your hand upon me. So shall I not fear the enemies of peace.
Your hand shall lead me and hold me in the everlasting way, until I know you, my Creator and lover of my soul, even as I am fully known.

Psalm 140

Prayer against poisonous words

Many tales are told of the days when Cambridge colleges locked up their formidable gates nightly at 10 p.m. and undergraduates not yet safely within were inclined to return in the small hours by scaling the walls. On one occasion, so it is related, a miscreant surmounted the wall only to see the Dean awaiting him below. 'O my God,' he exclaimed. 'No,' replied the Dean dryly, 'only his representative.'

The fact is that the expression 'my God' is commonly used, even in worship, with little sense of its wonderful meaning. In Hebrew it's just one word, as though we said 'God-of-me', and it expresses a close bond of love and obligation. This is clear in the psalm-prayers of David and the kings of his line. In Psalm 89, for example, it says that God has granted the king to pray intimately, saying, 'You are my Father, my God, and the Rock of my salvation.' It was felt as a wonderful thing that God, the Creator of the universe, should enter into such a close bond with this person, a bond of love and loyalty, promise and commitment.

In Psalm 140 we find a king appealing to God on the strength of this bond. He is in danger from cunning and ruthless enemies and calls to his God:

> I say to the LORD, You are my God;
> listen, O LORD, to the voice of my supplications.

> LORD God, my glorious Saviour,
> you cover my head on the day of battle.

Do not grant, LORD, the desires of the wicked;
do not let their evil purposes prosper.

In the conflicts of our time, whether outright war or the daily strife of politics, it is remarkable how much use is made of harmful words. In warfare words are spun to deceive the enemy, or for distorted propaganda to whip up support. In the politics of peacetime, contestants speak much to misrepresent their opponents. Good leaders are harried by malicious reports and beset by cunning traps until their careers are destroyed. It was not so different in biblical times, despite the absence of the media. The king in the psalm tells the Lord of his continual troubles:

Rescue me, LORD, from evil folk,
and guard me from the men of violence,

who think out harm in their heart,
and daily stir up war.

They make their tongue as sharp as a snake's;
a viper's poison is under their lips . . .

The arrogant have laid a snare for me
    and with cords have spread their net;
along the way they have set their traps for me.

Later in the psalm the king passes into confident statements that slanderers in the end will not be established on earth, and the violent will themselves be hunted down by harm. Then finally he supports his prayer by pointing to the humble and needy people he represents, and by picturing the worship and thanksgiving they will offer their Saviour.

Can we ourselves enter into the prayer of this troubled king? Certainly if we have great responsibilities or are moved by conscience to stand up for the right, certainly then we meet with those who wish us harm, daily stir up trouble or seek to lay a snare for us. But all of us are indebted to the brave ones who are so exposed, and we owe them the support of our prayers. The psalm indeed draws us all together as we perceive how it foreshadowed Christ. How fitting the words are for him who had daily to contend with those who wished him evil, slandered him, sought to entrap him, men who spared no violence and under whose tongue was a viper's poison. So we can readily pray the psalm for all who share his mission and suffer for the truth of God's kingdom. For them and for ourselves we can, through Christ, say the great 'My God'. As we are bound to Christ, so he binds us to the Father. Through him we have that great intimacy with the

Creator, the Infinite and Eternal who yet is 'my God'. For ourselves and for those in our heart we can take up the psalm's words: 'I say to the LORD, You are my God; listen, O LORD, to the voice of my supplications. LORD God, my glorious Saviour, you cover my head on the day of battle.'

Father, we lift to you those who for the sake of your people have become tar-
gets for the malice of the wicked. Turn aside the sharp arrows of slander.
Frustrate the cunning snares. Do not let the evil purpose prosper.
Grant us the faith and courage to stand with Christ as he confronts the evil
ones.
So may we abide before your face and give thanks for his victory of love.

Psalm 141

When angels mount guard

There was once a man who was just beginning to grow old. He thought he knew what symptoms to expect. Not only was it a matter of common observation. He was also familiar with several classic descriptions. There was the ancient Egyptian sage Ptah-hotep who said of himself: 'Oldness has arrived, old age descended. Eyes are weak, ears deaf, strength ebbs away. The heart cannot remember yesterday. Taste has gone. Standing or sitting is difficult' – and much more in the same vein. Then there was the coded description in the Book of Ecclesiastes: 'The years draw nigh when thou shalt say, I have no pleasure in them, or ever the sun and the light and the moon and the stars be darkened, and the clouds return after the rain, in the day when the keepers of the house shall tremble and the strong men shall bow themselves, and the grinders cease because they are few . . . and the almond tree shall blossom and the grasshopper shall be a burden . . .' Clearer was Shakespeare, describing the parts a man plays in his time on the world's stage: 'The sixth age shifts into the lean and slippered pantaloon, with spectacles on nose and pouch on side, his youthful hose well-saved a world too wide for his shrunk shank, and his big manly voice turning again towards childish treble.'

Yes, our friend thought he knew all about the symptoms of advanced years. But he was suddenly surprised to find in himself a symptom he had not expected. He found himself saying things he almost at once regretted. It was as though, from time to time, the watchmen who had always guarded the door of his mouth had fallen asleep. It was just one more vexing symptom of his oldness. But fortunately there was a prayer in Psalm 141 which he could use as a remedy:

> Set a watch, LORD, before my mouth;
> keep guard at the door of my lips.

With this prayer, our ageing friend was usually able to hold back the hasty word and activate that guard of the angels of patience and kindness at the door of his lips.

Whether the king praying in the psalm was also suffering from old age we cannot be sure, though it is quite possible. But it is clear that he calls to God from a time of danger. He supports his urgent prayer by humbly asking to be kept from wrongdoing. He would speak no evil, and he also asks to be strengthened against subtle temptations, including the flattery of those who would lure him into their evil company:

> Let my heart not incline to any evil thing,
>   to join in deeds of wickedness with evildoers;
> then I shall not partake of their pleasures.
>
> Let the faithful rebuke me strongly in friendship,
> but let the oil of the wicked not anoint my head.

It seems that some of the king's supporters have already been killed. His prayer rises urgently:

> But to you, LORD God, my eyes are turned;
> in you I take shelter, do not pour away my life.

Calling on God to come quickly, he asks that his prayer be acceptable as the offerings in the temple, offerings appointed by God. May his plea rise and reach heaven as does the incense and daily evening sacrifice:

> May my prayer be accepted as the incense before you,
> and the lifting up of my hands as the evening sacrifice.

All in all, the way this worshipper commends his prayer to God is rather distinctive, and it may help us in our own prayers. Like him, we cannot commend our prayers on the strength of our own merits. So he leads us at least to show a readiness to be kept by God's help from sin. We too, like him, can welcome the angels to guard the door of our lips. May their constant vigilance prevent us from hasty words we would later regret – words of anger or envy, words contrary to the love of Christ. And like the psalmist, we ask to be made strong against the lures and flatteries of evil. How much better that we receive an honest rebuke than be caught in the net of flattery!

But what can be made in our time of the psalmist's thought of incense and the evening sacrifice? What strengthening is here for our prayer? As we lift our hands in supplication we must think of Jesus who has lifted up his hands for us and made the perfect offering. And as incense rising up to heaven we think of the prayers of those good witnesses who have gone before us on the way of Christ, and who are granted by him to watch over us and pray for us.

Altogether, then, there is much in the psalm to encourage us to call to the Lord in faith. In a time of fear and danger, this singer can lead us with his prayer of humility and confidence that begins: 'LORD, I call to you. Come quickly to me.'

Set a watch, Lord, before my mouth, that I speak only in kindness and patience.
Let my heart not be lured into evil ways. Make me strong against oily flattery.
May my prayer come before you with the incense of the prayers of your faithful ones.
May my hands be raised in the power of the sacrifice of Jesus.
To you, Lord God, my eyes are turned. Come quickly to my help.

Psalm 142
A soul in prison

One of the most striking prayers in the psalms comes in Psalm 142. A sufferer cries to God: 'Bring my soul out of prison.' Do we ever feel that our soul is in prison – confined and fastened in, barred away from the space, freedom, happiness of life as it should be?

With the word 'soul' we probably think of our inmost being, sensitive and sympathetic, loving beauty and friendship. And there are times for all of us when this 'soul' seems confined, closed off from the light and air which it craves for.

Sometimes this imprisonment is caused by a numbing shock. There were some famous cases in the nineteenth century when the months of mourning for a spouse or parent were turned into a permanent imprisonment of the soul. Queen Victoria put up the bars around herself when her beloved husband Prince Albert died early.

In our time other forms of self-imprisonment are common. We have to ask ourselves what we may be allowing to imprison our souls. It could be an excess of activities, partly self-imposed. Through such an overcrowded schedule we may be shutting ourselves away from the light and air of the deeply satisfying experiences. It is only too easy to make ourselves prisoners of triviality, falling in with shallow fashions that waste the precious time God has given us.

Then again, our souls may be imprisoned through troubles not of our making. This seems to be the case with the sufferer in the psalm. He tells how he is brought very low. His very spirit faints because of hostility against him – as a king he would face many enemies. Foes gather and friends desert him, but he is sure the Lord knows and cares:

> When my spirit faints upon me, you know my path;
> in the way that I walk, they have laid a snare for me.
>
> I look to the right hand, but see,
> there is no one that will know me.
>
> I have no longer any refuge;
> there is no one to care for my soul.
>
> I cry to you, LORD, and say,
> You are my shelter, my portion in the land of the living.
>
> Give heed to my cry, for I am brought very low;
> save me from those who pursue me,
>   for they are too strong for me.

The situation is beyond his strength. His troubles shut him away from the space and light of true life. He prays with a promise of thanksgiving as he concludes:

> Bring my soul out of prison,
> to give thanks, LORD, to your name.
>
> The faithful will gather around me,
> when you act for me in all your goodness.

Whatever kind of imprisonment may beset our souls, we can follow the lead of this sufferer. We can follow him by speaking out to the Lord and by holding on to trust. As he says: 'I pour out my lament before him and tell him of my distress. You are my shelter, my portion in the land of the living.'

And do we not discern here a foreshadowing of Christ's Passion and resurrection? For him they laid snares. In his deepest need it seemed there was no one that would know him But then came the morning when his soul was brought out of prison. Death's prison door was broken and Christ rose in the glory of his new life. The Father had acted in all his goodness. And so he does still for all who gather to his Son in faith, hope and love.

With my voice I cry to the Lord. I tell him of my distress.
Lord, my spirit faints within me. But you know my plight and the way I must take to new freedom and joy.
My troubles are too much for me. O bring my soul out of prison, Lord, that I may joyfully give you thanks for deliverance.
Father, act for me in all your goodness, as you raised up the Lord Jesus to your eternal kingdom.

Psalm 143

Thirst for God

Some countries have a generous rainfall spread throughout the year. Surprisingly, their people are inclined to grumble about it. In other lands there is rejoicing when the limited season of rain comes round. In Rangoon, when the monsoon begins in May, people race through the streets in sheer delight, laughing and splashing water over everyone they meet.

In Bible lands the ground may be so hard after the long summer drought that the first rains stand on it in great pools. But in some areas the heat and drought of summer may have caused the ground to crack. The land then seems to be opening its mouth to heaven in extremity of thirst, now to be answered at last by a sweet downpour.

The singer of Psalm 143 had a bond of sympathy with the good earth. He had felt for her in her time of thirsty anguish. But now a time had come when it was his turn to be looking up to heaven, gasping for the help of God. To the Lord he sings:

> I spread out my hands to you;
> my soul longs for you like a thirsty land.

> Answer me quickly, Lord, for my spirit fails.

His thirst for God's help means that his sufferings have dragged on and on. It is significant that the immediately preceding psalms seem to be his prayers from the same situation. How often it is that such calls for help go apparently unanswered and we must keep on repeating our prayer! Jesus himself urges us to persevere. He gave us the ironical parable of the widow who so pressed upon the hard-hearted judge that he had to attend to her cause to get any peace. Well, our singer *is* persevering. And how earnest and direct his pleas:

> Lord, hear my prayer, give heed to my supplications;
> answer me in your faithfulness and goodness.

> My spirit has fainted upon me,
> and my heart is desolate . . .

> Answer me quickly, Lord, for my spirit fails;
> do not hide your face from me,
>> or I shall become like those gone down to the Pit.

In pleading with the Lord, the singer does not claim merit, but acknowledges that he shares the unworthiness of all living beings before God – they can only trust in his mercy. The words have echoed down the centuries, especially in the Church's daily services:

> Do not enter into judgement with your servant,
> for no one living shall be justified before you.

The singer supports his prayer by expressing his readiness to be guided by God; 'Show me the way that I should go. Teach me to do your will. Lead me by your good Spirit.' And further, he declares his trust in the faithful love and goodness of God, the grace gathered and given to us in his name. The theme sounds in many verses: 'Answer me in your faithfulness and goodness. Let me hear your faithful love in the morning. In your faithfulness you will silence my enemies. For the sake of your name, Lord, grant me life, and by your goodness bring my soul out of trouble.' Yes, all hope is centred in the mercy and steadfast love of God.

367

On Easter Eve, in those quiet, expectant hours before Easter Sunday, the Church has often sung this psalm with a profound application to Christ. The worshippers have thought of his coming in humility to share the lot of sinners. He accepted the sentence of death – as the psalm says:

> The enemy has pursued my soul and crushed my life into the earth;
> he has made me dwell in deep darkness like those long dead.

But the Church, in singing this psalm, added an antiphon, a theme-setting refrain repeated at various places. This was a verse taken from the Book of Ecclesiasticus (24.45, Latin): 'I will penetrate into the lower parts of the earth, and I will behold all that sleep, and I will give light to them that hope in the Lord.' In such Easter worship, the thought arising with our psalm is that Christ descended into the land of death and so brought the light of his salvation into that darkest of places.

It is for us to stand in this faith still today. Whether thinking of actual death or of the darkness of suffering, we too, following the psalm, can spread out our hands to God, longing for his salvation as the thirsty land longs for rain. And we too know that our hope is not in our merits, but in Christ's work. By his dying on the cross we have the great hope and confidence that we shall hear his faithful love in the morning and be gladdened by the rising light of his salvation.

In your faithfulness and goodness hear my prayer, O Lord. Enter not into judgement with your servant, for in your sight can none of the living be justified.

For the sake of your name, Lord, grant me life. By your goodness given in the name of Jesus bring my soul out of trouble.

I spread out my hands to you. My soul longs for you as a thirsty land. O send the rain of your mercy and grant me life.

Psalm 144

A royal prayer that became a prophecy

A regular feature of life in Bible times was fetching water from the well. It was no light task. Often there was a good walk downhill from the little town to reach the well, and then there was the return uphill with a heavy pitcher of water. The task usually fell to the women and especially the girls. Strenuous though it was, it could at least be an interesting event in the day's routine. Sometimes indeed it brought an encounter of romantic promise. This is hardly surprising, as the girls walked so gracefully, carrying the jars on head or shoulder.

Such graceful deportment was prized, as sometimes shown in a girl's name, such as 'Tamar' meaning a palm tree. The ideal also comes vividly near the end of a colourful psalm, Psalm 144. The singer is hoping for a happy time for the nation, a time of health and plenty. In such a time, he says, the girls would be graceful as finely carved columns in the temple, and the boys would grow up strongly like well-tended plants. The animals would breed safely. And in the streets there would be no cry of distress, no victim of violence or oppression. In the singer's own words:

> So may our sons in their youth be like well-nurtured plants,
> our daughters like pillars well shaped for the corners of the temple,
>
> our barns filled with all manner of store,
> our flocks bringing forth thousands and ten thousands in our
>   fields,
>
> our cattle heavy with young and bearing in safety,
> and no cry of distress in our streets.
>
> Happy the people for whom it is so;
> happy the people who have the LORD for their God.

Yes, the singer thinks, this would be a happiness of society which only the Lord could give, a time of health in earth and plants, in sons and daughters and animals, a time of peace and justice for the world.

But in the present situation this happy time is still a matter of prayer and hope. He is the king, representing his people and land and carrying them in his heart before God. He prays from a situation of need and suffering. Humankind, he says, is anyway frail, passing quickly like a breath of wind or a passing shadow. But more, he prays from a situation that is like being tossed in the wild waves of chaos, as far as could be from the peace and order of God. On every hand he fears enemies, treacherous and harmful. 'LORD, part your heavens and come down', he prays. 'Rescue me and pluck me out of the great waters. Rescue me from the cruel foes.'

We do not know the occasion of the psalm or what these dangers really were. It may indeed be that the psalm was part of a holy drama. The ceremony would have poetic depth expressing typical need, sufferings which again and again call for God's mercy. The royal person who prays in the psalm carries all this need before God and in trust and hope raises a mighty prayer on behalf of all.

At all events, the psalm is one of the many examples in the Book of Psalms of royal prayers which entered so deeply into the mystery of God's work in the world that they became prophecies of Christ. And this is in fact the last of such psalms in the collection, the last to foreshadow the person of Christ. So it is good that it is so eloquent and all-embracing, so rich in the poetry of suffering and deliverance, the vision of chaos overcome by the redemption that brings peace.

As the psalm thus foreshadows Christ's work, it helps us to see the reach of that work. In our own individual need, yes, he saves us, plucking us out of the swirling waters of our troubles. But also his death and risen life bring salvation to all creation. His prayer and love are for all, and upon all he will at last establish the happiness of peace with God. All will at last unite with him in the song of loving praise to the Father – in the psalm's words:

> O God, I will sing a new song to you,
> and make music for you with a ten-stringed harp.

Yes, all will be led by Christ to acknowledge the Father as our rock and sure help, our fortress, our deliverer, our shield in whom we shall ever trust.

Father, in the time of trouble we pray for ourselves and for all who suffer: reach down your hand from on high and pluck me out of the great waters.

Our days on earth are like a breath of wind and like a passing shadow, but you take thought for your creatures. In your knowledge and care is our enduring hope.

Happy those who know you as their Lord. Happy those who can give thanks for your work of redemption through your Son Jesus Christ.

Father, for his victory over chaos – the emptiness, the negation, the futility, the waste and the evil – for his victory I will sing a new song to you, make melody and bear witness to your salvation.

Psalm 145

Rays from the eternal kingdom

———•◆•———

A few friends used to meet together to pray and meditate on the Bible. A verse in one of the psalms led them to talk about looking after animals, especially about feeding them. Someone recalled a cat ever punctual in coming for his evening meal. At the due time he would bang the knocker on the front door. If that failed, he would jump onto a window ledge beside the door and press the bell. Another person spoke of the urgency of getting out crumbs, seeds, nuts and currants for the birds in the morning while the birds glared pointedly through the kitchen window. Everyone agreed it was a big job seeing that the animals had their requirements at the right time. Yet hardly to be compared with the huge task that fell to the devoted staff at the county's zoo park, with all their elephants, giraffes, lions, seals and many other hungry mouths, and each animal being individually checked for its health and contentment.

But what could the psalm have said to prompt these recollections? The psalm in question was 145, and it has a remarkable perspective on these matters of feeding. All living creatures, it says, including human beings, are fed punctually by the hand of God. And he too knows all about those staring eyes. This is how the singer puts it:

> The eyes of all look to you,
> and you give them their food at its proper time.
>
> You open your hand,
> and satisfy the wants of every living thing.

Now when we feed our animals, that is a chief part of our care for them – yet only a part. As the staff at the zoo park know well, there is much more to do for them if we are to look after them properly. Likewise God the Creator: for all living things he cares constantly and faithfully. And the psalm makes this care its main theme. So it blesses and praises the Lord again and again for his love of all his creatures.

The psalm follows the letters of the Hebrew alphabet, each verse beginning with the next letter. In this alphabetic pattern of poetry, each verse tends to make its own ringing declaration, and in this psalm each verse exclaims in wonder at the goodness of God. For example:

Let one generation to another praise your works . . .

Let them pour out the story of your abundant kindness,
and sing with joy of your goodness.

Gracious and compassionate is the LORD,
patient and great in faithful love.

The LORD is good to all,
and his compassion is over all that he has made . . .

The LORD is good in all his ways,
and faithful in all his deeds.

Near is the LORD to all who call upon him,
to all who call to him in truth . . .

My mouth shall speak the praise of the LORD,
and let all creatures bless his holy name for ever and ever.

Yes, each verse is a packet of praise in itself. And after each verse it was often the custom for the whole gathering of worshippers to answer the singer with a refrain of enthusiastic assent. This might be brief, just 'For ever and ever'. But according to an ancient manuscript found in the Dead Sea caves, some worshippers sang out after every verse: 'Blessed be the Lord and blessed be his name for ever and ever.'

In such joyful and interactive worship, the psalm nourished people in a positive faith – positive about the care of Almighty God. Their hearts were directed to the goodness of the Lord and his faithful care of every creature. It was as though, for a while, their souls were lit by rays from the ideal kingdom of God, the world as it should be, and one day will be. For some blessed days, these rays replenished the soul with faith, and gave hope and courage to walk positively again in the marred and mixed world of ordinary experience.

No less than those pilgrims of old, we too need that courage, that hope and faith. The wrongs and the sufferings of the world are still many, and now they are perpetually picked out and thrust at us by the media. How can we, of all generations, affirm the constant care of the Creator for all his creatures?

Surely we cannot explain, we cannot understand the contradictions. A verse in our psalm points us along the path of humility in our thinking and in our urge to understand:

> Great is the LORD and very glorious,
> and there is no searching out his greatness.

Yes, there is no searching out, no mastery of the mystery of God. It has been the same since the dawn of faith. The contradiction of suffering has been only too well known and not adequately explained.

And yet the praise of God's mercy and goodness has never ceased. Our psalm is a fine example. After so many psalms of distress, it marks a final turn in the collection. From here to the glorious finale in Psalm 150, all the songs will be of praise and thanksgiving, joy in the goodness of God. Here in the moment of worship, before the face of the Holy One, the rays of the kingdom shine through. Already we can hear the universal praise, already take part in it.

Our psalm leads us into this great sequence of praise by sounding out a simple but unfathomable message, the message of a truth that rises beyond the present sufferings. It is the message of God's faithful love, the love that never ends, the love that he has for every being he has made. Well may we join in this joy that sees more than this world's tragedies. We too can answer the singer with the refrain that defiantly affirms God's care and love as for all, for ever and ever and ever.

I will exalt you, my God, the King. I will bless your name for ever and ever.
Every day I will bless you, praising your name for ever and ever.
You are full of grace and compassion, patient and great in faithful love.
To all that you have made you are good, and for all eternity.
We who cannot search out your mystery, we bless your name with all you have
*   made, for ever and ever.*

Psalm 146
King, Saviour and Healer

We would all like people to think us trustworthy. But the leaders in industry, finance and politics have a hard time of it. Their work seems to require them to be less than frank, not to say devious. Still, these princes of governance and wealth-creation put a brave face on it. They take much care in manner and appearance to win people's trust.

It has always been so, to judge from the blunt advice given us in Psalm 146, which runs:

> Put no trust in princes nor in any child of earth,
> for there is no salvation from them.
>
> When their breath is gone they return to their earth;
> on that same day their thoughts will perish.

Not that the psalm is all gloom and depression. On the contrary, the singer is brimming over with enthusiasm, for he knows where trust will not be disappointed. 'Alleluia', he says,

> Praise the LORD, O my soul.
> Let me praise the LORD as long as I live,
> make music to my God all my life long . . .
>
> Happy those whose help is in the God of Jacob,
> who set their hope on the LORD their God.
>
> For he is the maker of heaven and earth,
> the sea, and all that is in them,
>
> keeping faith for evermore,
> doing justice for the oppressed.

Already in ancient times such concern for the oppressed was thought an essential mark of a true king. In our psalm the Lord is praised as the supreme King of all, active on behalf of all who are burdened or afflicted:

> . . . giving bread to the hungry,
> the LORD who sets the prisoners free,
>
> the LORD who gives sight to those who are blind,
> the LORD who raises those bowed down,
>
> the LORD who loves the faithful,
> the LORD who watches over strangers,
>
> who upholds the fatherless and widow,
> but overturns the way of the wicked.

Such is the compassionate and trustworthy character of God the King-Creator, and our psalm concludes:

> The LORD shall reign for ever,
> your God, O Zion, throughout all generations. Alleluia!

Thus the psalm bears witness to the mighty kingship of God, which is concerned for the lowly and suffering, quick to feed the hungry, liberate captives and heal the sick. It makes us think of Jesus. Just the first chapter of Mark's Gospel is enough to make the link. Mark brings before us Jesus the Messiah, the Son of God, whose coming has been prepared by prophets and John the Baptist. When Jesus himself is baptized it is like a royal anointing. The Spirit descends on this royal Son of God and brings him into the wilderness for 40 days of preparation. There the Tempter is repulsed and Jesus abides with the wild animals and the angels. Then he enters the region of Galilee, announcing that the time is fulfilled and the kingdom of God is at hand. By the great lake he gathers disciples to be with him. He teaches with unheard-of authority in the synagogue. He drives away spirits of sickness and heals many sufferers.

Our psalm helps us to recognize the pattern of these events. When Jesus announces the onrush of the kingdom of God and heals the sick, it is all of a piece. Jesus the Messiah is himself mediating the new kingdom, the new era of God's reign. On behalf of his Father, the heavenly king, he does the acts of the new reign. He frees captives, gives sight to the blind, raises those who are bowed down. He drives away the agents of harm. His actions speak at least as loud as his words. As he announces the new reign, he does the acts of the new reign, healing and helping by the finger of God. Words and acts together declare that the kingdom of God is indeed rushing upon the world.

Rushing – yes, there was an urgency in the preaching of Jesus. How quickly, too, the events unfolded! The ministry was forceful but brief. The arrest, the crucifixion, the resurrection, all followed swiftly. True, the centuries of faith and worship in Christ roll on at greater length, but the gospel is still urgent. We are called to lose no time in opening our hearts and eyes to the kingdom of God. Why should we lose one moment of the precious happiness of having God as our helper? 'Happy those whose help is in the God of Jacob, who set their hope on the LORD their God.' For he wonderfully upholds all who are in need and he will be our God and King for ever. So with the psalm we put our trust in him, taking up the heartfelt words: 'Let me praise the LORD as long as I live, make music to my God all my life long.'

O Lord our King, we hold up to your help all who suffer today. Many are hungry, many bowed down by sickness or grief.
For the strangers we pray, those thrust out of their homes, lost and in peril.
For the prisoners we pray. Open to them the gate of new life.

375

For the bereaved we pray. May they know you as the Comforter, the Beloved,
  companion of delight.
Save and heal today, Lord, according to the signs of your kingdom and your
  mercy that you gave in Jesus.

Psalm 147

Traveller's Joy and Wild Rose

A traveller was returning from a conference. He had spoken to the gathering about wisdom in the Bible and its international character. But now something was bothering him. One of his hearers, a clergyman familiar with the Psalms from daily recitation, remarked out of the blue that he could not abide the ending of Psalm 147, which he quoted as 'He sheweth his word unto Jacob, his statutes and ordinances unto Israel. He hath not dealt so with any other nation, neither have the heathen knowledge of his laws.' Our traveller was bothered now because he felt he had not given an adequate response to this accusation of narrow nationalism against a particularly beautiful psalm.

But then his thoughts turned to an experience on his journey to the conference. He had seen an exhibition of the original watercolours of some famous illustrations in a series of children's books. The artist, Cicely Mary Barker, was born in Croydon in 1895. Suffering from epilepsy, she had not been able to go to school. At home, however, she developed her artistic talent from an early age. When her father died young, she worked hard at her art to help support the family. In a series of books for children she painted her 'flower fairies'. In these entrancing compositions a flower is combined with its 'fairy' – in effect, a child expressive of the spirit of the flower. She also wrote a little poem for each painting as the fairy's song. Our traveller recalled how he was reading some of these innocent ditties, when he was surprised – taken aback even – by the song of the Wild Rose Fairy. Now this really did seem nationalistic! She calls herself 'the English Rose'. One word, she tells us, is her secret and her song, ''tis England, England, England all day long'.

After some musing, the traveller reckoned that what echoes here is not jingoism or the noisy patriotism heard at a sports stadium. Rather it is akin to the poet Rupert Brooke's affection when he describes the hedge roses at Grantchester: 'Unkempt about thee blows an unofficial English Rose.' So in Barker's surprising line there bursts out a deep and tender sympathy with the countryside she knows well, flowers and wild creatures, lanes and fields that she has watched and loved all her life. We must know from the spirit of all her paintings and poems that she means no offence to any other land. Only, this is where she happens to belong, this is what she has been given to love and be thankful for.

All this, our traveller decided, helped to enter into Psalm 147, and perhaps we can agree. Certainly the psalm as a whole can hardly be called narrow. Its praise moves to and fro from God's tenderness to individual sufferers to his guidance of stars, clouds, rains, snow and the greening of the good earth:

> He heals the broken-hearted,
> and binds up all their wounds.

> He counts the number of the stars,
> and calls them all by their names . . .

> He covers the heavens with clouds, preparing rain for the earth;
> and he makes the grass to grow on the hills . . .

> He gives the beasts their food,
> and feeds the young ravens when they cry . . .

> He gives the snow like wool;
> he scatters his frost like ashes.

And the singer declares that the Lord's pleasure is not in the champions of war, but in those who revere him and trust in his love:

> The Lord does not delight in the strength of the war-horse,
> and the warrior's strong legs he does not prize.

> But the Lord delights in those who fear him,
> who trustfully wait for his faithful love.

The psalm will have been set in a great festival at the temple in Jerusalem. It was natural for the singer to give thanks for God's care of the temple and holy city. Appropriately, too, he praised God for gathering back into the great family of worshippers any who might have been estranged or cast out. So he sings:

> The LORD builds up Jerusalem;
> he gathers together the outcasts of Israel . . .
>
> . . . O Zion, praise your God.
> He strengthens the bars of your gates;
> he blesses your children in your midst.

The massed pilgrims rejoiced in the life-giving presence of the Lord, and also gave thanks for the gift of his 'tora', that is, his teaching and commandments. This was his 'word' which bound people and God in a close relationship. So, when the psalm has given thanks for his commands and word that run swiftly to direct the great forces of nature, it concludes with appreciation of the word and commandments given to this people. It is in fact a striking chain of thought. As God sends his word to melt hailstones and ice and make the waters flow, so he sends it also as tora-teaching that will melt cold hearts and make the water of life flow through his people. Surely we may sympathize with the singer's wonder and gratitude for this unique gift to his people.

But we should remember that already in the collection of psalms Zion has been revealed as mother of *all* nations, sanctuary of all creation. God gives his peace, his well-being, 'throughout her borders'. All the more through Jesus we now recognize Zion's borders to be as wide as God's world. We see her children in her midst as all creatures God has made.

In one land Cicely Mary Barker was shown the depth of divine beauty and so could know it everywhere. In one people the psalmist knew the beauty of God's love, revealed in a unique form according to the divine purpose. He expressed a heartfelt appreciation which we easily adopt in thankfulness for the gospel of the unique Christ, who was given for all creation.

So the psalm stills leads us in the universal community of Christ, leads us to make music to our God. We thank him that he builds up his spiritual city, gathering in the outcasts and broken-hearted, healing and blessing all who will turn to him.

Mighty Lord, your wisdom is beyond all measure. You cover the heavens with light and clouds, you clothe the hills in green. You feed the fledglings and lift up the poor.

In every land your word runs swiftly and gives the stream of life. We thank you also that you declared your word to the generations on the way of your preparation for Jesus.

How good to make melody of praise to you! For in him you showed your glory to all the world, full of grace and truth.

Psalm 148

When the congregation cannot be counted

———⊷◆⊶———

'I must make a list!' How often we find that a useful thing to do – almost essential! It may be for an outing to the shops, or for sending out Christmas greetings, or for any day's programme. For many a task it helps to make a list. And those who have a talent for it put all the items in due order and categories.

Not so long ago, lists were a big part of education. Many were the lists to be learnt, such as lists of irregular verbs or of kings and queens. As a treat near the end of term, one old geography teacher had the class learn all the stations on the Trans-Siberian railway and then compete for speed of recitation, timed with a stopwatch. Elderly survivors from those distant days will still remember that on reaching Omsk they need to change for the branch lines to Tomsk and Semipalatinsk.

Some scholars became famous for their listing and classifying. Certainly it was the very heart of botany. The tradition goes back thousands of years. Already the ancient Egyptian sages compiled and ordered lists of things in nature. They thought it part of the task of living wisely in the order and beauty of the creation. And something of this kind of study can be glimpsed in the Bible, especially in lists of animals, tribes and ancestors. In the Books of Job and of Proverbs, listing of animals and aspects of nature is used to arouse our wonder and our adoration of the Creator. In the Psalms it is part of a glorious experience, the moment when all creatures together are praising the Lord.

This is especially the case in Psalm 148. Things vast and small, mysterious and commonplace are listed in order and kind. Not that we should in any way master them; rather, it is all an act of sharing – sharing in the praise of God. A voice goes out from the temple court, the voice of the precentor who interacts with a mighty choir, the chorus of all created things.

There are so many to call to, as he invites their response of praise, so many that he is glad of his list.

And a well-arranged list it is. It begins with beings in the heavenly regions, and each kind is invited to chant the praises of their Creator:

> Alleluia! Praise the LORD from the heavens,
> O praise him in the heights.
>
> Praise him, all his angels;
> O praise him, all his hosts.
>
> Praise him, sun and moon,
> praise him, all you stars of light.
>
> Praise him, heavens of heavens,
> and you waters above the heavens.

The precentor backs up his invitation to praise with reasons. He points to the sheer wonder of their creation and the divine command which keeps them in the cosmic harmony:

> Let them praise the name of the LORD,
> for he commanded and they were created.
>
> And he established them for ever and ever;
> he gave them a law which they might not transgress.

And now the precentor's list brings him to beings on and about the earth. What a rich variety of existences is here!

> Praise the LORD from the earth,
> you sea monsters and all ocean depths,
>
> fire and hail, snow and mists,
> stormy wind obeying his word.
>
> Mountains and all hills,
> fruitful trees and all you cedars,
>
> you beasts, both wild and tame,
> you creeping things and birds of the air.
>
> Kings of the earth and all you peoples,
> princes and all rulers of the earth,
>
> young men and maidens,
> old people and children together.

The singer rounds off this part of the list also with reasons that more than justify his call to praise. He declares that the Creator expresses his power and his love, as his name and glory shine out over all:

> Let them praise the name of the LORD,
> for his name alone is exalted, his glory over earth and heaven.

But the singer has something yet to add to his reasons for praise as the psalm draws to a close. He thinks of the worshippers actually standing in the temple courts, the Israelite assembly, and he is thankful that God has renewed their life and their strength. It's as though a wild ox, weary and weak, has found vigour again and raised its horns on high. As the singer puts it:

> And he has raised up the horn of his people,
> a cause for praise from all his faithful,
> the children of Israel, a people close to him.

And there the precentor ends. It is interesting that his thought of his own people is put like this. He makes no separate call to them. They are one with all the people on earth that he has already called to. But God's raising them up is just one extra reason why the world and they too should give thanks.

The key to the singer's thought here is in that word 'close', 'a people close to him'. It is in his mind that this people have been given a priestly role in the world. God enables them to stand near to the holy fire of his Presence, the overwhelming brilliance of his glory. So they have drawn near as priests, on behalf of all. And now, in the time of cosmic praise, when all creatures sing together to the Lord, the people at the temple, so close to the awesome glory of God, are there to lead the universal praises and pass on the blessing to all.

Christ's Church has inherited the vision of the psalm. She knows herself called to that particular ministry, bearing the responsibility of that nearness to the Presence. She does so until the kingdom is perfected, and the Church and all created life are one, and Christ is all and in all.

*O Spirit of God, grant us this vision of all creatures united in your praise.
Grant us the respect that does no harm to the creatures who there will
worship with us. For you will accept us as we love all beings in the cosmic
circle of your praise.*
*Grant us to learn from St Francis of the greater family – of Brother Sun
and Sister Moon, Brother Wind and Sister Water, Brother Fire, our sister*

*Mother Earth, and our Sister Death. With all your creatures we would
learn to praise and bless you and to serve you in great humility.*

Psalm 149
The sword of the Spirit

We get quite a number of surprises in the psalms. One comes in Psalm 149.
Many know the verse as 'Let the saints rejoice in their beds', or, 'Let them
sing praise in their beds.' You might think this is offering a comfortable
alternative to church attendance on Sunday mornings. But no. That
wouldn't fit the mood of this particularly energetic psalm. No lying in bed
here.

The psalm reflects the exciting climax in the dramatic flow of ceremonies at the chief festival in ancient Jerusalem. The call has gone out to
the massed assembly to greet the Lord with 'a new song' – one that befits
his new reign. They sense his presence as King and Creator, victorious over
chaos and evil. They are seized with the hope of new life for the world. So
their praise breaks out with a goodly noise of drums and joyful chants:

> Alleluia! Sing to the LORD a new song,
> his praise in the assembly of the faithful.

> Let Israel rejoice in their maker,
> the children of Zion exult in their king.

> Let them praise his name in the dance,
> with drums and lyres make music to him.

> For the LORD delights in his people,
> and adorns the humble with salvation.

But now, what about these saints still in their beds? It's even more
alarming when we seem to be told that, while still in bed, they are to bran-
dish deadly swords – as usually translated: 'Let them rejoice in their beds.
Let the praises of God be in their mouth and a two-edged sword in their
hands.' A strange picture indeed – holy folk rejoicing in their beds and
whirling two-edged swords!

Let's take the beds first. We should picture the vast gathering of pilgrim worshippers as arranged in orderly rows. During the numerous days and nights of the festival they would sometimes stand, sometimes rest on a garment or a mat. It is these resting places that the psalm refers to, and we might as well just translate:

> Let the faithful exult with glory,
> and sing praises from their ranks.

But as regards the swords, we probably just have a comparison, and a very significant one at that. The praises of God which the worshippers chant with such warmth and sincerity are *compared* to swords, the weapons of praise and faith which will defeat the forces of evil. 'Let the faithful sing praises from their ranks', sings the psalmist,

> with acclamations of God in their throat,
> as a two-edged sword in their hand.

The conclusion of the psalm also calls for our imagination. It speaks of a battle against nations, kings and nobles, of taking leaders captive and bringing them before God's justice:

> to bind their kings in chains,
> and their nobles with links of iron,
>
> to do among them the justice that is written;
> that will be glory for all his faithful.

In such passages the nations are symbolic of the world organized in neglect or defiance of the Creator. God himself wars against them until he establishes his kingdom of peace, when war is no more and the nations appear as beloved children of Zion, a world happy in God.

Our psalm sees God's warfare as not yet completed. His faithful people are called to have the courage of good soldiers. But their weapons are not those of the world. Theirs is the sword of the Spirit, the sword of praise and prayer. Yes, we might say, they will bind the godless kings and nobles, but bind them with the gold chains of prayer and the strong links of Christlike love.

The psalm's emphasis is on praise. It is seen as the expression of joy in God. Here is his humble people, seeing him by faith, touched and inspired by his beauty to speak, sing and live out their joy in him. They are transfigured by hope and love. With such arms from God they overcome the selfish world. The new song, the song of the new creation, is taken up at last by all that live, accompanied by the inspired lyres, drums and dances.

Help us, O God our King, to live in the spirit of praise. May we be thankful for the garment of your salvation. May we have the sure hope of your victory. By this spirit of praise may we overcome all adversity.

May we rejoice in you, our Maker and faithful Saviour, rejoice so that our hearts and mouths already sing the new song of your new creation.

Psalm 150

The orchestra of creation

Once a month the church organist was replaced with the church orchestra. Into the space at the front squeezed some twenty musicians. There was a trumpet, a trombone and a horn, strings in the form of violins and a cello, a set of drums, pipes in the shape of recorders, flutes, clarinets and an oboe, and, not least, the gentle percussion of a piano. The players were aged from eight to eighty. One Sunday, the oldest violinist, surveying his young colleagues, fell to musing about his first appearance in his school's orchestra some seventy years back. Having then only just begun on the violin, he was assigned the part of the quail in the 'Toy' Symphony of Haydn (or was it by Mozart's father?). The toy instrument for the quail was like a small bicycle horn, but gave out a chirp like that of the bird. You might think anyone could play it, but *when* to play and when *not* to play – ah, that was the art.

The symphony was a pleasant work to play in. To the usual instruments of the orchestra were added several toy instruments which echoed the sounds of nature. The toy cuckoo worked well, but the nightingale, which had to be filled with water, tended to splutter. The toy drum hinted at the knocking of the woodpecker. A rattle, turned with a handle, gave impressions of chattering insects. Yes, the melodious little symphony could transport you into a delightful Austrian countryside. But there the musing of our friend had to stop. Diana, the conductor, rapped her baton and launched them into 'When the Spirit of the Lord', teasingly slow until the exciting acceleration began.

As it happens, the orchestras used in worship in the first days of the psalms were also close to the sounds of nature. One common form of trumpet was in fact the horn of a wild goat. Its sound was not unlike the lowing of cattle. The stringed instruments – lyres and harps – were plucked and could sound like drops of rain falling into a pool. Among the drums, the dancer's hand-drum or tambourine was the most common, sounding like rain on the roof. From hollow reeds were made instruments that worked on the principles of our recorders, flutes, oboes and clarinets. Their voices readily took you into the world of birdsong or the sighs and melodies of the wind. Perhaps the closest to nature's sounds were the percussion instruments that included clackers, shakers, whirrers and, not least, the shivering and chiming cymbals.

In those psalm orchestras, then, you were not far from the voices of animals, birds and insects, tumbling waters, winds sighing over beds of reeds, dancing trees. The instruments combined with the singers to express the pleading of prayer and the jubilation of praise. In scenes of praise especially, the closeness of the music to nature was fitting, for the musicians, singers and dancers could take on the role of representing all creation.

This thought leads us into Psalm 150. The short psalm consists entirely of calls to praise. Since most are directed to the musicians and dancers but then rounded off with a call to everything that lives, it's clear that the music and movement has a representative character. There in the temple, the focus of God's universe, they represent all creatures in heaven and earth. They turn all the voices of the universe to praise. They lead every movement of life to become a tribute of adoration.

The little song is the conclusion of the Book of Psalms and so is especially awe-inspiring. Its content may seem restricted, but turns out to be inexhaustible. It is as though the Spirit speaking through the psalms intends to give us a final message, earnest and vital. We do well to take it to heart.

When we come to the place of praise – the Spirit seems to say – the place where God shows himself in his power and beauty, then we too speak for and with all living things. In that place, our love for the Lord must be one with love for all his creatures. Our praise will unite with the voices of all that are turned to him. And praise is the voice of love as we delight in the Lord, shift our regard from ourselves to him, put our trust in the Lord, live for the Lord.

But where is this wondrous place, the place of fullest praise before the revelation of the Holy One? Where must we come to see the firmament lit by his glory? The psalms themselves show that the way passes through strife and tears, through pain and loss. Anguished prayers mingle with early songs of hope and trust and the beginnings of praise. But as God wills, he brings us at last to his holy mountain, where the light of his presence and of his new creation shines upon us. The music of the Spirit sounds in the trumpets, strings, pipes and drums and dances, and in the mysterious shiver of the cymbals. The great alleluia rises, as every creature in its own way is led to tell out its love of our Lord:

Alleluia!
Praise God in his holy dwelling;
praise him in the firmament lit by his glory.

Praise him in his mighty acts;
praise him in the greatness of his power.

Praise him with the blowing of the trumpet;
praise him with the harp and lyre.

Praise him with the drums and dances;
praise him with the strings and pipes.

Praise him with the cymbals for proclamation;
praise him with the cymbals for acclamation.

Let every living thing
praise the LORD. Alleluia!

Lord Jesus, you are the way. As we trust in you and rejoice in you, already we make the pilgrimage to the sanctuary of God.

In every danger and perplexity you calm and guide me. You hear my cries and share my burdens.

You show us already the beauty of the Creator. You fill us with the love of God, that we may love all your creatures and through love join in their great hymn of praise. Alleluia.

Index of selected themes